A Generative Theory of Tonal Music

KU-511-884

Fred Lerdahl
Ray Jackendoff

The MIT Press
Cambridge, Massachusetts
London, England

© 1983 by The Massachusetts Institute of Technology

All rights reserved. No part of this book may be reproduced in any form or by any means, electronic or mechanical, including photocopying, recording, or by any information storage and retrieval system, without permission in writing from the publisher.

This book was set in VIP Sabon by Village Typographers, Inc., and printed and bound in the United States of America.

Library of Congress Cataloging in Publication Data

Lerdahl, Fred, 1943–
   A generative theory of tonal music.
   Includes bibliography and index.
   ISBN 978-0-262-62107-6 (paperback: alk. paper)
   1. Music—Theory.   2. Music—Psychology.   3. Music and language.
I. Jackendoff, Ray S.   II. Title.   III. Series.
MT6.L36G4   1983   781   82–17104

10 9 8

Contents

Contents

Contents

Preface

In the fall of 1973, Leonard Bernstein delivered the Charles Eliot Norton Lectures at Harvard University. Inspired by the insights of transformational-generative ("Chomskian") linguistics into the structure of language, he advocated a search for a "musical grammar" that would explicate human musical capacity. As a result of these lectures, many people in the Boston area took a fresh interest in the idea of an alliance between music theory and linguistics, and Irving Singer and David Epstein formed a faculty seminar on music, linguistics, and aesthetics at the Massachusetts Institute of Technology in the fall of 1974.

Our collaboration began as an outgrowth of that seminar. Consulting each other during the preparation of our individual talks, we soon found ourselves working together on an approach of some novelty. Our participation in the MIT seminar gave us frequent opportunities over the next three years to present and discuss our work in its formative stages. In addition, we had the good fortune to be invited in the spring of 1975 to a week-long seminar on music and language at the Institute de Recherche et Coordination Acoustique/Musique in Paris, organized by Nicolas Ruwet. We have also had the opportunity to present aspects of our work in talks at the Accademia Filarmonica in Rome, Brandeis University, Columbia University, the University of California at Irvine, and Yale University, and to the American Society of University Composers, the New York State Theory Society, a Sloan Foundation Conference on Cognitive Science, and the Third Workshop on Physical and Neuropsychological Foundations of Music in Ossiach, Austria.

In the course of preparing a written paper for the proceedings of the IRCAM conference (this paper eventually appeared as "Toward a Formal Theory of Tonal Music" in the *Journal of Music Theory*), we realized that the material we had worked out required book-length exposition. Hence this volume, written intermittently along with string quartets and books on linguistic theory.

We have tried to achieve a synthesis of the outlook and methodology of contemporary linguistics with the insights of recent music theory. There was a natural division of labor: Lerdahl, the composer, supplied musical insights, and Jackendoff, the linguist, constructed formal systems to express them. But of course it was hardly that cut and dried. Lerdahl had enough expertise in logic and linguistics to make substantial contributions on the formal side, and Jackendoff's experience as a performing musician enriched the purely musical aspect of the enterprise. Consequently, our individual contributions to the work are hopelessly intertwined, and neither of us could really have done any part of the work alone.

The result is a theory formulated in terms of rules of musical grammar. Like the rules of linguistic theory, these are not meant to be prescriptions telling the reader how one should hear pieces of music or how music may be organized according to some abstract mathematical schema. Rather, it is evident that a listener perceives music as more than a mere sequence of notes with different pitches and durations; one hears music in organized patterns. Each rule of musical grammar is intended to express a generalization about the organization that the listener attributes to the music he hears. The grammar is formulated in such a way as to permit the description of divergent intuitions about the organization of a piece.

We do not expect that these organizing principles will necessarily be accessible to introspection, any more than are the principles governing the ability to speak, walk, or see. The justification of the rules, therefore, lies not merely in whether they "look right" to ordinary intuition but in their ability to describe intuitions about a wide range of musical passages.

We conceive of a rule of musical grammar as an empirically verifiable or falsifiable description of some aspect of musical organization, potentially to be tested against all available evidence from contrived examples, from the existing literature of tonal music, or from laboratory experiments. Time and again in the course of developing the theory we discovered examples for which our musical intuitions did not conform to the predictions of our then-current set of rules. In such instances we were forced either to invent a new rule or, better, to come up with a more general formulation of the rules we had. Our exposition of the grammar here reflects some of this process of constant revision, but much more has been expunged in the interest of sparing the reader many of our blind alleys.

We consider this book a progress report in an ongoing program of research, rather than a pristine whole. We have taken care to leave the rough edges showing—to make clear where we have left problems unsolved or where our solutions seem to us inadequate. We present it at this stage partly because of limitations of time and patience and partly out of the realization that no theory ever reaches true completion. We feel, however, that we have gone far enough to be able to present a coherent and convincing overall view.

The book can be read from several perspectives. From the viewpoint of music theory as traditionally conceived it offers many technical innovations, not only in notation but also in the substance of rhythmic and reductional theory and the relation between the two. We feel that our approach has succeeded in clarifying a number of issues that have concerned recent tonal theory.

We hope that this work will interest a wider circle of readers than the usual treatise on music theory. As we develop our rules of grammar, we often attempt to distinguish those aspects of the rules that are peculiar to classical Western tonal music from those aspects that are applicable to a wide range of musical idioms. Thus many parts of the theory can be tested in terms of musical idioms other than the one we are primarily concerned with here, providing a rich variety of questions for historical and ethnomusicological research.

Beyond purely musical issues, the theory is intended as an investigation of a domain of human cognitive capacity. Thus it should be useful to linguists and psychologists, if for no other purpose than as an example of the methodology of linguistics applied to a different domain. We believe that our generative theory of music can provide a model of how to construct a competence theory (in Chomsky's sense) without being crippled by a slavish adherence to standard linguistic formalisms. In some respects our theory has turned out more like certain contemporary work in the theory of vision than like linguistic theory.

Our approach has led to the discovery of substantive as well as methodological connections among music, language, and vision. Some of these connections appear in the course of the theory's exposition (especially in sections 3.2, 3.4, 4.2, and 7.2), but we have reserved for chapter 12 a discussion of those connections that strike us as most significant. The matters treated there suggest that our theory is of more than peripheral interest to the cognitive sciences.

The exposition of the book reflects the diversity of its audience. On occasion we elaborate fairly obvious musical points for the sake of nonspecialists; more often we go into technical issues more deeply than nonspecialists may care for. Readers should feel free to use the book as their interests dictate. Linguists and psychologists should probably read chapters 1, 3, 11, 12, and the beginning of chapter 5 first. Musicians may want to start with chapters 1, 2, 5, 6, 8, and 11. All readers should bear in mind that the heart of the theory resides in the chapters on formalization: 3, 4, 7, and 9.

In the course of working out our ideas we have benefited greatly from the writings of Noam Chomsky, Edward T. Cone, Grosvenor Cooper and Leonard B. Meyer, Andrew Imbrie, Arthur J. Komar, David Lewin, Charles Rosen, Carl Schachter, Heinrich Schenker, Peter Westergaard, and Maury Yeston. We have also received valuable advice from many colleagues and students. Among the members of the MIT seminar, we must thank Jeanne Bamberger, Arthur Berger, David Epstein, John Harbison, David Lewin, and Irving Singer; among other musicians, Tim Aarset, Leonard Bernstein, Edward T. Cone, Gary Greenberg, Andrew Imbrie, Elise Jackendoff, Allan Keiler, Henry Martin, Gregory Proctor, Paul Salerni, Seymour Shifrin, James Snell, and James Webster; among linguists and psychologists, Morris Halle, Richard Held, Samuel Jay Keyser, Edward Klima, James Lackner, George Miller, Alan Prince, and Lisa Selkirk. Each of these people has contributed something essential to the content or form of this book. George Edwards and Louis Karchin read the entire manuscript and made many useful suggestions. The authors blame each other for any errors that remain.

We are also grateful to the School of Humanities at MIT for providing financial support to the Seminar on Music, Linguistics, and Aesthetics; to Brandeis University for support toward the preparation of the illustrations; to the John Simon Guggenheim Memorial Foundation for a fellowship to Lerdahl in 1974–75, ostensibly to compose; and to the National Endowment for the Humanities for a fellowship to Jackendoff in 1978, ostensibly to write on semantics. For the misuse of funds we can only apologize, and hope that this extracurricular activity has enriched our "real" work as much as we think it has.

We are deeply indebted to Allen Anderson for his splendid work in making our unusually difficult musical examples legible and attractive.

Earlier versions of portions of this book have appeared in the *Journal of Music Theory, The Musical Quarterly,* and the volume *Music, Mind, and Brain,* edited by Manfred Clynes.

Preface to the 1996 Reprint

This reprinting of *A Generative Theory of Tonal Music* incorporates a few minor corrections but otherwise leaves the text intact. Whatever its blemishes, *GTTM* is an integral whole whose main ideas appear to have stood up well since its publication thirteen years ago. We would not know how to revise it other than to start over and write a different book.

We often have been asked how a composer and a linguist came to collaborate on a music theory conceived as a branch of cognitive psychology. The answer is not far-fetched. A thinking composer in our confusing era has no choice but to be concerned with basic principles of musical organization. A linguist who is also a professional clarinetist finds it intriguing to extend his theory-building to the structurally rich domain of music. Intellectual currents in the 1970s encouraged the convergence of music, linguistics, and psychology within the emerging interdisciplinary field of cognitive science. And we were very lucky to find each other.

Each of us had in fact imagined doing such research independently before we met. But the ideas really took wing only in collaboration: neither of us could have done this work without the other. Our ability to collaborate depended on our geographical proximity in the Boston area during 1974–79. During that period we met weekly, hammering out ideas over kitchen tables, pianos, and typewriters. The give-and-take was unusually close; it would be pointless to try to disentangle who thought up this rule or wrote that paragraph. After 1979, when Lerdahl moved from Harvard to Columbia, our work was far enough along for us to complete it from a distance. Our close collaboration ended with the publication of *GTTM*, for it was not possible to develop new ideas together without the flow of weekly meetings.

One particular feature of *GTTM* bears mention in historical perspective. At the time that we were writing the book, a generative grammar was standardly conceived as a set of rewriting rules that generated "all and only" the grammatical expressions of the domain in question. This conception was consonant with the algorithmic style in which theories of cognitive processing were couched, as well as with then-current fashions in artificial intelligence. We discovered early in our work that such a notion of generative grammar could not be applied to musical structure; any grammar we could write generated too many "grammatical" structures that did not make musical sense. We found that we needed instead a grammar that generated a large number of alternative structures and then selected from among them the ones that were "most stable." This process of selection involved the use of "preference rules," violable principles that interacted according to relative weight. Worried by this curious innovation, we were relieved to learn, thanks to George Miller's timely advice, that antecedents existed in the work of the Gestalt psychologists of the first half of the century.

Our innovation did not fare especially well with readers who were hoping for a more traditional generative grammar. However, within a few years cognitive science was swept by new conceptions of computation (including neural nets) that replaced serial algorithms with parallel constraint-based architectures. Default logic became pervasive in artificial intelligence. Even linguistics, through the Optimality Theory of Alan Prince and Paul Smolensky, has begun to explore rule interactions very much like those in *GTTM*. In retrospect, then, we feel vindicated in our choice of how to formulate musical grammar.

Since the publication of *GTTM*, we have each independently built on our collaborative work. Jackendoff has further explored the relation between the theories of rhythm in music and in language, a process begun in *GTTM*; and he has shown how the *GTTM* theory can be adapted to the real-time processing of music. More generally, he has used the preference-rule formalism extensively in his work on lexical semantics and has used the multi-modular organization of musical grammar as a model for the organization of other kinds of mental computation. Lerdahl has significantly extended the music theory itself to include the analysis of chromatic and atonal music, timbral organization, musical schemas, mappings between music and poetry, and the relationship between compositional system and heard result in contemporary music. The most important extension has been the development of a precise model of pitch space, which replaces the underdefined "stability conditions" of *GTTM*. The hearing of a piece as it unfolds can now be understood in terms of paths in pitch space at multiple prolongational levels. These paths in turn enable the quantification of prolongational tension and melodic attraction.

As the paucity of references in our text attests, we did not know much music psychology when we wrote *GTTM*. But then the field barely existed in the 1970s. Music theorists were preoccupied with Schenker and pitch-class set theory; only Leonard Meyer's work suggested an alternative path. A few psychologists such as Robert Francés, Diana Deutsch, and W. J. Dowling published empirical research on music perception, but their work was marginal within psychology as a whole, and it rarely reached the levels of musical structure that would interest a musician. All of this changed dramatically in the 1980s. The Ossiach conferences, organized by Juan Roederer, encouraged contacts among psychoacousticians, brain scientists, cognitive psychologists, and music theorists. The launching of the journal *Music Perception* paved the way for conferences and for American, European, and Japanese organizations devoted to the study of music cognition. Important books such as those by John Sloboda, Albert Bregman, Carol Krumhansl, and Euguene Narmour appeared. We are proud that our work has been a central reference point for this growing field, both as a source of ideas and as material for experimental investigation.

Selected Works of Relevance to GTTM

By Ray Jackendoff

Semantics and Cognition. Cambridge: MIT Press, 1983.

Consciousness and the Computational Mind. Cambridge: MIT Press, 1987.

A Comparison of Rhythmic Structures in Music and Language. In *Phonetics and Phonology,* edited by P. Kiparsky G. Youmans, vol. 1, 15–44. New York: Academic Press, 1989.

Musical Parsing and Musical Affect. *Music Perception* 9 (1991): 199–230.

By Fred Lerdahl

Timbral Hierarchies. *Contemporary Music Review* 2 (1987): 135–160.

Cognitive Constraints on Compositional Systems. In *Generative Processes in Music,* edited by J. Sloboda. New York: Oxford University Press, 1988.

Tonal Pitch Space. *Music Perception* 5 (1988): 315–350.

Atonal Prolongational Structure. *Contemporary Music Review* 3 (1989): 65–87.

Underlying Musical Schemata. In *Representing Musical Structure,* edited by I. Cross and P. Howell. New York: Academic, 1991.

Some Lines of Poetry Viewed as Music. (Co-authored with John Halle.) In *Music, Language, Speech, and Brain,* edited by J. Sundberg, L. Nord, and R. Carlson. Wenner-Gren International Symposium Series. London: Macmillan, 1991.

Pitch-space Journeys in Two Chopin Preludes. In *Cognitive Bases of Musical Communication,* edited by M. R. Jones and S. Holleran. Washington, DC: American Psychological Association, 1991.

Tonal and Narrative Paths in *Parsifal.* In *Musical Transformation and Musical Intuition: Essays in Honor of David Lewin,* edited by R. Atlas and M. Cherlin. Roxbury, MA: Ovenbird Press, 1994.

Octatonic and Hexatonic Pitch Spaces. *Proceedings of the International Conference for Music Perception and Cognition,* 1994.

Calculating Tonal Tension. *Music Perception* 13 (Spring 1996).

1
Theoretical Perspective

1.1
Music Theory as Psychology

We take the goal of a theory of music to be a *formal description of the musical intuitions of a listener who is experienced in a musical idiom*. To explicate this assertion, let us begin with some general remarks about music theory.

Music can be discussed in a number of ways. First, one can talk informally about individual pieces of music, seeking to illuminate their interesting facets. This sort of explanation often can capture musical insights of considerable subtlety, despite—or sometimes because of—its unrigorous nature. Alternatively, one can attempt to create a systematic mode of description within which to discuss individual pieces. Here one addresses a musical idiom by means of an analytic method, be it as straightforward as classifying pieces by their forms or putting Roman numerals under chords, or as elaborate as constructing linear graphs. An analytic method is of value insofar as it enables one to express insights into particular pieces. The many different analytic methods in the literature differ in large part because of the nature and scope of the insights they are intended to convey.

At a further level of generality, one can seek to define the principles underlying an analytic system; this, in our view, constitutes a theory of music. Such a theory can be viewed as a hypothesis about how music or a particular musical idiom is organized, couched in terms of some set of theoretical constructs; one can have a theory of Roman numerals, or musical forms, or linear graphs.

Given a theory of music, one can then inquire as to the status of its theoretical constructs. Medieval theorists justified their constructs partly on theological grounds. A number of theorists, such as Rameau and Hindemith, have based aspects of music theory on the physical principle of the overtone series. There have also been philosophical bases for music theory, for instance Hauptmann's use of Hegelian dialectic.

In the twentieth century these types of explanations have fallen into relative disfavor. Two general trends can be discerned. The first is to seek a mathematical foundation for the constructs and relationships of music theory. This in itself is not enough, however, because mathematics is capable of describing any conceivable type of organization. To establish the basis for a theory of music, one would want to explain why certain conceivable constructs are utilized and others not. The second trend is to fall back on artistic intuition in constructing a theory, essentially ignoring the source of such intuition. But this approach too is inadequate, because it severs questions of art from deeper rational inquiry; it treats music as though it had nothing to do with any other aspect of the world.

All of these approaches downplay the obvious fact that music is a product of human activity. It is worth asking at the outset what the nature of this product is. It is not a musical score, if only because many musical traditions are partially or completely unwritten.[1] It is not a performance, because any particular piece of music can receive a great variety of performances. Music theory is usually not concerned with the performers' activities, nor is it concerned centrally with the sound waves the performers produce. There is much more to music than the raw uninterpreted physical signal.

Where, then, do the constructs and relationships described by music theory reside? The present study will justify the view that a piece of music is a mentally constructed entity, of which scores and performances are partial representations by which the piece is transmitted. One commonly speaks of musical structure for which there is no direct correlate in the score or in the sound waves produced in performance. One speaks of music as segmented into units of all sizes, of patterns of strong and weak beats, of thematic relationships, of pitches as ornamental or structurally important, of tension and repose, and so forth. Insofar as one wishes to ascribe some sort of "reality" to these kinds of structure, one must ultimately treat them as mental products imposed on or inferred from the physical signal. In our view, the central task of music theory should be to explicate this mentally produced organization. Seen in this way, music theory takes a place among traditional areas of cognitive psychology such as theories of vision and language.

This perspective sheds a different light on the two recent theoretical trends mentioned above. On the one hand, in principle it offers an empirical criterion for limiting mathematical formulations of musical structure; not every conceivable organization of a musical signal can be perceived by a human listener. One can imagine some mathematical relationship to obtain between every tenth note of a piece, but such a relationship would in all likelihood be perceptually irrelevant and musically unenlightening. On the other hand, this approach takes artistic intuition out of isolation and relates it to mental life in general. It becomes possible to explain artistically interesting aspects of musical structure in terms of principles that account for simpler musical phenomena. The insights of an "artistic" approach can thus be incorporated into a larger and more explanatory framework.[2]

We will now elaborate the notion of "the musical intuitions of the experienced listener." By this we mean not just his conscious grasp of musical structure; an acculturated listener need never have studied music. Rather we are referring to the largely unconscious knowledge (the "musical intuition") that the listener brings to his hearing—a knowledge that enables him to organize and make coherent the surface patterns of pitch, attack, duration, intensity, timbre, and so forth. Such a listener is able to identify a previously unknown piece as an example of the idiom, to recognize elements of a piece as typical or anomalous, to identify a performer's error as possibly producing an "ungrammatical" configuration, to recognize various kinds of structural repetitions and variations, and, generally, to comprehend a piece within the idiom.

A listener without sufficient exposure to an idiom will not be able to organize in any rich way the sounds he perceives. However, once he becomes familiar with the idiom, the kind of organization that he attributes to a given piece will not be arbitrary but will be highly constrained in specific ways. In our view a theory of a musical idiom should characterize such organization in terms of an explicit formal musical grammar that models the listener's connection between the presented musical surface of a piece and the structure he attributes to the piece. Such a grammar comprises a system of rules that assigns analyses to pieces. This contrasts with previous approaches, which have left it to the analyst's judgment to decide how to fit theoretical constructs to a particular piece.

The "experienced listener" is meant as an idealization. Rarely do two people hear a given piece in precisely the same way or with the same degree of richness. Nonetheless, there is normally considerable agreement on what are the most natural ways to hear a piece. A theory of a musical idiom should be concerned above all with those musical judgments for which there is substantial interpersonal agreement. But it also should characterize situations in which there are alternative interpretations, and it should have the scope to permit discussion of the relative merits of variant readings.

The concept of the "experienced listener," of course, is no more than a convenient delimitation. Occasionally we will refer to the intuitions of a less sophisticated listener, who uses the same principles as the experienced listener in organizing his hearing of music, but in a more limited way. In dealing with especially complex artistic issues, we will sometimes elevate the experienced listener to the status of a "perfect" listener—that privileged being whom the great composers and theorists presumably aspire to address.

It is useful to make a second idealization about the listener's intuition. Instead of describing the listener's real-time mental processes, we will be concerned only with the final state of his understanding. In our view it would be fruitless to theorize about mental processing before understanding the organization to which the processing leads. This is only a methodological choice on our part. It is a hypothesis that certain aspects of the phenomena under investigation can be cleanly separated. Of course, its value depends in the end on the significance of the results it yields.[3]

The two idealizations we have adopted, that of the experienced listener and that of the final state of his understanding, are comparable to idealizations made elsewhere in cognitive psychology. Without some initial simplification, the phenomena addressed by scientific inquiry have almost always proved intractable to rational investigation.

Having outlined this goal for a theory of a musical idiom, we envision a further sort of inquiry. A musical idiom of any complexity demands considerable sophistication for its full appreciation, and listeners brought up in one musical culture do not automatically transfer their sophistication to other musical cultures. And because one's knowledge of a musical style is to a great extent unconscious, much of it cannot be transmitted by direct instruction. Thus one may rightfully be curious about the source of the experienced listener's knowledge. To what extent is it learned, and to what extent is it due to an innate musical capacity or general cognitive capacity? A formal theory of musical idioms will make possible substantive hypotheses about those aspects of musical understanding that are innate; the innate aspects will reveal themselves as "universal" principles of musical grammar.

The interaction between this level of inquiry and a theory of a musical idiom is of great importance. If a listener's knowledge of a particular idiom were relatively uncomplicated (say, simply memorization of the musical surface of many pieces), there would be little need for a special theory of musical cognitive capacity. But the more the study of the listener's knowledge reveals complexity and abstraction with respect to the musical surface, the more necessary a theory of musical cognitive capacity becomes; it is no longer obvious how the listener obtains evidence for his structures from the musical surface. Thus a theory of a sufficiently intricate musical idiom will be a rich source of hypotheses about psychological musical universals.

In this book we develop a music theory along the lines suggested by these general considerations. Specifically, we present a substantial fragment of a theory of classical Western tonal music (henceforth "tonal music"), worked out with an eye toward an eventual theory of musical cognitive capacity. Our general empirical criteria for success of the theory are how adequately it describes musical intuition, what it enables us to say of interest about particular pieces of music, what it enables us to say about the nature of tonal music and of music in general, and how well it dovetails with broader issues of cognitive theory. In addition, we impose formal criteria common to any theoretical enterprise, requiring internal coherence and simplicity of the formal model relative to the complexity of the phenomena it accounts for. In short, we conceive of our theory as being in principle testable by usual scientific standards; that is, subject to verification or falsification on various sorts of empirical grounds.[4]

1.2 The Connection with Linguistics

In advocating these goals for inquiry about music, we are adopting a stance analogous to that taken in the study of language by the school of generative-transformational grammar, most widely known through the work of Noam Chomsky (see for example Chomsky 1965, 1968, 1975).[5] This approach has resulted in a depth of understanding about the nature of language unparalleled in previous approaches. Inasmuch as it has caused questions to be asked about language that could not even be imagined before, it has also revealed the extent of our ignorance; this too is progress.

Generative linguistic theory is an attempt to characterize what a human being knows when he knows how to speak a language, enabling him to understand and create an indefinitely large number of sentences, most of which he has never heard before. This knowledge is not on the whole available to conscious introspection and hence cannot have been acquired by direct instruction. Linguistic theory models this unconscious knowledge by a formal system of principles or rules called a *grammar*, which describes (or "generates") the possible sentences of the language.

Because many people have thought of using generative linguistics as a model for music theory, it is worth pointing out what we take to be the significant parallel: the combination of psychological concerns and the formal nature of the theory. Formalism alone is to us uninteresting except insofar as it serves to express musically or psychologically interesting generalizations and to make empirical issues more precise. We have designed our formalism with these goals in mind, avoiding unwarranted overformalization.[6]

Many previous applications of linguistic methodology to music have foundered because they attempt a literal translation of some aspect of linguistic theory into musical terms—for instance, by looking for musical "parts of speech," deep structures, transformations, or semantics. But pointing out superficial analogies between music and language, with or without the help of generative grammar, is an old and largely futile game. One should not approach music with any preconceptions that the substance of music theory will look at all like linguistic theory. For example, whatever music may "mean," it is in no sense comparable to linguistic meaning; there are no musical phenomena comparable to sense and reference in language, or to such semantic judgments as synonymy, analyticity, and entailment. Likewise there are no substantive parallels between elements of musical structure and such syntactic categories as noun, verb, adjective, preposition, noun phrase, and verb phrase. Finally, one should not be misled by the fact that both music and language deal with sound structure. There are no musical counterparts of such phonological parameters as voicing, nasality, tongue height, and lip rounding. (See also section 11.4.)

The fundamental concepts of musical structure must instead involve such factors as rhythmic and pitch organization, dynamic and timbral differentiation, and motivic-thematic processes. These factors and their interactions form intricate structures quite different from, but no less complex than, those of linguistic structure. Any deep parallels that might exist can be discussed meaningfully only after a music theory, in the sense defined in the preceding section, has been developed independently. If we have adopted some of the theoretical framework and methodology of linguistics, it is because this approach has suggested a fruitful way of thinking about music itself. If substantive parallels between language and music emerge (as they do in sections 4.2 and 12.3), this is an unexpected bonus but not necessarily a desideratum.

To help clarify in what sense our theory is modeled after linguistic methodology, we must mention some common misconceptions about generative-transformational grammar. The early work in the field, such as Chomsky 1957 and Lees 1960, took as its goal the description of "all and only" the sentences of a language, and many were led to think of a generative grammar as an algorithm to manufacture grammatical sentences. Under this interpretation, a musical grammar should be an algorithm that composes pieces of music.[7]

There are three errors in this view. First, the sense of "generate" in the term "generative grammar" is not that of an electrical generator that produces electricity, but the mathematical sense, in which it means to describe a (usually infinite) set by finite formal means. Second, it was pointed out by Chomsky and Miller (1963), and it has been an unquestioned assumption of actual research in linguistics, that what is really of interest in a generative grammar is the structure it assigns to sentences, not which strings of words are or are not grammatical sentences. The same holds for our theory of music. It is not intended to enumerate what pieces are possible, but to specify a *structural description* for any tonal piece; that is, the structure that the experienced listener infers in his hearing of the piece. A third error in the conception of a generative grammar as a sentence-spewing device is not evident from passing acquaintance with the early works of the generative school, but emerges as a prominent theme of Chomsky 1965, Lenneberg 1967, and subsequent work. Linguistic theory is not simply concerned with the analysis of a set of sentences; rather it considers itself a branch of psychology, concerned with making empirically verifiable claims about one complex aspect of human life: language. Similarly, our ultimate goal is an understanding of musical cognition, a psychological phenomenon.

**1.3
The Connection
with Artistic
Concerns**

Some readers may object to our use of linguistic methodology in studying an art form. One might argue that everyone speaks a language, but not everyone composes or performs music. However, this argument misses the point. For one thing, we are focusing on the listener because listening is a much more widespread musical activity than composing or performing. Composers and performers must be active listeners as well. And even if not every member of a culture listens to music, those who do are exercising a cognitive capacity; it is this capacity that we are investigating. (The fact that not everyone swims is not a deterrent to a physiological study of swimming.)

A related objection is that, whereas music characteristically functions as art, language does not. The data for linguistic study are the sentences of the everyday world, for which there is no musical counterpart. At first blush, poetry or drama would seem to provide a closer analogy to music. However, we feel that traditional comparisons between poetry or drama and music, though perhaps valuable in particular instances, have necessarily been superficial as a general theoretical approach. Our attitude toward artistic questions is somewhat different. In order to appreciate the poetic or dramatic structure of a poem in French, one must first understand the French language. Similarly, to appreciate a Beethoven quartet as art, one must understand the idiom of tonal music (where "understand" is taken in the unconscious sense discussed above).

Music theory that is oriented toward explicating masterpieces tends to address primarily those aspects of musical structure that are complex, ambiguous, or controversial. But such discussion takes for granted a vast substrate of totally "obvious" organization that defines the terms in which artistic options or questions are stated. For example, it rarely seems worth special mention that a piece is in a certain meter, that such-and-such is a motive, that a certain pitch is ornamental, and so forth. Throughout this study we come to grips with such musically mundane matters as a basis for understanding the more complex phenomena that an "artistic" theory deems worthy of interest.

Uninteresting though such an enterprise may at first seem, it has proved to us to yield two important benefits in the understanding of music. First, one comes to realize how intricate even the "obvious" aspects of musical organization are—perhaps more complex than any extant mathematically based conceptions of musical structure. These aspects only seem simple because their complexity is unconscious and hence unnoticed. Second, one can begin to see how artistically interesting phenomena result from manipulation of the parameters responsible for "obvious" intuitions. Many interesting treatments of motivic-thematic processes, such as Meyer's (1973) "implicational" theory, Epstein's (1979) *"Grundgestalt"* organization, and aspects of Schenkerian analysis, rely on an account of what pitches in a piece are structurally important. In the present study we show how the notion of structural importance depends on more elementary intuitions concerning the segmentation and rhythmic analysis of the musical surface; thus we offer a firmer foundation for the study of artistic questions. We consider our work to complement rather than compete with such study.

Our interest in the musically mundane does not deter us from taking masterpieces of tonal music as the analytic focus for our inquiry. As will be seen, it is often easiest to motivate principles of the theory with invented examples that are, roughly, "musical prose." But there are two reasons for then going on to grapple with existing works of art, one preferential and the other methodological. First, it is less rewarding to specify structural descriptions for normative but dull examples than for works of lasting interest. Second, if we were to restrict ourselves to contrived examples, there would always be the danger, through excessive limitation of the possibilities in the interest of conceptual manageability, of oversimplifying and thereby establishing shallow or incorrect principles with respect to music in general. Tonal masterpieces provide a rich data sample in which the possibilities of the idiom are revealed fully.[8]

An artistic concern that we do not address here is the problem of musical affect—the interplay between music and emotional responses. By treating music theory as primarily a psychological rather than a purely analytical enterprise, we at least place it in a territory where questions of affect may meaningfully be posed. But, like most contemporary music theorists, we have shied away from affect, for it is hard to say anything systematic beyond crude statements such as observing that loud and fast music tends to be exciting. To approach any of the subtleties of musical affect, we assume, requires a better understanding of musical structure.[9] In restricting ourselves to structural considerations, we do not mean to deny the importance of affect in one's experience of music. Rather we hope to provide a steppingstone toward a more interesting account of affect than can at present be envisioned.

1.4 The Overall Form of the Theory

A comprehensive theory of music would account for the totality of the listener's musical intuitions. Such a goal is obviously premature. In the present study we will for the most part restrict ourselves to those components of musical intuition that are hierarchical in nature. We propose four such components, all of which enter into the structural description of a piece. As an initial overview we may say that *grouping structure* expresses a hierarchical segmentation of the piece into motives, phrases, and sections. *Metrical structure* expresses the intuition that the events of the piece are related to a regular alternation of strong and weak beats at a number of hierarchical levels. *Time-span reduction* assigns to the pitches of the piece a hierarchy of "structural importance" with respect to their position in grouping and metrical structure. *Prolongational reduction* assigns to the pitches a hierarchy that expresses harmonic and melodic tension and relaxation, continuity and progression.

Other dimensions of musical structure—notably timbre, dynamics, and motivic-thematic processes—are not hierarchical in nature, and are not treated directly in the theory as it now stands. Yet these dimensions play an important role in the theory in that they make crucial contributions to the principles that establish the hierarchical structure for a piece. The theory thus takes into account the influence of nonhierarchical dimensions, even though it does not formalize them.

We have found that a generative music theory, unlike a generative linguistic theory, must not only assign structural descriptions to a piece, but must also differentiate them along a scale of coherence, weighting them as more or less "preferred" interpretations (that is, claiming that the experienced listener is more likely to attribute some structures to the music than others). Thus the rules of the theory are divided into two distinct types: *well-formedness rules,* which specify the possible structural descriptions, and *preference rules,* which designate out of the possible structural descriptions those that correspond to experienced listeners' hearings of any particular piece. The preference rules, which do the major portion of the work of developing analyses within our theory, have no counterpart in standard linguistic theory; their presence is a prominent difference between the forms of the two theories (see section 12.2 for further discussion).

The need for preference rules follows from the nature of intuitive judgments involved in motivating the theory. In a linguistic grammar, perhaps the most important distinction is grammaticality: whether or not a given string of words is a sentence in the language in question. A subsidiary distinction is ambiguity: whether a given string is assigned two or more structures with different meanings. In music, on the other hand, grammaticality per se plays a far less important role, since almost any passage of music is potentially vastly ambiguous—it is much easier to construe music in a multiplicity of ways. The reason for this is that music is not tied down to specific meanings and functions, as language is. In a sense, music is pure structure, to be "played with" within certain bounds. The interesting musical issues usually concern what is the most coherent or "preferred" way to hear a passage. Musical grammar must be able to express these preferences among interpretations, a function that is largely absent from generative linguistic theory. Generally, we expect the musical grammar to yield clear-cut results where there are clear-cut intuitive judgments and weaker or ambiguous results where intuitions are less clear. A "preferred" structural description will tend to relate otherwise disparate intuitions and reveal regular structural patterns.

Certain musical phenomena, such as elisions, require structures not expressible by the well-formedness rules. These structures are described

Chapter 1

1.1

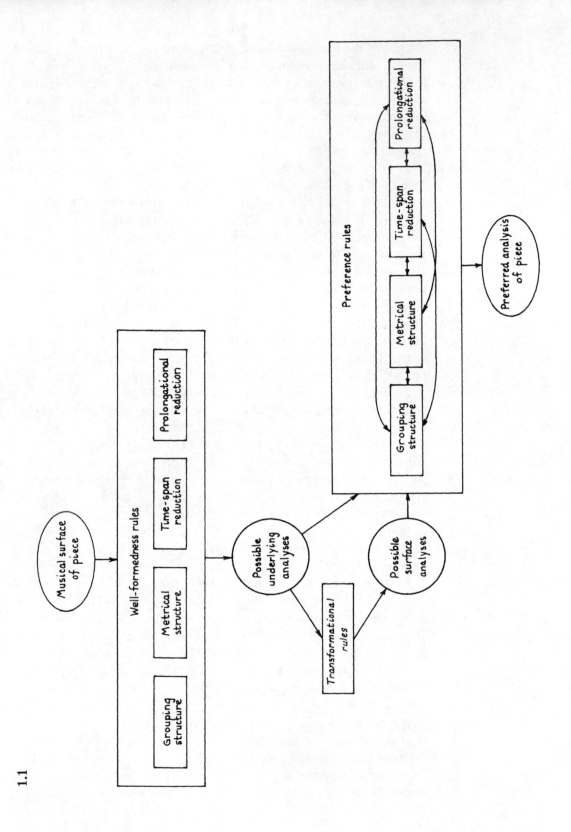

by adding a third rule type, *transformational rules,* to the musical grammar. The transformational rules apply certain distortions to the otherwise strictly hierarchical structures provided by the well-formedness rules. Although transformational rules have been central to linguistic theory, they play a relatively peripheral role in our theory of music at present.[10]

Figure 1.1 summarizes the form of the theory. The rectangles stand for sets of rules, the ellipses and circles stand for inputs and outputs of rules, and the arrows indicate the direction of formal derivation. Overall, the system can be thought of as taking a given musical surface as input and producing the structure that the listener hears as output. The meaning of the intermediate steps will become clear as our exposition of the theory proceeds.

In presenting the theory we discuss each component twice. First we present its *analytic system,* the conceptions and notations needed to express intuitions relevant to that component. At the same time we deal with the interaction of that component with the others and relate our formulations to contrasting theoretical approaches. Then we present each component's *formal grammar,* the system of rules that assigns that component's contribution to the structural description of a piece. These chapters are followed by further illustrations of the analytic system and by remarks on various musical, psychological, and linguistic implications of the theory.

2
Introduction to Rhythmic Structure

This chapter introduces those aspects of rhythmic structure inferred by the listener that do not directly involve pitch. A guiding principle throughout will be that rhythmic intuition must not be oversimplified. In our view, an adequate account of rhythm first of all requires the accurate identification of individual rhythmic dimensions. The richness of rhythm can then be seen as the product of their interaction.

The first rhythmic distinction that must be made is between grouping and meter. When hearing a piece, the listener naturally organizes the sound signals into units such as motives, themes, phrases, periods, theme-groups, sections, and the piece itself. Performers try to breathe (or phrase) between rather than within units. Our generic term for these units is *group*. At the same time, the listener instinctively infers a regular pattern of strong and weak beats to which he relates the actual musical sounds. The conductor waves his baton and the listener taps his foot at a particular level of beats. Generalizing conventional usage, our term for these patterns of beats is *meter*.

Sections 2.1 and 2.2 present grouping structure and metrical structure as independent components of rhythmic organization and develop their analytic notations. Section 2.3 sketches how these two components interrelate. Section 2.4 discusses the notion of "structural accent" and shows how it interacts with grouping and meter. Aspects of rhythm directly involving pitch structure will be dealt with in the chapters on time-span and prolongational reduction.

Whatever intrinsic interest our formulations of grouping and meter may have, they are not merely ends in themselves. We originally developed these formulations because no principled account of pitch reduction was possible without them. In this sense the purely rhythmic part of this book (chapters 2–4) is an extended preliminary to the reductional part (chapters 5–9).

The process of grouping is common to many areas of human cognition. If confronted with a series of elements or a sequence of events, a person spontaneously segments or "chunks" the elements or events into groups of some kind. The ease or difficulty with which he performs this operation depends on how well the intrinsic organization of the input matches his internal, unconscious principles for constructing groupings. For music the input is the raw sequences of pitches, attack points, durations, dynamics, and timbres in a heard piece. When a listener has construed a grouping structure for a piece, he has gone a long way toward "making sense" of the piece: he knows what the units are, and which units belong together and which do not. This knowledge in turn becomes an important input for his constructing other, more complicated kinds of musical structure. Thus grouping can be viewed as the most basic component of musical understanding.

The most fundamental characteristic of musical groups is that they are heard in a hierarchical fashion. A motive is heard as part of a theme, a theme as part of a theme-group, and a section as part of a piece. To reflect these perceived hierarchies we represent groups by slurs placed beneath the musical notation. A slur enclosed within a slur signifies that a group is heard as part of a larger group. For example, in 2.1 the groups marked p are heard as part of the larger group marked q.

2.1

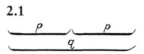

The concept *hierarchy* must be examined with some precision. A hierarchical structure, in the sense used in this theory, is an organization composed of discrete elements or regions related in such a way that one element or region subsumes or contains other elements or regions. A subsumed or contained element or region can be said to be *subordinate* to the element or region that subsumes or contains it; the latter can be said to *dominate*, or be *superordinate* to, the former. In principle this process of subordination (or domination) can continue indefinitely. Thus all elements or regions in a hierarchy except those at the very top and bottom of the structure are subordinate in one direction and dominating in the other. Elements or regions that are about equally subordinate within the entire hierarchy can be thought of as being at a particular hierarchical *level*. A particular level can be spoken of as *small-scale* or *large-scale,* depending on the size of its constituent elements or regions.

In a strictly hierarchical organization, a dominating region contains subordinate regions but cannot partially overlap with those regions. Hence the grouping structure in 2.2a represents a possible organization, but the grouping structure in 2.2b represents an impossible organization: at *i* two regions overlap at both levels 1 and 2, at *j* two regions overlap each other at level 2 and completely overlap a region at level 1, and at k a boundary at level 3 overlaps a region at level 2.

2.2

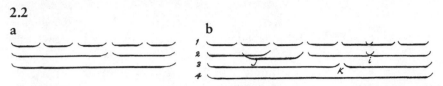

Whereas k never happens in music, j is at least conceivable, and i occurs commonly (in the form of grouping overlaps and elisions). Thus musical grouping is not *strictly* hierarchical in the sense just described. However, the conditions under which overlaps and elisions are perceived are highly constrained. These cases require special treatment. For now we merely acknowledge their existence and notate them as at i where appropriate.[1] We will return to them in section 3.4.

Hierarchically correct grouping structures are illustrated in 2.3. The beginning of the scherzo of Beethoven's Sonata op. 2, no. 2 (2.3a) shows a typical, regular kind of grouping structure in classical music: a 4-bar antecedent phrase is balanced by a 4-bar consequent phrase; both phrases divide internally into $1+1+2$ bars, and, at the next larger level, into $2+2$ bars. By contrast, the opening of Beethoven's Eighth Symphony (2.3b) is an instance of a less symmetrical, more complex grouping structure: although there are regular 4-bar groups at the smallest level indicated, measures 5–12 group together (because of thematic parallelism) at the next larger level to counterbalance measures 1–4, and to produce at the still next larger level a 12-bar phrase. And there is a legitimate, indeed prototypical case of grouping overlap at measure 12 in 2.3b: the event at the downbeat of measure 12 simultaneously cadences one group (or set of groups) and begins another group (or set of groups).

Two further general points about musical groups are already implicit in this discussion of hierarchical organization. The first concerns the relation among subordinate and dominating groups. This relation does not differ from level to level or change in some substantive way at any particular level, but is essentially the same at all levels of musical structure. For example, it never happens that one kind of overlap is allowed at one level but disallowed at another. Or, to put the matter rather differently, any abstract grouping pattern could stand equally for local or global levels of musical structure. Thus the abstract grouping in 2.1— two groups enclosed within a larger one—occurs at three pairs of levels in 2.3a: at the 1- and 2-bar levels at the beginning of each phrase ($1+1=2$), at the 2- and 4-bar levels within each phrase ($2+2=4$), and at the 4- and 8-bar levels within the passage as a whole ($4+4=8$). Because

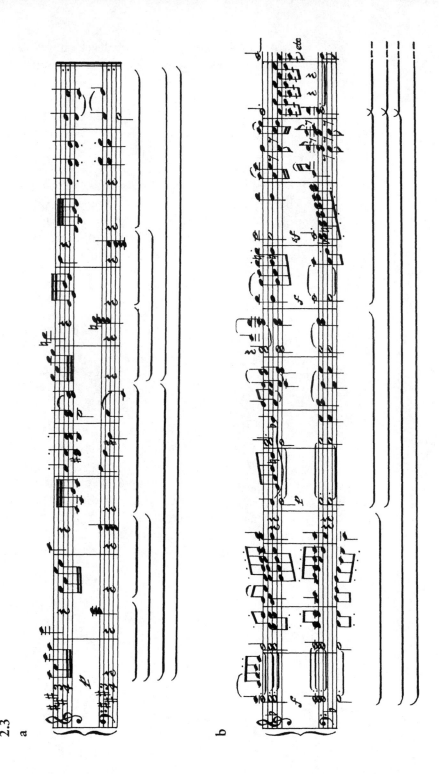

2.3
a

b

Rhythmic Structure

of this uniformity from level to level, we can assert that grouping structure is *recursive;* that is, it can be elaborated indefinitely by the same rules.

The second point follows from the nonoverlapping condition for hierarchical structures: nonadjacent units cannot group together at any particular level of analysis. To see what this means, consider the sequence in 2.4. On the basis of identity, one might wish to group all the *a*s together and all the *b*s together (2.4a). Although such a grouping is conceivable in principle, it is not the kind of grouping structure intended here. Translated into the slur notation, 2.4a would yield the impermissible overlaps in 2.4b (in which, as a visual convenience, the *a*s are grouped by dashed slurs and the *b*s by solid slurs). The correct grouping analysis of this sequence is instead 2.4c, which captures the larger repetition of the *aab* pattern.

2.4

a   **b**   **c**

The Beethoven scherzo of 2.3 (repeated in 2.5) provides an approximate analog to 2.4 if we consider it (plausibly enough) to consist of three motivic cells: the 16th-note arpeggio (*a*), the single chord (*b*), and the cadential figure (*c*). Linking these cells together produces some structure such as that indicated in 2.5. Although the listener undoubtedly makes such associations, they are not the grouping structure that he hears. Rather he hears the grouping in 2.3a, in which the motivic cells are related to their surrounding contexts and parallel motivic cells form parallel parts of groups.

2.5

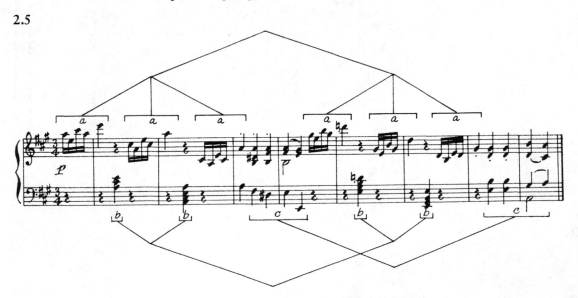

More generally, the web of motivic associations (and of textural and timbral associations as well)—let us call it *associational structure*—is a highly important dimension in the understanding of a piece. But this web is not hierarchical in the restricted sense described above, and it must not be confused with grouping structure. It is a different dimension of musical structure, one that interacts with grouping structure. Because associational structure is not hierarchical, however, our theory at present has little to say about it. (See further remarks in section 11.4.)

To sum up: Grouping structure is hierarchical in a nonoverlapping fashion (with the one exception mentioned above), it is recursive, and each group must be composed of contiguous elements. These conditions constitute a strong hypothesis about the nature of musical cognition with respect to grouping. As will be seen, they are all the more significant in that they also pertain to the other three components of the theory.

2.2 Metrical Structure

Kinds of Accent

Before discussing metrical structure (the regular, hierarchical pattern of beats to which the listener relates musical events), we must clarify the concept of *accent*. Vague use of this term, often in connection with meter, has caused much confusion. In our judgment it is essential to distinguish three kinds of accent: phenomenal, structural, and metrical. By *phenomenal accent* we mean any event at the musical surface that gives emphasis or stress to a moment in the musical flow. Included in this category are attack points of pitch-events, local stresses such as sforzandi, sudden changes in dynamics or timbre, long notes, leaps to relatively high or low notes, harmonic changes, and so forth. By *structural accent* we mean an accent caused by the melodic/harmonic points of gravity in a phrase or section—especially by the cadence, the goal of tonal motion. By *metrical accent* we mean any beat that is relatively strong in its metrical context.[2]

Phenomenal, structural, and metrical accents relate in various ways. Section 2.4 deals with the interaction of structural and metrical accents, and chapter 4 is concerned in detail with the relation of phenomenal accent to metrical accent. Nonetheless, a general characterization of the latter relation is now in order, if only because it will help locate the conception of metrical structure in concrete experience.

Phenomenal accent functions as a perceptual input to metrical accent—that is, the moments of musical stress in the raw signal serve as "cues" from which the listener attempts to extrapolate a regular pattern of metrical accents. If there is little regularity to these cues, or if they conflict, the sense of metrical accent becomes attenuated or ambiguous. If on the other hand the cues are regular and mutually supporting, the sense of metrical accent becomes definite and multileveled. Once a clear metrical pattern has been established, the listener renounces it only in the face of strongly contradicting evidence. Syncopation takes place where cues are strongly contradictory yet not strong enough, or regular enough, to override the inferred pattern. In sum, the listener's cognitive task is to match the given pattern of phenomenal accentuation as closely as possible to a permissible pattern of metrical accentuation; where the two patterns diverge, the result is syncopation, ambiguity, or some other kind of rhythmic complexity.

Metrical accent, then, is a mental construct, inferred from but not identical to the patterns of accentuation at the musical surface. Our concern now is to characterize this construct. However, because "metrical accent" is nothing but a relative term applied to beats within a regular metrical hierarchy, we can instead describe what constitutes a metrical pattern. Specifically, we need to investigate the notions of "beat," "periodicity," and "metrical hierarchy." In the course of this discussion we will develop an analytic notation for metrical structure and outline the range of permissible metrical patterns.

Before proceeding, we should note that the principles of grouping structure are more universal than those of metrical structure. In fact, though all music groups into units of various kinds, some music does not have metrical structure at all, in the specific sense that the listener is unable to extrapolate from the musical signal a hierarchy of beats. Examples that come immediately to mind are Gregorian chant, the alap (opening section) of a North Indian raga, and much contemporary music (regardless of whether the notation is "spatial" or conventional). At the opposite extreme, the music of many cultures has a more complicated metrical organization than that of tonal music. As will emerge, the rhythmic complexities of tonal music arise from the interaction of a comparatively simple metrical organization with grouping structure, and, above all, from the interaction of both components with a very rich pitch structure.

The Metrical Hierarchy
The elements that make up a metrical pattern are *beats*. It must be emphasized at the outset that beats, as such, do not have duration. Players respond to a hypothetically infinitesimal point in the conductor's beat; a metronome gives clicks, not sustained sounds. Beats are idealizations, utilized by the performer and inferred by the listener from the musical signal. To use a spatial analogy: beats correspond to geometric points rather than to the lines drawn between them. But, of course, beats occur in time; therefore an interval of time—a duration—takes place between successive beats. For such intervals we use the term *time-span*. In the spatial analogy, time-spans correspond to the spaces between geometric points. Time-spans have duration, then, and beats do not.[3]

Because beats are analogous to points, it is convenient to represent them by dots. The sequences of dots in 2.6 stand for sequences of beats.

2.6

a

· · · · · · ·

b

· · · · · · · · · · · · ·

The two sequences differ, however, in a crucial respect: the dots in the first sequence are equidistant, but not those in the second. In other words, the time-spans between successive beats are equal in 2.6a but unequal in 2.6b. Though a structure like 2.6b is conceivable in principle, it is not what one thinks of as metrical; indeed, it would not be heard as such. The term *meter,* after all, implies measuring—and it is difficult to measure something without a fixed interval or distance of measurement. Meter provides the means of such measurement for music; its function is to mark off the musical flow, insofar as possible, into equal time-spans. In short, metrical structure is inherently periodic. We therefore assert, as a first approximation, that beats must be equally spaced. This disqualifies the pattern of beats in 2.6b from being called metrical.

Curiously, neither is the pattern of beats in 2.6a metrical in any strict sense. Fundamental to the idea of meter is the notion of periodic alternation of strong and weak beats; in 2.6a no such distinction exists. For beats to be strong or weak there must exist a *metrical hierarchy*—two or more levels of beats.[4] The relationship of "strong beat" to "metrical level" is simply that, if a beat is felt to be strong at a particular level, it is also a beat at the next larger level. In 4/4 meter, for example, the first and third beats are felt to be stronger than the second and fourth beats, and are beats at the next larger level; the first beat is felt to be stronger than the third beat, and is a beat at the next larger level; and so forth. Translated into the dot notation, these relationships appear as the structure in 2.7a. At the smallest level of dots the first, second, third, and fourth beats are all beats; at the intermediate level there are beats under numbers 1 and 3; and at the largest level there are beats only under number 1.

2.7

a

| Beats | / | 2 | 3 | 4 | / | 2 | 3 | 4 | / |

b

	/	2	3	4	/	2	3	4	/
	−	∪	−	∪	−	∪	−	∪	−
	−		∪		−		∪		−

The pattern of metrical relations shown in 2.7a can also be represented by "poetic" accents, as shown in 2.7b ("−" means "strong" and "∪" means "weak"); but this traditional prosodic notation is inferior to the dot notation in three respects. First, it does not treat beats as points in time. Second, the distinction between strong and weak beats is expressed by two intrinsically unrelated signs rather than by patterns made up of one sign. Third, by including strong and weak markings at each "level" (that is, by turning two levels into one), the prosodic notation obscures the true relationship between metrical level and strength of beat.

Observe that the beats in 2.7a are equally spaced not only at the smallest level but at larger levels as well. This, the norm in tonal music, provides what might be called a "metrical grid" in which the periodicity of beats is reinforced from level to level. Because of the equal spacing between beats at any level, it is convenient to refer to a given level by the length of its time-spans—for example, the "quarter-note level" and the "dotted-half-note level." As in 2.8, we indicate this labeling of metrical levels by showing the appropriate time-span note value to the left of each level.

2.8

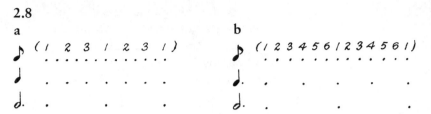

An important limitation on metrical grids for classical Western tonal music is that the time-spans between beats at any given level must be either two or three times longer than the time-spans between beats at the next smaller level. For example, in 4/4 (2.7a) the lengths of time-spans multiply consistently by 2 from level to level; in 3/4 (2.8a) they multiply by 2 and then by 3; in 6/8 (2.8b) they multiply by 3 and then by 2.

It is interesting to see how the three restrictions on grouping hierarchies—nonoverlapping, adjacency, and recursion—transfer to the very different formalism of metrical structure. The principle of nonoverlapping prohibits situations such as 2.9a, in which the time-spans from beat to beat at one level overlap the time-spans from beat to beat at another level. Rather, a beat at a larger level must also be a beat at all smaller levels; this is the sense in which meter is hierarchical.

2.9

The principle of adjacency means that beats do not relate in some such fashion as suggested by the arrows in 2.9b; rather, they relate successively at any given metrical level. The principle of recursion says that the elements of metrical structure are essentially the same whether at the level of the smallest note value or at a hypermeasure level (a level larger than the notated measure). Thus the pattern in 2.7a not only expresses 4/4 meter, but could apply equally to a sequence of 16th notes or a sequence of downbeats of successive measures. Typically there are at least five or six metrical levels in a piece. The notated meter is usually a metrical level intermediate between the smallest and largest levels applicable to the piece.

However, not all these levels of metrical structure are heard as equally prominent. The listener tends to focus primarily on one (or two) intermediate level(s) in which the beats pass by at a moderate rate. This is the level at which the conductor waves his baton, the listener taps his foot, and the dancer completes a shift in weight (see Singer 1974, p. 391). Adapting the Renaissance term, we call such a level the *tactus*. The regularities of metrical structure are most stringent at this level. As the listener progresses away by level from the tactus in either direction, the acuity of his metrical perception gradually fades; correspondingly, greater liberty in metrical structure becomes possible without disrupting his sense of musical flow. Thus at small levels triplets and duplets can easily alternate or superimpose, and at very small levels—imagine, say, a cascade of 32nd notes—metrical distinctions become academic. At large levels the patterns of phenomenal accentuation tend to become less distinctive, blurring any potentially extrapolated metrical pattern. At very large levels metrical structure is heard in the context of grouping structure, which is rarely regular at such levels; without regularity, the sense of meter is greatly weakened. Hence the listener's ability to hear global metrical distinctions tapers and finally dies out. Even though the dots in a metrical analysis could theoretically be built up to the level of a whole piece, such an exercise becomes perceptually irrelevant except for short pieces. Metrical structure is a relatively local phenomenon.

Problems of Large-Scale Metrical Structure
It may be objected that the listener measures and marks off a piece at all levels, and that metrical structure therefore exists at all levels of a piece. For example, the listener marks off a sonata movement into three parts; the time-spans created by these divisions form the piece's basic proportions. In reply, we of course acknowledge such divisions and proportions; the question is whether these divisions are metrical, that is, whether the listener senses a regular alternation of strong and weak beats at these levels. Does he really hear the downbeat beginning a recapitulation as metrically stronger than the downbeat beginning the development, but metrically weaker than the downbeat beginning the exposition? We argue that he does not, and that what he hears instead at these levels is grouping structure together with patterns of thematic parallelism, cadential structure, and harmonic prolongation. As will be seen, all these factors find their proper place in our theory as a whole, and together account for the sense of proportion and the perception of relative large-scale "arrival" in a piece.[5]

To illustrate the difficulties involved in large-scale metrical analysis, let us see how far we can carry the intuition of metrical structure in a not untypically complex passage: the beginning of Mozart's G Minor Symphony. The metrical analysis of the first nine bars appears in 2.10.

The cues in the music from the 8th-note level to the 2-bar level unambiguously support the analysis given. For example, at the 2-bar level, the introductory bar, the down-up pattern of the bass notes, the motivic structure of the melody, and the harmonic rhythm all conspire to produce strong beats at the beginnings of odd-numbered bars. (Chapter 4 will develop this analysis in detail.) The case is quite otherwise at the next larger level, the 4-bar level. Should the beats at this level be placed at the beginnings of measures 1, 5, and 9, or at those of measures 3 and 7? The cues in the music conflict. The harmonic rhythm supports the first interpretation, yet it seems inappropriate to hear the strongest beats in each 4-bar theme-group (measure 2–5, 6–9) as occurring at the very end of those groups (the downbeats of measures 5 and 9). Rather, the opening motive seems to drive toward strong beats at the beginnings of measures 3 and 7. We incline toward this second interpretation—this is the reason for the dots in parentheses at measures 3 and 7 in 2.10. But the real point is that this large level of metrical analysis is open to interpretation, whereas smaller levels are not.

The problems of large-scale metrical analysis become more acute if we consider 2.11, a simplified version of the first 23 bars of Mozart's G Minor Symphony.

First, observe that since measures 21–23 are parallel to measures 2–4, it is impossible even at the measure level to maintain a regular alternation of strong and weak beats; the strong beats at odd-numbered bars must at some point give way to strong beats at even-numbered bars. Let us investigate where this point might be.

In 2.11 we have indicated only two metrical levels, the measure level and the 2-measure level. The analysis of the first eight bars duplicates the analysis in 2.10, where the downbeats of the odd-numbered bars were stronger than those of the even-numbered bars. Whatever the case may be in measures 9–13, however, it is clear that the downbeats of measures 14 and 16 are strong in relation to the downbeat of measure 15. The reasons for this are that the melody forms what is felt to be an appoggiatura on D in measure 14, which resolves to C♯ in measure 15, and that the harmonic rhythm moves decisively from measure 14 to measure 16. Once this new pattern of strong beats on the downbeats of even-numbered bars has been established, it continues without serious complication to the restatement of the theme at measures 21 ff. Where in measures 9–13, then, has the metrical shift taken place?

Imbrie 1973 makes a useful distinction between "conservative" and "radical" hearings of shifting metrical structures. In a conservative hearing the listener seeks to retain the previous pattern as long as possible

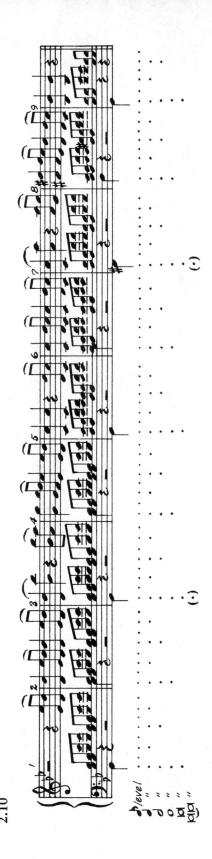

2.10

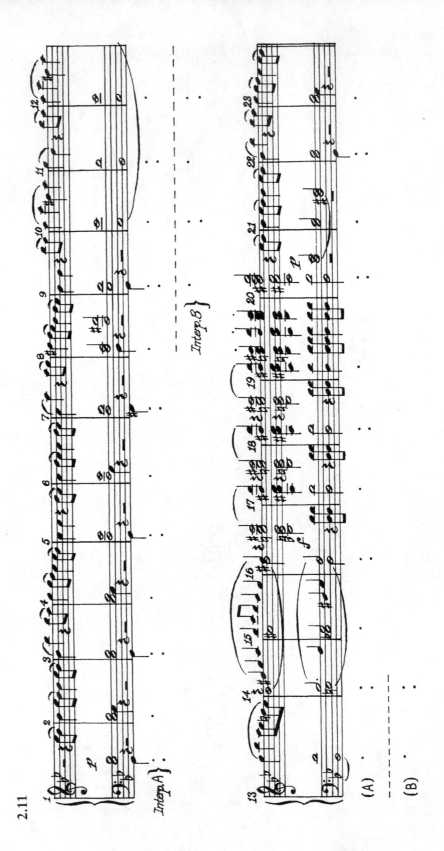

2.11

against conflicting new evidence; in a radical hearing he immediately readjusts according to new evidence. Applied to measures 9–13, interpretation A in 2.11 represents a conservative hearing. It retains the previous pattern until it is forced to relinquish the downbeats of measures 13 and 15 in favor of the downbeats of measures 14 and 16 as strong. This hearing has the advantage of giving the thematic structure in measures 10–11 the same metrical structure that it had in measures 2–3, 4–5, 6–7, and 8–9, and it lends significance to the motivically unique thematic extension in measure 13—that is, the extension is not merely thematic, but serves as well to bring about the metrical shift from the downbeat of measure 13 to the downbeat of measure 14 as strong. Interpretation B, on the other hand, represents a radical hearing: it immediately reinterprets the harmonies in measures 10 and 12 as hypermetrical "appoggiatura chords," thus setting up a parallelism with the ensuing measure 14. We will refrain from choosing between these competing alternatives; suffice it to say that in such ambiguous cases the performer's choice, communicated by a slightly extra stress (in this case, at the downbeat of either measure 10 or measure 11), can tip the balance one way or the other for the listener.[6]

But if the 2-bar metrical level has proved so troublesome, what is one to do with the 4-bar level? If the downbeats of measures 3 and 7 are beats at this level, then the downbeats of measures 11, 16, and 20 appear to follow (allowing for a 5-bar time-span somewhere in the vicinity of measures 9–16 because of the adjustment at the 2-bar level). But it seems implausible to give such a metrical accent to the downbeat of measure 11; and two bars are unhappily left over between measure 20 and measure 22. If, on the other hand, the downbeats of measures 5 and 9 are beats at this level, then the downbeats of measures 14, 18, and 22 apparently follow. But it stretches matters to hear a metrical accent at the downbeat of measure 18, placed as it is in the middle of the dominant pedal in measures 16–20. Neither alternative is satisfactory.

There is a third alternative: to posit a regular, more "normal" version of these measures—a "model"—and derive the actual music from that.[7] But it is extremely difficult to know which model to construct, other than somehow to make the downbeats of measures 16 and 22—the major points of harmonic arrival—strong beats at this level. In other respects this exercise is so hypothetical that it would seem wise to give up the attempt altogether. The 4-bar metrical level (not to mention larger levels) simply does not have much meaning for this passage.

2.3
The Interaction of Grouping and Meter

We have established that the basic elements of grouping and of meter are fundamentally different: grouping structure consists of *units* organized hierarchically; metrical structure consists of *beats* organized hierarchically. As we turn to the interaction of these two musical dimensions, it is essential not to confuse their respective properties. This admonition is all the more important because much recent theoretical writing has confused their properties in one way or another. Two points in particular need to be emphasized: groups do not receive metrical accent, and beats do not possess any inherent grouping. Let us amplify these points in turn.

That groups do not receive metrical accent will be conveyed if we compare two rhythmic analyses of the opening of the minuet of Haydn's Symphony no. 104, the first (2.12) utilizing the notations proposed above and the second (2.13) taken from Cooper and Meyer 1960 (p. 140).

2.12

2.13

Beneath the music in 2.12 appear the grouping and metrical structures heard by the listener. Considered independently, each structure is intuitively straightforward and needs no further justification in the present context. What must be stressed is that, even though the two structures obviously interact, neither is intrinsically implicated in the other; that is, they are formally (and visually) separate. By contrast, Cooper and Meyer (1960) are concerned from the start with patterns of accentuation within and across groups. Though this concern is laudable, it leads them to assign accent to groups as such. And, since groups have duration, the apparent result is that beats are given duration. In 2.13 these difficulties do not emerge immediately at level 1, which—notational differences aside—corresponds closely (until measure 7) to the smaller levels of grouping and metrical analysis in 2.12. But at level 2 in 2.13, each group of level 1 is marked strong or weak in its entirety. If metrical accent is intended (as it evidently was at level 1), this result is plainly wrong, since the second and third beats of each bar must all be equally weak regardless of metrical distinctions on the first beats. What is meant, we believe, is not that a given group is stronger or weaker than another group, but rather that the strongest beat in a given group is stronger or weaker than the strongest beat in another group. These relationships are represented accurately in 2.12.

If level 2 in 2.13 was problematic, level 3 is doubly so. Here the "accent" covers measures 5–8, presumably because of the "cadential weight" at measure 8. Thus the sign "–", which at level 1 stood for metrical accent, now signifies structural accent. Whether or not this structural accent should coincide with a large-scale metrical accent (we think not, for reasons discussed in the next section), it clearly does not spread over the 4-bar group.

These (and other) difficulties in 2.13 derive from a common source. The methodology of Cooper and Meyer—an adaptation from traditional prosody—requires that any group contain exactly one strong accent and one or two weak accents, and any larger-level group must fill its accentual pattern by means of accents standing for exactly two or three smaller-level groups. Thus only two levels of metrical structure ("–" and "‿") can be represented within any group, regardless of the real metrical situation. Far more serious, however, is that this procedure thoroughly interweaves the properties of, and the analysis of, grouping and meter. Once these components are disentangled and analyzed separately, as in 2.12, all these difficulties disappear.[8]

To illustrate briefly the kind of analytic insight that can emerge from our proposed notation for grouping and meter, let us look again at the opening of Mozart's G Minor Symphony (2.14a), this time with both structures indicated. Examples 2.14b and 2.14c isolate fragments of the analysis for comparison. It is significant that the metrical structure of the first two-measure group (2.14c) is identical with that of the initial motive (2.14b), but at larger metrical levels. No doubt the theme as a whole sounds richer, more "logical," because of this rhythmic relationship.

2.14

a

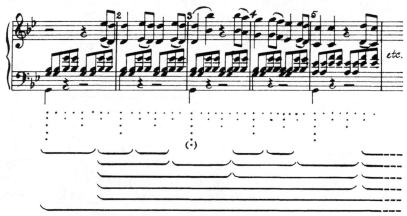

2.14 (cont.)

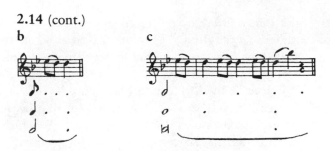

b   c

Now consider the proposition that beats do not possess inherent grouping. This means that a beat as such does not somehow belong more to the previous beat or more to the following beat; for instance, in 4/4 the fourth beat belongs no more to the third beat than to the following first beat. In metrical structure, purely considered, a beat does not "belong" at all—rather, it is part of a pattern. A metrical pattern can begin anywhere and end anywhere, like wallpaper.

But once metrical structure interacts with grouping structure, beats do group one way or the other. If a weak beat groups with the following stronger beat it is an *upbeat;* if a weak beat groups with the previous stronger beat it is an *afterbeat.* In the Haydn minuet (2.12) the third beat is consistently heard as an upbeat because of the presence of a grouping boundary before it, whereas in the scherzo of Beethoven's Second Symphony (2.15) the third beat is consistently heard as an afterbeat because of the presence of a grouping boundary after it. This difference between the two passages is all the more salient because in other respects their grouping and metrical structures are almost identical.[9]

2.15

Another example of how grouping and meter interact emerges if we consider a simple V–I progression. If it occurs at the beginning or in the middle of a group it is not heard as a cadence, since a cadence by definition articulates the end of a group. If the progression occurs at the end of a group it is heard as a full cadence—either "feminine" or "masculine," depending on whether the V or the I is metrically more accented. If a grouping boundary intervenes between the two chords, the V does not resolve into the I; instead the V ends a group and is heard as a half cadence, and the I is heard as launching a new phrase. Metrical structure alone cannot account for these discriminations, precisely because it has no inherent grouping. Both components are needed.

This completes our argument that the properties of grouping and meter must be kept separate. En route we have also shown that some fundamental rhythmic features—patterns of metrical accentuation in grouping, upbeats and afterbeats, aspects of cadences—emerge in a direct and natural way when the components interact. Now we need to generalize their interaction in terms of time-span structure.

Although time-spans can be drawn from any beat to any other beat, the only time-spans that have relevance to perceived metrical structure are those drawn between successive beats at the same metrical level; these spans reflect the periodicity inherent in metrical structure. The hierarchy of such spans can be represented by brackets as shown in 2.16, where a bracket begins on a given beat and extends up to (but does not include) the next beat at that level.

2.16

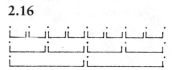

Groups, of course, also take place over spans of time. But in this case, even though a group begins on a given beat and extends up to another beat (the norm in tonal music, in which even the smallest detail is almost always given a metrical position), there is no prior restriction that the group extend between beats at the same metrical level. A group can have any arbitrary length. If, however, a group does extend between beats at the same metrical level, and if the first beat in the group is its strongest beat, then the span produced by the group coincides with a metrical time-span. An instance of this common phenomenon appears in 2.17a, where the span for the third level of dots is coextensive with the smallest grouping span.

2.17

a

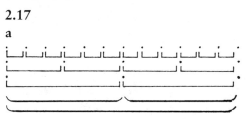

2.17 (cont.)

b

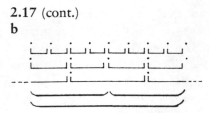

In such cases we can speak of the grouping and metrical structures as *in phase*. An example is the Beethoven scherzo in 2.15. However, if a group begins on a beat weaker than the strongest beat in the group (that is, if it begins on an upbeat), then the grouping and metrical structures are *out of phase*—that is, the grouping boundaries cut across the periodicity of the metrical grid, as in 2.17b.

Grouping and meter can be in or out of phase in varying degrees. To clarify this point, we define *anacrusis* as the span from the beginning of a group to the strongest beat in the group. (The term *upbeat* will not do here, since beats do not have duration; an anacrusis can include many upbeats at various levels.) If the anacrusis is brief, as in the Haydn minuet (2.12), grouping and meter are only slightly out of phase. On the other hand, if the anacrusis takes up a major portion of the relevant group, as in the theme of the G Minor Symphony (2.14), grouping and meter are acutely out of phase. Acutely out-of-phase passages are more complicated for the listener to process because the recurrent patterns in the two components conflict rather than reinforce one another. Generally, the degree to which grouping and meter are in or out of phase is a highly important rhythmic feature of a musical passage.

2.4
The Relation of Structural Accent to Grouping and Meter

Unlike metrical structure, pitch structure is a powerful organizing force at global levels of musical structure. The launching of a section, the return of a tonal region, or the articulation of a cadence can all have large-scale reverberations. Pitch-events functioning at such levels cause "structural accents" because they are the pillars of tonal organization, its "points of gravity." In Cone's simile (1968, pp. 26–27), a ball is thrown, soars through the air, and is caught; likewise, events causing structural accents initiate and terminate arcs of tonal motion. The initiating event can be called a *structural beginning,* and the terminating event a *structural ending* or *cadence.* (Chapter 6 will show how these events emerge from time-span reduction.)

The relation of structural accent to grouping is easily disposed of: Structural accents articulate the boundaries of groups at the phrase level and all larger grouping levels. To be sure, a structural beginning may occur shortly after the onset of a group, especially if there is an anacrusis; more rarely, an extension after a cadence may cause a group to stretch beyond the cadence proper. In general, however, these events form an arc of tonal motion over the duration of the group. The points of structural accent occur precisely at the attack points of the structural beginning and cadence; if the cadence has two members (as in a full cadence), the terminating structural accent takes place at the moment of resolution, the attack point of the second member of the cadence. Thus, even without a postcadential extension, there is a short time-span—the duration of the (second) cadential event—between the terminating structural accent and the end of the group. These remarks are summarized in figure 2.18, with b signifying "structural beginning" and c signifying "cadence."

2.18

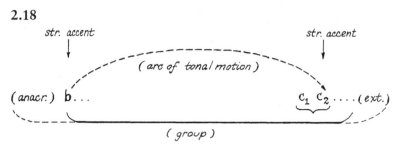

The relation of structural accent to meter requires lengthier discussion, because recently there have been several attempts to equate structural accents with strong metrical accents. We will argue against such a view and hold instead that the two are interactive accentual principles that sometimes coincide and sometimes do not.

Before proceeding to the details, let us observe in passing that the proposed equation of structural and metrical accents would mean giving up the traditional distinction between cadences that resolve at weak metrical points and cadences that resolve at strong metrical points. Thus there would be no distinction between "feminine" and "masculine" cadences, or between metrically unaccented large-scale arrivals and large-scale structural downbeats. In our view this would be an unacceptable impoverishment of rhythmic intuition.

Taking a closer view, we can schematize the issue as follows. Figure 2.19 represents a normal 4-bar phrase (it could just as well be an 8-bar phrase), with the b (most likely a tonic chord in root position) at the left group boundary on the downbeat of the first bar and the c (either a half or a full cadence) on the downbeat of the fourth bar. For present purposes only two levels of metrical structure need to be indicated: the measure level and the 2-measure level. Typically, the downbeats of successive measures are in a regular alternation of strong and weak metrical accent. Thus either the downbeats of measures 1 and 3 or the downbeats of measures 2 and 4 are relatively strong. But since the structural accents occur on the downbeats of measures 1 and 4, there is a conflict: either the c occurs at a relatively weak metrical point, as in hypothesis A, or the b occurs at a relatively weak metrical point, as in hypothesis B. The only way out of this apparent conundrum is to place strong beats both on bs and on *c*s, as in hypothesis C. But this solution is not feasible if one is to keep the notion of equidistant beats as a defining condition for meter; for when the next phrase starts, its *b* is closer to the previous *c* than each *b* is to the *c* within its own phrase, with the result that the dots at the larger metrical level are not equally spaced. In sum, hypotheses A and B do not satisfy the equation of structural and metrical accents, and hypothesis C does not satisfy the formal or intuitive requirements for metrical structure.[10]

2.19

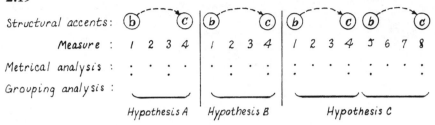

Hypothesis C becomes all the more untenable if, as often happens, the terminating structural accent takes place later in the fourth bar than its first beat. The opening of Mozart's Sonata K. 331 provides a characteristic instance; if hypothesis C is followed, the resulting "metrical" structure becomes the pattern shown in 2.20.

2.20

Here the two smaller levels follow conventional metrical accentuation, and the third level of dots represents the initial and cadential structural accents. This third level not only is wildly irregular in the spacing between beats, unlike the two smaller levels, but also makes the second beats of measures 4 and 8 stronger than their first beats. Surely this cannot be true; it creates havoc with the notion of meter. Hypothesis C—the equation of structural and metrical accents—must be rejected.

This leaves hypotheses A and B. In both, structural accent can be regarded as a force independent of meter, expressing the rhythmic energy of pitch structure across grouping structure. A dogmatic preference for either hypothesis would distort the flexible nature of the situation; one or the other—or perhaps something more complicated—pertains in a given instance. In a broad sense, in-phase passages usually yield hypothesis A and out-of-phase passages usually yield hypothesis B. The K. 331 passage (2.21a) is an instance of the former and the opening of the third movement of Beethoven's Fifth Symphony (2.21b) an example of the latter.

2.21

a

b

The case for the separation of metrical and structural accent can be supported at more global levels by a consideration of the notions of structural anacrusis and structural downbeat. A *structural anacrusis* is like a local anacrusis except that it spans not just a beat or two but a whole passage or section—for example, the transition to the finale of Beethoven's Fifth Symphony, or the introduction to Beethoven's First Symphony (analyzed in section 7.4), or measures 1–20 of Beethoven's "Tempest" Sonata (analyzed in section 10.2). In such cases a large-scale group closes on a harmonic arrival (typically through an overlap or an elision) in a strong metrical position. The effect is one of prolonged tension followed by instantaneous release. In analytic terms, significant articulations in three different musical parameters—grouping structure, metrical structure, and harmonic structure—converge at a single moment, producing a *structural downbeat*. Thus there is an asymmetry between structural anacrusis and structural downbeat: the former stretches over a long time-span, and the latter coincides with a beat.

Viewed purely as a structural accent, a structural downbeat is so powerful because it combines the accentual possibilities of hypotheses A and B: the structural anacrusis drives to its cadence (as in hypothesis B), which simultaneously, by means of a grouping overlap, initiates a new impulse forward at the beginning of the following section (as in hypothesis A). This situation is diagrammed in figure 2.22.

2.22

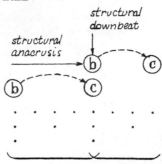

If all large-scale harmonic arrivals were metrically strong, there would be nothing special about structural downbeats. Yet it is undeniably significant to the rhythmic flow of a piece whether its cadences articulate phrases or sections on weak beats before the next phrases or sections begin (as in a Schubert waltz or a Chopin mazurka), or whether its cadences arrive on strong beats in an overlapping fashion with ensuing phrases or sections (as in the Beethoven examples cited above). The former case produces formal "rhyme" and balance; the latter is dynamically charged. The difference is theoretically expressible only if metrical and structural accents are seen as independent but interacting phenomena.

Measures 5–17 of the first movement of Beethoven's "Hammerklavier" Sonata (2.23) illustrate both possibilities nicely. The antecedent phrase (measures 5–8) cadences in a metrically weak position (marked p in 2.23), but the consequent phrase is extended in a metrically periodic fashion so that its cadence (marked q) arrives on a strong hypermetrical beat and overlaps with the succeeding phrase. In other words, the local anacrusis immediately after p begins a structural anacrusis that tenses and resolves on a structural downbeat at q.

These various discriminations would not be possible if structural and metrical accents were equated. Perhaps attempts have been made to equate them because the profound distinction between grouping and meter has not been appreciated. In any case, structural accents articulate grouping structure, not metrical structure. Groups and their structural accents stand with respect to meter in a counterpoint of structures that underlies much of the rhythmic richness of tonal music.[11]

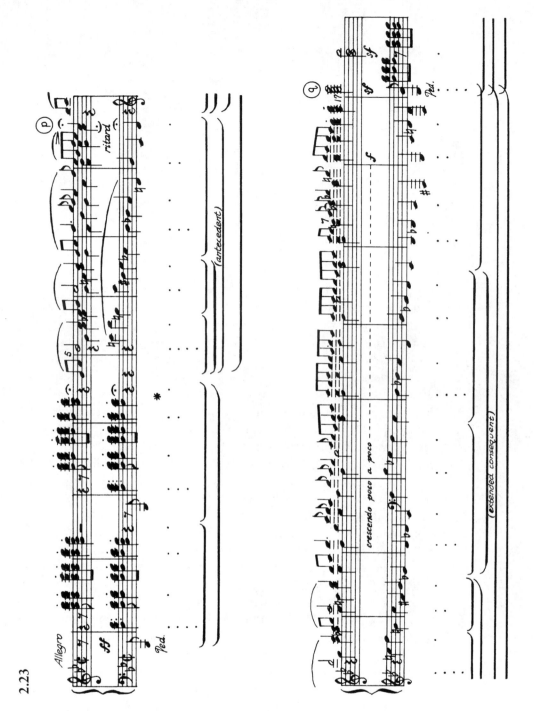

2.23

3
Grouping Structure

Chapter 2 presented the analytic system for two aspects of musical structure: grouping and meter. This chapter and the next address the formalization of these two components of the analytic system, showing how the structures used in analysis are rigorously characterized and how they are related to actual pieces of music in a rule-governed way.

In presenting our hypotheses about the grammar of tonal music we will attempt to motivate as fully as possible each rule, so that the reader can follow each step in building up what turns out to be a rather intricate system. Ideally we would explore a number of alternative formulations and defend our choice against them, but limitations of space and patience preclude doing so to any great extent. The reader should nevertheless be aware that alternative formulations are possible, and that defects in one aspect of the theory often can be remedied by relatively minor modifications.

This chapter is devoted to the organization of the musical surface into groups. From a psychological point of view, grouping of a musical surface is an auditory analog of the partitioning of the visual field into objects, parts of objects, and parts of parts of objects. More than any other component of the musical grammar, the grouping component appears to be of obvious psychological interest, in that the grammar that describes grouping structure seems to consist largely of general conditions for auditory pattern perception that have far broader application than for music alone. Moreover, the rules for grouping seem to be idiom-independent—that is, a listener needs to know relatively little about a musical idiom in order to assign grouping structure to pieces in that idiom.

Like the other components of the musical grammar, the grouping component consists of two sets of rules. Grouping well-formedness rules (GWFRs) establish the formal structure of grouping patterns and their relationship to the string of pitch-events that form a piece; these rules are presented in section 3.1. Grouping preference rules (GPRs) establish which of the formally possible structures that can be assigned to a piece correspond to the listener's actual intuitions; these are developed in sections 3.2 and 3.3. Section 3.4 deals with grouping overlap. Section 3.5 briefly addresses some questions of musical performance. Section 3.6 presents two additional analyses.

Before beginning to discuss the grammar of grouping structure, we must enter an important caveat. At the present stage of development of the theory, we are treating all music as essentially homophonic; that is, we assume that a single grouping analysis suffices for all voices of a piece. For the more contrapuntal varieties of tonal music, where this condition does not obtain, our theory is inadequate. We consider an extension of the theory to account for polyphonic music to be of great importance. However, we will not attempt to treat such music here except by approximation.

3.1 Grouping Well-Formedness Rules

This section defines the formal notion *group* by stating the conditions that all possible grouping structures must satisfy. In effect these conditions define a strict, nonoverlapping, recursive hierarchy in the sense discussed in section 2.1. As a sample of the notation, 3.1 repeats the grouping for the first few bars of melody in the Mozart G Minor Symphony, K. 550.[1]

3.1

The first rule defines the basic notion of a group.

GWFR 1 Any contiguous sequence of pitch-events, drum beats, or the like can constitute a group, and only contiguous sequences can constitute a group.

GWFR 1 permits all groups of the sort designated in 3.1, and prevents certain configurations from being designated as groups. For example, it prevents all the eighth notes in 3.1 from being designated together as a group, or the first six occurrences of the pitch D. (The contiguity condition is what makes the slur notation a viable representation of grouping intuitions; if there could be discontinuous groups some other notation would have to be devised.)

The second rule expresses the intuition that a piece is heard as a whole rather than merely as a sequence of events.

GWFR 2 A piece constitutes a group.

The third rule provides the possibility of embedding groups, evident in 3.1.

GWFR 3 A group may contain smaller groups.

The next two rules state conditions on the embedding of groups within groups.

GWFR 4 If a group G_1 contains part of a group G_2, it must contain all of G_2.

This rule prohibits grouping analyses such as 3.2, in which groups intersect.

3.2

In these examples G_1 contains part of G_2 but not all of it. On the other hand, all the groups in 3.1 satisfy GWFR 4, resulting in an orderly embedding of groups.

There are in fact cases in tonal music in which an experienced listener has intuitions that violate GWFR 4. Such *grouping overlaps* and *elisions* are inexpressible in the formal grammar given so far. However, since overlaps and elisions occur only under highly specific and limited conditions, it would be inappropriate simply to abandon GWFR 4 and permit unrestricted overlapping of groups. Instead overlaps and elisions receive special treatment within the formal grammar, involving *transformational rules* that alter structure. We turn to these phenomena in section 3.4.

The second condition on embedding is perhaps less intuitively obvious than the other GWFRs. It is, however, formally necessary for the derivation of time-span reduction in chapter 7.

GWFR 5 If a group G_1 contains a smaller group G_2, then G_1 must be exhaustively partitioned into smaller groups.

GWFR 5 prohibits grouping structures like those in 3.3, in which part of G_1 is contained neither in G_2 nor in G_3.

3.3

a
b

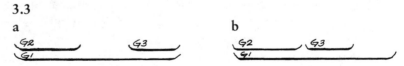

Note however that GWFR 5 does not prohibit grouping structures like 3.4, in which one subsidiary group of G_1 is further subdivided and the other is not. Such situations are common; one occurs in example 3.1.

3.4

These five well-formedness rules define a class of grouping structures that can be associated with a sequence of pitch-events, but which are not specified in any direct way by the physical signal (as pitches and durations are). Thus, to the extent that grouping structures truly correspond to a listener's intuitions, they represent part of what the listener brings to the perception of music. This will become clearer as we discuss the preference rules in the next two sections.

3.2
Perceptual
Motivation for
the Preference Rule
Formalism

Although the GWFRs rule out as ill-formed certain possible groupings such as 3.2 and 3.3, they do not preclude the assignment of grouping structures such as those in 3.5 to the opening of the Mozart G Minor Symphony.

3.5

a

b

Though these groupings conform to GWFRs 1–5, they do not, we trust, correspond to anyone's intuition of the actual grouping of this passage. One might conceivably attempt to deal with this problem by refining the well-formedness and transformational rules, but in practice we have found such an approach counterproductive. A different type of rule turns out to be more appropriate. We will call this type of rule a *preference rule,* for reasons that will soon be obvious.

To begin to motivate this second rule type, we observe that nothing in the GWFRs stated in the previous section refers to the actual content of the music; these rules describe only formal, not substantive, conditions on grouping configurations. To distinguish 3.1 from 3.5 it is necessary to appeal to conditions that refer to the music under analysis. In working out these conditions we find that a number of different factors within the music affect perceived grouping, and that these factors may either reinforce each other or conflict. When they reinforce each other, strong grouping intuitions result; when they conflict, the listener has ambiguous or vague intuitions.

Some simple experiments comparing musical grouping with a visual analog suggest the general principles behind grouping preference rules. Intuitions about the visual grouping of collections of small shapes were explored in detail by psychologists of the Gestalt tradition such as Wertheimer (1923), Köhler (1929), and Koffka (1935). In 3.6a the left and middle circles group together and the right circle is perceived as separate; that is, the field is most naturally seen as two circles to the left of one circle. In 3.6b, on the other hand, the middle and right circles are seen as grouped together and the left circle is separate.

3.6

The principle behind this grouping obviously involves relative distance: the circles that are closer together tend to form a visual group. The grouping effect can be enhanced by exaggerating the difference of distances, as in 3.7a; it can be weakened by reducing the disparity, as in 3.7b. If the middle circle is equidistant from the outer circles, as in 3.7c, no particular grouping intuition emerges.

3.7

As Wertheimer 1923 observes, similar effects exist in the grouping of musical events. Consider the rhythms in 3.8.

3.8

The perceptions about grouping for these five examples are auditory analogs to the visual perceptions in 3.6 and 3.7. The first two notes of 3.8a group together (the example is heard as two notes followed by one note); the last two notes group together in 3.8b; the grouping of the first two is very strong in 3.8c and relatively weak in 3.8d; 3.8e has no particular perceived grouping. These examples make it evident that on a very elementary level the relative intervals of time between attack points of musical events make an important contribution to grouping perception.

Examining simple visual perception again, we see that like shapes tend to be grouped together. In 3.9a the middle shape tends to form a group with the two left shapes, since they are all squares; in 3.9b the middle shape groups with the two right shapes, which are circles.

3.9

Similarly, as Wertheimer points out, equally spaced notes will group by likeness of pitch. In 3.10a the middle note is grouped most naturally with the two left notes; in 3.10b with the two right notes (assuming all notes are played with the same articulation and stress and are free of contrary harmonic implications, since these factors can also affect grouping intuitions).

3.10

Considerably weaker effects are produced by making the middle note not identical in pitch to the outer pitches, but closer to one than the other, as in 3.11a and 3.11b. If the middle pitch is equidistant from the outer pitches, as in 3.11c, grouping intuitions are indeterminate.

3.11

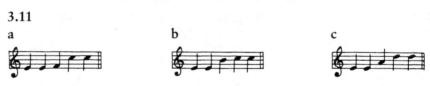

These examples have demonstrated two basic principles of visual and auditory grouping: groups are perceived in terms of the *proximity* and the *similarity* of the elements available to be grouped. In each case, greater disparity in the field produces stronger grouping intuitions and greater uniformity throughout the field produces weaker intuitions.

Next consider fields in which both principles apply. In 3.12a the principles of proximity and similarity reinforce each other since the two circles are close together and the three squares are close together; the resulting grouping intuition is quite strong. In 3.12b, however, one of the squares is near the circles, so the principles of proximity and similarity are in conflict. The resulting intuition is ambiguous: one can see the middle square as part of either the left or the right group (it may even spontaneously switch, in a fashion familiar from other visually ambiguous configurations such as the well-known Necker cube). As the middle square is moved still farther to the left, as in 3.12c, the principle of proximity exerts an even stronger effect and succeeds in overriding the principle of similarity; intuition now clearly groups it with the left group, though some conflict may still be sensed. Parallel musical examples appear in 3.13.

3.12

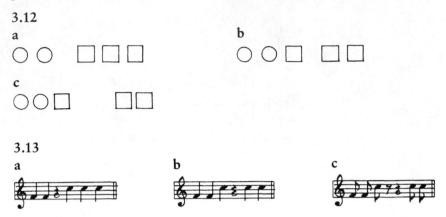

Thus three important properties of the principles of grouping have emerged. First, intuitions about grouping are of variable strength, depending on the degree to which individual grouping principles apply. Second, different grouping principles can either reinforce each other (resulting in stronger judgments) or conflict (resulting in weak or ambiguous judgments). Third, one principle may override another when the intuitions they would individually produce are in conflict. The formal system of preference rules for musical perception developed in this study possesses these same properties. The term *preference rule* is chosen because the rules establish not inflexible decisions about structure, but relative preferences among a number of logically possible analyses; our hypothesis is that one hears a musical surface in terms of that analysis (or those analyses) that represent the highest degree of overall preference when all preference rules are taken into account. We will call such an analysis the "most highly preferred," or "most stable."[2]

We have illustrated the intuitions behind preference rules with elementary visual examples as well as musical ones in order to show that the preference-rule formalism is not an arbitrary device invented solely to make musical analyses work out properly. Rather it is an empirical hypothesis about the nature of human perception. Cognitive systems that behave according to the characteristics of preference rules appear to be widespread in psychological theories. But the identification of preference rules as a distinctive and general form of mental representation seems to have gone unnoticed since the time of Wertheimer (whose work lacked the notion of a generative rule system). The introduction of preference rules as a rule type is an innovation in the present theory. (More discussion of this general point appears in chapter 12.)

With this background, we turn to stating in some detail the preference rules for musical grouping.

3.3 Grouping Preference Rules

Two types of evidence in the musical surface are involved in determining what grouping is heard by an experienced listener. The first is local detail—the patterns of attack, articulation, dynamics, and registration that lead to perception of group boundaries. The second type of evidence involves more global considerations such as symmetry and motivic, thematic, rhythmic, or harmonic parallelism. We explore these two types of evidence in turn.

Local Detail Rules

There are three principles of grouping that involve only local evidence. The first is quite simple.

GPR 1 Strongly avoid groups containing a single event.

Perhaps the descriptive intent of the rule would be clearer to some readers if the rule were stated as "Musical intuition strongly avoids choosing analyses in which there is a group containing a single event" or "One strongly tends not to hear single events as groups." Readers who may be initially uncomfortable with our formulation may find such paraphrases helpful as they continue through the rules.

The consequence of GPR 1 is that any single pitch-event in the normal flow of music will be grouped with one or more adjacent events. GPR 1 is overridden only if a pitch-event is strongly isolated from the adjacent events, or if for some reason it functions motivically all by itself. Under the former of these conditions, GPR 1 is overridden by another of the rules of local detail, which we will state in a moment. Under the latter condition, GPR 1 is overridden by the preference rule of parallelism, to be stated as GPR 6. But the comparative rarity of clearly sensed single-note groups attests to the strength of GPR 1 as a factor in determining musical intuition. (An example of an isolated note functioning as a group is the fortissimo C♯ in measure 17 of the finale of Beethoven's Eighth Symphony. An example of a single element functioning motivically occurs at measure 210 of the first movement of Beethoven's Fifth Symphony: elements of the motive have been progressively deleted in the preceding measures, until at this point one event stands for the original motive.)

An alternative formulation of GPR 1 is somewhat more general. Some evidence for it will appear in section 3.6.

GPR 1, alternative form Avoid analyses with very small groups—the smaller, the less preferable.

The effect of this version is to prohibit single-note groups except with very strong evidence, and to prohibit two-note groups except with fairly strong evidence. By three- or four-note groups, its effect would be imperceptible. Put more generally, this rule prevents segmentation into groups from becoming too fussy: very small-scale grouping perceptions tend to be marginal.

The second preference rule involving local detail is an elaborated and more explicit form of the principle of proximity discussed in the preceding section. It detects breaks in the musical flow, which are heard as boundaries between groups. Consider the unmetered examples in 3.14.

3.14

Our judgment is that, all else being equal, the first three notes in each example are heard as a group and the last two are also heard as a group. In each case the caret beneath the example marks a discontinuity between the third and fourth notes: the third note is in some sense closer to the second, and the fourth note is closer to the fifth, than the third and fourth notes are to each other. In 3.14a the discontinuity is a break in a slur; in 3.14b it is a rest; in 3.14c it is a relatively greater interval of time between attack points. (The examples of proximity in the preceding section involved a combination of the last two of these.)

In order to state the preference rule explicitly, we must focus on the transitions from note to note and pick out those transitions that are more distinctive than the surrounding ones. These more distinctive transitions are the ones that intuition will favor as group boundaries.

To locate distinctive transitions the rule considers four consecutive notes at a time, which we designate as n_1 through n_4. The sequence of four notes contains three transitions: from the first note to the second, from the second to the third, and from the third to the fourth. The middle transition, $n_2 - n_3$, is distinctive if it differs from both adjacent transitions in particular respects. If it is distinctive, it may be heard as a boundary between one group ending with n_2 and one beginning with n_3.

The distance between two notes can be measured in two ways: from the end of the first note to the beginning of the next, and from the beginning of the first note to the beginning of the next. Both these ways of measuring distance contribute to grouping judgments. The former is relevant when an unslurred transition is surrounded by slurred transitions, as in 3.14a, or when a transition containing a rest is surrounded by transitions without rests, as in 3.14b. The latter is relevant when a long note is surrounded by two short notes, as in 3.14c. Thus the rule of proximity has two cases, designated as a and b in the following statement of GPR 2.

GPR 2 (Proximity) Consider a sequence of four notes $n_1n_2n_3n_4$. All else being equal, the transition n_2–n_3 may be heard as a group boundary if

a. (Slur/Rest) the interval of time from the end of n_2 to the beginning of n_3 is greater than that from the end of n_1 to the beginning of n_2 and that from the end of n_3 to the beginning of n_4, or if

b. (Attack-Point) the interval of time between the attack points of n_2 and n_3 is greater than that between the attack points of n_1 and n_2 and that between the attack points of n_3 and n_4.

It is important to see exactly what this rule says. It applies in 3.14 to mark a potential group boundary where the caret is marked. However, it does not apply in cases such as 3.15.

3.15

Consider 3.15a. There are two unslurred transitions, each of which might be thought to be a potential boundary. But since neither of these transitions is surrounded by slurred transitions, as GPR 2a requires, the conditions for the rule are not met and no potential group boundary is assigned. This consequence of the rule corresponds to the intuition that grouping in 3.15a is far less definite than in 3.14a, where GPR 2a genuinely applies. Examples 3.15b and 3.15c are parallel illustrations of the nonapplication of GPR 2 when rests and long notes are involved.

Another rule of local detail is a more complete version of the principle of similarity illustrated in the preceding section. Example 3.16 shows four cases of this principle; the first of these corresponds to the earlier examples of similarity.

3.16

As in 3.14, the distinctive transitions are heard between the third and fourth notes. What makes the transitions distinctive in these cases is change in (a) register, (b) dynamics, (c) pattern of articulation, and (d) length of notes. We state the rule in a fashion parallel to GPR 2:

GPR 3 (Change) Consider a sequence of four notes $n_1n_2n_3n_4$. All else being equal, the transition n_2-n_3 may be heard as a group boundary if

a. (Register) the transition n_2-n_3 involves a greater intervallic distance than both n_1-n_2 and n_3-n_4, or if

b. (Dynamics) the transition n_2-n_3 involves a change in dynamics and n_1-n_2 and n_3-n_4 do not, or if

c. (Articulation) the transition n_2-n_3 involves a change in articulation and n_1-n_2 and n_3-n_4 do not, or if

d. (Length) n_2 and n_3 are of different lengths and both pairs n_1,n_2 and n_3,n_4 do not differ in length.

(One might add further cases to deal with such things as change in timbre or instrumentation.)

This rule too relies on a transition as being distinctive with respect to the transitions on both sides. Example 3.17, like 3.15, illustrates cases where transitions are distinctive with respect only to the transition on one side; grouping intuitions are again much less secure than in 3.16.

3.17

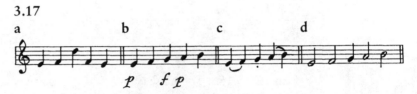

As observed in the preceding section, the various cases of GPRs 2 and 3 may reinforce each other, producing a stronger sense of boundary, as in 3.18a. Alternatively, different cases of the rules may come into conflict, as in 3.18b–3.18d. In these examples each caret is labeled with the cases of GPRs 2 and 3 that apply.

3.18

In 3.18b–3.18d there is evidence for a group boundary between both the second and third notes and between the third and fourth notes. However, GPR 1 prohibits both being group boundaries at once, since that would result in the third note alone constituting a group. Thus only one of the transitions may be a group boundary, and the evidence is conflicting. This prediction by the formal theory corresponds to the intuition that the grouping judgment is somewhat less secure in 3.18b–3.18d than in 3.18a, where all the evidence favors a single position for the group boundary.

Although judgments are weaker for 3.18b–3.18d than for 3.18a, they are not completely indeterminate. Close consideration suggests that one probably hears a boundary in 3.18b and 3.18d after the second note, and in 3.18c after the third note (though contextual considerations such as parallelism could easily alter these judgments if they occurred within a larger piece). These intuitions can be reflected in the theory by adjusting the relative strengths of the different cases of GPRs 2 and 3 so that in these configurations the slur/rest rule (GPR 2a) overrides the attack-point rule (GPR 2b), the slur/rest rule overrides the register rule (GPR 3a), and the dynamics rule (GPR 3b) overrides the attack-point rule. In general, all cases of GPR 3, with the possible exception of the dynamics rule, appear to have weaker effects than GPR 2. As in the examples in section 3.2, judgments should change depending on the degree to which different conditions are satisfied. For example, if the G in 3.18b is lengthened to four quarters, increasing the disparity in time between attacks, the evidence for the attack-point rule becomes stronger than the evidence for the slur/rest rule, and the G is heard as grouped with the E and the F.

In order to make the theory fully predictive, it might be desirable to assign each rule a numerical degree of strength, and to assign various situations a degree of strength as evidence for particular rules. Then in each situation the influence of a particular rule would be numerically measured as the product of the rule's intrinsic strength and the strength of evidence for the rule at that point; the most "natural" judgment would be the analysis with the highest total numerical value from all rule applications. We will not attempt such a quantification here, in part for reasons discussed below. Our theory is nevertheless predictive, even at its present level of detail, insofar as it identifies points where the rules are and are not in conflict; this will often be sufficient to carry the musical analysis quite far. Furthermore, the construction of simple artificial examples such as those in 3.18 can serve as a helpful guide to the relative strengths of various rules, and these judgments can then be applied to more complex cases. We will often appeal to this methodology when necessary rather than try to quantify rule strengths.[3]

Before stating the remaining grouping preference rules, let us apply GPRs 1, 2, and 3 to the opening of Mozart's G Minor Symphony. Besides illustrating a number of different applications of these rules, this exercise will help show what further rules are needed. Example 3.19 repeats the Mozart fragment. For convenience, the notes are numbered above the staff. Below the staff, all applications of GPRs 2 and 3 are listed as in 3.18.

3.19

Grouping Structure

In order to make clearer the application of the preference rules, we examine their application to 3.19. Consider first the sequence from notes 2 to 5. The time between attack points of 2 and 3 is an eighth, and so is that between 4 and 5; that between 3 and 4 is a quarter. Therefore the conditions of the attack-point rule (GPR 2b) are met and a potential group boundary is marked at transition 3–4. Similar considerations motivate all the rule applications marked. On the other hand, one might be tempted to think that the slur/rest rule (GPR 2a) would mark a potential boundary between 2 and 3. However, since there is no slur at transition 3–4 either, the conditions for the rule are not met and no boundary is marked.

Next observe that, with three exceptions, the potential group boundaries marked by GPRs 2 and 3 in 3.19 correspond to the intuitively perceived group boundaries designated in 3.1 (repeated here).

The exceptions are at transitions 8–9, 9–10, and 18–19, at which the rules mark potential boundaries but none are perceived. Transition 9–10 is easily disposed of. Because GPR 1 strongly prefers that note 10 alone not form a group, a boundary must not be perceived at both 9–10 and 10–11. Thus one of the rule applications must override the other. Example 3.18c showed a similar conflict between GPRs 2a and 3a. There the former rule overrode the latter, even with a relatively shorter rest. Hence GPR 2a should predominate here too. Further weight is put on transition 10–11 by the attack-point rule, GPR 2b, so the application of GPR 3a at 9–10 is easily overridden.

Let us ignore transitions 8–9 and 18–19 for the moment. The remaining transitions marked by GPRs 2 and 3 are exactly the group boundaries of the lowest level of grouping in example 3.1: 3–4, 6–7, 10–11, 13–14, and 16–17. Thus the bizarre grouping analysis *a* in example 3.5 (repeated here), though permitted by the well-formedness rules, is shown by GPRs 1–3 to be a highly nonpreferred grouping for the passage.

Chapter 3

However, consider again the analysis in grouping *b* of 3.5, which has all the low-level boundaries in the right place, but whose larger boundaries are intuitively incorrect. GPRs 1–3 do not suffice to prefer 3.1 over grouping *b* of 3.5, since they deal only with placement of group boundaries and not with the organization of larger-level groups. Further preference rules must be developed in the formal theory to express this aspect of the listener's intuition.

Organization of Larger-Level Grouping

Beyond the local detail rules, a number of different principles reinforce each other in the analysis of the larger-level groups in 3.1. The first of these depends on the fact that the largest time interval between attacks, and the only rest, are at transition 10–11. This transition is heard as a group boundary at the largest level internal to the passage. The most general form of this principle can be stated as GPR 4.

GPR 4 (Intensification) Where the effects picked out by GPRs 2 and 3 are relatively more pronounced, a larger-level group boundary may be placed.

A simple example that isolates the effects of GPR 4 from other preference rules is 3.20, which is heard with the indicated grouping.

3.20

GPRs 2a and 2b (the slur/rest and attack-point rules) correctly mark all the group boundaries in 3.20, but they say nothing about the second level of grouping, consisting of three groups followed by two groups. GPR 4, however, takes note of the fact that there is a rest at the end of the third small group, strongly intensifying the effects of GPR 2 at that particular transition. It is this more strongly marked transition that is responsible for the second level of grouping.

A second principle involved in the larger-level grouping of example 3.1 is a general preference for symmetry in the grouping structure, independent of the musical content:

GPR 5 (Symmetry) Prefer grouping analyses that most closely approach the ideal subdivision of groups into two parts of equal length.

GPR 5 is involved in the larger-level grouping of 3.21a in which the smaller groups are further grouped two and two rather than, say, one and three.

3.21

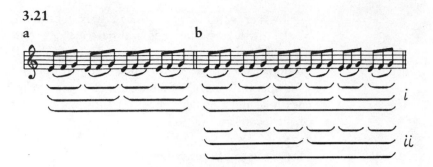

In a case such as 3.21b, where there are six small groups, GPR 5 cannot apply in the ideal fashion. The ideal can be achieved in the relation between the small and intermediate-level groups, or in the relation between the intermediate-level and large groups, but not both. The result is an ambiguous intermediate-level grouping, shown as analyses *i* and *ii* in 3.21b. In a real piece the ambiguity may be resolved by metrical or harmonic considerations, but then the result is not due solely to GPR 5. In general, it is the impossibility of fully satisfying GPR 5 in ternary grouping situations that makes such groupings somewhat less stable than binary groupings.

In the Mozart passage (example 3.19), GPR 5 has effects of two sorts. First, it reinforces GPR 4 (the intensification rule) in marking transition 10–11 as a larger-level boundary, since this divides the passage into two equal parts. Second, the resulting intermediate-level groups each contain three groups, the first two of which are two quarter notes in duration and the third four quarter notes. GPR 5 therefore groups the first two together into a group four quarter notes in duration, producing the ideal subdivision of all groups. (Note that GPR 5 does not require all groups to be subdivided in the same way; it is irrelevant to GPR 5 that the first and third four-quarter-note groups are subdivided but the second and fourth are not.)

In addition to GPRs 4 and 5, a third very important principle is involved in the larger-level grouping of 3.19: the motivic parallelism of events 1–10 and 11–20. We can isolate the effects of this principle in passages such as those shown in example 3.22.

3.22

Other things being equal, 3.22a is most naturally grouped in threes and 3.22b in fours. Since both examples have uniform motion, articulation, and dynamics, the grouping preference rules so far make no prediction at all about their grouping. Hence a further preference rule is necessary to describe these intuitions. We state it as GPR 6.

GPR 6 (Parallelism) Where two or more segments of the music can be construed as parallel, they preferably form parallel parts of groups.

The application of GPR 6 to 3.22 is obvious: the maximal parallelism is achieved if the "motive" is three notes long in 3.22a and four notes long in 3.22b.

However, consider what happens if a contrary articulation is applied to 3.22a, as in 3.23.

3.23

One's intuition is that a grouping into threes is now relatively unnatural. The theory accounts for this as follows: the slur/rest rule places rather strong potential group boundaries in 3.23 after every fourth note, where the slurs are broken; thus each of the three-note segments so obvious in 3.22a comes to have an internal group boundary in a different place. Since motivic parallelism requires (among other things) parallel internal grouping, 3.23 cannot be segmented into three-note parallel groups nearly as easily as 3.22a can. Thus GPR 6 either is overridden by the slur/rest rule or actually fails to apply.

GPR 6 says specifically that parallel passages should be analyzed as forming parallel parts of groups rather than entire groups. It is stated this way in order to deal with the common situation in which groups begin in parallel fashion and diverge somewhere in the middle, often in order for the second group to make a cadential formula. (More rarely, parallelism occurs at ends of groups.) A clear example is 3.24, the opening of Beethoven's Quartet op. 18, no. 1.

3.24

GPR 6, reinforced by the slur/rest rule, analyzes the first four measures as two two-measure groups. The fifth measure resembles the first and third, but at that point the similarity ends. If GPR 6 demanded total parallelism it could not make use of the similarity of measures 1, 3, and 5. But as we have chosen to state the rule above, it can use this parallelism to help establish grouping.

In the Mozart example (3.19), GPR 6 has two effects. First, it reinforces the intensification and symmetry rules in assigning the major grouping division at the middle of the passage. Second, recall that GPR 2a, the slur/rest rule, marks a possible group boundary at transitions 8–9 and

18–19, and that these group boundaries did not appear to correspond to intuition. Consider transition 8–9; 18–19 is treated similarly. GPR 6 is implicated in the suppression of this potential boundary by detecting the parallelism between the sequences of events at transitions 1–3, 4–6, and 7–9. If a group boundary appeared at transition 8–9, parallelism would require it at 2–3 and 5–6 as well. But this would in turn make notes 3 and 6 form single-note groups, in violation of GPR 1. Hence the only way to preserve parallelism is to suppress the possible group boundary at 8–9. Indirectly, then, GPR 6 overrides the slur/rest rule here.

The parallelism rule is not only important in establishing intermediate-level groupings such as those in the brief examples examined here; it is also the major factor in all large-scale grouping. For example, it recognizes the parallelism between the exposition and the recapitulation of a sonata movement, and assigns them parallel groupings at a very large level, establishing major structural boundaries in the movement.

Finally, a seventh preference rule for grouping is concerned primarily with influencing large-scale grouping. Different choices in sectionalization of a piece often result in interesting differences in the time-span and prolongational reductions, and often the choice cannot be made purely on the basis of grouping evidence. Rather, the choice of preferred grouping must involve the relative stability of the resulting reductions. Without a full account of the reductions we obviously cannot motivate such a preference rule here, but we state it for completeness; it plays a role in several analyses in chapter 10.

GPR 7 (Time-Span and Prolongational Stability) Prefer a grouping structure that results in more stable time-span and/or prolongational reductions.

Having stated the system of GPRs, we conclude this section with a few remarks on the notion of parallelism mentioned in GPR 6 and on the nature of the formalism used in stating our rules. The grouping preference rules are applied to two other brief examples in section 3.6.

Remarks on Parallelism

The importance of parallelism in musical structure cannot be overestimated. The more parallelism one can detect, the more internally coherent an analysis becomes, and the less independent information must be processed and retained in hearing or remembering a piece. However, our formulation of GPR 6 still leaves a great deal to intuition in its use of the locution "parallel."

When two passages are identical they certainly count as parallel, but how different can they be before they are judged as no longer parallel? Among the factors involved in parallelism are similarity of rhythm, similarity of internal grouping, and similarity of pitch contour. Where one passage is an ornamented or simplified version of another, similarity of relevant levels of the time-span reduction must also be invoked. Here knowledge of the idiom is often required to decide what counts as ornamentation and simplification. It appears that a set of preference rules for parallelism must be developed, the most highly reinforced case of which is identity. But we are not prepared to go beyond this, and we feel that our failure to flesh out the notion of parallelism is a serious gap in our attempt to formulate a fully explicit theory of musical understanding. For the present we must rely on intuitive judgments to deal with this area of analysis in which the theory cannot make predictions.

The problem of parallelism, however, is not at all specific to music theory; it seems to be a special case of the much more general problem of how people recognize similarities of any sort—for example similarities among faces. This relation of the musical problem to the more general problem of psychology has two consequences. On one hand, we may take some comfort in the realization that our unsolved problem is really only one aspect of a larger and more basic unsolved problem. On the other hand, the hope of developing a solution to the musical problem in terms of the preference-rule formalism suggests that such a formalism may be more widely applicable in psychological theory.

Remarks on Formalism

Some readers may be puzzled by our assertion that grouping well-formedness rules 1–5 and grouping preference rules 1–7 constitute a formal theory of musical grouping. There are two respects in which our theory does not conform to the stereotype of a formal theory. First, the rules are couched in fairly ordinary English, not in a mathematical or quasimathematical language. Second, even if the rules were translated into some sort of mathematical terms they would not be sufficient to provide a foolproof algorithm for constructing a grouping analysis from a given musical surface. This seems an appropriate place to defend our theory against such possible criticisms.

The first criticism is rather easily disposed of. As we have said above, our interest is in stating as precisely as possible the factors leading to intuitive judgments. Mathematicization of the rules rather than precise statement in English is useful only insofar as it enables us to make more interesting or more precise predictions. Consider the grouping well-formedness rules, which together define a class of hierarchical grouping structures connected in a simple way to musical surfaces. One could presumably translate these rules into the mathematical language of set theory or network theory without difficulty. But no empirical content would be added by such a translation, since there are no particularly interesting theorems about sets or networks that bear on musical problems. In fact, the adoption of such a formalism would only clutter our exposition with symbolic formulas that would obscure the argument. Hence we have chosen to state our rules in ordinary English, but with sufficient precision that their consequences, both for and against the theory, are as clear as we can make them.

The second argument against the theory is more substantive. The reason that the rules fail to produce a definitive analysis is that we have not completely characterized what happens when two preference rules come into conflict. Sometimes the outcome is a vague or ambiguous intuition; sometimes one rule overrides the other, resulting in an unambiguous judgment anyway. We suggested above the possibility of quantifying rule strengths, so that the nature of a judgment in a conflicting situation could be determined numerically. A few remarks are in order here to justify our decision not to attempt such a refinement.

First, as pointed out earlier, our main concerns in this study are identifying the factors relevant to establishing musical intuition and learning how these factors interact to produce the richness of musical perception. To present a complex set of computations involving numerical values of rule applications would have burdened our exposition with too much detail not involving strictly musical or psychological issues.

But our decision was not merely methodological. Reflection suggests that the assignment of numerical values to rule applications is not as simple a task as one might at first think. Winston (1970), in developing a computer program for certain aspects of visual pattern recognition, utilizes procedures not unlike preference rules. Because the computer must make a judgment, Winston puts numerical strengths on the rules and sets threshold values that rule applications must attain in order to achieve a positive judgment. Winston himself notices the artificiality of this solution. For one thing, it allows only positive and negative judgments; not ambiguous or vague ones, which we showed necessary in section 3.2. Moreover, the choice of threshold values is to a certain extent arbitrary: should the threshold be, say, 68 or 72? A simple numerical solution of this sort provides an illusion of precision that is simply absent from the data.

A more formidable conceptual problem lies in the need for the preference rules to balance local and global considerations. Although it is not hard to imagine numerically balancing the length of a rest against the size of an adjacent change in pitch, it is much more difficult to balance the strength of a parallelism against a break in a slur. Part of the difficulty lies in the present obscurity of the notion of parallelism, but part also lies in a lack of clarity about how to compare parallelism with anything else. Even worse is the difficulty of balancing intercomponent considerations such as those introduced by GPR 7, the rule of time-span and prolongational stability. How much local instability in grouping, or loss of parallelism, is one to tolerate in order to produce more favorable results in the reductions? Evidently, if we are to quantify strength of rule application, nothing short of a global measure of stability over all aspects of the structural description will be satisfactory. Thus we feel that it would be foolish to attempt to quantify local rules of grouping without a far better understanding of how these rules interact with other rules whose effects are in many ways not comparable.

Both the problem of overprecision and that of global considerations are acknowledged by Tenney and Polansky (1980), whose theory of musical grouping in many ways resembles ours (see note 3). They state quantified rules of local detail, which are used by a computer program to predict grouping judgments. They point out, however, that their system does not comfortably account for vague or ambiguous grouping judgments, because of its numerical character, and they note the essential arbitrariness in the choice of numerical weights. And, although aware of the need for global rules such as those of symmetry and parallelism, they do not incorporate these rules into their system. It is our impression that they do not really confront the difficulty of how in principle one balances global against local considerations.

To sum up: Our theory cannot provide a computable procedure for determining musical analyses. However, achieving computability in any meaningful way requires a much better understanding of many difficult musical and psychological issues than exists at present. In the meantime we have attempted to make the theory as predictive as possible by stating rules clearly and following through their consequences carefully, avoiding *ad hoc* adjustments that make analyses work out the way we want. We believe that the insights the theory has been able to afford are sufficient justification for this methodology.

3.4 Grouping Overlaps

The term *overlap* has had a number of uses in the music literature. This section is devoted to overlaps in grouping structure, an important class of counterexamples to the grouping well-formedness rules. The discussion is in two parts. The first discusses the perceptual phenomena of grouping overlap and elision; the second describes some of the mechanisms needed to incorporate overlap and elision into the formal theory.

The Perception of Grouping Overlaps and Elisions

In section 3.1 we remarked that there is a discrepancy between the predictions of GWFR 4 ("If a group G_1 contains part of a group G_2, it must contain all of G_2") and certain actual musical intuitions according to which groups overlap. A typical case is the beginning of Mozart's Sonata K. 279 (example 3.25).

In this example, the beginnings of the third and fifth measures are heard as belonging to two intersecting groups at once, at various levels of grouping. This situation is a violation of GWFR 4, since there are groups that contain part but not all of other groups. Such situations are common

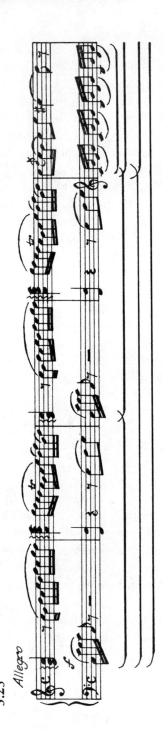

3.25

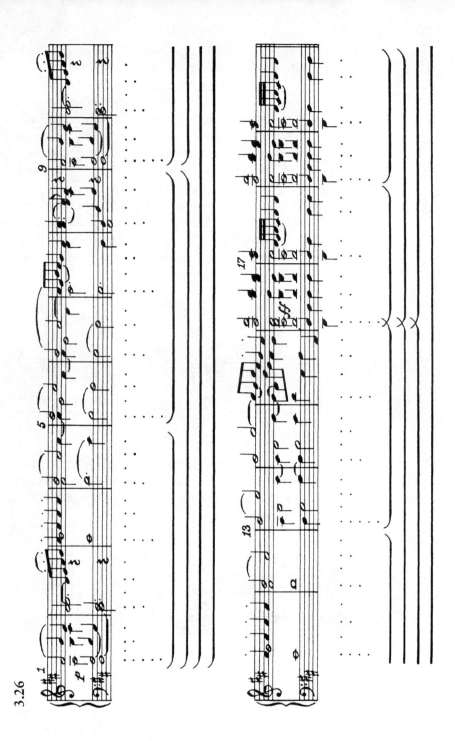

in tonal music, especially in "developmental" pieces such as sonata-form movements, where they have a great deal to do with the sense of continuity: overlaps at major group boundaries prevent the piece from reaching a point of rhythmic completion.

In addition to true overlap, in which an event or sequence of events is shared by two adjoining groups, there is another overlap situation more accurately described as *elision*. Consider the opening of the allegro of the first movement of Haydn's Symphony no. 104 (example 3.26).

The groups ending in measure 16 are interrupted by the new fortissimo group. One's sense is not that the downbeat of measure 16 is shared, as if the group ending in measure 16 were heard as 3.27a; a more accurate description of the intuition is that the last event of 3.27b is elided by the fortissimo.

3.27
a   **b**

A second and somewhat rarer type of elision occurs when a group ending forte obscures the beginning of a group starting piano, as in the ending of the first movement of Schubert's "Unfinished" Symphony (example 3.28).

3.28

The pianissimo group is not heard as beginning with a fortissimo chord, but as beginning with an unheard pianissimo attack. We will refer to the two kinds of elisions exemplified in 3.26 and 3.28 as *left elision* and *right elision* respectively: part of the left group is elided in the former and part of the right group in the latter.

In thinking about grouping overlaps, it is useful again to invoke a visual parallel. Consider 3.29a. It is most likely perceived as two abutting hexagons that share a vertical side; in other words, it is resolved perceptually as 3.29b rather than as 3.29c or 3.29d.

3.29

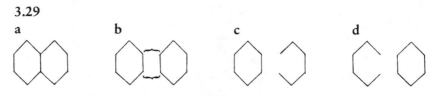

A single boundary element functions as part of two independent figures. This is comparable to overlap in music.

For a parallel to elision, consider 3.30a, which is most likely to be resolved perceptually into a square partially obscured by a triangle (3.30b), not as any of the other configurations shown.

3.30

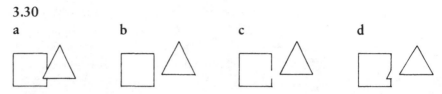

The unlikely reading 3.30d is the closest visual parallel to the musical example 3.27a. In both cases the left boundary of the right figure has been used as the right boundary of the left figure, with inappropriate results. The more natural interpretation in both cases is to infer a hidden boundary.

These visual examples appear not to be just trivial analogs to the musical phenomena. As in the discussion of preference rules, the possibility of drawing parallels between auditory and visual domains points to the operation of fundamental processes of perception and/or cognition. In both cases of overlap a single element of the field presented to perception is perceived as belonging simultaneously to two adjacent figures, neither of which is part of the other. In both cases of elision a boundary element of one figure obscures an inferred boundary of an adjacent figure. In the visual case the figures are perceived in space; in the musical case they are perceived in time. But the perceptual effect is the same. (For further discussion, see section 12.1.)

The Formal Representation of Overlaps and Elisions

Because the musical intuitions encountered in grouping overlaps and elisions correspond to grouping structures that violate GWFR 4, the grouping well-formedness rules must be modified in order to be empirically correct. However, the appropriate alteration is not to abandon GWFR 4 totally, for such an alteration predicts the existence of grouping structures such as 3.31, which do not occur.

a   b   c

In 3.31a the intermediate level of grouping bisects one element of the smallest level of grouping; in 3.31b the intermediate level of grouping has an overlap and the smallest level does not; in 3.31c the small groups overlap and the intermediate ones do not.

A more empirically sound alteration of the theory is to modify the effects of GWFR 4 in such a way as to make possible only those particular types of violations that actually occur in music. To make the appropriate modifications, we propose to distinguish two formal steps in describing a piece's grouping structure. The first, *underlying grouping structure,* is described completely by means of the grouping well-formedness rules of section 3.1; that is, it contains no overlaps or elisions. The second step, *surface grouping structure,* contains the overlaps and elisions actually observed. These two steps are identical except where the surface grouping structure contains an overlap or elision. At points of overlap, the underlying grouping structure resolves the overlapped event into two occurrences of the same event, one in each group. At elisions, the underlying structure contains the event understood as being elided. Thus the underlying grouping structure of a piece has two important properties: it conforms to the GWFRs, and it explicitly represents the double function of the overlapped or elided event.

The following rule expresses the desired relationship between underlying and surface grouping structure for overlap. The last two conditions in the rule are safeguards to ensure that all groups meeting at a boundary are overlapped in exactly the same way. They prevent the rule from creating situations like 3.31b and 3.31c, in which overlapping is not uniform from one level to the next.

Grouping Overlap Given a well-formed underlying grouping structure G as described by GWFRs 1–5, containing two adjacent groups g_1 and g_2 such that

g_1 ends with event e_1,

g_2 begins with event e_2, and

$e_1 = e_2$,

a well-formed surface grouping structure G' may be formed that is identical to G except that

it contains one event e' where G had the sequence $e_1 e_2$,

$e' = e_1 = e_2$,

all groups ending with e_1 in G end with e' in G', and

all groups beginning with e_2 in G begin with e' in G'.

When notating surface grouping structure, we designate grouping overlaps by overlapping slurs beneath the music, as in 3.32a. When notating underlying grouping structures, we join by a brace events that come to be overlapped in the surface, as in 3.32b.

3.32

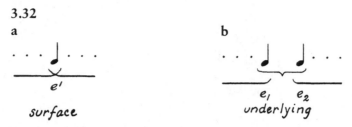

a

surface

b

underlying

The formal rule for elision is almost exactly identical to that of overlap. The only difference lies in the relationships of the boundary events e_1, e_2, and e'. For the more common left elision (3.26), e_1 (the underlying event to be elided) is harmonically but not totally identical to e_2; typically it is at a lower dynamic and has a smaller pitch range. The corresponding event in surface grouping structure, e', is identical to e_2. For right elision (3.28), the roles of e_1 and e_2 are reversed. The description of a grouping structure containing an elision thus contains in its underlying grouping structure a description of the intuitively elided event.

Grouping Elision   Given a well-formed underlying grouping structure G as described by GWFRs 1–5, containing two adjacent groups g_1 and g_2 such that

g_1 ends with event e_1,

g_2 begins with event e_2, and

(for left elision) e_1 is harmonically identical to e_2 and less than e_2 in dynamics and pitch range or

(for right elision) e_2 is harmonically identical to e_1 and less than e_1 in dynamics and pitch range,

a well-formed surface grouping structure G' may be formed that is identical to G except that

it contains one event e' where G had the sequence e_1e_2,

(for left elision) $e' = e_2$,

(for right elision) $e' = e_1$,

all groups ending with e_1 in G end with e' in G', and

all groups beginning with e_2 in G begin with e' in G'.

The rules for overlap and elision have the desired effect of expanding the class of well-formed grouping structures to include the observed counterexamples to GWFR 4. In doing so, they express the musical intuitions behind these counterexamples and they restrict the predicted range of counterexamples to three very specific related types.

In addition, the separation of underlying and surface grouping structure entailed by these rules will be advantageous in the description of the time-span reduction (chapter 7). The overlapped and elided events in all the passages cited above serve two different functions: as the end of a cadence in the left group and as the beginning of the right group. By stating the time-span reduction, which expresses these functions explicitly, in terms of underlying grouping structure, we can separate these two functions cleanly.

In looking for analogs of the overlap and elision rules in linguistic theory, two different parallels come to mind. First, with respect to their place in the formal description, they resemble syntactic transformations in linguistics, in that they increase the class of well-formed structures by applying certain optional distortions to underlying structures. However, in their substance they do not particularly resemble linguistic transformations, in that the distortions they introduce do not include such things as movement of constituents (as in the passive or subject-auxiliary inversion transformations of English). Rather, their effects are most like those of highly local phonological rules that delete or assimilate material at word boundaries (for example, the process that results in the pronunciation of only one slightly elongated *d* in the middle of the phrase *dead duck*).

Having introduced a mechanism for the formal description of overlaps and elisions, we must ask what evidence in the musical surface leads the listener to hear them. Though we cannot at this point produce a detailed account of the preference-rule mechanisms involved in the perception of overlap and elision, the general outlines of a solution are fairly clear. In example 3.25, for instance, parallelism suggests that a group begins on the first beat of measure 3, but the local details suggest instead that a group ends *after* the first beat of measure 3. If a group boundary could be drawn after the V chord at the end of measure 2, the first group might be perceived as ending in a half cadence. But local detail, particularly the position of the V in the last eighth of the measure, does not support the perception of a half cadence. Hence there is strong pressure toward hearing the I at the beginning of measure 3 as the completion of a full cadence. The two desiderata, motivic parallelism and cadence, can be achieved simultaneously only if the groups overlap at the first beat of measure 3.

This situation seems typical of overlaps and elisions: thematic considerations require the start of a new group at a point where local detail and cadential considerations strongly favor the continuation of an ongoing group. We leave for future research a formal characterization of these phenomena. Such a characterization clearly will involve not only grouping structure but also metrical structure and time-span reduction. Some overlaps and elisions are accompanied by metrical irregularities; these will be discussed briefly in chapter 4.

The performer of a piece of music, in choosing an interpretation, is in effect deciding how he hears the piece and how he wants it heard. Among the aspects of an interpretation will be a (largely unconscious) preferred analysis of the piece with respect to the grammatical dimensions addressed by our theory. Because grouping structure is a crucial link between the musical surface and the more abstract time-span and prolongational reductions, the perception of grouping is one of the more important variables the performer can manipulate in projecting a particular conception of a piece.

The principal influence the performer has on grouping perception is in his execution of local details, which affect the choice of small-level grouping boundaries through GPRs 2 and 3 (the local detail rules) and of larger boundaries through GPR 4 (the intensification rule). For example, consider the very beginning of the Mozart Sonata K. 331. In 3.33 it is supplied with two possible groupings. (We favor grouping *a*, but grouping *b* has not been without its advocates; see Meyer 1973.)

3.33

The musical surface is in conflict between these two groupings. Since the longest duration between attacks is after the quarter note, local detail favors grouping *b*. But maximal motivic parallelism favors grouping *a*. (If the piece began with an upbeat eighth, parallelism would favor *b*.) The variations that follow take advantage of the potentialities in this grouping ambiguity, tipping the balance in favor of grouping *b* in variations 1, 2, and 5 and in favor of grouping *a* in variations 3, 4, and 6.

A performer wishing to emphasize grouping *a* will sustain the quarter note all the way to the eighth and will shorten the eighth and diminish its volume. He thereby creates the most prominent break and change in dynamics at the bar line, enhancing the effects of GPRs 2 and 3 there. On the other hand, a performer who wishes to emphasize grouping *b* will shorten the quarter, leaving a slight pause after it, and sustain the eighth up to the next note. The effect of GPRs 2 and 3 is then relatively greater before the eighth and less after it.

A second and less noticeable alteration the performer may make is a slight shift in the attack point of the eighth, playing it a little early for grouping *a* and a little late for grouping *b*. This slight change in attack-point distance also affects preferred grouping through its influence on GPR 2.

Grouping Structure

These subtle variations in articulation are typical of the strategies used by performers to influence perceived grouping. However, it is important to emphasize that the performer's conscious awareness of these strategies often does not go beyond "phrasing it this way rather than that way"; that is, in large part these strategies are learned and used unconsciously. In making explicit the effect of such strategies on musical cognition, we have suggested how our theory potentially addresses issues relevant to performance problems.

3.6
Two More
Examples

In support of the claim that the rules of grouping are not style-specific, we analyze the grouping structure of the opening of Stravinsky's *Three Pieces for Clarinet Solo* (example 3.34) in terms of the rules developed here. As in the Mozart G Minor Symphony fragment, each note is numbered for convenience in discussion, and applications of GPRs 2 and 3 are marked at appropriate transitions. We assume that the breath mark is in effect an indication to the performer to produce a grouping boundary by means of one or both of the strategies just discussed: shortening the preceding note and leaving a space (which provides evidence for the slur/rest rule, GPR 2a), and perhaps lengthening the time between attack points (which provides evidence for the attack-point rule, GPR 2b). In addition to rule applications, the example shows the smallest levels of grouping predicted by the rules.

3.34

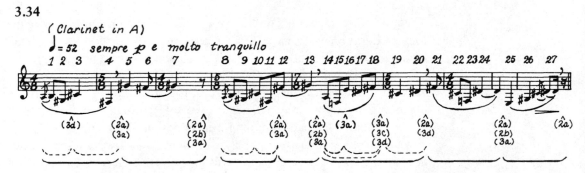

The dashed slurs in 3.34 require some explanation. Consider first transition 2–3. Although there is weak evidence for a grouping boundary at this point due to the change in note values, one tends to hear events 1–4 grouped together and to suppress the smaller groups. In section 3.3 we suggested an alternative version of GPR 1: "Avoid analyses with very small groups—the smaller, the less preferable." This version of the rule would say that the weak evidence at transition 2–3 is insufficient to establish a group boundary there, because of the shortness of the resulting groups.

At transition 9–10 there is no local evidence to support a group boundary, but parallelism with transition 2–3 and its context would argue for a boundary if one were chosen at 2–3. Similar (though weaker) parallelism plus the change in register are evidence for a boundary at 15–16; finally, a number of relatively weak rules apply at transition 18–19. Placement of a group boundary at each of these points results in one or more two-note groups, which the revised GPR 1 attempts to avoid. The overall effect of the revised GPR 1, then, is to suppress or at least make far less salient all the groups represented by dashed lines in 3.34.

On the other hand, at all the other marked transitions there are applications of the more influential preference rules of proximity. In general these rule applications cause no difficulty. However, at one point they also lead to a two-event group: notes 12 and 13. We have retained this group in the analysis for two reasons: because the local evidence for a boundary at transition 11–12 is relatively strong, and because group 1–4 followed by group 5–7 is paralleled motivically by group 8–11 followed by group 12–13. Thus both relatively strong local evidence and motivic parallelism support a grouping boundary at transition 11–12, overriding the preference of the revised GPR 1 against the two-note group 12–13.

The result of the local evidence interacting with GPR 1, then, is to establish the small-scale grouping indicated by solid lines in 3.34. In attempting to establish larger-level grouping, we first observe that motivic parallelism of the groups beginning at 1, 8, and (to a lesser extent) 14 and 21 favors larger-level boundaries at transitions 7–8, 13–14, and 20–21. In addition, the strongest local rule applications in the passage are at transitions 7–8 and 13–14; the breath at 20–21 also establishes it as a relatively strong application of GPR 2a (the slur/rest rule). So far, then, GPRs 6 (parallelism) and 4 (intensification) suggest the grouping shown in 3.35.

3.35

1 – 4 5 – 7 8 – 11 12 – 13 14 – – 20 21 – 24 25 – 27

There are two possible ways to construct still larger groups. Symmetry (GPR 5) suggests the grouping shown in 3.36a.

3.36

a

1 – 4 5 – 7 8 – 11 12 – 13 14 – – 20 21 – 24 25 – 27

b

1 – 4 5 – 7 8 – 11 12 – 13 14 – – 20 21 – 24 25 – 27

c

1 – 4 5 – 7 8 – 11 12 – 13 14 – – 20 21 – 24 25 – 27

On the other hand, transition 7–8 has the strongest application of GPR 2 in the passage, because of its rest and the preceding long note; thus GPR 4 (intensification) favors grouping 3.36b, in which this transition is the most important grouping boundary. Moreover, the strongest motivic parallelism in the passage obtains between events 1–4 and 8–11; since the rule of parallelism prefers these to be parallel parts of groups, this rule too favors grouping 3.36b. (If, in addition, purely binary grouping is desired in 3.36b, to minimally satisfy the symmetry rule, the relatively strong motivic parallelism between 8–10 and 14–16 favors an additional group, including events 14–27, as shown in 3.36c.)

The choice between 3.36a and 3.36b is the first point where the preference rules result in an ambiguous grouping in this passage. We personally incline toward 3.36b, treating the second large group in effect as an extended repetition of the first group. The resulting asymmetry is characteristic of the piece's style, in which symmetry is deliberately avoided so as to thwart the possibility of maximal reinforcement of preference rules. That is, the difference between this style and Mozart's with respect to grouping is not in its grammar as such, but in what structures the composer chooses to build using the grammar.

In the Mozart and Stravinsky passages we have examined, the grouping preference rules have encountered at least minor conflicts. Consider what an example would look like in which the preference rules encountered no conflicts and strongly reinforced each other at all points. Such an example would have strongly marked group boundaries; the major group boundaries would be more strongly marked than the minor ones; and the piece would be totally symmetrical, would have only binary subdivisions of groups, and would display considerable parallelism among groups. The theory predicts that the grouping of such a passage would be totally obvious. Example 3.37, part of the anonymous fifteenth-century French instrumental piece *Dit le Bourguignon*, is just such a case. As usual, applications of GPRs 2 and 3 are marked at relevant transitions.

3.37

Little comment on this example is necessary. The total repetition of phrases is of course the strongest form of parallelism. The smallest groups group by twos with adjacent groups of equal length; these intermediate groups again group by twos with groups of equal length. Furthermore, the intermediate-level boundaries are marked by both rests and greater duration between attack points, whereas the less important boundaries are marked only by the latter distinction, and to a lesser degree. Thus the rules of intensification, symmetry, and parallelism are all simultaneously satisfied by the grouping suggested by the local evidence; there is no ambiguity or vagueness. In addition, the grouping is maximally in phase with the meter, in the sense discussed in section 2.3, and this contributes to the stability of the analysis.

Many folk songs and nursery rhymes also exhibit this sort of regularity in the application of grouping preference rules. Pieces of this sort are often thought of as having "stereotypical" grouping structure, which in terms of the present theory means maximal reinforcement of grouping preference rules. And here lies a danger for research. Some attempts at a generative description of music (such as Sundberg and Lindblom 1976) have treated such stereotypical grouping structures as basic and assumed they could be extended to more complex structures. Furthermore, because the grouping is in phase with the meter, Sundberg and Lindblom make the same mistake as Komar 1971 (discussed in section 2.2): grouping is confused with large-scale metrical structure. If the present theory is correct, however, the stereotypical structures are totally unrevealing, since they represent the confluence of a great number of interacting factors whose individual effects therefore cannot be identified. It is essential to begin with more sophisticated examples in order to arrive at any notion of what is going on.

4
Metrical Structure

This chapter is concerned with the information the listener uses to associate a metrical structure with a musical surface. As in the grouping
component, the principles governing this association are divided into
well-formedness rules and preference rules. The former define the set of
possible metrical structures, and the latter model the criteria by which the
listener chooses the most stable metrical structure for a given musical
surface. We begin with well-formedness rules, then turn to preference
rules. Sections 4.4 and 4.5 present further discussion of well-formedness
rules.

To review the formalism for metrical structure, recall that each row of
dots below the music symbolizes a level of metrical structure. If a beat at
a given level L is also a beat at a larger level, we call it a *strong* beat of L;
if it is not, it is a *weak* beat of L. Example 4.1 illustrates the formalism.

4.1

At the eighth-note level the beats at 2, 5, 8, and 11 are strong and all
other beats are weak. In turn, at the dotted quarter-note level 2 and 8 are
strong and 5 and 11 are weak. At the dotted half-note level 2 and 8 are
beats; however, since no larger level of beats is present in this structure,
the distinction strong-weak at this level is undefined. It is the interaction
of different levels of beats (or the regular alteration of strong and weak
beats at a given level) that produces the sensation of meter.

This section first states a simple set of well-formedness rules for metrical structure in tonal music. It then points out a number of empirical problems with these rules and suggests how to improve them.

First approximation

The first well-formedness rule establishes the relation of beats to attack points.

MWFR 1 Every attack point must be associated with a beat at the smallest level of metrical structure.

The second rule establishes the relationship among metrical levels.

MWFR 2 Every beat at a given level must also be a beat at all smaller levels.

Example 4.2a, in which not every note corresponds to a beat, illustrates a violation of MWFR 1. Example 4.2b is a violation of MWFR 2; the second beat on the largest level is not also a beat on the intermediate level.

4.2

a   b

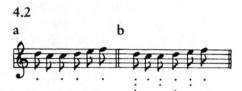

MWFRs 1 and 2 are defining conditions for metrical structures and are universal. (However, see the next subsection for refinements.)

The other MWFRs define the metrical regularities possible within a given musical idiom. Since metrical traditions differ, these MWFRs are idiom-specific. Some other idioms are discussed in section 4.4. For classical Western tonal music, the necessary rules are MWFRs 3 and 4.

MWFR 3 At each metrical level, strong beats are spaced either two or three beats apart.

MWFR 4 Each metrical level must consist of equally spaced beats.

MWFR 3 prohibits analyses like 4.3a, in which strong beats on the smaller level are six beats apart. In order for the structure to be well-formed an intermediate level must be added, either as in 4.3b or as in 4.3c.

4.3

a

(*ill formed*)

· ˌ · · · · ˌ · · · · ˌ ·
 ˌ   ˌ   ˌ

4.3 (cont.)

b

(well formed)

. . . .
. . . .
. . . .

c

(well formed)

. . . .
. . . . .
. . .

MWFR 4 holds for the smaller levels of metrical structure in tonal music, with such extremely rare exceptions as the second movement of Tchaikovsky's *Pathetique* Symphony (in five) and the third movement of the Brahms C Minor Trio op. 101 (in seven). In much of tonal music this metrical regularity also obtains beyond the measure level, producing regular "hypermeasures" of two, four, and even eight measures.[1]

In music where regular hypermeasure metrical levels are sensed, certain irregularities are heard as *metrical deletions*—violations of the metrical regularity required by MWFR 4. As with grouping overlaps and elisions, we do not account for these irregularities by dropping MWFR 4 altogether; we add a transformational rule that modifies permissible metrical structures in a constrained way. We deal with hypermeasure irregularities and metrical deletions in section 4.5.

Second Approximation

There are some difficulties in the account of metrical structure given by MWFRs 1–4. This section shows that some of these have a common source, and suggests some appropriate refinements.

First, we have assumed that each metrical level has evenly spaced beats. In a passage played with rubato or with the numerous minute temporal inflections added by a sensitive performer, spacing is uneven in the musical surface. Normally, however, the listener treats these local deviations from the metrical pattern as though they did not exist; a certain amount of metrical inexactness is tolerated in the service of emphasizing grouping or gestural patterns. Though the study of such local metrical deviations is of interest to the theory of musical cognition, we have nothing more to say about it here.

A problem that we will deal with, however, is an overexplicitness in the notation for metrical structure. Consider a piece with predominantly quarter-note and eighth-note motion, but with an occasional sixteenth note—the Mozart A Major Sonata again is a good example. Because of the presence of the sixteenth notes, the MWFRs require an overly fussy sixteenth-note level throughout the piece, as shown in 4.4.

4.4

This overexplicitness becomes a descriptive liability in dealing with the not uncommon passages in tonal music that mix incommensurate subdivisions of the beat, such as example 4.5 (from the Brahms Clarinet Sonata op. 120, no. 2, measures 9–11).

4.5

As stated above, MWFR 1 requires that each attack point in this passage be associated with a beat on the smallest level. MWFR 4 requires that this smallest level of beats must be equally spaced. Thus the smallest beat level must be spaced at the least common denominator of all the different subdivisions—in this case 1/60 of the quarter note, an absurdly small time interval.

These mechanical difficulties in the formal notation reflect a more basic metrical intuition that the rules as stated fail to express. The metrical structures described by MWFRs 1–4 treat each metrical level, from smallest to largest, as though it is as salient as every other. Yet metrical intuitions about music clearly include at least one specially designated metrical level, which we are calling the *tactus*. This is the level of beats that is conducted and with which one most naturally coordinates foot-tapping and dance steps. When one wonders whether to "feel" a piece "in 4" or "in 2," the issue is which metrical level is the tactus. In short, the tactus is a perceptually prominent level of metrical structure that the rules so far fail to designate as in any way special.

We can incorporate this notion into the formal theory by designating a particular level in a metrical structure as the tactus. The tactus is required to be continuous throughout the piece, but levels smaller than the tactus are permitted to drop out when unnecessary. Normally, two or three metrical levels larger than the tactus are continuous as well, extending to what is usually notated as the measure level; regular metrical units of two and four measures are not uncommon. Example 4.6 illustrates the conception of metrical structure that arises from incorporating this notion of tactus. The tactus is either the eighth-note or the dotted quarter-note level; the sixteenth-note level appears only where an eighth-note level beat is subdivided in the surface.

4.6

To accommodate this analysis, MWFRs 1 and 2 must be slightly modified as follows:

MWFR 1 (revised) Every attack point must be associated with a beat at the smallest metrical level present at that point in the piece.

MWFR 2 (revised) Every beat at a given level must also be a beat at all smaller levels present at that point in the piece.

This modification is still not quite enough to deal with the Brahms example (4.5), since the quarter-note tactus cannot be subdivided in a uniform way throughout the passage, as required by MWFR 4. The intuition behind the tactus, however, is that its subdivision can be relatively free, whereas the alternation between strong and weak beats of the tactus is relatively fixed. This suggests that MWFR 4 be weakened for subtactus levels. The revised version of MWFR 4 is the point in the well-formedness rules where the tactus is explicitly mentioned:

MWFR 4 (revised) The tactus and immediately larger metrical levels must consist of beats equally spaced throughout the piece. At subtactus metrical levels, weak beats must be equally spaced between the surrounding strong beats.

This revision makes the tactus the minimal metrical level that is required to be continuous (though there is nothing prohibiting smaller levels from being continuous too). It also permits the tactus to be subdivided into threes at one point and twos at another, as long as particular beats of the tactus are evenly subdivided.

The quintuplet in example 4.5 still poses a problem, since MWFR 3 does not allow subdivisions into five, and since there is no possible intermediate metrical level with evenly spaced beats, as required by MWFR 4. The correct solution here does not appear to be to allow subdivision into fives, since quintuplets are so rare in the metrical idiom we are considering. Rather, there is a class of musical devices that do not receive metrical structure: grace notes, trills, turns, and the like. These *extrametrical* events normally are fast relative to the tactus. Intuition suggests they are exempt from the MWFRs. The quintuplet in 4.5 appears to belong to this category, as do the lengthy ornamental flourishes of Chopin. A refinement to include extrametrical events is possible, but we will not pursue it here.

It should be noted that the revised MWFR 4, though it allows incommensurate subdivisions of the tactus level, prohibits them at immediately larger metrical levels, just as the original MWFR 4 prohibited them at all levels. For instance, it says that the rhythm of example 4.7 (as in Bruckner's Eighth Symphony, first movement) is possible only with a half-note or larger tactus, not with a quarter-note tactus.

4.7

This prediction corresponds with the intuition that 4.7 is most likely "felt" in half-note metrical units. It also is borne out by the fact that, in the literature of tonal music, triplets in predominantly duple metrical environments are not uncommon at small metrical levels but are rare at large metrical levels.

Which metrical level of a piece is heard as the tactus? The fact that there are often disputes about this indicates that a preference-rule mechanism is at work. Although we cannot provide a full account of how the tactus is chosen, certain influences are fairly clear. The first is absolute speed: the tactus is invariably between about 40 and 160 beats per minute, and often close to the traditional Renaissance tactus of 70. (The relationship of this rate to the human pulse has often been noted, though an explanation of why there should be such a relation between physiological and psychological rates is far less obvious than one might first think.) Second, the tactus cannot be too far away from the smallest metrical level: a succession of notes of short duration is generally an indication of a relatively fast tactus, unless the subdivisions are introduced gradually, as often happens in slow movements or variation movements. On the other hand, the tactus is usually not faster than the prevailing note values. Thus the radical change in note values during the first theme in the finale of Mozart's *Jupiter* Symphony (4.8) sets up a conflict in choice of tactus: the whole notes in measures 1–4 suggest a whole-note tactus, while the eighth and sixteenth notes in measures 6–8 (plus the eighth-note accompaniment) suggest a faster tactus. The conflict is resolved by a compromise at the half-note level.

4.8

Finally, the choice of tactus is related to harmonic rhythm. A piece with frequent functional harmonic change is heard with a faster tactus than a piece with equal note values but less frequent harmonic change. Roughly, each beat of the tactus must have only a single functional harmony. This last intuition involves the rules of time-span and prolongational reduction in a way not completely clear to us. We leave a formalization of the preference rules determining the tactus for future research.

The revisions proposed in this section create a stratified rather than a uniform metrical structure. The tactus is the central and most prominent of the metrical levels, and is regular throughout. The levels immediately smaller and immediately larger than the tactus likewise tend to be regular and aurally prominent. As the structure extends to extremely small and large levels, metrical intuition tends to fade out. Irregularity and extra-metricality are tolerated at small levels; levels larger than one or two measures are often somewhat irregular, if present at all.

4.2
Metrical Preference
Rules

Having defined the possible metrical structures for tonal music, we turn to the problem of relating these structures to a presented musical surface. To make the problem clear, note that all three metrical structures assigned to the beginning of the Mozart G Minor Symphony in example 4.9 conform to the metrical well-formedness rules, but only the first describes real musical intuition. It is the task of the preference rules to select, out of the possible metrical structures, just those that the listener hears.

This example, like succeeding ones in this chapter, is presented without bars and beams so as not to prejudice the preferred reading. Bars and beams are notational devices that convey preferred metrical structure to the performer, but they are not present in the musical surface (the sequence of pitches and durations).

4.9

Parallelism and Connection with Grouping
As we develop the metrical preference rules, it will be useful to investigate patterns that are to be repeated an indefinite number of times. The length of the pattern, three or four eighth notes, determines whether the metrical

structure must be triple or duple; it remains to find out which of the beats within the pattern are heard as strong. Since the starting point for the pattern sometimes affects judgments of metrical structure, optional notes have been added at the beginning in some examples to indicate alternative starting points in cases where it might make a difference.

The use of repeating patterns as evidence for metrical structure depends on the existence of a preference for metrical parallelism, which we state as MPR 1.

MPR 1 (Parallelism) Where two or more groups or parts of groups can be construed as parallel, they preferably receive parallel metrical structure.

MPR 1 accounts for the fact that example 4.10a is preferably heard with a metrical structure that repeats after four eighths, and 4.10b with a structure that repeats after six eighths. Where the strong beats fall in these patterns (and whether 4.10b is in 3/4 or 6/8) is still unclear.

4.10

a   b

Next consider a uniform sequence of equal-length notes of the same pitch, such as in 4.11. No beat is more metrically prominent than any other, and the sequence is totally vague metrically.

4.11

As in grouping, differentiation is required to establish perceived structure.

There is, however, a slight preference for hearing the starting point as strong in 4.11. The generalization under which this judgment falls is revealed more clearly by 4.12.

4.12

In this example one has a tendency to hear a strong beat on the A, though one can easily hear it elsewhere. This effect is connected with the fact that the downward leap after each D creates a succession of A-B-C-D sequences as the most plausible grouping. If one deliberately hears a less favored grouping, such as B-C-D-A, the metrical structure is most naturally heard with the strong beat on B rather than on A. Thus there seems to be some connection between grouping and metrical structure besides the ubiquitous factor of parallelism:

Metrical Structure

MPR 2 (Strong Beat Early) Weakly prefer a metrical structure in which the strongest beat in a group appears relatively early in the group.

A place in real music where the effect of MPR 2 is evident is 4.13, the beginning of the coda of Beethoven's *Leonore* Overture no. 3 (measures 514–525).

4.13

At this point there is a new tempo, so there is no previous metrical evidence to guide the listener. One tends to hear strong beats at each upward leap—despite the fact that at the seventh group, marked here with an asterisk, the regularity begins to come at the unmetrical distance of seven notes.

Inception of Events and Local Stress

A further and more obvious source of metrical differentiation is the distinction between beats occupied by the inception of pitch-events and those occupied by rests or continuations of pitch-events. In 4.14, for instance, strong beats at the eighth-note level occur much more naturally at the attack points of notes than between them: metrical structure *i* is preferred over metrical structure *ii*. (Structure *ii* is intuitively somewhat less unstable in 4.14a than in 4.14b. This difference will be accounted for below.)

4.14

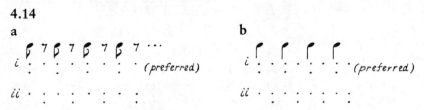

The preference for structure *i* over structure *ii* is expressed in MPR 3.

MPR 3 (Event) Prefer a metrical structure in which beats of level L_i that coincide with the inception of pitch-events are strong beats of L_i.

It often happens that the attack pattern of a given musical surface is such that there is no way to satisfy MPR 3 fully. Example 4.15 is one such case. (Applications of MPR 3 are marked.)

4.15

Chapter 4

The metrical well-formedness rules for tonal music require strong beats to be equally spaced. When attacks are not evenly spaced, the only solution for the preference rules is to choose a structure that minimizes violations of MPR 3. In 4.15 the points where MPR 3 is overridden are marked with asterisks. Between points x and y, the metrical structure assigned is from the local point of view the less preferred one; it is identical to structure ii in 4.14a. But this less preferred structure must be accepted in order to meet the requirement of metrical regularity. Hence this part of the passage is heard as syncopated. In general the phenomenon of syncopation can be formally characterized as a situation in which the global demands of metrical well-formedness conflict with and override local preferences. The more severe and extended in time the conflict is, the more prominent the syncopation.

Next observe that, when attacks occur on adjacent beats, MPR 3 applies to both of them, saying that both should be heard as strong beats. But since the well-formedness rules do not permit two adjacent beats to be equally strong, one must give way to the other. Example 4.16, in which applications of MPR 3 have been marked, illustrates this situation. The reader is cautioned to hear these examples without accents (local stresses), except where specifically marked. We will take up the effect of such accents shortly.

4.16

a

```
 (♭)♭ 7 ♭ ♭ 7 ♭ ♭ 7 ...
      3  3    3  3    3  3
i     .  .  .  .  .  .  .  .  ⎫
         *        *        *  ⎬ (equally
                              ⎭  preferred)
ii    .  .  .  .  .  .  .  .
      *        *        *
iii   .  .  .  .  .  .  .  . : (less preferred)
      *  *  .  *  *  .  *  *
```

b

```
 (x)(x)♭ 7 ♭ ♭ ♭ 7 ♭ ♭ ♭ 7 ...
       3 3 3    3 3 3    3 3 3
i      .  .  .  .  .  .  .  .  .  . (preferred)
          *        *        *
ii     .  .  .  .  .  .  .  .  .  . : (less preferred)
       *  *  *  *  *  *  *  *  *
```

Where there are only two adjacent attacks, as in 4.16a, two equally stable structures exist: either the first attack is the strong beat, as in structure i, or the second is, as in structure ii. In either case MPR 3 is violated once in every three beats. (Violations are again marked with asterisks.) The third possible structure that conforms to the rule of parallelism (MPR 1) places the strong beat on the rest, as in structure iii in example 4.16a. Here there are two violations of MPR 3 in every three beats, and so the structure is predicted to be less stable than the other two. This prediction corresponds to the musical intuition that structures i and ii are about equally plausible, and that structure iii is a less natural way to hear the surface pattern of 4.16a in the absence of other information.[2]

Next consider 4.16b, in which there are three adjacent attacks. A metrical structure that satisfies the well-formedness rules and the requirements of parallelism must have strong beats at the eighth-note level spaced two beats apart; the two possibilities are given as structures *i* and *ii*. Structure *i* contains only one violation of MPR 3 per four beats; structure *ii* contains two. Therefore MPR 3 predicts, in conformance with intuition, that structure *i* should be the more stable of the two.

Because the regularity of 4.16b involves a span of four eighths, there is an additional metrical level to account for. Example 4.17a gives the two possible half-note levels for structure *i* of 4.16b; example 4.17b gives them for structure *ii*.

4.17

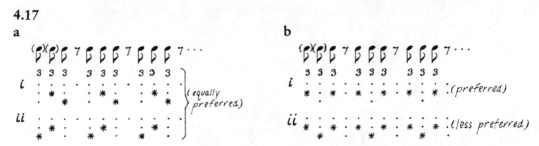

In 4.17a every beat at the quarter-note level coincides with an attack. Hence either choice for the half-note level results in alternate violations of MPR 3 (marked by asterisks at the half-note level), and structures *i* and *ii* are predicted to be commensurate in naturalness. In 4.17b, on the other hand, beats of the quarter-note level fall alternately on attacks and rests. Hence structure *i*, with half-note beats falling on attacks, produces no new violations of MPR 3; but structure *ii*, with half-note beats falling on rests, does produce further violations. The result is that structure *i* is predicted to be more natural than structure *ii*.

Having demonstrated the behavior of MPR 3 with respect to a number of rhythmic configurations, we now consider another source of metrical differentiation with similar properties: local stress (accent). By local stress we mean extra intensity on the attack of a pitch-event. We include as kinds of stress not only those marked by the signs > and ∧, but also those indicated by *sf, rf, fp,* and *subito f.* In a regular sequence of attacked notes, those with stress will preferably be heard as strong beats. In 4.18, for instance, one most naturally hears structure *i*; structure *ii* is heard as syncopation or cross-accent.

4.18

The relevant preference rule is MPR 4.

MPR 4 (Stress) Prefer a metrical structure in which beats of level L_i that are stressed are strong beats of L_i.

Note the similarity between MPRs 3 and 4. MPR 3 distinguishes beats that are inceptions of events from those that are not; MPR 4 distinguishes beats that have intense inceptions from those that do not. A comparison of examples 4.14 and 4.18 reveals this similarity: where 4.14 has inceptions of events, 4.18 has stresses; and where 4.14 has noninceptions, 4.18 has nonstresses. Thus MPR 4 has the same effect in 4.18 as MPR 3 has in 4.14. Because of this similarity, we can demonstrate the behavior of MPR 4 simply by making corresponding substitutions in 4.15–4.17. Example 4.19 corresponds to 4.15, 4.20 to 4.16, and 4.21 to 4.17. (In each of these MPR 3 applies at every beat, so it makes no differentiation.)[3]

4.19

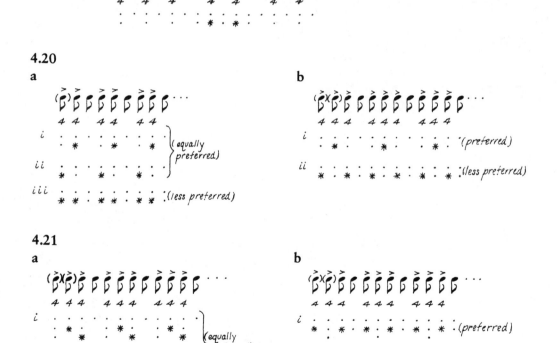

4.20

4.21

In 4.20a structures *i* and *ii* are about equally natural, and preferable to *iii*. In 4.20b structure *i* is preferable to structure *ii*. In 4.21a structures *i* and *ii* are about equally natural, but in 4.21b structure *i* is preferable to structure *ii*.

Metrical Structure

Length

Next consider example 4.22, which differs from 4.16a only in that the second eighth note in each group has been lengthened into a quarter note.

4.22

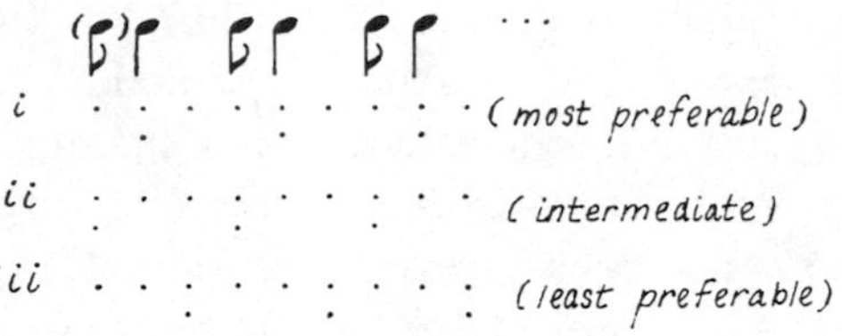

Intuitions about 4.22 are interestingly different from those about 4.16a. Here structure *i* is considerably more natural than structure *ii* (unless the eighth is stressed, invoking MPR 4), and both are far preferable to structure *iii*. Similarly, in 4.23 the quarter note attracts the strong beat on both the quarter-note level (since structure *i* is more natural than structure *ii*) and the half-note level (since structure *iii* is slightly more natural than structure *iv*). Notice how these examples differ in preferred structure from 4.16b and 4.17a, which have the same attack pattern but lack the long note.

4.23

These examples suggest a fifth metrical preference rule.

MPR 5 (Length), first version Prefer a metrical structure in which relatively strong beats occur at the inception of notes of relatively long duration.

According to this rule, the quarter notes in 4.14b, 4.22, and 4.23 receive an extra preference-rule marking, which the eighth notes followed by rests in 4.14a, 4.16a, and 4.16b lack. Thus the presence of quarter notes creates exactly the observed biases in metrical structure.

This is only a first approximation to a far more interesting rule. The notion of length appears to generalize to a number of phenomena other than simply how long a particular pitch-event is sustained. For example, the alternation of forte and piano in 4.24 creates a preferred metrical structure in which strong beats occur on the changes. (In addition, the changes to forte are preferably heard as stronger than the changes to piano, because the sudden forte functions as a local stress and triggers MPR 4.)

4.24

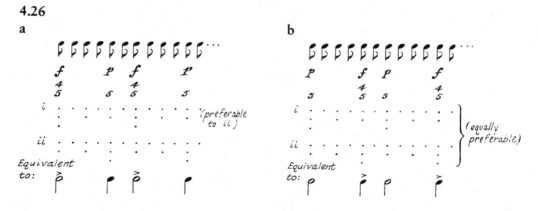

We can account for the fact that this is heard most naturally as 6/8, with strong beats at the changes in dynamic, by extending MPR 5 so it counts the length of a particular dynamic as a kind of length indicative of metrical structure. Then MPR 5 will apply at the changes in dynamics in 4.24, setting up a preference in metrical structure. In other words, from the point of view of MPRs 4 and 5, example 4.24 behaves analogously to 4.25.

4.25

For a slightly more complex example consider 4.26, in which applications of preference rules have been marked.

4.26

The spacing of changes of intensity establishes a preferred quarter-note level: both passages in 4.26 are preferably in 3/4, with quarter-note beats on the changes of dynamics. However, the two passages differ in the factors determining where the strong beats of the quarter-note level lie.

From the point of view of MPRs 4 and 5, the passages are equivalent to the durational patterns at the bottom of the example. In 4.26a the forte lasts longer than the piano, so MPR 5 says that the onset of the forte should be relatively stronger. In addition, the stress perceived at the onset of the forte reinforces the impression of a strong beat. Hence structure *i* is far more natural than structure *ii*. On the other hand, 4.26b has reversed the durations of forte and piano. The greater length of the piano now attracts the strong beat, but so does the stress of the forte. Because of the conflict, either structure *i* or structure *ii* can be heard, but with more equivocation than structure *i* in 4.26a. Thus the two passages in 4.26 present the familiar contrast between reinforcement and conflict of preference rules.

Continuing with the generalization of MPR 5, we observe that the beginning of a slur is indicative of a strong beat. In example 4.27 the most highly preferred pattern places the beginning of the slur at a strong beat on both the quarter-note and half-note levels, as indicated below the passage.

4.27

Furthermore, the longer of two slurs most naturally occurs on a relatively stronger beat: in 4.28 structure *i* is preferable to structure *ii*. Thus slurring has the same properties with respect to metrical preference rules as long notes and changes of dynamics.

4.28

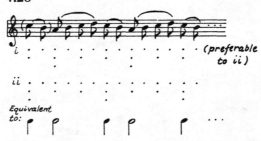

A third extension of MPR 5 concerns the length of a consistent pattern of articulation. An especially salient example is 4.29, from the Courante of the fourth Bach Cello Suite, in which it is difficult to hear the downbeats at any point other than at the change from triplets to sixteenths and back again.

4.29

Again, the longer of two alternating patterns of articulation attracts the stronger beat. In 4.30 the beginning of the triplet pattern is somewhat more likely to be heard as the strong beat at the dotted-half level than the beginning of the sixteenths. In other words, from the point of view of MPR 5, example 4.30 behaves like the rhythmic pattern shown below it.

4.30

So far pitch has not been implicated in the metrical preference rules. But the repetition of a pitch also counts as a kind of length, as shown by the preference for 4.31 to be heard with the first C on a strong beat of the quarter-note level and (less decisively) the half-note level.

4.31

The rule of length applies to repeated pitches not only at the surface, but also at relevant levels of the time-span reduction.[4] Consider the upper line in 4.32, which has the preferred metrical structure shown.

4.32

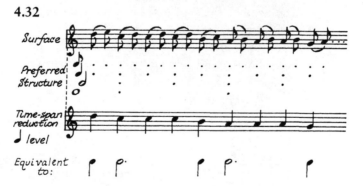

The slurring establishes the preferred placement of beats at the quarter-note level, but beyond that there is nothing in the musical surface to account for larger metrical levels. On the other hand, as will emerge in chapters 6 and 7, the time-span reduction at the quarter-note level (given below the metrical structure) contains pitch repetitions that do produce the desired metrical structure. Hence metrical preference with respect to pitch repetition must be derived in this case from the time-span reduction of the proper level.

Finally, the related phenomenon of harmonic rhythm produces strong cues for metrical structure. Harmonic rhythm can be regarded as the pattern of durations created by successive changes in harmony, not only at the musical surface but at underlying reductional levels. The relevance of harmonic rhythm to metrical structure can be incorporated into the present theory by treating duration of a harmony as still another kind of length in MPR 5. As in the case of individual lines, the rule may invoke the time-span reduction in order to abstract away from nonharmonic tones and ornamental changes in harmony.

Having noted all these generalizations of the notion of length, we now can state the final version of MPR 5.

MPR 5 (Length), final version Prefer a metrical structure in which a relatively strong beat occurs at the inception of either
a. a relatively long pitch-event,
b. a relatively long duration of a dynamic,
c. a relatively long slur,
d. a relatively long pattern of articulation,
e. a relatively long duration of a pitch in the relevant levels of the time-span reduction, or
f. a relatively long duration of a harmony in the relevant levels of the time-span reduction (harmonic rhythm).

As in the case of preference rules for grouping, not all cases of MPR 5 are of the same intrinsic strength. For instance, example 4.33a presents a conflict between a prolonged pitch-event and a slur of the same length. The beat of the half-note level falls most naturally on the long note, indicating that MPR 5a overrides MPR 5c in this situation. (If a performer wants to project the strong beat on the E, he will typically accent it and both shorten and remove stress from the quarter-note D, affecting the application of preference rules.) Similarly, 4.33b places MPRs 5c and 5e in conflict. Here it is unclear which rule should dominate.

4.33

a   b

The strongest case of MPR 5 seems to be case f (harmonic rhythm). For example, the long note in 4.34a clearly attracts the strong beat; but given the harmonic context in 4.34b, the strong beat falls most naturally on the second eighth of each group, where the harmony changes, and the quarter note is heard as syncopated. Hence MPR 5f has overridden MPR 5a here.

4.34

We will not work out all the combinations of relative strengths of rules here. Nor will we attempt to quantify rule strengths, for reasons discussed in section 3.3. The reader should, however, be aware that relative intrinsic strength of preference rules plays an important role in determining the most stable analysis.

A Linguistic Parallel

It should not be without interest that the last two metrical preference rules discussed (those for stress and length) are reminiscent of the principles governing prosodic features in language. It is well known (see for example Trubetzkoy 1939, chapter IV.5) that there are a limited number of discrete ways in which languages mark the distinction between strong and weak syllables. Some languages use stress (differentiation in intensity), others length, and others higher pitch as a mark of strength. Among other things, the opposition between strong and weak often plays an important role in the metrical structure of poetry, where linguistic material is fitted to an abstract metrical pattern (see Halle and Keyser 1971).

That stress and length function as markers of metrical strength in music as well as in language can hardly be a coincidence. Rather it seems that we are dealing with a more general cognitive organization that has manifestations in both musical and linguistic structure. This lends the theory of metrical preference rules a significance beyond its usefulness for musical purposes. (In section 12.3 we discuss a related parallel of music and language in considerable detail.)

An Example

In section 2.2 we discussed some questions about the larger-level metrical structure of the opening of Mozart's G Minor Symphony. We now apply the metrical preference rules developed so far to derive the smaller levels of metrical structure—those levels not open to question. Again the example is given without bars and beams; beats at the eighth-note level are numbered for convenience. We treat the theme and bass line alone; we have omitted the beginning of the first measure and the viola accompaniment as an exercise, in order to bring more rules into play.

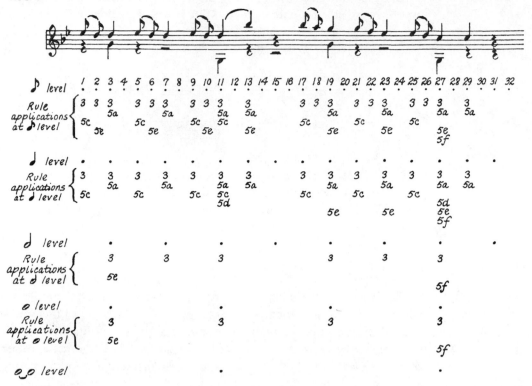

We start with the eighth-note level, which is of course assigned by the MWFRs (MWFR 1 requires a beat at the attack point of each note, and MWFR 4 fills the level in evenly). Those beats at the eighth-note level that coincide with beginnings of notes are marked by MPR 3 (the event rule); rests and continuations of notes are not marked. There are no local stresses, so MPR 4 has no effect (though stresses are often added at 11 and 27 in performance to reinforce the metrical structure). MPR 5a (length of pitch-event) marks the beginning of the quarter notes; MPR 5c (length of slur) marks the beginning of the slurs. The beginnings of repeated pitches are marked by MPR 5e. Finally, MPR 5f (length of harmony) applies at the change at 27 (beat 1 has been preceded by accompaniment, so it is not a harmonic change).[5]

Examining the totality of rule applications at this level, we find a situation not unlike 4.16b above: clusters of three adjacent beats where rules apply, followed by a beat with no rule applications. As in 4.16b, rule applications on weak beats can be minimized by assigning strong beats to the first and third beats of each cluster, giving the quarter-note level shown in 4.35.

Now let us determine the strong beats at the quarter-note level. At this level, every beat except 15 and 31 occurs at the inception of a pitch-event and therefore is marked by MPR 3. The quarter notes are relatively long pitch-events, so they are marked by MPR 5a. The strongest application of MPR 5c (length of slur) is at beat 11, the beginning of the longest slur. Beat 11 is also the only place where MPRs 5a and 5c reinforce each other. A consistent pattern of articulation—two quarter notes in a row—begins at beats 11 and 27, so MPR 5d applies at those points. Pitch prolongations into the next beat are marked by MPR 5e at beats 19, 23, and 27; again the harmonic change is marked at beat 27.

In addition to the rule applications marked, MPR 1 (parallelism) requires that each pattern of two eighths followed by a quarter receive the same metrical structure. This requires that strong beats of the quarter-note level be spaced two quarter notes apart.

In trying to find a half-note level that minimizes overall MPR violations, we see that MPRs 5a and 5c alternate throughout much of the passage, superficially giving the appearance of a predicted ambiguity. But we saw in 4.33a that MPR 5a overrides 5c in such an environment; hence rule violations are minimized if beats of the half-note level are placed where MPR 5a applies. This fits the multiple applications of rules at beats 11 and 27 and the bass attacks at 3, 11, 19, and 27, so that the half-note level shown is quite stable throughout.

Next consider MPR applications at the half-note level. First, MPR 3 applies straightforwardly to the melody, giving again the clusters of three adjacent applications separated by one beat. As before, the most favorable analysis of this is to place strong beats on the endpoints of the clusters. Second, the bass attacks strengthen the application of MPR 3 at beats 3, 11, 19, and 27, further weighting the analysis toward the endpoints of the clusters. Third, the harmonic change again triggers MPR 5f at beat 27. Fourth, parallelism again requires a duple pattern. Fifth, in the time-span reduction the beginning of the melody has been reduced to a sequence of half-note Ds by this level, so the pitch-repetition rule (MPR 5e) applies at beat 3.

At the whole-note level, the time-span repetition of D beginning at beat 3 and the harmonic change at 27 are again relevant. But since parallelism requires the two halves of the passage to be the same metrically, this evidence is globally inconsistent, and one rule must give way. The decision in favor of treating beats 11 and 27 as strong is favored by the relative strength of the harmonic rhythm rule and reinforced by factors discussed in the next subsection. We have thus successfully derived the desired metrical structure for this passage.

**4.3
Further Metrical
Preference Rules**

This section discusses briefly four further metrical preference rules and the analysis of a more complex example.

Effects of Bass, Cadence, Suspension, and Time-Span Reduction
The first of the four rules deals specifically with polyphonic factors. In tonal music, the bass tends to be metrically more stable than the upper

parts: when it plays isolated notes, they are usually strong beats; when it plays sustained notes, they are much less likely to be syncopated than an upper part is, and so forth. In other words, MPRs 3, 4, and 5 are given extra weight when they apply to the bass. We express this tendency as MPR 6; we have already alluded to its effects in the G Minor Symphony above, where the bass attacks create extra metrical prominence.

MPR 6 (Bass) Prefer a metrically stable bass.[6]

The next rule concerns the behavior of the metrical preference rules at cadences. It is generally the case in tonal music and in earlier idioms within Western music that metrical disruptions such as syncopations and cross-accents are extremely rare within cadences. In example 4.36 the fourth measure of the Mozart A Major Sonata has been changed to show what does *not* happen.

4.36

Of course, syncopations and cross-accents are common elsewhere, and the approach to a cadence is not infrequently marked by a metrical complexity such as a hemiola. An extreme case where the cadence is practically the only point of metrical stability in the phrase is 4.37, measures 9–16 of the second movement of the Beethoven Sonata op. 110.

4.37

It seems fairly clear that cadences are an important factor in fixing metrical as well as tonal structure. MPR 7 is a preliminary statement showing the place of this aspect of metrical structure in the present theory.

MPR 7 (Cadence) Strongly prefer a metrical structure in which cadences are metrically stable; that is, strongly avoid violations of local preference rules within cadences.

Note that MPR 7 does not dictate whether a cadence should fall into a metrical pattern of weak-strong ("masculine" cadence) or one of strong-weak ("feminine" cadence). It says only that, whatever the metrical pattern, the metrical evidence within the cadence should not conflict with the prevailing global pattern. In particular, when surrounding metrical evidence is in conflict, as in 4.37, MPR 7 implies that the cadence is decisive in settling on a preferred metrical structure.

From this rule and from MPR 6 follows the traditional principle that the cadential $^6_4$ chord should be on a stronger beat than the dominant it precedes. The bass arrives at the fifth degree of the scale at the $^6_4$ and maintains it through both chords, so the metrical stability of the bass with respect to MPR 5a (length of event) requires the stronger beat on the $^6_4$. The requirement is particularly stringent because it is within a cadence.

Another place where contrapuntal considerations affect metrical structure is at suspensions. In tonal music, the examples in 4.38 are heard with structure *i* in strong preference to structure *ii;* that is, the dissonant suspensions are heard as metrically stronger than their consonant preparations and resolutions.

4.38

In 4.38a this preference is reinforced by MPR 6, since the lower voice moves to create the dissonance. In 4.38b, by contrast, this preference is in conflict with MPR 6, since the upper voice creates the dissonance and the bass is suspended; hence the preference for structure *i* is somewhat weaker here. Nonetheless, the fact that MPR 6 can be overruled here demonstrates the need for another preference rule:

MPR 8 (Suspension) Strongly prefer a metrical structure in which a suspension is on a stronger beat than its resolution.

Finally, we deal with a preference rule alluded to in the previous subsection in connection with the larger-level metrical structure in example 4.35. The bass in this passage alternates between G in the upper octave on beats 3 and 19 and G in the lower octave on beats 11 and 27. The lower G is sensed to be some indication of a stronger beat on the whole-note level. To add this effect to the existing rules, one might be tempted simply to formulate a preference rule favoring lower bass positions. However, the typical "oom-pah" accompanimental figure (4.39) argues against such a treatment, since in this example one would hardly be tempted to hear the lower bass note as the strongest beat.

4.39

What really influences the metrical structure is the stability of the bass within the harmonic context: the lower bass is favored, but not at the expense of choosing an inversion (especially a $^6_4$ chord) over root position. These principles of bass stability play a role in determining the time-span reduction, and it would miss a generalization to repeat them in the metrical rules. Rather, the appropriate account seems to be a metrical preference rule that takes into account the interaction with the time-span reduction.

The preference rules for time-span reduction are concerned with the relative structural importance of events (see chapters 6 and 7). Broadly speaking, the factors involved are pitch stability, metrical stability, and articulation of groups. It often happens that pitch considerations and metrical considerations are at odds, for example in a suspension. In such a case the choice of time-span reduction is conflicted, with the result that the reduction is less stable at that point than it would be if all the factors were reinforcing.

Now consider the G Minor Symphony. If the higher bass note were chosen as the strong beat at the whole-note level, the rules of time-span reduction would encounter a conflict between metrical and pitch considerations, since the more stable pitch-event (the low G) would fall in the weaker metrical position. On the other hand, if the low G is chosen as the strong beat, metrical and pitch considerations reinforce each other, resulting in a more stable time-span reduction. Similarly, in 4.39 the C in the bass is far more stable than the G in terms of pitch, since it forms a root-position chord and the G forms a $^6_4$; hence the least conflicted time-span reduction results from a metrical analysis with the C on a stronger beat. These considerations suggest the following preference rule:

MPR 9 (Time-Span Interaction) Prefer a metrical analysis that minimizes conflict in the time-span reduction.[7]

A More Difficult Example
Example 4.40 is the opening of the finale of the Haydn Quartet op. 76, no. 6. The smallest metrical level is of course supplied by the metrical well-formedness rules; we will show how the next two levels are derived by the metrical preference rules. As usual, the example is presented without bars and beams. The dashed vertical lines are added as a visual aid.

The first half of the passage is characterized by tremendous metrical ambiguity. The reader is invited to demonstrate to himself how many

different metrical structures (3/4 versus 6/8 and six possible positions for the downbeat) are viable possibilities for beats 1–24. As Rosen 1972 points out (pp. 339–340), Haydn makes extensive use of this ambiguity throughout the movement. The second half of the passage intuitively rules out most of these possible analyses, but is itself full of metrical complexity due to syncopation and cross-accents. In the course of our analysis, we will show how the intuitive metrical complexity of the entire passage is reflected in the application of metrical preference rules.

First consider the grouping. Parallelism and symmetry clearly establish the grouping of beats 1–24 into sixes. Because of the counterpoint, the grouping of the second half of the passage is somewhat more difficult to motivate. However, it seems reasonable that the motivic parallelism between the first violin in the first four groups and the cello at 31–35 and 37–40 establishes the grouping illustrated, although this is to some extent in conflict with the grouping suggested by the inner parts between about 28 and 40.

Beneath the eighth-note level of beats are marked the applications of the metrical preference rules at this level. From 1 to 24, metrical evidence at the eighth-note level is not highly differentiated. Since there are no regularities at either two-beat or three-beat intervals, it is not at all obvious whether the six-note groups imply 3/4 or 6/8. Furthermore, though it is clear that the harmony changes somewhere in each group, it is not clear where. In particular, the fact that each of the chords (6, 12, 18, and 24) is immediately preceded by one of its pitches suggests that the chords themselves are not the point of harmonic change. Hence no applications of the harmonic-change rule (MPR 5f) can be marked with any certainty at this level.

The first solid indications of meter are the attacks of long notes at 28, 30, and 36 and the clear harmonic changes at 30, 34, and 36, which establish a spacing of metrical evidence consistent with a 3/4 meter. (The harmony at 40 lasts only for a single eighth, so it does not constitute evidence for MPR 5f, which looks for the onset of a *prolonged* harmony.)

Next, observe that in 40–48 the alternating quarter notes in the bass and the upper parts create a generally high level of metrical evidence on all beats. However, MPR 6 emphasizes the contribution of the bass, establishing a differentiation that again favors spacing strong beats two rather than three apart. Furthermore, the counterpoint sets up suspensions at 44 and 46, creating pressure from MPR 8 to place strong beats there.

All of this metrical evidence is consistent with the well-formed metrical level shown as the quarter-note level in 4.40, and much more so than with any other choice. Thus the second half of the passage, rich in metrical evidence, forces the interpretation of the first half, which alone provides only meager evidence for a metrical interpretation.

Turning to the derivation of the next metrical level, we see in 4.41 the application of MPRs to the quarter-note level. Only those applications of the length rule (MPR 5) that span more than a quarter-note's duration have been marked.

First consider the second half of the passage, which is again richer in evidence. Since the dominants initiated at 30 and 36 are prolonged into the following quarter, these beats receive applications of MPR 5f. Similarly, the long notes beginning at 28, 30, and 36 extend into the next quarter and are marked by MPRs 5a and 5e. The change from eighth-note to quarter-note motion in the bass at 40 is marked by MPR 5d (length of pattern of articulation).

At beat 46 the situation is more complicated. Within the time-span 46–47, the time-span reduction chooses the V chord as more important, since it is more consonant than the $\frac{6}{4}$ chord on beat 46. The V is then heard as prolonged into the next quarter, beat 48, since the pitch at 48 is consistent with that harmony. Hence beat 46 is marked for the inception of a prolonged harmony as well as for the repetition of the pitch B♭. In addition, beats 46–48 form a cadence, so MPR 7 applies in this area.

Let us consider the implications of these rule applications for the choice of the next metrical level. Parallelism throughout the passage requires that strong beats at the quarter-note level be spaced three apart. Thus there are three possible placements for the next level of beats in the portion of the passage examined·so far: 26, 32, 38, and 44; 28, 34, 40, and 46; and 30, 36, 42, and 48. The first of these is readily eliminated. There are no applications of MPR 5 on any of these beats, and applications of MPRs 3 and 6 are weak because they are always adjacent to another beat where these rules also apply.

The second possibility is more promising. MPR 5 applies on beats 28, 40, and 48, and in the latter two of these it is not adjacent to another application. In addition, the beginning of the long-held treble B♭ at 28 favors this analysis, even more so because it is held so long. The change in articulation in the bass at 40 and the harmonic change at 46 also reinforce this analysis. Moreover, this analysis makes the correct predictions about relative metrical weight within the cadence at 46–48, so MPR 7 (cadence) strongly favors it.

Finally, the third possible analysis is favored by the strong applications of MPR 5 at 30 and 36. But it makes exactly the wrong prediction about the cadence at 46–48: the local metrical evidence strongly favors 46 as the strong beat, whereas this analysis places the strong beat on 48. MPR 7 therefore strongly disfavors this analysis. In sum, the metrical evidence for the second half of the passage favors the dotted-half metrical level shown in 4.41, though not without some uncertainty at points preceding the cadence. In particular, there is little direct evidence to override the strongly marked 30 and 36, which are therefore heard as cross-accents.

4.41

Now turn to the first half of passage 4.41. The musical surface apparently provides no new applications of preference rules, but a consideration of the time-span reduction reveals evidence for metrical structure. The issue concerns where the harmony is heard to change in each group. As pointed out already, each chord is immediately preceded by a pitch that is consistent with it, so the chords are not heard as the points of change. However, example 4.42, the time-span reduction of beats 1–24 at the quarter-note level, shows pitches inconsistent with the preceding harmony at 10, 16, and 22, suggesting that these beats are the point of harmonic change; we have indicated this in 4.41.[8]

4.42

As evidence that this indirect source of metrical prominence derived through the time-span reduction is the correct one, consider 4.43, in which the pitches at 5 and 11 have been changed from Haydn's.

4.43

Whatever the musical sins of this alteration, it results in a radically different metrical intuition—the strongest beats are most naturally heard at 6 and 12 rather than at 4 and 10. The theory proposed here accounts nicely for this difference: because the chords in 4.43 are not preceded by pitches consistent with them, they can this time be heard as the points of harmonic change. Hence 6 and 12 rather than 4 and 10 will be marked by MPRs 5e and 5f, altering the distribution of metrical weight.

In choosing the preferred dotted half-note level for this part of 4.41, we are faced with a conflict between the harmonic changes at 4, 10, 16, and 22 on one hand and the chords at 6, 12, 18, and 24 on the other. Though the strength of the harmony rule (MPR 5f) is undoubtedly sufficient to prevail, the metrical evidence for the chords causes them to be heard as cross-accents, parallel to those in the second half of the passage at 30 and 36.

Thus the rules predict that the analysis shown in 4.41 should be favored for both halves of the passage. However, the indirectness of metrical evidence in the first half of the passage and the syncopation in the second half together create an overall complexity in deriving the preferred metrical interpretation, and this seems to reflect accurately the complexity that this passage presents to musical intuition.

By contrast, the Mozart example 4.35 provides clear evidence for a metrical interpretation at every level and at nearly every point in the passage; applications of metrical rules are numerous and mutually reinforcing. The nature of the derivation predicts that the passage will be heard as metrically straightforward, in accordance with intuition. Thus we have seen how the preference-rule formalism not only can derive a final analysis for a passage, but can also express finer intuitions about the degree of metrical complexity and the reasons it arises. This is one of the ways in which the theory bridges the gap between artistic and psychological concerns, one of the principal goals of the present study.

With one exception, to appear in the next section, this completes our discussion of metrical preference rules. To sum up: The preference rules decide which of the many possible well-formed metrical structures assignable to a piece represents its intuitively preferred metrical interpretation. The rules of local detail—MPRs 3 (event), 4 (stress), and 5 (length)—are supplemented by considerations having to do with stability of the bass (MPR 6), of cadences (MPR 7), and of suspensions (MPR 8). In addition, interaction with grouping structure (MPR 2) and time-span reduction (MPR 9) and the ubiquitous and powerful considerations of parallelism (MPR 1) affect the choice of metrical structure.

There is reason to believe that much of this preference-rule system is not peculiar to classical Western tonal music, but is universal. The rules of local detail seem to us especially strong candidates. We should make clear what such a claim of universality means. Take the rule of local stress, for example. There are of course musical idioms in which local stresses do not appear; Renaissance choral music for instance can arguably be said not to have them. But we would feel fairly confident in conjecturing that there is no musical idiom employing stress in which it does not mark potential metrical strength. In this sense we can say that the preference rule for stress is always available to musical intuition; the differences between idioms in this respect lie only in whether they ever give the rule opportunities to apply.

We conclude this chapter by returning to metrical well-formedness rules, briefly discussing two topics: well-formedness rules for other metrical traditions, and metrical irregularities.

4.4 Variations on the Metrical Well-Formedness Rules

In section 2.2 we observed that, unlike the grouping well-formedness rules, which appear to be essentially universal across musical idioms, the metrical rules are in part idiom-specific. This section will illustrate some possible variants of the rules that lead to metrical idioms other than that of classical Western tonal music.

For convenience, we repeat here MWFRs 1–4 as stated in section 4.1.

MWFR 1 Every attack point must be associated with a beat at the smallest metrical level present at that point in the piece.

MWFR 2 Every beat at a given level must also be a beat at all smaller levels present at that point in the piece.

MWFR 3 At each metrical level, strong beats are spaced either two or three beats apart.

MWFR 4 The tactus and immediately larger metrical levels must consist of beats equally spaced throughout the piece. At subtactus metrical levels, weak beats must be equally spaced between the surrounding strong beats.

MWFRs 1 and 2 define respectively the association of metrical structure with a musical surface and the hierarchical nature of metrical structure, conditions common to all types of music. However, MWFRs 3 and 4 are open to variation. For a simple example, a metrically more rigid idiom that allowed only duple meters could be characterized by dropping "or three" from the statement of MWFR 3. Alternatively, a much more loosely structured metrical idiom such as *recitativo* might be characterized by dropping MWFRs 3 and 4 altogether, permitting strong beats at arbitrarily distant points of articulation. In such an idiom, only local detail detected by preference rules would determine the location of beats.

By keeping MWFR 3 but dropping MWFR 4 we describe a metrical idiom of considerable irregularity, in that strong beats at each level can be indiscriminately two or three beats apart. Such structures appear, for instance, in some of Stravinsky's music—reflected notationally by his use of constantly changing meters. Note that the lack of rigidity in the metrical structure means that there is no prevailing pattern to which local details can be set in opposition; rather, strong beats will be heard wherever there are appropriate local details. This predicts that it will be more difficult in such a metrical idiom to produce effects of syncopation, which depend on the conflict of a rigid metrical pattern with local evidence.

Certain other metrical idioms have more complex rules in place of MWFR 4, permitting structured alternation of different-length metrical units. One such metrical idiom is found in the late sixteenth-century settings of French *vers mesuré* by Claude le Jeune. The metrical principle behind these settings is that the length of notes is determined by accentual properties of the corresponding syllables: strong syllables receive a half note and weak syllables a quarter. A brief sample, accompanied by a plausible metrical structure, is given in 4.44.

U.C.B.
LIBRARY

Metrical Structure

4.44

Claude le Jeune's metrical experiment apparently did not form the basis of any larger tradition. However, another complex metrical tradition, studied extensively in Singer 1974, is found in a large body of folk music from Macedonia and Bulgaria. Though this music has metrical regularity at the sixteenth-note and measure levels, the level of metrical structure with which dance steps are most closely correlated (the tactus) is irregular, consisting of units which Singer classifies as slow (*S*) and quick (*Q*); the *S* units are one and a half times the length of the *Q* units. Meter in this music is most easily represented as a repeating pattern of slows and quicks; for example, *QQS* (2+2+3). Singer quotes the dance tune "Racenitsa," reproduced in part in 4.45, as a typical example of the *QQS* meter.

4.45

Singer points out that not all possible combinations of *S*s and *Q*s are possible meters in this metrical idiom; *QSS* (2+3+3), for example, never appears. The meters that actually occur group into a number of families; Singer states well-formedness rules that express the generalizations among these possible meters. Within the present theory, the Macedonian metrical idiom would be described in part by replacing MWFR 4 with Singer's rules. We will not take the space here to discuss the rules, but Singer's list of basic meters in example 4.46 gives some idea of the complexity involved. This example omits compound meters, which complicate the situation further.

4.46

SS	QQ	SQQSQ	SQ	QS	QSQQ	SQS
	QQQ		SQQ	QQS	QQSQQ	SQQS
	QQQQ		SQQQ	QQQS	QQQSQQ	SQQQS
			SQQQQ	QQQQS		
			SQQQQQ	QQQQQS		

The point of our brief foray into other metrical idioms is that, in developing a theory of tonal music that addresses the issues of musical universals and acquisition of musical knowledge, one should construct formalisms that are adequate to express the facts of other idioms, and one should try to localize the similarities and differences between idioms in the statements of particular rules. In the cases presented here, the differences lie in what corresponds in other idioms to MWFRs 3 and 4. These differences in rules represent what one must learn about an idiom to become an experienced listener.

4.5 Metrical Irregularities at Hypermeasure Levels

As mentioned in section 4.1, tonal music often has from one to three levels of metrical structure that are larger than the level notated by bar lines, corresponding to regularities of two, four, and even eight measures. Except in the most banal music, these levels are commonly subject to a certain degree of irregularity. The metrical well-formedness rules proposed in section 4.1, however, require that a metrical level be unswervingly regular throughout a piece or at least a major section of a piece. They are therefore incapable of allowing for irregularity in a metrical level except by abandoning that level altogether—which amounts to claiming that there is no regularity at all. This section will show how two important kinds of larger-level metrical irregularity can be incorporated into the theory. Both depend on the interaction of metrical structure and grouping. The first involves irregular-length groups, the second grouping overlap and elision.

As will be seen more clearly in the discussion of time-span reduction, the segmentation of the musical surface forms a hierarchy whose levels can be divided roughly into three zones. At the smallest levels, metrical structure is responsible for most factors of segmentation; at the largest levels, grouping structure bears all the weight of segmentation. In between lies a transitional zone in which grouping gradually takes over responsibility from metrical structure, as units of organization become larger and as metrical intuitions become more attenuated because of the long time intervals between beats. It is in this zone of musical organization that metrical irregularities appear in tonal music.

In this transitional zone one hears metrical structure, but parallelism among groups of irregular length often forces metrical structures into irregularity above the measure level. The openings of the Mozart C Major Quintet K. 515 and the *Chorale St. Antoni* used in the Brahms "Haydn" Variations (see section 8.5) are well-known cases of five-measure phrases; examples of this sort are numerous. In order to make it possible for these phrases to receive a metrical analysis, MWFR 4 must cease to enforce strict metrical regularity at more than two or three levels above the tactus (usually the one- or two-measure levels). Nonetheless,

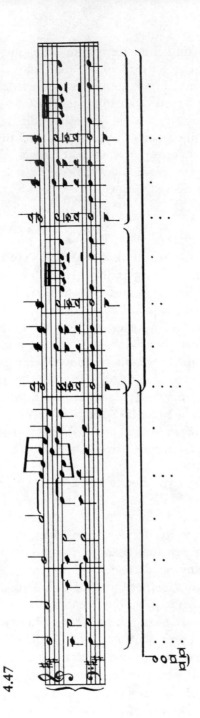

4.47

the preference for regularity, especially binary regularity, remains. Apparently there is a preference rule operating at these levels—the metrical counterpart of the grouping rule of symmetry (GPR 5):

MPR 10 (Binary Regularity) Prefer metrical structures in which at each level every other beat is strong.

MPR 10 allows metrical irregularity, but, in the absence of other information, imposes duple meter. This seems to reflect musical intuition about hypermetrical structure. At smaller metrical levels, the more rigid requirements of MWFR 4 obscure the effects of MPR 10, since such levels will be all duple or all triple (that is, either completely obeying or completely violating MPR 10).

A second kind of metrical irregularity is the result not of irregular group lengths but of grouping overlaps and elisions. It comes in two varieties. The first gives the impression of a jarring metrical readjustment. An example is the passage from Haydn's Symphony no. 104 quoted in section 3.4 in connection with its grouping elision, repeated here as 4.47.

Beneath the example appear the grouping and metrical structures from the half-note (tactus) level up. At the point of grouping elision, the metrical structure is distorted: a beat at the four-measure level occurs only three measures after the previous one. Such a metrical distortion commonly occurs in conjunction with left elision in the grouping structure.

The association with elision suggests that a part of the metrical structure, in this case the time-span of a measure, has been deleted from an otherwise regular metrical structure, along with the elided pitch-events.[9] The alteration can be represented as in 4.48; the parenthesized beats on the left are deleted. In effect, the strong beat comes too soon.

4.48

A second and more rare kind of metrical deletion gives the intuitive effect of a retrospective awareness that a metrical shift has taken place. An example occurs in the last seven measures of the Schumann song "Wehmut," from *Liederkreis*, op. 39, shown in 4.49.[10]

At the point of grouping overlap (not elision this time) the voice part must end on a weak beat of the dotted-half level; however, the same point must function as a strong beat of that level with respect to the piano postlude, and this does not become clear until the following measure. The effect in the analysis of the musical surface is a metrical structure containing two weak beats in a row at the measure level. Again the coalescence of underlying pitch-events in the overlap suggests a corresponding

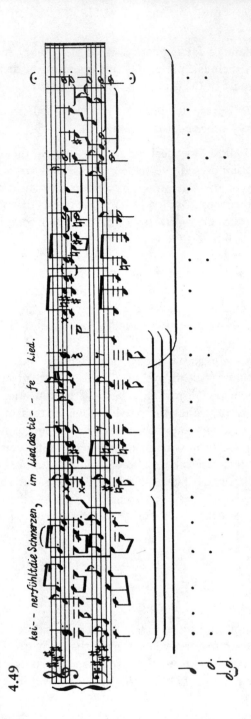

metrical deletion, this time of a time-span starting with a strong beat as shown in 4.50.

4.50

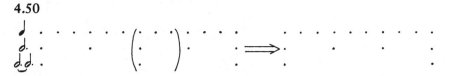

Examples 4.48 and 4.50 help show what these two kinds of metrical irregularity have in common. In a situation where two groups are joined by an overlap or elision, the right group seems invariably to begin with a strong metrical position in the underlying form. If the left group also ends with a strong metrical position, as in the Mozart Sonata K. 279 discussed in section 3.4, a well-formed regular metrical structure can be assigned to the musical surface without problem. If, however, the left group ends in a relatively weak metrical position, the conflict in the region of overlap must be resolved by deleting one or the other of the metrical functions. In 4.47 the weak position has been deleted, in a manner consistent with the elision of the associated pitch-events; in 4.49 the strong position has been deleted.

In formalizing a transformation rule for metrical deletion, it is not sufficient to delete the strong or weak beat itself. Notice in 4.48 and 4.50 that a number of beats at a smaller metrical level have also been deleted to regularize the pattern. This will be included in the statement of the rule. The rule as stated here encompasses the two types of metrical deletion observed above.

Metrical Deletion, first version From a well-formed metrical structure M as described by MWFRs 1–4, in which B_1, B_2, and B_3 are adjacent beats at level L_i, and B_2 is also a beat at level L_{i+1} (that is, a strong beat of level L_i), another well-formed metrical structure M' can be created by deleting from M either

a. B_1 and all beats at all levels between B_1 and B_2 (deletion of weak position), or

b. B_2 and all beats at all levels between B_2 and B_3 (deletion of strong position).

It can be seen that cases a and b are deletions of the sort illustrated in examples 4.47 and 4.49 respectively.

This version of the rule does not mention the connection with grouping elision and overlap. The rule can be made more specific as follows:

Metrical Deletion, second version Given a well-formed metrical structure M in which

i. B_1, B_2, and B_3 are adjacent beats of M at level L_i, and B_2 is also a beat at level L_{i+1},

ii. T_1 is the time-span from B_1 to B_2 and T_2 is the time-span from B_2 to B_3, and

iii. M is associated with an underlying grouping structure G in such a way that both T_1 and T_2 are related to a surface time-span T' by the grouping transformation performed on G of

    (a) left elision or

    (b) overlap,

then a well-formed metrical structure M' can be formed from M and associated with the surface grouping structure by

    (a) deleting B_1 and all beats at all levels between B_1 and B_2, and associating B_2 with the onset of T', or

    (b) deleting B_2 and all beats at all levels between B_2 and B_3, and associating B_1 with the onset of T'.

As in the case of grouping overlaps and elisions, we will not explore the preference-rule mechanisms involved in detecting the presence of metrical deletions. However, if they are linked as closely to grouping as we believe, and if the presence of cadences is as crucial to grouping overlap and elision as has been suggested in section 3.4, then it becomes clearer how a powerful confluence of factors can accumulate in the musical surface to break the established pattern. We leave for future research the incorporation of these observations into the formal system.

5
Introduction to Reductions

5.1
The Need for
Reductions

Although the concept of reduction is familiar in current musical analysis, we will review some elementary intuitions that justify the claim that a reduction represents something that one perceives in a piece of music. Besides aiding those readers not familiar with the notion, this discussion may help to ground it in ordinary experience and clarify what claims we are and are not making.

An obvious observation about music is that some musical passages are heard as ornamented versions, or *elaborations,* of others. For instance, despite the surface differences in pitches and durations between examples 5.1a and 5.1b, from the finale theme of Beethoven's *Pastoral* Symphony, the listener has no difficulty in recognizing 5.1b as an elaboration of 5.1a.

5.1

The inverse of elaboration also occurs, for example when a popular song is played in "stop time" to accompany a tap dancer. Despite the fact that the "stop time" version has fewer notes in it and the notes are in different rhythmic relationships, the listener readily accepts it as a version of the song.

More complex is the situation where two or more passages are both heard as elaborations of an abstract structure that is never overtly stated. Bach's *Goldberg* Variations is a particularly magnificent example of this kind of organization. Why is the listener able to recognize, beneath the seemingly infinite variety of its musical surface, that the aria and 30 variations are all variations of one another? Why do they not sound like

31 separate pieces? It is because the listener relates them, more or less unconsciously in the process of listening, to an abstract, simplified structure common to them all.

Such relationships are needed not just for the analysis of written-out music. In any musical tradition that involves improvisation on a given subject (such as jazz or raga), the performer must actively employ knowledge of principles of ornamentation and variation to produce a coherent improvisation.

In all these cases, the listener or performer has an intuitive understanding of the relative structural importance of pitches. If a pitch is heard as ornamenting another pitch, it is felt as structurally less important than the other pitch—it is subordinate to the other pitch. In short, the pitch relations involved in these intuitions are hierarchical.

Music theorists have of course been aware of these principles for hundreds of years. But it was especially the insight of the early twentieth century theorist Heinrich Schenker that the organization of an entire piece can be conceived of in terms of such principles, and that such organization provides explanations for many of the deeper and more abstract properties of tonal music. For present purposes, this insight might be phrased as follows:

Reduction Hypothesis The listener attempts to organize all the pitch-events of a piece into a single coherent structure, such that they are heard in a hierarchy of relative importance.

This hypothesis is central to Schenkerian analysis and its derivatives. (It is emphatically not a claim of "implication-realization" theories, like that of Narmour 1977.) A consequence of the claim is that part of the analysis of a piece is a step-by-step simplification or *reduction* of the piece, where at each step less important events are omitted, leaving the structurally more important events as a sort of skeleton of the piece. In Schenkerian theory, the steps closest to the musical surface are called "foreground," and successive steps lead in turn to "middleground" and "background" levels.

Within our theory we have found it desirable to tighten the Reduction Hypothesis by adding the following conditions:

a. Pitch-events are heard in a strict hierarchy (in the sense described in section 2.1).
b. Structurally less important events are not heard simply as insertions, but in a specified relationship to surrounding more important events.

We will use the term *Strong Reduction Hypothesis* to refer to this tighter version of reduction. Not all notions of reduction in the literature share these conditions.

The Strong Reduction Hypothesis leaves three areas of freedom in fleshing out what constitutes a proper reduction of a piece: (1) what the criteria of relative structural importance are, (2) what relationships may obtain between more important and less important events, and (3) precisely what musical intuitions are conveyed by the reduction as a result of 1 and 2. We will develop two distinct conceptions of reduction within our theory that differ in just these respects.

To convey an initial feeling for intuitions about structural importance, consider the suspension chain in 5.2a. If the resolutions are omitted or "reduced out," as in 5.2b, the sense of the passage is changed much more radically than if the suspensions are omitted, as in 5.2c. In other words, suspensions are heard as subordinate to, and hence as elaborations of, their resolutions.

5.2

This sort of testing by omission is generally a useful guide for checking reductional intuitions. To give another example, suppose that we were listening to a recording of the scherzo of Beéthoven's Sonata op. 10, no. 2 (5.3), and that a speck of dust obliterated the sound of event *m*. The effect would be one of mild interruption. But if the cadence *n* were obliterated, the effect would be far more disconcerting, because *n* is structurally more important than *m*. In other words, it would change the sense of a phrase more if its goal—a cadence—were omitted than if an event en route toward that goal were omitted.

5.3

Example 5.4 presents in preliminary form a complete reduction of the first phrase of the Bach chorale "O Haupt voll Blut und Wunden." The first musical system represents the musical surface, and the systems below stand for successive steps of omitting relatively ornamental events. At the final step only the structurally most important event remains, in this analysis the initial D major chord. (Other plausible reductions of this passage are of course possible. Furthermore, note that in giving this preliminary reduction we have as yet specified neither our criteria for structural importance nor the relationships between important events

and their elaborations. These will be detailed gradually in the course of the following chapters.)

5.4

The best way to read 5.4 is to hear the successive levels approximately in rhythm. If the analysis is satisfactory, each level should sound like a natural simplification of the previous level. As in 5.2 and 5.3, alternative omissions should make the process of simplification sound less like the original.

In assessing one's intuitions about reductions, it is important not to confuse structural importance with surface salience. These often coincide, but not always. For example, the IV chord at the beginning of measure 1 in 5.4 is prominent because of the relative height of the soprano and bass notes and because of its metrical position. But from a reductional viewpoint it is perhaps best considered as an "appoggiatura chord," just as are the events on the following strong beat 3 of measure 1 and beat 1 of measure 2. Likewise (to take a more extreme case), perhaps the most striking moment in the first movement of Beethoven's *Eroica* Symphony is the dissonant climax in measures 276–279 (example 5.5).

But in terms of structural importance, this event resolves into (i.e., is less stable than, and hence structurally less important than) the dominant of E minor in measures 280–283, which in turn is subordinate to the E minor chord at the beginning of measure 284. And, through a process we will not trace here, the ensuing E minor episode is relatively subordinate within the set of relationships emanating from the fact that the piece is in E♭ major. Thus the chord in measures 276–279, despite its conspicuousness, would be deeply subordinate within a reduction of the whole movement. The tension of this moment is due in part to the disparity between its surface salience and its reductional status.

We do not deprecate the aural or analytic importance of salient events; it is just that reductions are designed to capture other, grammatically more basic aspects of musical intuition. A salient event may or may not be reductionally important. It is within the context of the reductional hierarchy that salient events are integrated into one's hearing of a piece.

Some readers may balk at extending the notion of reduction to "background" levels—so that, for example, an E♭ major triad is ultimately all that is left of the first movement of the *Eroica*. Such an extension, it may be felt, is mechanical, abstract, and irrelevant to perception. There are two responses to this view. First, exactly where should a reduction stop? There is no natural place, for there is no point in the musical hierarchy where the principles of organization change in a fundamental way. Classical theorists were aware of this when they derived sonata form from the structure of the phrase. Rosen 1972 (pp. 83–88) illustrates the point beautifully by showing how Haydn, in his G Minor Piano Trio, actually develops a miniature sonata form out of a period form. If a phrase can be reduced, so can the *Eroica*.

Second, how would our reader feel if an E minor chord, derived from measures 284 ff. (see example 5.5), stood at the end of a reduction of the *Eroica*? Surely he would feel that the piece had been misrepresented. That solitary, reduced-out E♭ major triad means something after all: it is a way of saying what key the piece is in—and, indeed, that it has a tonic at all. To be sure, at this level it is scarcely differentiated from Schumann's *Rhenish* Symphony, which is also in E♭. But if a listener hears a piece as beginning and ending in the same key, he knows (however tacitly) a great deal about its global structure. There is nothing abstract or perceptually irrelevant about this. Nor does it deny the many important things that distinguish one piece from another; these emerge at more detailed levels of analysis.

Granted human frailty and inattention, it is rare for a listener on a particular occasion to hear a reduction in its entirety from the smallest

5.5

detail to the most long-range connection. Most likely, he will hear fairly accurately the details (except when his mind wanders) and the largest connections, but will be vague about some of the intervening relationships. A complete reduction of the *Eroica* is in this sense an idealization.

A final remark on the need for reductions: The Gestalt psychologists, for example Koffka (1935), recognized transposition of a musical passage as a way of changing a musical surface that preserves recognizability. They took this as important evidence for a mental representation that involves not just a list of pitches, but an abstract representation in which relations among pitches are more important than the actual pitches themselves. However, for whatever reasons, comparatively little seems to have been done within psychology to extend these observations in any significant way (though a certain degree of generalization appears in Dowling 1978, for example). The concepts, examples, and arguments just presented are exactly the sort that should be of interest in this regard, because they provide evidence for musical cognition of relationships not just between events adjacent on the musical surface, but between structurally important events at various reductional levels that are potentially far apart on the musical surface. Thus the study of musical reductions and of the processes producing them from musical surfaces is of great value in extending to a richer class of cases what has long been acknowledged as a psychologically important phenomenon.

5.2 Possible Formal Approaches to Reduction

If Schenkerian thought is central to the notion of reduction, and if there are significant parallels between Schenkerian theory and generative linguistics,[1] it seems logical to ask what is required to convert Schenkerian theory into a formal theory. For example, one might set out to develop a set of rules that would generate little pieces, perhaps without durational values, from the triad to the *Ursatz* (the "fundamental structure," made up essentially of a tonic-dominant-tonic progression supporting a linear melodic descent to the tonic note), and from there to simple harmonic and contrapuntal elaborations. Such an enterprise, however, would be utterly unrevealing from a psychological standpoint. "Generating" trivial musical examples says nothing about how people hear.[2]

It would be more promising to take Schenkerian analyses of actual tonal pieces—pieces that are intrinsically interesting as well as sufficiently complex to be informative about cognitive processes—and then to develop a rule system capable of generating these analyses. This approach would reveal the lacunae in Schenkerian theory, and, generally, would put the theory on a solid intellectual foundation.[3] We might have taken this tack, except that it seemed a doubtful strategy to launch a theory of musical cognition by filling in the gaps in somebody else's "artistic" theory, no matter how brilliant it may be in numerous respects.

Besides, it is not clear to us how such an approach would address cognitive issues.

We have found it far preferable to reverse the generative process from elaboration to reduction. This allows us to begin not by trying to justify a prior model, but by directly investigating actual musical surfaces and seeing what reductional structures emerge. If the results turn out like Schenkerian analyses, fine; if not, that too is interesting. This strategy permits us to ask, "What reduction or reductions does an experienced listener infer from a given musical surface, and by what principles?" In our view, this is the central question about reductions.

This strategy is consistent with our approach to rhythmic structure in chapters 2–4. It is also consistent with the methodology of generative linguistics, for, despite the term "generative," the goal in linguistic theory is to find the rules that assign correct structures to sentences. Consequently the sentences as such in linguistic theorizing are usually taken as given (recall the discussion in section 1.2 on misconceptions about generative grammar). In addition, our strategy is amenable to experimental methods in cognitive psychology, in which subjects are typically given a "stimulus object" (such as the musical surface of an existing piece) to which they react under controlled conditions. We want our theory to be testable.

This is not to preclude the possibility that a sophisticated alternative approach of constructing computational rules to "compose" pieces might not also be valuable. It is conceivable that such an enterprise could dovetail with our theoretical paradigm.

5.3 The Tree Notation for Reductions

To construct reductions one must have an adequate notation. Schenkerian notation, though attractive, is not explicit enough; it typically combines a number of levels at one putative level ("background," "middleground," or "foreground"), it often does not show what is an elaboration of what, and it utilizes too many signs (beams, slurs, quasidurational values) to express similar relationships. The formal nature of our inquiry necessitates a completely unambiguous and efficient notation, one that reflects in a precise way the hierarchical nature of reductions. To this end it is convenient to borrow from linguistics the notion of a "tree" notation.

The notion, however, cannot simply be transferred, because linguistic syntactic trees relate grammatical categories, which are absent in music. This basic fact is one of the crucial differences between language and music. All natural languages have nouns, verbs, adjectives, and the like. Linguistic trees represent *is-a* relations: a noun phrase followed by a verb phrase is a sentence, a verb followed by a noun phrase is a verb phrase, and so forth. There is no musical equivalent to this situation. Rather, the fundamental hierarchical relationship among pitch-events is that of one pitch-event being an *elaboration of* another pitch-event; the latter is the structurally more important event of the two. Thus a suspension is an elaboration of its resolution, the events en route in a phrase are elaborations of either the phrase's structural beginning or its cadence (as the case may be), and so forth.

In these musical cases the event that is elaborated is retained along with the event(s) that elaborate it; the structural beginning and the cadence of a phrase do not disappear or convert into something else in the course of fleshing out the phrase as a whole. In language, by contrast, grammatical categories are not retained in the tree structure from level to level, but break down into other categories; a verb phrase may break down into a verb plus a noun phrase, which in turn may break down into an article plus a noun, and so on. A mere transference of linguistic trees into their musical counterpart would be misguided from the start.[4]

With these considerations in mind, we will develop purely musical trees, having nothing to do with linguistic trees except that both express hierarchical structures with precision. There is nothing esoteric about this—the organization of a corporate bureaucracy might best be represented by a tree diagram; it is just a notation.

Given two pitch-events x and y, if y is an elaboration of x (see figure 5.6a), then its "branch" attaches to the branch of x, which continues upward (presumably to attach to the branch of another event of which it in turn is an elaboration); the converse can be said if x is an elaboration of y (5.6b). The first case (5.6a) is called a "right branch," and signifies the subordination of an event to a preceding event; the second case (5.6b) is called a "left branch," and signifies the subordination of an event to a succeeding event. (Sometimes, for purposes of discussion, it is useful to indicate simply that the branches of two events attach, without any concern for which dominates the other. In such cases we just connect their branches neutrally, as in 5.6c.)

5.6

a   b   c

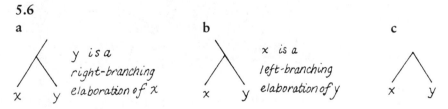

In accordance with the Strong Reduction Hypothesis, these branching structures must meet the well-formedness conditions of strict hierarchical structure. Thus the trees must satisfy the requirements of nonoverlapping, adjacency, and recursion, just as did the grouping and metrical structures (see sections 2.1 and 2.2). We will illustrate with a sequence of four arbitrary pitch-events (figure 5.7). The principle of nonoverlapping prohibits the crossing of branches (5.7a, 5.7b). It also disallows the assignment of more than one branch to the same event (5.7c), since that

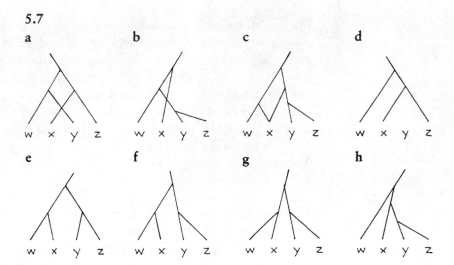

would be tantamount to saying that an event (x in 5.7c) is an elaboration of two different events.[5] The principle of adjacency means that events are heard in the context of their surrounding events at any given level of analysis. Hence, not only can branches not cross, but a sequence of events at any level must be exhaustively analyzed. This prohibits such analyses as 5.7d, in which y does not receive a branch. We emphasize here that "adjacency" does not necessarily mean adjacency on the musical surface; w, x, y, and z in 5.7 might well form a sequence at an underlying reductional level, and hence might be far apart on the musical surface. Finally, the principle of recursion says that an indefinite number of events could be analyzed by means of these branchings, forming an indefinite number of reductional levels. This is what permits the *Eroica* as well as a Bach chorale phrase to be reduced.

In contrast with 5.7a–5.7d, 5.7e–5.7h are well-formed trees. By way of example, 5.7e can be read as follows: x is an elaboration of w, and y is an elaboration of z; at the next larger level, z is an elaboration of w (thus y is recursively an elaboration of w).[6]

As an illustration of the tree notation, example 5.8 repeats the reduction of "O Haupt" given in 5.4, this time with the tree added above. (Of course, we have not yet stated the criteria that determine what branches from what.) The correspondence between the tree and the musical notation should be clear: one can think of each musical level as representing a horizontal slice across the tree, showing only the events whose branches appear in that slice. The dashed lines across the tree in 5.8 illustrate this correspondence.

One objection that might be raised against expressing reductions by means of these trees is that it might be thought arbitrary to have to attach a subordinate event—say, the neighboring chord in 5.9—either to the preceding event (5.9a) or to the ensuing event (5.9b).

5.8

Level a

Level b

Level c

Level d

Level d

Level c

Level b

Level a

5.9

a   b   c

One might argue instead that subordinate events should appear simply in between structurally more important events at the next smaller reductional level, and therefore that a "network" notation (5.9c) is more appropriate. In response, we observe that the sheer geometry of networks creates insuperable notational difficulties once even a moderate number of events are considered together; network notation is simply impracticable for the analysis of real pieces. It would be preferable to allow, say, just right branching, and interpret that as signifying plain insertion (for example, to let 5.9a signify 5.9c). A more substantive reason for maintaining both right and left branching is that it enforces the generally pervasive intuition that subordinate events are elaborations of particular dominating events, not just elaborations within a certain context. If this restriction can be maintained for all cases, it represents a great advance from a systematic point of view. Furthermore, the geometrical possibility of right and left branching provides a significant opportunity for structural interpretation. The task is to establish interpretations for these branchings that are both consistent and psychologically meaningful; these are discussed in chapters 6 and 8. As will be seen, the reductional components would be far less rich without these interpretations.

A second objection to the use of tree notation is more critical. Inherent in the notation is that a specific branch leads to a specific pitch-event (where by *pitch-event* we mean any pitch or group of simultaneous pitches that has an independent attack point). Hence pitch structure is seen as a sequence of discrete events. This leads to an excessively vertical representation of musical experience; highly polyphonic music in particular is slighted, and basic voice-leading techniques, such a central concern in Schenker's work, do not receive adequate treatment either. In response, we observe that this objection pertains not to the tree notation per se but to the very nature of hierarchical organizations, which by definition are made up of discrete elements or regions. The difficulty is not with the horizontal dimension as such, since the theory is as capable of providing structural descriptions for individual lines as it is for harmonic progressions. But in truly contrapuntal music there is an important sense in which each line should receive its own separate structural description. Although it is possible in principle to extend the theory to simultaneous multiple descriptions, the formal complications would be so enormous that they would obscure the presentation of other, perhaps more fundamental aspects of musical structure. We reserve such an extension for future research. (See section 10.4 for further discussion.)

A related objection concerns the fact that Schenker's underlying voice-leading lines not only form counterpoints with each other, but also have motivic content. Our concentration on a single tree for all voices often shortchanges this aspect of musical structure. However, Schenker's mature thought combines two modes of pitch organization, the hierarchical and the "linear-motivic" (for want of a better term). Since the linear-motivic aspects of pitch structure cannot be given proper systematic treatment without a theory of the hierarchical structures within which they are heard, we feel justified for now in concentrating on the hierarchical aspects.

This emphasis denies neither the importance of the linear-motivic aspects nor their influence on the hierarchical dimensions. Their influence is dealt with in the preference rules for reductions; that is, the linear-motivic is not part of reductions per se, but an input to reductions. Moreover, specific levels of reduction provide further material for linear-motivic analysis (see section 10.2 for examples). Thus the purely reductional approach, though one-sided, is not so one-sided as one might at first suppose. (Ultimately, one would also want an independent formal component for assigning linear-motivic structure. See the general discussion in section 11.4.)

A final possible objection to the trees is not substantive but practical: they are too hard to read. In response, we can only say that their difficulty lies solely in their novelty. If we had been able to invent an equally efficient and accurate representation through traditional musical notation, we would have done so. As it is, we will often supply a secondary and more traditional musical notation as an aid to reading the tree, as we did in 5.8 above.

<table>
<tr><td>

5.4
Preliminary
Construction of
Reductions

</td><td>

Now we are ready to explore what is needed to construct a reduction. First we will attempt a reduction based only on pitch criteria. The need for rhythmic criteria will lead us to the conception of time-span reduction. This will prove to be only partly successful, so we will then develop the conception of prolongational reduction. All of this will be a mere sketch in preparation for the extensive discussions in chapters 6–9.

In what follows, we can take as given the classical Western tonal pitch system—the major-minor scale system, the traditional classifications of consonance and dissonance, the triadic harmonic system with its roots and inversions, the circle-of-fifths system, and the principles of good voice-leading. Though all of these principles could and should be formalized, they are largely idiom-specific, and are well understood informally within the traditional disciplines of harmony and counterpoint. Nothing will be lost if we conveniently consider them to be an input to the theory of reductions.

What is needed, in addition, is a scale of stability among pitch configurations, derived from the raw material of the given tonal system. Broadly, the relative stability of a pitch-event can be thought of in terms of its relative consonance or dissonance. For example, a local consonance is more stable than a local dissonance, a triad in root position is more stable than its inversions, the tonic is the most stable harmony, the relative stability of two chords is a factor of the relative closeness to the tonic (or

</td></tr>
</table>

the local tonic) of their roots on the circle of fifths, conjunct linear connections are more stable than disjunct ones, and so forth.

Rhythmic Criteria and Time-Span Reduction

Granted all these criteria for relative pitch stability, we might now hypothesize that the listener seeks maximal stability among pitch relations and mentally constructs pitch hierarchies (reductions) that express such stability. Thus, if a pitch-event were adjacent to and less stable than another event, it would automatically be subordinate to it. In other words, according to this hypothesis, structural importance would be equated with pitch stability.

But is this hypothesis adequate for the construction of a coherent reduction? A glance at any tonal piece will reveal that it is not. For example, in the first phrase of Mozart's Sonata K. 331 (5.10),[7] the most "stable" events are the four root-position tonic chords with C♯ on top. Purely according to pitch criteria, they must attach equally, because they are identical; all other events, being less "stable," must somehow be subordinate to them. Among other things, this means that the cadential dominant—even though it is the goal of the phrase—can do no better than to attach as a right branch to the closest root-position I chord, as a kind of afterthought to the phrase. The result is the partial tree in 5.10, which is intuitively so ludicrous that we might as well discontinue the exercise. Criteria of pitch stability may be necessary, but they are not sufficient for the construction of reductions.

5.10

What other criteria are needed? Intuitively, the structurally most important events in the phrase are its first and last events, the opening I and the cadential V; as described in section 2.4, these are the *structural accents* of the phrase.[8] The intervening I chords are heard as comparatively local phenomena: the one on the third eighth of measure 1 is a mere repetition of the opening I; the one in measure 2 is scarcely a chord at all, but a neighboring motion within a V^6; and the one in measure 4, though important within the phrase, is not as important as the structural accents.

These intuitions all have to do with rhythm—specifically, with grouping and meter. The V in measure 4 is heard as cadential only because it articulates the end of a large group; this in itself is enough to raise it above the I in measure 4, which by pitch criteria alone is the more stable of the two. The opening I also occurs at a large grouping boundary, and besides is in a strong metrical position. By contrast, the I on the third eighth of measure 1 and the I in measure 2 do not stand next to grouping boundaries, and are in weak metrical positions. The I in measure 4 occurs on a fairly strong beat, but is in the middle of a group.

The solution, then, lies in the proper integration of criteria of pitch stability with rhythmic criteria based on the grouping and metrical components. Schenkerian reductions rely heavily on a tacit knowledge of these areas. Indeed, Schenkerian analysis is workable at all only because the analyst himself supplies (consciously or unconsciously) the requisite rhythmic intuitions. A formal cognitive theory must make this knowledge manifest through a set of explicit rules.

A reductional theory based only on pitch criteria is deficient in another respect: it does not restrict in the slightest way the domains over which events can attach. The criteria for pitch stability alone are "free floating"—they can connect up events anywhere, as long as the resultant trees are well formed and the principles of relative consonance and dissonance are observed. For example, there is nothing in principle to prevent the I "chord" in measure 2 of 5.10 from attaching at the level of the whole phrase, even though intuitively it is an elaboration only within the context of the first half of measure 2.

Again the metrical and grouping structures fill the need, for they offer a principled way of segmenting a piece into domains of elaboration at every level—a hierarchy of *time-spans.* At the most local levels, the metrical component marks off the music into beats of equal time-spans; at larger levels, the grouping component divides the piece into motives, subphrase groups, phrases, periods, theme groups, and sections. Thus it becomes possible to convert a combined metrical and grouping analysis into a *time-span segmentation,* as diagrammed for the beginning of K. 331 in 5.11. (As in section 2.3, the brackets represent time-spans from beat to beat.) This time-span segmentation can define the domains over which reduction takes place.

Consequently, the grouping and metrical components serve a double function in constructing reductions: they segment the music into rhythmic domains, and within these domains they provide rhythmic criteria to supplement pitch criteria in the determination of the structural importance of events.

5.11

The problem now becomes simply to select the structurally most important event in each time-span, in a cyclical fashion from level to level. This process is illustrated schematically in 5.12. (In the example, we have omitted the events below the dotted-quarter-note level. The vi⁷ is given in quotes because it is hardly a chord in a normal sense; the labeling is for convenience.)

5.12

For each time-span in 5.12, a single event is chosen as the most important event, or *head*. For instance, in the span covering measure 2, the V^6 is chosen over the V_3^4, and proceeds for consideration in the span covering measures 1–2; here it is less stable than the opening I, so it does not proceed to the next larger span; and so forth. As a result of this procedure, a particular time-span level produces a particular *reductional level* (the sequence of heads of the time-spans at that level).

Note how the events marked *m* and *n* in 5.12, which were unhappily so prominent in 5.10, have already disappeared at the half-measure level. This is a result of their having had to "compete" in an environment (the span of the half-measure) in which they "lost" to another event; they never had a chance to attach at larger levels. Thus meter and grouping have placed constraints on how the pitch structure is heard.

Such in principle is time-span reduction.[9] When we develop it in the next chapter, we will explain more fully how it represents the interaction of pitch and rhythmic structure.

Motivation for Prolongational Reduction

It would be disappointing to stop at time-span reduction. Too many aspects of musical intuition, of exactly the kind one would want from a reduction, are not expressed by it. For instance, it is common for a group or phrase to begin with an event identical or almost identical to the event that ended the previous group or phrase; this is a major means for establishing continuity across group boundaries. Characteristic examples are the beginning of Beethoven's Sonata op. 2, no. 3 (example 5.13a), in which the V carries across a group boundary, and the beginning of Mozart's G Minor Symphony (reduced to a harmonic and linear skeleton in 5.13b), in which the ii$^4_2$ carries across a group boundary.

5.13

Now it is obvious that the first group in 5.13a progresses from I to V, and the second from V to I; likewise, the first group in 5.13b progresses from i to ii$^4_2$, and the second from ii$^4_2$ through V^6 to i. These elementary perceptions are expressed in time-span reduction, since its function is to relate pitch structure at every level to the segmentation produced by meter and grouping. But it is equally obvious that the harmonic rhythm in both cases prolongs across group boundaries.[10] Time-span reduction fails to express this sense of continuity.

For a related problem, return to the Mozart K. 331 phrase. There is a sense in which the opening tonic is prolonged, through lower-neighbor motion in measures 2–3, into measure 4, at which point the first real structural movement takes place, in three ways at once: contrapuntally, by the first independent motion of the outer voices (which until then are in parallel tenths); harmonically, through the "cadential preparation" (the ii^6 chord) to the cadential V; and melodically, by the underlying motion from the third to the second scale degree. The overall effect of the phrase is very much due to these three dimensions working in concert, as indicated in 5.14.

5.14

Time-span reduction cannot express the structural relationships sketched in 5.14 because it is constrained in its selection of significant events by the time-span segmentation established by the metrical and grouping analyses. It chooses single events over more or less equal time-spans, that is all. Thus, in 5.11, only one event (the I chord) can be selected within the span of the first half of measure 4, with the result that the syntactically essential ii⁶ is assigned less structural importance than, say, the merely arpeggiated V$^4_3$ in measure 2. And at the span of the measure, the I in measure 4, even though it is heard as a significant prolongation of the opening sonority, must give way to the cadential V, while in measures 2–3 neighboring events remain. If, as often happens, events of equivalent structural importance were to unfold at a regular rate, one per time-span, these particular difficulties would not emerge. But here—and this often happens, too—the structural action of the phrase is delayed until the fourth bar, where it precipitates all at once. Time-span reduction is not equipped to handle such situations.

Example 5.14 also suggests a "psychological" interpretation that sheds more light on the limitations of time-span reduction. One might say that the phrase begins in relative repose, increases in tension (second half of measure 1 to the downbeat of measure 3), stretches the tension in a kind of dynamic reversal to the opening (downbeat of measure 3 to downbeat of measure 4), and then relaxes the tension (the rest of measure 4). It would be highly desirable for a reduction to express this kind of musical ebb and flow. Time-span reduction cannot do this, not only because in such cases as this it derives a sequence of events incompatible with such an interpretation (5.12 as opposed to 5.14), but because the kind of information it conveys, while essential, is couched in completely different terms. It says that particular pitch-events are heard in relation to a particular beat, within a particular group, but it says nothing about how music flows across these segments.

It is through such considerations as these that we have been led to the conception of two independent but interactive reductional components: time-span reduction and prolongational reduction. Recall that the Strong Reduction Hypothesis posits a hierarchy of events such that less important events are heard in a specified relationship to surrounding more important events. Whereas in time-span reduction this relationship concerns relative stability within rhythmic units, in prolongational reduction it concerns relative stability expressed in terms of continuity and progression, the movement toward tension or relaxation, and the degree of closure or nonclosure. The prolongational component not only expresses intuitions of connection and continuity such as those suggested in 5.13 and 5.14, but also provides "psychological" interpretations for them in precise structural terms, by means of a tree notation to be described in section 8.1.

In order to define the notion of prolongational importance, we again need more than purely pitch criteria, so that incorrect reductions such as 5.10 may be avoided. We will show in chapters 8 and 9 that prolongational importance is derived not from the musical surface, but from the associated time-span reduction, with all its encoded rhythmic structure. Thus, indirectly, grouping and meter are also implicated in prolongational structure. The inclusiveness of this hypothesis mirrors the intuitive judgment that patterns of tension and relaxation are at the heart of musical understanding.

The two kinds of reduction interact in a fashion not unlike the in-phase or out-of-phase relationship between grouping and meter. If the domains produced by the two reductions correspond, the reductions can be said to be *congruent;* if not, they are *noncongruent.* As with the "phase" relationship, congruence and noncongruence are relative terms. A good example of an acutely noncongruent passage is the K. 331 phrase, since at a certain prolongational level the region of the opening tonic extends to the downbeat of measure 4 (as shown in 5.14), in contrast with the pitch hierarchy heard through the time-span segmentation in 5.12. If the prolongationally significant events were evenly distributed across the time-spans—say, if the I in measure 4 had arrived on the downbeat of measure 3—the phrase would be fairly congruent. As it is, the opening tonic seems to stretch like a rubber band, which in measure 4 belatedly springs loose. In general the interaction of the two kinds of reduction has a great deal to do with the "shape" of a passage. Congruent passages seem relatively straightforward and square; noncongruent passages have a more complex, elastic quality.

We will now devote two chapters in turn to each kind of reduction.

6
Time-Span Reduction: The Analytic System

In this chapter we discuss time-span segmentation and time-span tree structure in some detail and conclude with a complete time-span reduction. The rules that assign analyses within this component are developed in chapter 7.

6.1
Time-Span
Segmentation

Recall from section 5.4 that in time-span reduction the hierarchy of time-spans derives from the metrical and grouping components, and that a single structurally most important event is chosen as *head* for each time-span. Time-spans can thus be thought of as apprehended rhythmic units in terms of which pitch structure is heard. We will first explore the organization of these units.

We begin with relatively global levels. Consider the finale theme of Beethoven's Ninth Symphony. We may say, unexceptionally, that it segments into six 4-bar phrases, which group together on the basis of parallelism (A A′ B A′ B A′) into the structure shown in example 6.1.

6.1

Furthermore, in the context of the whole movement, the theme is the first of a set of orchestral variations, preceded by an elaborate introduction; then all the foregoing is paired with an ensuing introduction and variations, this time with voices; and so forth. All these formal articulations would be reflected in a grouping analysis of the entire movement. In brief, at intermediate and large levels the apprehended rhythmic units of a piece correspond to its grouping analysis. We therefore can assert that any group is a time-span.

Considering now only the first phrase of the theme, we note that motivic parallelism divides the phrase into two smaller groups, as shown in 6.2a. Beneath this level, however, there is little in the music that permits the assigning of still smaller groupings. At these local levels we must turn to the metrical analysis in 6.2a for segmentation of the music into time-spans. Here intuition suggests that there is a rhythmic unit corresponding to each beat of each level of metrical structure. Example 6.2b represents these rhythmic units in the form of what we call *subgroup bracketing*. Each bracket is associated with a particular beat, commencing at that beat and continuing up to but not including the next beat at the level in question.

6.2

a

b

In 6.2b the largest levels of subgroup bracketing, the 2- and 4-bar levels, are coextensive with the small grouping levels shown in 6.2a. In such cases, both meter and grouping support the intuition that these are rhythmic units. But what happens if the subgroup bracketing conflicts with the grouping, as in measures 12–13 and 20–21 of the theme? Example 6.3 interprets the span from the fourth beat of measure 12 to the downbeat of measure 13 in incompatible ways: in the subgroup bracketing the span belongs to measure 12 (by virtue of the regular

Time-Span Reduction

metrical structure), but in the grouping it belongs to measure 13 (as an anticipation of the next phrase).

6.3

Although such an interpretation may shed light on the unique tension of this moment in the theme, it will not do as a procedure for constructing reductions. The Strong Reduction Hypothesis requires that the F♯ on the fourth beat of measure 12 cannot attach both ways at once. This moment is an isolated instance in this particular theme of a more general phenomenon: grouping and meter that are out of phase (see section 2.3). The bracketing procedure outlined so far applies only to in-phase passages.

The solution for out-of-phase passages lies in the strong intuitive notions of *upbeat* and *afterbeat*. As discussed in section 2.3, a weak beat is heard as an afterbeat to the immediately preceding strong beat unless a grouping boundary intervenes between the two. If a grouping boundary intervenes, the weak beat is associated as an upbeat with the immediately following strong beat. If we compare all the fourth beats in 6.3, we indeed find that those of measures 11, 13, and 14 are heard as afterbeats, but that this hearing is not possible for the fourth beat of measure 12 because of the grouping articulation immediately to its left. Instead, the primary sense of the F♯ on the fourth beat of measure 12 is that it belongs as an anacrusis to the succeeding phrase.

The revised subgroup bracketing in 6.4 reflects these intuitions.

6.4

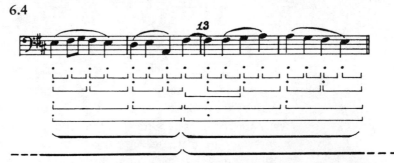

Measures unaffected by out-of-phase conditions, such as 11 and 14, receive subgroup bracketings as above. Any such bracketing we call a *regular time-span*. But in the out-of-phase region, the grouping structure forces alterations: the brackets at the half-note level and larger are truncated just to the left of the fourth beat of measure 12, and the corresponding brackets to the right of this beat are enlarged so as to include it as an upbeat. Any such enlarged bracketing we call an *augmented time-span*. In this way a unified time-span segmentation is achieved in a manner compatible with the criterion that a group is a time-span.

In 6.4 an additional bracket is required at the half-note level at the beginning of measure 13: beats 1 and 2 are bracketed together within a regular time-span, since their relation is unmodified by the grouping boundary in measure 12, and then beat 4 of measure 12 is added to form the augmented time-span. Because the augmented time-span contains the regular time-span, this procedure grants a slight prominence to events on upbeats. This formal detail appears to mirror perceptual experience.

Example 6.5 illustrates the subgroup bracketing for a thoroughly out-of-phase passage, the opening theme of Mozart's G Minor Symphony. The inner tension of this music is in part a product of the rhythmic conflict between the periodicity of the metrical structure (reinforced by the accompaniment) and the complexity of the time-spans resulting from such out-of-phase conditions.

6.5

Previous approaches to time-span reduction have been based exclusively on some metrical conception. We surmise that this has been so only because it has not been customary to develop grouping and meter as independent yet interactive components. In any case, we have just shown that a purely metrical approach to time-span segmentation is accurate only for in-phase passages.

A second argument against an exclusively metrical conception of time-span reduction is that the perception of meter fades at large levels (as argued in section 2.2). Thus a reductional procedure based on large-scale metrical relations would have little basis in musical experience. A related argument concerns the fact that time-span segmentation is often irregular at intermediate levels because of surface irregularities in the music. An exclusively metrical conception would have to make these spans regular at an underlying level. This approach may be satisfactory for certain cases (essentially, for clear-cut extensions or contractions within an otherwise regular context), but in general it is problematic.

Many passages are simply heard as irregular; in such cases it would be sheer speculation to choose one "regularized" version over another. A reliance on grouping structure, on the other hand, poses no such theoretical difficulties, because there is no requirement that groups be periodic.[1]

To sum up: At the smallest levels, metrical structure is the only influence on the choice of time-spans, and the time-spans are regular in length. At some intermediate level, grouping boundaries may interrupt the regularity imposed by the metrical pattern, and the time-spans result from the interaction of meter and grouping. At still larger levels, the time-spans are totally determined by grouping structure, and metrical structure is irrelevant.

6.2 Time-Span Trees and Metrical Structure

Now let us begin to construct trees for sequences of pitch-events as they occur within the time-span segmentation. Figure 6.6 schematizes the general case: if events *x* and *y* are the most important events in time-spans *a* and *b* respectively, and if at the next larger level they are contained in time-span *c,* then either *x* dominates *y* (a right branch) (6.6a) or *y* dominates *x* (a left branch) (6.6b). This process continues recursively through the time-span segmentation until one event dominates the time-span of the entire piece.

6.6

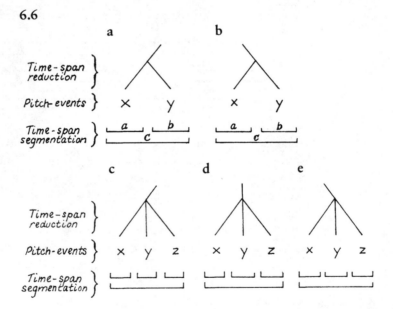

Sometimes the time-span segmentation includes three spans within the next larger span. This happens most frequently at local levels of pieces in triple meter, but can also occur at large levels if phrases or sections group together in threes. Such segmentation causes ternary branching when there is an event for each span at the level in question. Diagrams 6.6c–6.6e complete the branching possibilities: if event x dominates, y and z attach to it equally; and similarly if y or z dominates. (See section 12.3 on the possibility of restricting time-span trees to binary branching.)

At local levels, as we have just seen, metrical structure determines time-span structure. Thus we can relate right and left branching to metrical structure in a musically significant way. In 6.7 two levels of metrical structure and time-span segmentation have been indicated, to produce, along with the two kinds of branching, four paradigmatic situations.

6.7

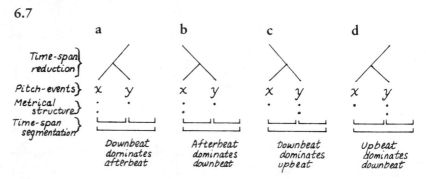

Cases *a* and *b* pertain to afterbeats: in *a*, event *y* on the afterbeat is the less stable event, as in the case of a passing or neighboring tone or chord; in *b*, event *x* on the downbeat is the less stable event, as in the case of a suspension or an appoggiatura tone or chord. Cases *c* and *d* pertain to upbeats: in *c*, event *x* on the upbeat is the less stable event; in *d*, event *y* on the downbeat is the less stable event. Viewed differently, the more stable events in *a* and *c* occur on strong beats, and those in *b* and *d* occur on weak beats. (These distinctions function for ternary branching as well.)

A time-span reduction of local levels of the first two phrases of Bach's chorale "O Haupt Voll Blut und Wunden" will illustrate these pitch-meter relationships. Example 6.8 presents the time-span segmentation.

6.8

Let us construct the tree step by step. Example 6.9 applies the principles of pitch stability to the events at the quarter-note time-span level. If
there is only one event in a span, its branch extends upward by a dotted
line, to be connected at a later stage to another branch. If there are two
events in the span, they attach as in 6.6a or 6.6b. As an aid, we label each
branching according to the paradigmatic situations shown in 6.7.

6.9

If we omit ("reduce out") the events designated as subordinate in 6.9, a
single event remains as head of each time-span at the quarter-note level.
Example 6.10 is a convenient musical notation—a "secondary notation"—for representing this stage of analysis.

6.10

In this notation, if the head in 6.9 is on the weaker beat, it is placed in
6.10 on the associated stronger beat. This procedure expresses three
related intuitions: that an appoggiatura (in its broadest sense) is a structural delay, that strong beats "attract" stable events within a group, and
that the ear seeks, insofar as possible, a regular underlying harmonic
rhythm.

The next level in the time-span segmentation, the half-note level, contains both regular and augmented time-spans (see 6.8). Example 6.11a
shows the branching for events in the regular time-spans; 6.11b shows it
for the augmented time-spans as well.

Observe how the levels of branching correspond to the levels of subgroup
bracketing. Again, the labeling specifies the paradigmatic situations from
6.7. Example 6.11c converts 6.11b into the secondary notation.

6.11

a

b

c

The pattern of the four paradigmatic situations in 6.9 and 6.11a,b is musically revealing. At both levels cases *b* and *d* pervade the first phrase, *a* and *c* the second. Remember that in *b* and *d* the head is on the weak beat, whereas in *a* and *c* it is on the strong beat. In other words, an important feature of the first phrase is that at various levels of detail the more stable events occur on the weaker beats, until the phrase cadences on the comparatively strong third beat of measure 2. In the second phrase, by contrast, at various levels of detail the more stable events appear on the stronger beats; and when the phrase cadences, it happens on a stronger beat than the cadence of the first phrase. The coherence of each phrase individually, and the sense that the second answers the first, depend crucially on these relationships between pitch and meter. (The one exception, case *b* in measure 3 of 6.11a, is in itself revealing: in every phrase of the entire chorale, a suspension occurs at the equivalent place at that particular time-span level. Thus the one pitch-meter irregularity in the opening phrases yields a greater global regularity.)

Example 6.12 compresses the information conveyed in 6.9–6.11. This is our normal format for time-span reduction.

6.12

Here the letters labeling branchings signify not pitch-meter relationships (we assume acquaintance with these from now on), but reductional levels. Specifically, in the tree and at the left in the secondary notation, *c* stands for the eighth-note level, *b* for the quarter-note level, and *a* for the half-note level of this example. Beneath the actual music and above the secondary notation appear the grouping and metrical analyses. We omit the subgroup bracketing (with which we also henceforth assume acquaintance) because it does not constitute a separate component in the sense that grouping, meter, and the two kinds of reduction do.

To carry the reduction of the chorale farther than level *a* in 6.12, we must first develop the treatment of cadences—the subject of section 6.4. A complete reduction will be presented in section 6.6.

In closing this section we must caution that the formal theory resides only in the trees, not in the secondary notation, even though the latter is a close translation of the former. We retain both because the tree notation is unfamiliar, and because, as will become clearer in longer examples, the two notations serve somewhat different purposes. The tree gives a picture of all the levels in relation to one another; the notation below the music is useful in hearing any particular level.

A further cautionary word is needed about the labeling of levels. This, too, is not part of the formal theory. It will turn out that the formal theory does not require that one branching at level n correspond strictly to another branching at level n in some other part of a piece. This restriction is not feasible because of the frequent irregularity of depth of embedding in the time-span segmentation, especially at global levels of analysis. Nonetheless, we keep the labeling of levels because in this kind of reduction it has a meaning—namely, that the time-spans partition a piece into approximately equal parts at any given level, and therefore the structurally most important event in one span can be ranked with another such event in another span of about the same length. No doubt music is perceived, to a degree, as progressing at an even rate of events from level to level. This is what the labeling of levels addresses.

<table>
<tr><td>

**6.3
Time-Span Trees
and Structural
Accents**

</td><td>

In section 2.4 we claimed that the structural accents of the phrase—its structural beginning (abbreviated b) and its structural ending, or cadence (abbreviated c)—belong in a music theory not as part of metrical structure but as part of time-span reduction. It is time to make good that claim. Again we begin schematically. We revive the analogy of section 2.4: like a ball thrown and caught, the overarching elements of a phrase are its structural beginning and its cadence. In section 2.4 we diagrammed this state of affairs as in 6.13a. Now we can be less impressionistic: the b and c of a phrase must emerge as its structurally most important events in the time-span reduction, in the form of either 6.13b or 6.13c, depending on whether the b dominates the c (6.13b) or vice versa (6.13c).

</td></tr>
</table>

6.13

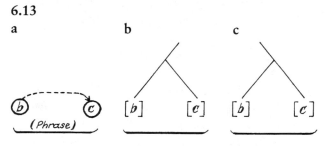

Our first task is to see how the *b* and *c* dominate all other events in a phrase. There is no problem with the *b:* it results naturally from the reductional process; it is whatever emerges as the most stable event before the cadence in a phrase. Often the *b* is the first event in a phrase, as in the Mozart K. 331 phrase (see example 5.12) or the first phrase of the Bach chorale; often it is the second or third event, as in the second phrase of the chorale (as suggested in example 6.12). More rarely it occurs in the middle of a phrase. The germane point is that a *b* is always heard as associated with a corresponding *c;* if a time-span lacks a *c,* then it lacks a *b.* A phrase can be characterized roughly as the smallest level of grouping in which there is a *b* and a *c.*

The treatment of cadences is more complicated, for two reasons. First, the half cadence or the deceptive cadence might not emerge simply on grounds of pitch stability as structurally important at the phrase level. Second, the full cadence and the deceptive cadence possess two members, joined together as a unit; in both, neither member would have remotely the same meaning if the other did not function with it. This suggests that in certain respects the two-membered cadence should be counted as one event.

The Mozart K. 331 theme illustrates both points. One hears the first phrase as progressing from I to a half-cadential V and the second phrase as progressing from I to a V–I full cadence (6.14a). The tree should express this hearing. But unless the cadences are treated specially, the I in measure 4 dominates the half cadence because its pitch structure is more "stable" (as discussed in section 5.4); and the V in the full cadence already disappears at a local level because it has not been joined to the final I. The absurd result is sketched in the incomplete reduction in 6.14b.

To avoid results such as 6.14b, we must regard cadences as signs, or conventional formulas, that mark and articulate the ends of groups from phrase levels to the most global levels of musical structure. In any well-established style, the repertory of cadences is very limited—for classical tonal music, only V–I, V, and V–vi, with occasional variants. (Because the plagal cadence is always an elaboration of the I in the full cadence, it need not be specified.) The theory can therefore "find" these signs when they occur at the ends of groups, and label them as functioning cadentially for all the levels of grouping that terminate with them. The labeling retains cadences regardless of other reductional criteria, and unifies both elements of two-membered cadences.

The need for such labeling of cadences can be approached in another way. If they were not labeled, global levels of reduction would simply calculate the duration of harmonic areas in a piece; that is, each large-level group would be reduced to just the tonic or local tonic. For example, the minuet and trio of Beethoven's Sonata op. 10, no. 3, would

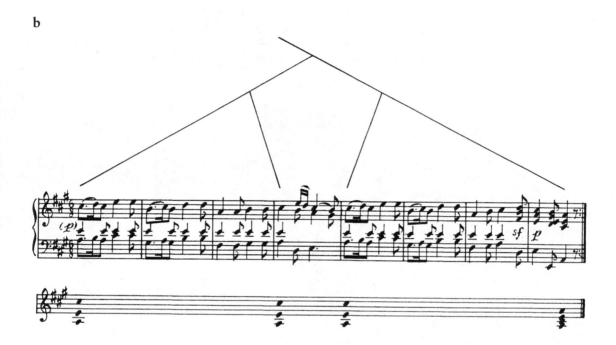

eventually boil down to a I–IV–I progression, and Schubert's song "Ihr Bild" would become a i–VI–i progression. Though such harmonic relationships are important, they are idiosyncratic, and they obscure the generalization that virtually every tonal piece progresses from the tonic to a full cadence on the tonic. The most global levels of reductions should represent relations characteristic of the tonal idiom as a whole. Relations characteristic of a particular piece should begin to emerge at somewhat more intermediate levels, showing precisely how the piece is a unique instance of the tonal idiom.

Granting, then, cadential labeling and the resulting dominance of the *b* and *c* over all other events within a phrase, let us see how the *b*s and *c*s of different phrases interact to produce larger hierarchies. Here it will be convenient to view all cs, regardless of type, as undifferentiated entities; the details of cadential reduction are reserved for the next section.

Imagine a piece in four phrases, grouped together as in 6.15a. As an aid, we place a number, signifying the number of measures spanned, within each grouping slur. We find the bs and cs and supply each with one or more subscripts corresponding to the groups that it begins or cadences. Suppose (not implausibly) that each b is about as stable, purely by pitch criteria, as each c. In short, disregard all factors except the bs, the cs, and the regions over which they operate.

6.15

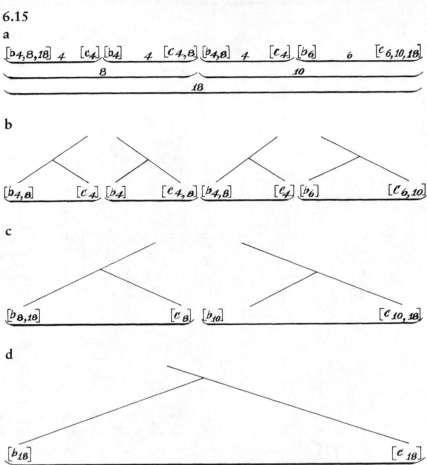

Example 6.15b connects the b and c of each phrase as in 6.13b,c. Whether the b or the c is structurally most important in a particular phrase is determined by the role each plays in the larger grouping structure; that is, by whether it functions as a b or c for a larger group. Thus, as indicated by the subscripts, the c of the first phrase is a c only for that phrase, but its b is also a b at the next larger grouping level; hence the b is

the head of the phrase. In the second phrase, by similar considerations, the *c* instead is the head; and so forth. This process continues cyclically from level to level. Finally, in 6.15d, the *c* dominates the *b* because the ending of a piece is usually more stable than its beginning.

Pitch relations among *b*s and *c*s can reinforce or undermine this scheme. If, for instance, the *b* of the first phrase were far less stable than its *c* (think, for example, of the opening of Beethoven's Sonata op. 31, no. 3), the *c* might emerge as the structurally most important event of the phrase and thus be retained at larger levels instead of the *b*. In such a case, pitch stability (the *c*) would override adjacency to a larger grouping boundary (the *b*). Since these cases are exceptional, however, we will not pursue them now; an example appears in section 7.4.

Example 6.16 compresses the information conveyed in 6.15. As a convenience, we give the subscript for only the largest level of grouping for which a *b* or a *c* functions.

6.16

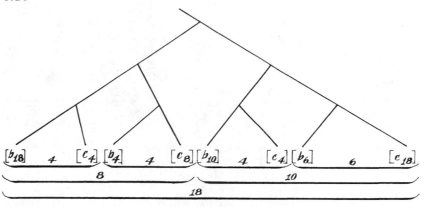

At these levels right and left branchings no longer express pitch-meter relationships, but pitch-*grouping* relationships. The translation of 6.16 into the "ball-throwing" representation of 6.17 should clarify this point.

6.17

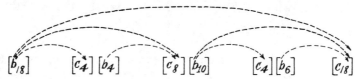

The arrows signify the arcs of tonal motion over which structural accents function. In any time-span tree, large-scale branchings connecting *b*s and *c*s are always to be interpreted as arcs of tonal motion articulating grouping structure.

The tree in 6.16 still simplifies the cadential structure for two-membered cadences. Although they function as a unit, they also comprise two events, each of which must receive its own branch in accordance with the Reduction Hypothesis. In the full cadence, because the I is next to the grouping boundary and is more stable than the V, the V must be subordinate to the I. The deceptive cadence, being a deviation merely in bass motion from the full cadence, receives the same structure (see sections 7.2 and 9.4 for further discussion).

The internal analysis of a two-membered cadence must violate normal principles of time-span branching. In retaining a feminine cadence, two branches instead of one are retained within one bracket (6.18a). In retaining a masculine cadence, the V attaches to the ensuing I instead of being compared with another event x in its own bracket (6.18b). These exceptions are necessary if the V is to function at larger reductional levels.

6.18

a   b

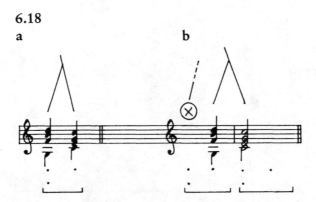

The treatment of events subordinate to a two-membered cadence must also be special. Sometimes a local detail is subordinate to just one member of the cadence. In 6.19a, for example, the $^6_4$ elaborates only the V; in 6.19b the appoggiatura elaborates only the I. At somewhat larger levels, however, where the cadence has been labeled as a unit, an event may be subordinate not to one element of the cadence but to the cadence as a whole. We represent this situation by attaching the subordinate branch to both cadential branches with an egglike shape, as in 6.19c. At still larger levels, the cadence may be subordinate to a b; in this case the V attaches to the I and the I to the dominating b, as in 6.19d. Example 6.19e combines 6.19a–6.19d into one hypothetical tree.

With these considerations in mind, we convert 6.16 into 6.20, this time with actual chords indicated for each b and c. This is in fact the time-span analysis for the structural accents of the entire 18-bar variation theme of Mozart's K. 331.

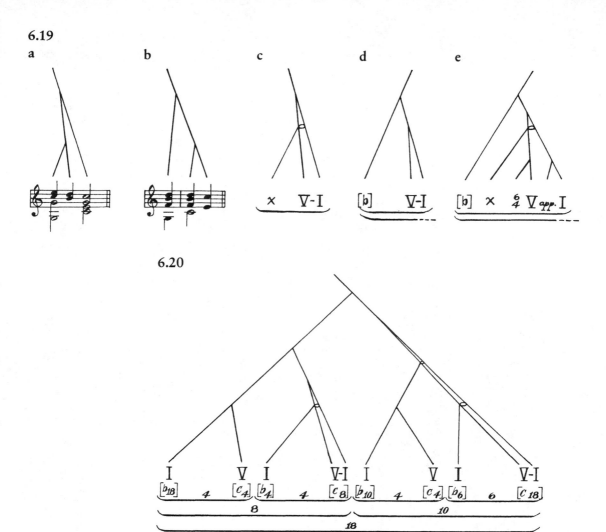

6.20

**6.5
Background
Structures and the
Location of the
Structural
Dominant**

Readers familiar with Schenkerian theory will have noticed that the procedures outlined here produce an *Ursatz*-like structure at the most global level of analysis. Specifically, the *b* for an entire piece is bound to be the tonic, and the *c* is bound to be a full cadence; together these create a I–V–I progression. In many cases, moreover, the $\hat{3}$–$\hat{2}$–$\hat{1}$ quasi-*Urlinie* ("fundamental line," the melodic aspect of the *Ursatz*—a stepwise diatonic descent to the tonic note from another member of the tonic triad) also results.

What is one to make of this correlation? From our perspective, the *Ursatz* constitutes the most stable "background" structure expressible within the tonal system, in that it embodies many of the basic harmonic and melodic principles of tonality (prolongation of the tonic, the circle of fifths, stepwise linear motion, and so forth). As a consequence, a piece structured on such principles will tend to reveal an *Ursatz* at the most global reductional level; it is not necessary to posit such a structure in advance. The *Ursatz* is an effect, not a cause, of tonal principles.

From this it follows that reductions of tonally unstable pieces probably will not result in a stepwise melodic descent, or possibly even a I–V–I progression. Rather than make such cases conform somehow to an *a priori* conception, it is illuminating to see how they deviate from prototypical cases. (An intriguing example in this respect will be discussed in section 9.6. For a general discussion of "models," see section 11.4.)

A related issue of interest to Schenkerian theory concerns the location of the *structural dominant* (the most important V in a piece or passage). It is obvious that a typical tonal piece begins and ends on the tonic. Less clear is where that crucial V occurs, particularly in the pervasive "interruption" forms (which include, among others, the antecedent-consequent period and sonata form). Figure 6.21 diagrams the essentials of an interruption form: the tonic moves to a half cadence (or possibly to a tonicizing cadence on V); then a reprise on the tonic leads to a completion of the interrupted half cadence by a full cadence. Is the structural dominant the V at the half cadence, or the V at the final cadence?[2]

6.21

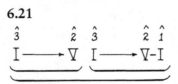

Because of the labeling of cadences and their relation to grouping structure, our theory asserts unequivocally that the structural dominant, in interruption form or any other tonal form, is the V at the full cadence that resolves the piece (or passage) as a whole. The tree shown in 6.22 for the structural accents of the opening eight bars of K. 331 will illustrate: the half cadence (measure 4) plays a role only in measures 1–4, but the final V functions cadentially for both measures 5–8 and measures 1–8. (If necessary, consult the ball-throwing representation in 6.17.)

We offer the following general arguments in support of this position. First, the selection of the V in measure 4—or, more generally, any merely centrally located and salient dominant—would not reflect tonal principles as a whole, since many passages or pieces do not have an available V at the equivalent place. For instance, where would one find the structural dominant in the entire 18-bar theme of K. 331 (6.20) if not in the final cadence? The most centrally located dominant, the V in measure 8, clearly resolves in measure 8. More plausible is the half-cadential V in measure 12; but this is too deeply embedded in the grouping structure, especially if the repeats are observed, to function for the theme as a whole. Thus the final V is the only satisfactory choice.

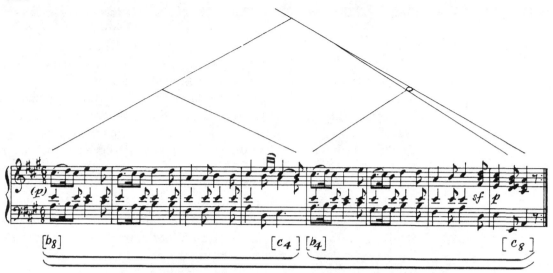

$[b_8]$ $[c_4]$ $[b_4]$ $[c_8]$

Second, to take a large class of instances, how are we to analyze pieces in the minor mode? Many passages in the minor mode move to III rather than V for the intermediate cadence (think, for example, of the main theme of the second movement of Beethoven's Seventh Symphony). This rules out parallel treatment across the two modes if the intermediate V is selected in the major mode as the structural dominant. Surely one would not want to assign opposing trees to structural accents in the minor and major modes, especially when they are otherwise formally parallel. By contrast, the final cadence in the minor mode cannot be a III–i progression. That the final cadence in the minor mode must be V–i points to the real location of the structural dominant in the major mode.

A final argument against choosing an intermediate V as the structural dominant is that this would create an unfavorable prolongational reduction. In the Mozart K. 331 passage, for example, it would suggest that the V in measure 4 prolongs across the repeat of the opening (measure 5) to the V in measure 8 (6.23a) rather than that the opening I prolongs across the half cadence to the repeat of the opening (6.23b). It seems to us essential that the latter relationship obtain. (See section 8.3 for discussion.)

6.23

a   b

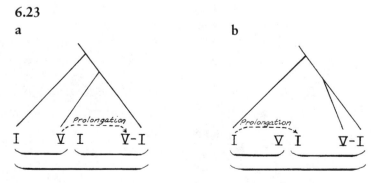

6.6
A Complete
Time-Span
Reduction

In this section we will present a time-span reduction of the chorale "O Haupt voll Blut und Wunden" from Bach's *St. Matthew Passion*. Example 6.24 gives one of Bach's harmonizations of the chorale; 6.25 supplies its time-span reduction. To avoid a thicket of branches, we have already reduced the music in 6.25 to the quarter-note level. The repeat has been written out for reasons that will be explained in a moment.

Some details in the secondary notation in 6.25 require explanation. First, the events at global levels are notated merely in black note-heads because at these levels there are no longer any dots in the metrical analysis with which durational values could be associated. This is our equivalent to Schenker's dictum (1935, paragraph 21) that rhythm does not exist at background levels. The critical factor here is the fading of the perception of meter over large time-spans. Second, at local levels we do not displace an event metrically beyond an aurally plausible point (evidently the tactus is a factor in this regard). For example, the V in measure 2 is heard as rhythmically delayed by the preceding ii§, so we place it beneath the ii§ at level *f*. But at level *e* it does not seem meaningful to say that the I in measure 2 has been delayed by the immediately preceding V, so we retain the original vertical alignment of the I. In any case, regardless of whether an event is displaced, we give it the full durational value (at local levels) of the time-span for which it stands. By this notational compromise, readers may hear the various levels in the presented durational values without being under the misapprehension that events "really" belong somewhere else.

The reduction itself proceeds for the most part in a straightforward manner, but a few features deserve comment. First, observe that the functioning harmony at beat 3 of measure 11, a root-position E minor chord, is not in fact present at the musical surface because the suspension in the alto resolves only after the bass has changed. To reduce this passage correctly, we have inserted this understood chord (by a transformational rule that will be introduced in section 7.2) and treated it as head of the relevant time-span. Second, this same E minor chord is retained at levels *e* and *d* not because it is cadentially labeled—this phrase ends in a half cadence—but because it is structurally parallel to such labeling in all the other phrases. Third, the preference rules (developed in sections 7.3 and 7.4) conflict as to whether the B minor chord in measure 8 or the D major chord in measure 10 dominates the phrase in measures 8–10 (see level *d*). The former is next to a larger grouping boundary and is more stable within the harmonic context of measures 7–12; the latter is more stable within the context of the whole. We have made the B minor chord dominate in the tree, but have hinted at the alternative in the secondary notation.

This conflict does not point to a deficiency in the rules, but represents a truly ambiguous musical situation that pertains to the piece as a whole.

6.24

The chorale oscillates throughout between the tonic and its relative minor. In fact, in its last, chromatic harmonization (just after Christ's death in the Passion story), this tonal relationship is virtually reversed, by means of the tentative beginning on the relative minor and the ineffable close on the dominant of the relative minor.

A reduction such as 6.25 can be a valuable source for analytic insights, locating them within a coherent design. Consider for example level *e,* in which only the structural accents of each phrase remain. Here, as sketched in 6.26, the inner logic of the melody becomes manifest.

6.26

Every odd-numbered phrase returns to its structural origin via lower-neighbor motion; every even-numbered phrase progresses and resolves by descending stepwise a third. (The only exception, the last phrase, by not resolving to D but returning to F♯, repeats the underlying structure of the opening phrase.) This melodic alternation is complemented and clarified by registral alternation from phrase to phrase. In the second half, however, the registers reverse from a low-high, low-high pattern to a high-low, high-low pattern, while the melodic alternation continues as before. This reversal highlights the symmetrical organization of the piece, in particular the obligatory nature of the repeat of the first two phrases. Not only does each even-numbered phrase answer the previous odd-numbered phrase, but the second half answers the first half.

Such observations could of course be continued. The point to emphasize here is that, although time-span reduction may not itself draw such connections, it does provide the framework for them. Without the framework the connections would not exist.

7
Formalization of Time-Span Reduction

In formalizing the time-span reduction, we begin by defining the time-span structure—the segmentation of a piece into rhythmic units within which relative structural importance of pitch-events can be determined. Then, as in previous chapters, we take up in turn well-formedness rules and preference rules.

7.1 Time-Span Segmentation

We begin by defining the term time-span in terms of metrical structure:

A *time-span* is an interval of time beginning at a beat of the metrical structure and extending up to, but not including, another beat.

This is the minimal condition on time-spans.[1] It must be developed further in order to establish the time-span segmentation of a piece.

Section 6.1 discussed the intuitions behind time-span segmentation. At relatively large levels, we argued that the group is the unit of segmentation:

Segmentation Rule 1 Every group in a piece is a time-span in the time-span segmentation of the piece.

Because, for purposes of deriving a time-span reduction, a piece must be exhaustively segmented into time-spans at every level, it is necessary to guarantee that no such grouping structure as 7.1 arises. The gaps between groups would constitute domains not subject to time-span reduction.

7.1

The need to prevent such situations is one of the motivations for grouping well-formedness rule 5 ("If a group G_1 contains a smaller group G_2, G_1 must be exhaustively partitioned into smaller groups").

Though we will encounter no grouping overlaps until near the end of this chapter, their effect on time-span segmentation is best described here. Essentially, we want to say that an overlapped event has a function in both groups of which it is a member. We can most simply express this in the theory by stipulating that the time-span segmentation and reduction are based on underlying group structure rather than the musical surface. In this way the overlapped event will correspond to two events in time-span reduction, one in the left group and one in the right.

Section 6.1 also argued that time-span segmentation is determined by metrical structure at small levels and by the interaction of metrical and grouping structure at intermediate levels. It was shown there that when meter and grouping are out of phase, metrically determined time-spans cross over grouping boundaries. Such crossing would violate the requirement for the time-span segmentation to form a strict hierarchy in the sense of section 2.1. We proposed to solve this problem by appealing to the distinction between afterbeats and upbeats. An afterbeat forms a rhythmic unit with the preceding strong beat. An upbeat (a weak beat such that a grouping boundary intervenes between it and the preceding strong beat) forms a rhythmic unit with the following strong beat.

We formalize these considerations as follows.

Segmentation Rule 2 In underlying grouping structure,
a. each beat B of the smallest metrical level determines a time-span T_B extending from B up to but not including the next beat of the smallest level,
b. each beat B of metrical level L_i determines a *regular time-span* T_B, which is the union (or sum) of the time-spans of all beats of level L_{i-1} (the next smaller level) from B up to but not including
   (i) the next beat B' of level L_i or
   (ii) a group boundary, whichever comes sooner, and
c. if a group boundary G intervenes between B and the preceding beat of the same level, B determines an *augmented time-span* T'_B, which is the interval from G to the end of the regular time-span T_B.

Segmentation Rule 2 produces the time-span segmentation shown in 7.2 for the relevant portion of the finale theme of Beethoven's Ninth Symphony.

In measure 13, the first beat of the half-note level determines two time-spans, marked w and x. The regular time-span w is assigned by rule 2b; the augmented time-span x, which includes the upbeat from measure 12, is assigned by rule 2c.

7.2

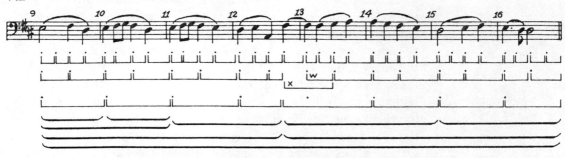

Notice that the whole-note level time-span in measure 13 automatically incorporates the upbeat, because of the way rule 2b defines it: it is the union of all half-note level time-spans determined by the half-note level beats of measure 13—including the augmented time-span *x*. On the other hand, the whole-note level time-span corresponding to measure 12 is only three quarters long, because one half-note level time-span within it has been truncated by the group boundary.

As additional justification for this solution to the interaction of grouping and metrical structures in time-span segmentation, consider the first phrase of Bach's "O Haupt" in 7.3. To what time-span does the quarter-note anacrusis belong at the larger levels of time-span segmentation?

7.3

One possibility is that the anacrusis belongs to *no* time-spans at larger levels; it is disregarded at larger levels of time-span segmentation. However, this would result in either 7.4a or 7.4b as the half-note level reduction of 7.3.

7.4

a   b

(Disregard upbeat)

Neither of these is intuitively adequate, since they do not express the structural importance of the tonic chord on the upbeat; they claim that at this level the piece is heard as not beginning on a root-position tonic.

To capture the importance of the initial tonic, the anacrusis must be included in some half-note level time-span. One solution is to posit, before the upbeat, a hypothetical beat at the half-note level, within whose time-span the anacrusis could be included. Example 7.5a shows the resulting reduction; the hypothetical beat is enclosed in parentheses.

7.5

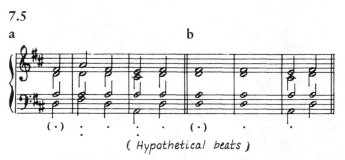

(Hypothetical beats)

This is better than 7.4a or 7.4b, in that the importance of the initial tonic is expressed. But in order to retain the tonic at the next step of reduction, the whole-note level, we must posit a hypothetical beat at this level too—three quarter-notes before the actual beginning of the piece, as in 7.5b. (In the third measure of 7.5b, the entire cadence is retained, following the discussion in section 6.4.) The hypothetical beats in 7.5, unlike the extra structure we have posited in grouping overlaps and elisions and in metrical deletions, do not express any musical intuition; they are only there to provide a time-span for the structurally important anacrusis to occupy.

In the solution we have adopted, expressed in segmentation rule 2, the upbeat belongs to an augmented time-span determined by the first beat at the half-note level, as shown in 7.6a. Since the upbeat is structurally more important than the other events in this time-span, the half-note-level reduction is 7.6b.

7.6

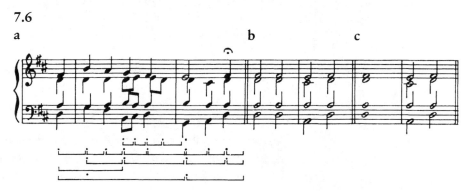

Note that the upbeat has disappeared from the rhythmic representation at this level, as in 7.4, but the structural importance of the upbeat has been expressed, as in 7.5. The reduction from 7.6b to the whole-note level is then 7.6c, a root-position tonic followed by a full cadence.

Example 7.7 illustrates the application of segmentation rule 2 to a more complex example, measures 6–8 of the finale of Beethoven's First Symphony.

7.7

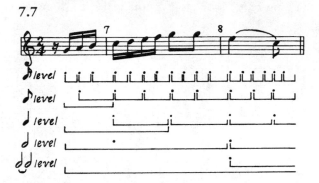

This passage is strongly out of phase, since the strongest beat, marked by the entrance of the accompaniment, falls at the beginning of measure 8. Moreover, the anacrusis is triply embedded. The first sixteenth is an anacrusis to the second two at the eighth-note level; the first three sixteenths form an anacrusis to the downbeat of measure 7 at the quarter-note level; and the first three sixteenths plus all of measure 7 form an anacrusis to the downbeat of measure 8 at the two-measure level. This triple embedding is reflected in the time-span segmentation by the presence of three levels at which both a regular and an augmented time-span exist. It is an important test of our theory of rhythm that it can express this upbeat-within-upbeat intuition by elaboration of the technique used to describe ordinary upbeats.

The time-span segmentation in 7.7 gives rise to the time-span reduction in 7.8, given in tree form and in secondary notation. The inclusion of the initial G in the first augmented time-span of the eighth-note level makes it possible for this note to be the most important event at the beginning of this level and the next while still giving the reduction a rhythmically satisfying form.[2]

A final comment on the segmentation rules: We surmise that they are universal, except for one interesting idiom-specific variation. In classical tonal music, the strong beat of a regular time-span falls at the beginning. This seems to be the normal case across idioms. However, in the gamelan idiom described in Becker and Becker 1979, it appears that the strong beat is at the end of each subgroup. The typical grouping, metrical, and subgrouping organization of this music is shown in 7.9.

7.8

7.9

In order to produce this segmentation, it suffices to change condition b of segmentation rule 2 to include in T_B the preceding rather than the following time-span of the next smaller level. The possibility of such a mirror reversal of the usual situation will be of particular interest when time-span reduction is compared with phonological theory in section 12.3.

Given the rules for segmentation of the musical surface into time-spans, we now turn to a formal description of the possible time-span trees.

The Reduction Hypothesis and the Tree Notation

Chapters 5 and 6 have developed many of the ideas we need to state the well-formedness rules for time-span reduction. The most basic is that every time-span has a most important event, or *head,* selected from the pitch-events in it; the other pitch-events are said to be *subordinate* to the head.

Chapter 5 also presented what we called the Strong Reduction Hypothesis, namely that all the pitch-events of a piece can be organized into a single structure by hierarchical relationships of subordination. It is essential to this hypothesis that the relationship of subordination be transitive; that is, if pitch-event x is subordinate to pitch-event y, and y is subordinate to z, then x is subordinate to z. More intuitively, if a particular event is the structurally most important event of some large time-span, then it must also be the structurally most important event of all smaller time-spans to which it belongs. Were this not the case, a strictly ordered hierarchy would be impossible; for example, an event could be subordinate to itself.

In turn, the transitivity of subordination enables us to represent all levels of time-span reduction of a piece perspicuously in the tree notation introduced in chapter 5. Each pitch-event in the piece is connected to a branch of the tree; each branch but the longest terminates on another branch. Termination of a branch b_1 on another branch b_2 signifies that there is a step of time-span reduction in which the pitch-event e_1 connected to b_1 is eliminated in favor of the pitch-event e_2 connected to b_2. In this situation we will say that e_1 is *directly subordinate* to e_2. In addition, because of the transitivity of subordination, e_1 is subordinate to all the pitch-events to which e_2 is subordinate; these can be found by tracing upward in the tree to the termination of branch b_2 on another branch b_3, and so on to the top of the tree.

Thus the tree notation is possible only if subordination is transitive. If the Strong Reduction Hypothesis turns out to be false, the notation for reduction will have to be modified accordingly. On the other hand, we find it difficult to envision a theory lacking the Strong Reduction Hypothesis that would be both sufficiently rich and sufficiently constrained to constitute a plausible account of musical cognition.

We sum up this discussion by giving a preliminary statement of the well-formedness rules. One definition will make the rules clearer. We will say that a time-span T_i *immediately contains* another time-span T_j if T_i contains T_j and if there is no time-span T_k such that T_i contains T_k and T_k contains T_j. Informally, T_i immediately contains T_j when T_j is exactly one level smaller than T_i.

Time-Span Reduction Well-Formedness Rules (preliminary version)

TSRWFR 1 For every time-span T, there is an event e that is the *head* of T; all other events in T are subordinate to e.

TSRWFR 2 If T does not contain any other time-spans (that is, if T is at the smallest level of time-spans), e is whatever event occurs in T.

TSRWFR 3 If T contains other time-spans, let $T_1,...,T_n$ be the (regular or augmented) time-spans immediately contained in T, and let $e_1,...,e_n$ be their respective heads. Then the head of T is one of the events $e_1,...,e_n$.

Observe how the Strong Reduction Hypothesis is incorporated into these rules. First, the segmentation rules guarantee that a piece is exhaustively segmented into time-spans, arranged hierarchically from the smallest metrical level up to the level of grouping encompassing the entire piece. Second, each time-span has a head, chosen from the heads of those time-spans it immediately contains. This method of choice guarantees that each level of reduction can be constructed from the next smaller level and does not have to refer to events eliminated at earlier stages of reduction. Hence these rules create a class of unified hierarchical structures for the entire piece.

The rules just stated deal only with cases of reduction in which the head of a time-span is a single event chosen from among the events in that time-span. Let us call this situation *ordinary reduction*. Though the majority of situations produce ordinary reduction, three other sorts of heads can also appear, resulting from reductional processes which we will call *fusion, transformation,* and *cadential retention.* We take them up in turn, before incorporating them into a final statement of the well-formedness rules later in this section.

Fusion

This process can be exemplified by 7.10, a passage from the prelude of the first Bach Cello Suite.

7.10

A reduction at the eighth-note level should obviously show the existence of the rising line, but it should also reflect awareness of the pedal D. Similarly, in an Alberti bass, the reduction should represent the fact that one hears a single chord spread out over a time-span. If the rules for selecting the head of a time-span were to allow only the selection of a single event in a time-span, we would not be able to represent such intuitions in a time-span reduction. Accordingly we will introduce another possible relation between the head of a time-span and the events within it: the head may be the *fusion* of the events into a single event; or, conversely, the surface events may be an *arpeggiation* of the head.

We will represent the fusion of two events in the tree by joining their branches with a crossbar. Example 7.11 illustrates the reduction of 7.10 by fusion, giving the lower branches of the resulting tree.

7.11

Example 7.12 is the beginning of the same movement; its tree contains multiple levels of fusion, showing that each half-measure is heard as the arpeggiation of a chord. (The dissonant neighbor tones are eliminated by ordinary reduction at the eighth-note level.)[3]

7.12

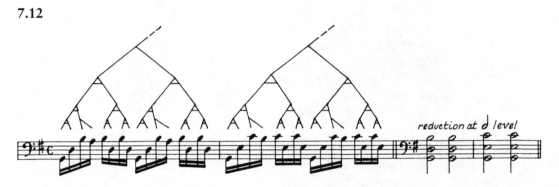

Fusion, unlike ordinary reduction, is limited to relatively local levels. Although one may hear long-range arpeggiation of a chord, one does not fuse the elements into a single chord heard over the entire interval of time. The proper delimitation appears to be that events cannot be fused if they are separated by a group boundary. This "locality" condition is provisionally incorporated into the well-formedness rules below. Its effect is shown in the reduction in 7.12: each pair of half-measures is not fused into a single event at the whole-note level; rather, the second half-measure is treated as a repetition of the first that is eliminated by ordinary reduction. This follows from the locality condition, because each half-measure forms a group.

Fusion in time-span reduction corresponds to the perceptual phenomenon of "auditory stream segregation," where one hears two voices instead of a single oscillating one (Bregman and Campbell 1971). The fact that auditory stream segregation is not confined to musical inputs suggests that time-span reduction has some connection to nonmusical auditory perception. We see two opposing ways in which such a connection could be made. An extremely restrictive account would claim that auditory stream segregation is an independent phenomenon that happens to have an effect on musical perception just at this point. By contrast, an extremely comprehensive account would claim that the rules of time-span reduction are completely subsumed by more general principles of auditory perception, and thus that the rule resulting in fusion in the Bach suite is just a special case of the principle of auditory stream segregation. We suspect that the truth lies somewhere between these two extremes—that the rules of time-span reduction are in part determined by general properties of auditory perception, but that there is a certain degree of specialization for musical cognition. Section 12.3 discusses this issue further, presenting evidence from linguistics bearing on the cognitive generality of rules for time-span reduction.

Transformation

A process somewhat rarer than fusion occurs in 7.13a, part of the Bach chorale "O Haupt."

7.13

a   b

Within the bracketed time-span, neither of the two surface pitch-events is heard as the structurally more important, as ordinary reduction would require. Rather, as suggested in section 6.6, the head of this time-span is a hypothetical root-position E minor chord, composed out of mutually consonant fragments of the two-surface events in the time-span.

Example 7.13b illustrates the representation we adopt. The hypothetical chord is inserted in brackets into the musical surface, between the two events out of which it is constructed; the tree represents both actual events as directly subordinate to the hypothetical one. In this situation we will call the head of the time-span a *transformation* of the events within the time-span.[4]

Like fusion, transformation occurs only at quite local levels of reduction. Again, we provisionally incorporate a restriction into the well-formedness rule to express this fact.

Cadential Retention

Sections 6.3 and 6.4 observed that there is one situation in which more than a single event is retained in a step of reduction: at a full or deceptive

Formalization of Time-Span Reduction

cadence, the dominant as well as the resolution to I or vi must be retained in order for the reduction to make musical sense. The resulting two-event sequence acts like a grammatical unit. To permit such a reduction to be well formed, the condition for selecting the head of a time-span must be enriched to allow a sequence of events forming a cadence to serve as the head.

For convenience, we will call the last event of a cadence the *final* and the element preceding it the *penult*. In a full cadence the penult is V and the final is I; in a deceptive cadence the penult is V and the final is vi; in a half cadence there is no penult and the final is V.[5]

Section 6.4 discussed various details of reductions involving cadences. It suffices here to elaborate a few technical points. Example 7.14 illustrates the retention of the cadence in measures 7–8 of Mozart's K. 331. The full cadence, labeled [*c*], is retained in reducing to the measure level.

7.14

Example 7.14 represents the retention of a feminine cadence. In reducing to the dotted quarter-note level, the $^6_4$ at the beginning of measure 8 is eliminated in favor of the V. Hence in the tree the $^6_4$ is connected by an ordinary branch to the V. In reducing to the measure level, because of the metrical structure of a feminine cadence, the penult and the final occupy a single time-span. Thus the cadence can be retained simply by refraining from eliminating the penult. Finally, in the next step of reduction, the head of measure 7 is subordinate to the entire cadence, so it is attached in the tree to both elements of the cadence with a small "egg shape."

The retention of a masculine cadence raises a slightly more difficult problem. Example 7.15 shows some steps in reducing measures 5–6 of "O Haupt." Reduction to the half-note level proceeds as usual. At the whole-note level, the head of measure 6 is obviously the D major chord

7.15

on the third beat; the appoggiatura covering the first and second beats is eliminated. However, in measure 5 there is a conflict. The B minor chord in the first half, originating as an anacrusis in the surface, is the structural beginning for the phrase, but the chord in the second half of the measure is the dominant (vii^6) of the cadence. Neither can be eliminated at the whole-note level without losing the musical sense. In order to resolve this conflict, we permit the B minor chord to be the head of measure 5, but let measure 6 "borrow" the head of the second half of measure 5 for the sake of retaining the cadence. In this way, both halves of measure 5 are retained at the whole-note level.

The general solution to the reduction of cadences, therefore, is to permit the retention of a dominant penult just in case it is the head of a time-span immediately preceding the time-span headed by the final. In a feminine cadence the penult will fall in a larger time-span with the final, but in a masculine cadence the penult will be "borrowed" from a preceding time-span.

Example 7.15 also shows how a cadence is reduced out when it is directly subordinate to another event. The essential intuition is that the penult is heard most saliently in relation to its final. Thus when the cadence is about to be eliminated there is a preliminary step in which the penult is reduced out in favor of the final, followed by the ordinary reduction of the final itself. This special case of reduction must be incorporated into the time-span reduction well-formedness rules in order to "undo" the effects of retaining two elements at once.

Though the subordination of the dominant to the final is uncontroversial in the case of a full cadence, one might question whether it is appropriate for a deceptive cadence, where the final is harmonically less stable than the penult. Since less stable events are in general subordinate to more stable ones (see section 7.3), one might want to reverse the dependency of the cadential elements here. However, such a reversal would lose the intuition that the vi of the deceptive cadence is perceived as the rhythmic goal of the phrase. We propose instead that the structural difference between full and deceptive cadences appears only in prolongational reduction, where conditions of pitch stability and connection override rhythmic considerations. Thus the musical character of a deceptive cadence arises from the disparity between its rhythmic and harmonic endings. (See section 9.4 for further discussion.)

Final Statement of Time-Span Reduction Well-Formedness Rules

TSRWFR 1 For every time-span T, there is an event e (or a sequence of events $e_1 e_2$) that is the *head* of T.

TSRWFR 2 If T does not contain any other time-span (that is, if T is at the smallest level of time-spans), then e is whatever event occurs in T.

TSRWFR 3 If T contains other time-spans, let $T_1,...,T_n$ be the (regular or augmented) time-spans immediately contained in T and let $e_1,...,e_n$ be their respective heads. Then:

a. (Ordinary Reduction) The head of T may be one of the events $e_1,...,e_n$.

b. (Fusion) If $e_1,...,e_n$ are not separated by a group boundary ("locality" condition), the head of T may be the superimposition of two or more of $e_1,...,e_n$.

c. (Transformation) If $e_1,...,e_n$ are not separated by a group boundary, the head of T may be some mutually consonant combination of pitches chosen out of $e_1,...,e_n$.

d. (Cadential Retention) The head of T may be a cadence whose final is e_n (the head of T_n, the last time-span immediately contained in T) and whose penult, if there is one, is the head of a time-span immediately preceding T_n, though not necessarily at the same level.

TSRWFR 4 If a two-element cadence is directly subordinate to the head e of a time-span T, the final is directly subordinate to e and the penult is directly subordinate to the final.

The two segmentation rules plus TSRWFRs 1–4 are now sufficiently rich to express the class of time-span reductions that we have motivated. However, as was the case with the grouping and metrical components, the definition of a set of possible structures is insufficient. How is the theory to choose the head of a time-span from among the heads of the immediately contained time-spans? This question is addressed by the time-span reduction preference rules.

**7.3
Preference Rules
Within Phrases**

The principles for selecting the head of a time-span fall into three categories. *Local rules* attend exclusively to the rhythmic structure and pitch content of the events within the time-span itself. *Nonlocal rules* bring into play the pitch content of other time-spans (essentially considerations of voice-leading and parallelism). *Structural accent rules* involve articulation of group boundaries. This section deals with the first two types; section 7.4 discusses the third.

An initial caveat: We will not specify what factors motivate the choice of fusion or transformation rather than ordinary reduction in a time-span. Nonetheless, we will not hesitate to use fusion and transformation in our analyses where they are intuitively appropriate.

Local Influences
Consider the reduction of example 7.16a at the quarter-note level.

Formalization of Time-Span Reduction

7.16

Of the two choices presented below it, 7.16b is intuitively the more natural. Because the heads in 7.16b fall on beats at the quarter-note level and those in 7.16c fall on beats only at the eighth-note level, this example suggests the following preference rule:

TSRPR 1 (Metrical Position) Of the possible choices for head of a time-span *T*, prefer a choice that is in a relatively strong metrical position.

A second principle involves pitch stability. Section 6.2 discussed the treatment of local dissonances: an ordinary passing or neighboring tone is subordinate to the preceding note, whereas a suspension or appoggiatura is subordinate to its resolution. The principle behind these choices is that a consonant vertical configuration must be chosen as head in preference to a dissonant one, regardless of metrical weight. In the case of a passing tone, which falls in weak metrical position, this choice reinforces the preference of TSRPR 1 for strong metrical position. By contrast, an appoggiatura is in strong metrical position and its resolution is in a weak position; the resulting conflict between harmonic and rhythmic principles is what creates the expressive force of the appoggiatura. This principle filters out most of the absolute dissonances in a musical surface within one or two stages of reduction. But an extension of the principle to include relative degrees of consonance and dissonance allows it to operate at larger levels, and expands its application at smaller ones.

If we are to state this principle fully, the theory must include a definition of the relative degrees of consonance and dissonance of all possible vertical configurations. These are well known from traditional theory and will simply be assumed here. It only needs to be pointed out that there are two distinct measures of vertical consonance and dissonance. The first is the intrinsic consonance of the pitch-event itself. According to this criterion, major and minor triads in root position are the most stable, followed by their first inversions. The second inversion is dissonant, because of the fourth between the bass and another part; likewise, seventh chords are dissonant and require resolution. But, in addition, a pitch-event has a stability relative to the local tonic, measured essentially in terms of closeness on the circle of fifths, with additional points of stability defined through the diatonic collection and relative and parallel major-minor relationships. (See sections 9.4 and 11.5 for further discussion.)

These two measures of relative stability interact in what is by now the expected fashion. For example, a root-position V chord is intrinsically more stable than a I⁶, but the latter is closer to the tonic. Hence a choice between these two is less highly determined than a choice between, say, a I and a V⁶, where the two kinds of stability reinforce each other. The preference rule can therefore be stated as follows:

TSRPR 2 (Local Harmony) Of the possible choices for head of a time-span *T*, prefer a choice that is
a. relatively intrinsically consonant,
b. relatively closely related to the local tonic.

Example 7.17, the opening of "O Haupt," illustrates TSRPR 2 in some detail. In the stages of reduction given, TSRPR 1 is consistently overruled. In the first half of measure 1, the IV and the I⁶ are approximately in balance with respect to the factors of TSRPR 2, but voice-leading considerations favor the I⁶. In the augmented time-span, the anacrusis I is

7.17

chosen as head over the I⁶ by TSRPR 2a. At the third beat of measure 1, the IV⁶ and the V⁶₅ are again approximately in balance with respect to TSRPR 2, so voice-leading considerations come into play, choosing the dominant chord as head. At the fourth beat, the consonance in the second eighth is a clear choice by TSRPR 2. In combining the third and fourth beats of measure 1 into a time-span, the I (despite its weaker metrical position) is harmonically more stable than the V⁶₅ with respect to both criteria in TSRPR 2. Finally, in the first half of measure 2, the V on the second beat is both intrinsically more stable and closer to the tonic than the ii⁶₅ on the first beat.

In addition to the two local TSRPRs discussed so far, a third and somewhat weaker principle can be stated as follows:

TSRPR 3 (Registral Extremes) Of the possible choices for head of a time-span *T*, weakly prefer a choice that has
a. a higher melodic pitch
b. a lower bass pitch.

In practice, this consideration rarely has a decisive effect unless the harmony and the metrical position are otherwise identical, but it may have a supplementary reinforcing or weakening influence.

Example 7.18 illustrates cases where TSRPR 3a affects judgments.

7.18

In 7.18a, from the finale of Beethoven's Wind Octet, op. 103, one tends to hear the E♭ of the anacrusis as more prominent, despite its weaker metrical position. That this is due to its higher pitch is clear from comparison with 7.18b, where the G is heard as primary.

Example 7.18c returns to Mozart's K. 331. Schenker (1925) analyzes the E in the second half of the first measure as the structurally most important event in spite of its relatively weak metrical position. The plausibility of this judgment is due to the higher pitch of the E. If the pitches were changed to those of 7.18d it would be implausible to choose the event in weaker metrical position, because it is now lower. Thus, although we disagree with Schenker here (because of the bass and the metrical structure), his analysis does receive support from TSRPR 3a. (See section 10.4 for further discussion of Schenker's alternative.)

For cases where relatively low pitch of the bass has an influence, consider 7.19.

7.19

a

b

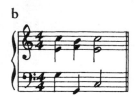

Example 7.19a, from the Mozart G Minor Symphony, brings back an issue raised in section 4.3. There we argued that the low G in the bass reinforces the choice of metrical structure, because it is more important than the high G in the time-span reduction. TSRPR 3b brings about the desired distinction in importance. (If the high and low bass notes were exchanged in 7.19a, metrical perceptions would be affected.)

Example 7.19b illustrates an octave drop of the bass beneath a I_4^6–V progression in a cadence. In the first half of the measure, the V^7 on the second beat is chosen over the I_4^6 by TSRPR 2a. However, the progression would be somewhat weaker if the low G in the bass were on the first rather than the second beat. This suggests that the low G on the second beat helps the V^7 overcome the strong metrical position of the I_4^6. In fact, the bass line in 7.19b is a cliché of tonal music, but an upward leap of an octave rarely occurs. The reinforcing interaction of TSRPRs 2a and 3b, overriding TSRPR 1, demonstrates a principled basis for this disparity.

Nonlocal Pitch Influences

Time-span reduction preference rules 1–3 describe factors internal to a time-span that affect the choice of its head. We now turn to influences that involve material outside of the time-span as well. In general it is difficult to separate these principles, because of their constant interaction with local principles and with each other, so our motivation for them will be more suggestive than rigorous.

The first of these principles is the inevitable rule of parallelism. For example, consider again the opening of K. 331 (7.18c). Suppose someone were, for whatever reason, to adopt the analysis in which the quarter-note E in the first measure is the structurally most important event. Then, because of the parallelism of the first two measures, it would be absurd

Formalization of Time-Span Reduction

not to take the D rather than the B as most important in the second measure. More elaborate examples could be cited, but this simple case seems sufficient to make the point.

TSRPR 4 (Parallelism) If two or more time-spans can be construed as motivically and/or rhythmically parallel, preferably assign them parallel heads.

We next examine a point in K. 331 that appears to be a counter-example to the interaction of preference rules proposed so far. The time-span reduction of the first four measures proceeds straightforwardly to the dotted-quarter level (7.20a). At the next level, however, the intuitively most important event in the third measure is the "vi[7]" rather than the V⁶; that is, the reduction from 7.20a should be 7.20b rather than 7.20c.

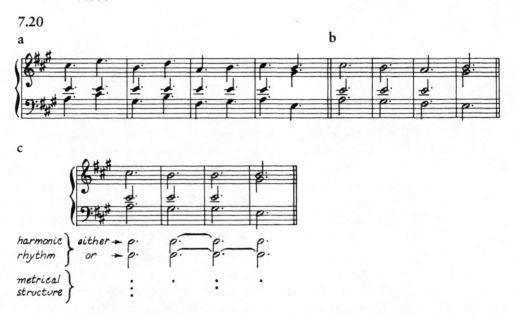

7.20

In all other cases we have seen up to this point, harmonic stability has been sufficient to override metrical position. Yet in this case the highly unstable chord in strong metrical position has managed to override the more stable chord in weak metrical position. This suggests that one or more additional preference rules must apply here, adding strength to the analysis in 7.20b.

We discern two principles at work in this example, having to do with harmonic rhythm and linear bass motion. Consider first harmonic rhythm. In 7.20b the harmony changes in every measure, whereas in 7.20c it does not change in the third measure and it only changes by inversion in the fourth. In other words, the harmonic rhythm in 7.20c is syncopated with respect to the metrical structure. If the difference in harmonic rhythm is significant in choosing 7.20b over 7.20c—as we believe it is—we might state a preference rule such as "Prefer a time-span reduction with harmonic changes on relatively strong beats."[6]

But this formulation can be improved if we recall that there is a metrical preference rule (MPR 5f) that addresses the effect of harmonic rhythm on metrical structure: "Prefer a metrical structure in which relatively strong beats are associated with the inception of relatively long durations of harmony in time-span reduction." If the time-span reduction of 7.20a were 7.20c, MPR 5f would create pressure for placing the strongest beat of the passage at the beginning of the second measure, conflicting with other metrical evidence. By contrast, reduction 7.20b creates no such pressure, because all the harmonies are of equal length.

This suggests that the choice of 7.20b is influenced by the fact that it permits a less highly conflicted metrical analysis. In other words, in addition to a metrical preference rule that considers metrical effects on time-span reduction, there is a time-span reduction preference rule that considers time-span effects on metrical structure:

TSRPR 5 (Metrical Stability) In choosing the head of a time-span *T*, prefer a choice that results in more stable choice of metrical structure.

Though the reasoning that leads to TSRPR 5 is less direct than that involved in the preliminary formulation above, we find TSRPR 5 a more theoretically satisfying proposal, in that it claims that harmonic rhythm affects time-span reduction not according to an arbitrary additional principle but by means of the effect that time-span reduction is independently known to have on metrical structure. TSRPR 5 therefore creates one of the pressures that helps the strong metrical position of the "vi⁷" override its harmonic instability.

The second factor involved in the choice of 7.20b is the stepwise motion of the bass that emerges in 7.20b but not in 7.20c. Similar linear factors were used implicitly in the reduction of "O Haupt" in 7.17. For instance, in the first half of the first measure, there is a choice between a IV on the first beat and a I⁶ on the second. Example 7.21 presents the two possibilities.

7.21

The I^6 presents a more stable melodic line, since it represents an unfolding of the tonic chord. The influence of linear connection in both 7.20 and 7.21 can be stated as TSRPR 6a:

TSRPR 6a (Linear Stability, preliminary version) In choosing the head of a time-span *T*, prefer a choice that results in more stable linear connections with events in adjacent time-spans.

The analysis of "O Haupt" in 7.17 also made implicit use of a second nonlocal influence. In the third quarter of the first measure there is a choice between a IV^6 on the first eighth and a V$^6_5$ on the second. Since the IV^6 is in strong metrical position and is intrinsically more consonant, the principles discussed so far would seem to favor it. But compare the two choices within the context of the reduction, in example 7.22. Example 7.22a has the IV^6 and 7.22b the V$^6_5$, marked by asterisks.

7.22

Example 7.22b is intuitively preferable, despite the apparent predictions of the rules mentioned above. What favors it? TSRPR 6a might select it because of the stepwise motion of the bass from the third to the fourth beat, and TSRPR 4 (parallelism) might pick out the parallelism between this stepwise bass motion and that in the first halves of the first and second measures (marked by braces in 7.22b). However, a further consideration is the greater stability of the V$^6_5$–I progression in 7.22b over the IV^6–I in 7.22a. This suggests TSRPR 6b:

TSRPR 6b (Harmonic Progression, preliminary version) In choosing the head of a time-span *T*, prefer a choice that results in more stable harmonic connections with events in adjacent time-spans.

We have left unspecified in TSRPRs 6a and 6b what constitutes a relatively stable linear or harmonic connection. To provide this information, the relative stability of various connections could be stipulated directly within the statement of the preference rules. But there is an alternative. Looking ahead to chapters 8 and 9, two primary factors affect the choice of prolongational reduction: time-span importance and stability of connection among events. Now if the events that are important in time-span reduction also form stable linear and harmonic connections, a highly reinforced choice of prolongational reduction is possible. On the other hand, if the time-span reduction does not follow the strongest possible connection, the choice of prolongational reduction will be conflicted. It seems conceivable, therefore, that the influence of linear and especially harmonic connection on time-span reduction should not be stated directly in the TSRPRs, but rather it arises through the effect of time-span reduction on the stability of the prolongational reduction. This solution can be expressed in the theory by replacing TSRPRs 6a and 6b with the following rule:

TSRPR 6 (Prolongational Stability) In choosing the head of a time-span *T*, prefer a choice that results in more stable choice of prolongational reduction.

Note the similarity between this and TSRPR 5. These rules encode the interdependence of the different components of musical cognition on each other. It is the feedback among the various components that makes it so difficult to isolate these principles.

TSRPR 6 is crucially involved in the choice of fusion or transformation rather than ordinary reduction for a time-span. For example, in the Bach Cello Suite quoted in 7.10–7.12, fusion is plausible in part because it results in a consistent multivoiced texture that follows principles of good voice leading and harmonic progression. (In addition, fusion is favored by relatively great distance between the two lines and by relatively rapid alternation between them; these factors are intuitively relevant, but we have for the moment not formalized them.) Similarly, in the passage from "O Haupt" quoted in 7.13, transformation is necessary because neither of the choices available through ordinary reduction produces a good progression in the next level of reduction. Thus, although we have no complete account of how fusion and transformation are chosen, TSRPR 6 provides a starting point for such a study.

7.4 Structural Accents of Groups

Retention of Cadences

The preference rules stated so far make two errors in their treatment of cadences. First, the rules provide no way to choose a two-element cadence as head of a time-span, since they all deal with ordinary reduction. Second, as pointed out in section 6.3, the rules of rhythmic and harmonic stability (TSRPRs 1 and 2) often lead to incorrect choices where half cadences are involved. For example, in measure 4 of K. 331 (see 7.20a), the rules so far say unequivocally that the I rather than the cadential V should be chosen as head for the measure. Both of these failings of the rules motivate an additional preference rule:

TSRPR 7 (Cadential Retention, preliminary form) Of the possible choices for head of a time-span *T*, strongly prefer an event or pair of events that forms a cadence.

The term "strongly" in this rule is meant to indicate that this preference rule is sufficient to override the powerful combination of harmonic and metrical strength, as in measure 4 of K. 331.

To state TSRPR 7 more carefully, we must work out the conditions under which an event or a pair of events in some level of time-span reduction functions as a cadence. First, the correct harmonic sequence must be present for a full, half, or deceptive cadence. Second, the final element must actually mark the end of a group. For example, in measures 9–12 of the Chopin A Major Prelude (7.23), the sequence V–I cannot be heard as a cadence because of the V/ii following the I in the group.[7]

7.23

To refine this requirement, we observe that intuitively a cadence must be a cadence *of something;* a group that consisted only of the articulation of its ending would be unsatisfying. For instance, measures 1–8 of the same prelude (7.24) consists of two V–I progressions. (For convenience, the reduction in 7.24 simplifies the voice leading to the essential soprano and bass lines.) The first of the V–I progressions, since it completely occupies the first four-measure group, is not really heard as a cadence. Therefore, only the V or the I may be retained at the next level. By contrast, the V–I progression in measures 5–8 is a cadence for the entire eight-measure group, and therefore should be retained as a whole in the reduction. As a result, the reduction at the four-measure level contains either the V or the I of the first group followed by the cadence. (The piece is genuinely ambiguous here between the reduction in 7.24 and that with an initial I instead. For a number of reasons, including parallelism with the second half, we find that the choice of V yields a more stable analysis overall. This piece is discussed further in section 9.6.)

We can make the intuition about the first four measures of 7.24 more precise by introducing the notion of a *cadenced group:* a group that at some level of reduction reduces to two elements, the second of which is a cadence. The first of these elements is the *structural beginning* of the group, and the cadence is the *structural ending.* In section 6.3 we labeled these with the notations [b] and [c], followed by a subscript to indicate for which groups they were structural accents.

Cadenced groups are to be contrasted with lower-level groups, which do not contain bs and cs. The smallest levels of cadenced groups correspond rather closely to the traditional notion of musical *phrase.*

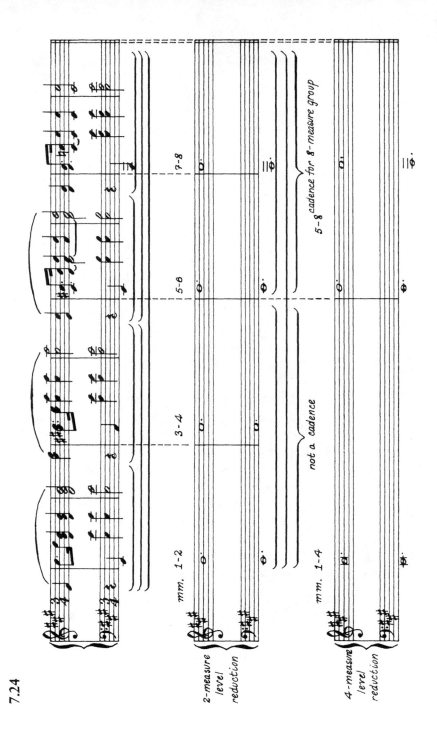

7.24

Returning to the refinement of TSRPR 7, we can now stipulate that a progression counts as a cadence only if it functions as structural ending for a group. More precisely, there must be a cadenced group G that has a reductional level consisting of one other event (the b) followed by the progression in question. If such a level does not exist in the reduction, an apparent cadential progression (such as the first V–I in 7.24) does not perform the function of articulating a group ending. This condition is global, in that it depends on the outcome of higher-level analysis.

These considerations can be summed up in a final statement of the preference rule for cadences:

TSRPR 7 (Cadential Retention) If the following conditions obtain in a time-span T, then label the progression as a cadence and strongly prefer to choose it as head:

   i. There is an event or sequence of two events $(e_1)e_2$ forming the progression for a full, half, or deceptive cadence.
   ii. The last element of this progression is at the end of T or is prolonged to the end of T.
   iii. There is a larger group G containing T for which the progression can function as a structural ending.

Retention of Structural Beginnings

The articulation of structural beginnings of groups is in part symmetrical to the use of cadences at the ends of groups. But since there are no formulaic progressions to mark the beginnings of groups, a preference rule for structural beginnings need contain no condition analogous to condition i of the cadence rule. Moreover, though the resolution of a cadence must be prolonged to the end of its group, a structural beginning may be preceded by contrasting material.

However, groups in which the structural beginning is not near the actual beginning are felt as distinctly less stable. There seems to be a preference for the structural beginning to be near the beginning:

TSRPR 8 (Structural Beginning) If, for a time-span T, there is a larger group G containing T for which the head of T can function as structural beginning, then prefer as head of T an event relatively close to the beginning of T (and hence to the beginning of G as well).

Note the parallelism between the condition in this rule and condition iii of the cadence rule above. They are both "top-down" conditions, concerning the function of the chosen event within the larger structure of the piece. It is these two rules that embody the importance of structural beginnings and endings of groups within the present theory of musical grammar.

Examples To make the operation of TSRPRs 7 and 8 clearer, let us work through the larger levels of reduction for some examples. We begin with a case where pitch stability plays a minimal role, so that TSRPRs 7 and 8 operate freely. Then we turn to a case where pitch stability conflicts with TSRPR 8 to create an asymmetrical large-scale tree.

Example 7.25 gives the reduction of the last six measures of the Mozart K. 331 theme, from the measure level up. In measures 16 and 18, the full cadences satisfy conditions i and ii of TSRPR 7. The cadence in measure 16 forms the structural ending for the group consisting of measures 13–16, and that in measure 18 forms the ending for groups 17–18, 13–18, 9–18, and the entire theme. Thus all the conditions of TSRPR 7 are met, and both cadences are retained in level *f*.

Level *e* of 7.25 shows the heads of all the two-measure groups. We will examine them in order. In group 13–14, TSRPR 2 (harmonic stability) favors the I in measure 13 over the V^6 in measure 14. Since the event selected here will be the *b* for groups 13–16 and 13–18, TSRPR 8 also favors the I, the earlier of the two events. In group 15–16, the cadence is chosen because of its stability as well as its function as the *c* for group 13–16. In group 17–18, the head of the group will not form a *b* for a larger group, as required by the condition of TSRPR 8; hence TSRPR 8 does not apply here. On the other hand, the cadence does form the *c* for a number of larger groups, so TSRPR 7 applies to retain it.

Level *d* of 7.25 shows the selection of head for the four-measure group 13–16. The first and last chords of this time-span in line *e* are essentially identical, so TSRPR 2 does not choose between them. Moreover, the time-span is large enough that metrical considerations no longer play a role. Thus the choice is determined only by TSRPRs 7 and 8. The head of this time-span will form the *b* of the larger group 13–18, so the condition of TSRPR 8 is met, favoring the earlier I. Since there is no larger group for which the head of this time-span will function as a *c*, condition iii of TSRPR 7 is not met, and this rule does not apply. Hence the cadence is reduced out.

In level *c*, that of the head of the entire six-measure group, we find that the head of this time-span will function as the *c* for the second half of the theme. Hence condition iii of TSRPR 7 is met and the condition of TSRPR 8 is not. As a result, the cadence is selected as head.

Example 7.26 represents the largest levels of the entire theme (as in 6.20). Levels *c* and *d* are the same as levels *c* and *d* in 7.25. The derivation of this analysis is straightforward, given what we have already seen in 7.25. There are no conflicts from other TSRPRs; thus, whenever a particular time-span falls at the beginning of a larger group, TSRPR 8 applies and the first event in the time-span is chosen. Similarly, whenever a time-span falls at the end of a larger group, TSRPR 7 applies and the cadence is chosen. The result is the symmetrical tree in 7.26.

The reduction from level *b* to level *a* constitutes a special case. Assume for the moment that these eighteen measures are the entire piece, so there are no further levels of reduction. Then neither event of level *b* will be a *b*

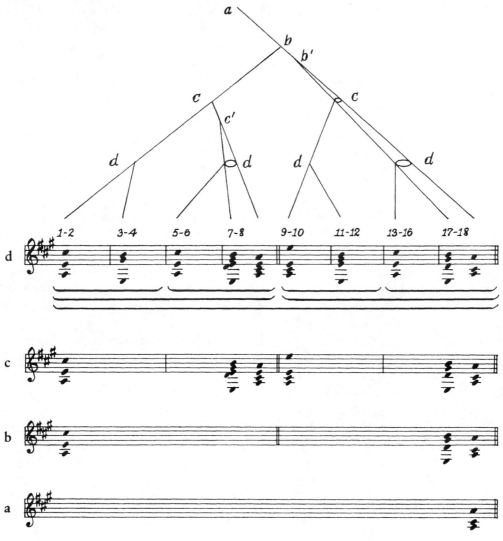

Formalization of Time-Span Reduction

or a *c* for a larger group. This means that neither condition iii of TSRPR 7 nor the condition of TSRPR 8 is met. There are two consequences: first, there is no way to retain both elements of the cadence, since only TSRPR 7 would permit this; second, the choice between the first and last events is determined only on the basis of harmonic and melodic stability. In the present case the ending is favored, but this might not be so in every case. It may be desirable to add a special rule to deal with the highest level of reduction:

TSRPR 9 In choosing the head of a piece, prefer the structural ending to the structural beginning.

Behind this rule lies the intuition that tonal pieces are fundamentally goal-oriented.

We next examine a passage where the large-scale reduction is not symmetrical: the introduction of Beethoven's First Symphony (7.27). It has often been noted that, although the symphony is in C, its first measure appears superficially to be a cadence in F. The time-span reduction will show how, as a consequence of this unusual beginning, the entire passage functions as a sequence of structural anacruses to the beginning of the allegro in measure 13.

Before discussing the reduction in 7.28, we must make two comments on the grouping. First, the largest subdivision of the passage sets off the first 3½ measures from the rest, as a sort of preintroduction consisting only of wind chords supported by pizzicato; in the rest of the introduction the melodic line is dominated by the violins. Second, the grouping contains three overlaps. As argued in section 7.1, time-span reduction is based on the underlying grouping structure, so that an overlapped event can be assigned different functions in the two groups to which it belongs. The overlapped event corresponds to two events in time-span reduction, one in the left group and one in the right. This dual function appears in 7.28 in measures 8 and 13 (the overlap in measure 10 has already been reduced out).

Example 7.28 is the reduction of 7.27 from approximately the measure level to the level of the whole passage. Measures 7 and 10 still contain more than one event in level *e* because they are broken by group boundaries. We have placed a double bar after the "preintroduction" as a visual aid.

With the exception of measure 1, to which we will return shortly, the reduction from the musical surface to level *e* is relatively straightforward and requires no comment. The reduction of group 5–13 proceeds down to level *c* according to principles familiar from previous examples, leading to an approximately symmetrical tree in which beginnings and endings of cadenced groups are of greatest importance. In reducing this group to level *b* the final cadence is most important, since it is the *c* for the entire introduction.

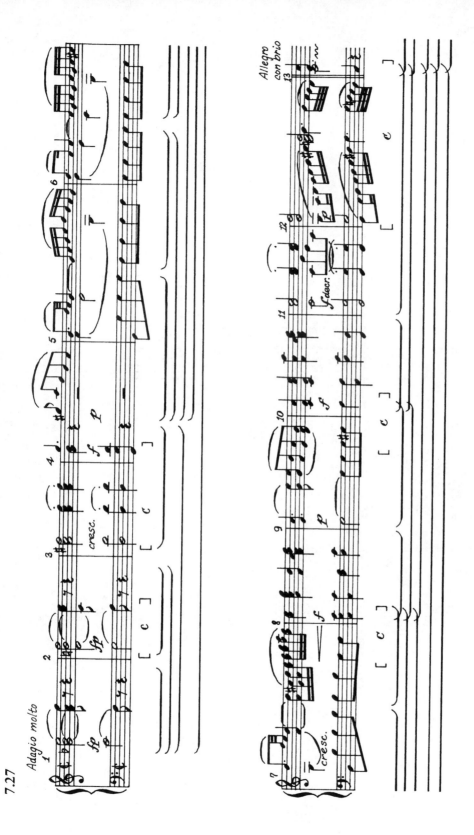

7.27

Adagio molto

Allegro con brio

Formalization of Time-Span Reduction

7.28

The reduction of the preintroduction, however, follows different lines. First, return to the reduction of measure 1. Though measure 1 contains the correct sequence of chords to form a cadence, it is not the c for any larger group; so, as in measures 1–2 of the Chopin prelude in 7.24, the cadence cannot be retained as a whole. The head of the measure will form the b of group 1–2; thus TSRPR 8 applies, creating a preference for the first chord, a V^7/IV, as head. But this chord is less stable than the IV following it, on grounds of both intrinsic consonance (TSRPR 2) and harmonic connection to the next time-span (TSRPR 6). The combination of these two factors accounts for the choice of the IV in level e of 7.28.

Next consider the reduction of the preintroduction from level e to level d. The head of group 1–2 will form a b for group 1–4, so TSRPR 8 applies, choosing the IV in measure 1 over the deceptive cadence in measure 2. In addition, the IV is harmonically more stable than the vi, reinforcing this choice. In group 3–4 the V is chosen as head, on all possible grounds.

In reducing from level d to level $c,$ we first note that the head of group 1–4 will function as the b for the entire introduction; hence TSRPR 8 favors the IV chord. Moreover, since the head of this group will not form the c for a larger group, there is no pressure from TSRPR 7 to retain the V in a cadential role. On the other hand, the V is in a stronger metrical position and harmonically closer to the tonic, and it forms a more stable progression with the V^7 following it in measure 5. These three factors appear to override TSRPR 8. Hence, as in the reduction of measure 1, the final event rather than the initial event is chosen as head.

Finally, in reducing from level b to level a—finding the head of the entire introduction—we confront exactly the same situation: the V chord representing the preintroduction is less stable than the I representing the cadence of the entire passage. Thus, despite the fact that TSRPR 8 would prefer the V, the I is chosen as head.

In the reduction as a whole, the picture emerges of a series of beginnings that turn out to be not structural beginnings but structural anacruses: first the initial V^7/IV, then its resolution, then the V at the end of the preintroduction. The "real" beginning of the piece—the event to which all that precedes is subordinate—is the final I of the introduction, which overlaps with the first event of the allegro. This characteristic of the passage is revealed by the predominance of left branching in the tree.

The introduction to Beethoven's Second Symphony presents an interesting contrast to the analysis just developed, in spite of their similar large-scale grouping structures. Because its first event is a tonic, there is never a harmonic reason to select anything else as the b, as there is in 7.28. Hence TSRPR 8 consistently is reinforced by harmonic factors and can select the initial I as the b of all the cadenced groups it belongs to. As a result, this introduction lacks the embedded structural anacruses found in the First Symphony.

This completes the discussion of the time-span reduction preference rules, which take into account local rhythmic considerations (TSRPR 1), local harmonic considerations (TSRPR 2), local pitch extremes (TSRPR 3), parallelism (TSRPR 4), metrical and prolongational stability across time-spans (TSRPRs 5 and 6), the presence of cadences (TSRPR 7), the importance of early structural beginnings (TSRPR 8), and the overall structure of the piece (TSRPR 9).

This chapter has gone a long way toward providing a principled account of what the experienced listener must know in order to sense the relative structural importance of events in a musical surface. In particular, the rules of time-span reduction provide the crucial link between local rhythmic and pitch detail and the notions of structural accent crucial to any theory of large-scale musical structure.

We end the chapter with some speculation about musical universals. One important way in which musical idioms differ is in the principles of relative pitch stability. Here we have simply assumed the pitch principles of classical Western tonal music; the relation of these to other tonal systems will be discussed briefly in section 11.5. Insofar as the principles of pitch stability play a role in the preference rules for harmonic stability (TSRPR 2), linear progression (TSRPR 6), and retention of cadences (TSRPR 7), their influence on time-span reduction is pervasive. On the other hand, it seems possible that the preference rules themselves are universal—for example, that TSRPR 2 says to prefer harmonically stable events as head no matter how the idiom chooses to define harmonic stability.

There is no problem extending the segmentation rules and the well-formedness rules to any idiom that is as highly structured in both grouping and meter as classical Western tonal music. (We did, however, mention one possible variant of the segmentation rules in section 7.1, in which regular subgroups include a weak beat preceding rather than following a strong beat.) However, in an idiom where meter is largely absent, one could not necessarily build time-span structure up to the group level using meter as we have done here. Similarly, if grouping in some idiom were not as strongly hierarchical as in classical Western tonal music, time-span segmentation as we have defined it might not be highly structured enough at larger levels to permit meaningful decisions about the relative global importance of events. However, even tentative conclusions about cross-idiom variation in time-span reduction require far deeper investigation than do grouping and meter, so we hesitate to speculate further.

8
Prolongational Reduction: The Analytic System

As with time-span reduction, we divide the exposition of prolongational reduction into two parts. In this chapter we develop the meaning of and notation for prolongational trees, and gradually work our way toward a complete prolongational analysis; in chapter 9 we will develop the system of rules that assigns prolongational analyses.[1]

8.1
Intuitions
About Tension
and Relaxation

In the grouping, metrical, and time-span components there is nothing that expresses the sense of tension and relaxation involved in the ongoing progress of music. To be sure, we have described local tensions arising from conflict of preference rules—for example, the rhythmic tension of syncopation. But the opposite of such tension is the absence of tension. The kind of tension we wish to address here is the more elastic sort whose opposite is relaxation—the incessant breathing in and out of music in response to the juxtaposition of pitch and rhythmic factors. We wish to be able to speak of points of relative tension and repose and the way music progresses from one to the other. This is the function of prolongational reduction. By viewing prolongational reduction in this way, we are dealing not only with pitch reduction but with an essential aspect of musical rhythm, for tension and relaxation are rhythmic properties.[2]

We conceive of tension and relaxation as relative terms defined with respect to particular events. For example, an arrival at an event such as the end of a phrase normally constitutes a point of relative relaxation; departure from this event normally constitutes the beginning of an increase in tension as the music progresses toward the next goal. An event such as the dominant of a full cadence gives the sense of being a step in an ongoing process of relaxation. Other events, such as the climax of a phrase, may give the sense of being at a stage of maximal tension. We would like to express such intuitions in an articulate and systematic way. Let us survey some elementary examples to motivate our general approach.

A single pitch (say, the tonic note C) produces no particular tension. A repetition of this pitch may create rhythmic tension, but no real melodic tension; the C is merely prolonged. However, the insertion of another pitch between the two Cs creates a tensing, then a relaxing, of melodic progression, as illustrated by the neighboring motion in 8.1 (*t* and *r* stand for tensing and relaxing). This effect is due to the comparative dissonance of the D within its context.

8.1

Next consider the motion from E to C in 8.2a. Because the second event is more "consonant," the progression is felt as a relaxation. We can then elaborate 8.2a by the insertion of a passing tone between the E and the C (8.2b), thereby superimposing a second, more local, pattern of tension and relaxation like that in 8.1.

8.2

a   b   c

Adding a bass line converts the dissonant passing tone in 8.2b into a root-position (implied) triad, yielding the quasi-*Ursatz* in 8.2c. The overall pattern of tension and relaxation, however, does not change between 8.2b and 8.2c; musical particulars can vary within a specific pattern of tensing and relaxing.

In 8.3 we elaborate 8.2b further, by inserting a D and an E in the middle.

8.3

a   b

Here the contrasting durational values produce different prolongational perceptions: in 8.3a the first D is heard as a lower neighbor within the context of a prolonged E; in 8.3b the second E is heard as an upper neighbor within the context of a prolonged D. It is apparent that rhythmic as well as pitch factors affect intuitions about tension and relaxation.

This brief survey has shown the possibility of speaking of intuitions about tension and relaxation in terms of superimposing simple patterns in a hierarchical fashion to produce more complex patterns. But the notation of these patterns in 8.3 is already unwieldy. Before considering longer examples, we must develop an adequate notation.

We begin by defining tension and relaxation in terms of right and left prolongational branching. As diagrammed in 8.4, a tensing motion will be represented by a right branch, a relaxing motion by a left branch. These are structural interpretations placed on the elaborational hierarchies of prolongational trees. Henceforth we can dispense with the arrow notation.

8.4

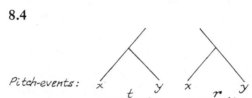

For both right and left branching we distinguish three possible kinds of connection between two events. First, a simple joining of branches (8.5a) signifies what we call a *progression*. This occurs when the harmonic roots of the two events are different. (If a single line is analyzed, branching is decided largely on the basis of the implied harmony. Even the simplest tunes in Western tonal music involve harmonic implications.)

8.5
a

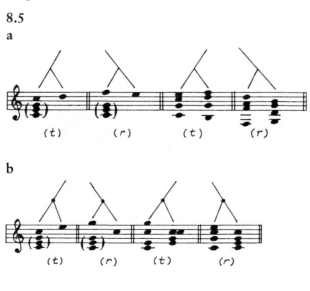

c

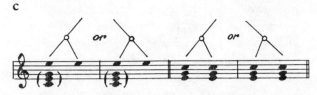

Second, a joining of branches by a filled-in circle (8.5b) signifies what we call a *weak prolongation:* the roots of the two events are identical, but one of the events is in a less consonant position, either with respect to the bass (chordal inversion) or—secondarily—with respect to the melodic note. Third, a joining of branches by an open circle (8.5c) signifies what we call a *strong prolongation:* the roots, bass notes, and melodic notes of the two events are identical. Here pitch factors alone produce no increase or decrease in tension, so rhythmic factors must be invoked to decide right or left branching. We will take up this issue in the next section.

The different kinds of right and left branching do not represent the same degrees of tension or relaxation. Consider right branching first. A repetition of the same event is intrinsically nontensing (8.6a). A repetition in a less consonant form induces some degree of tension (8.6b). Most tensing is a progression to a completely different and less consonant event (8.6c).

8.6

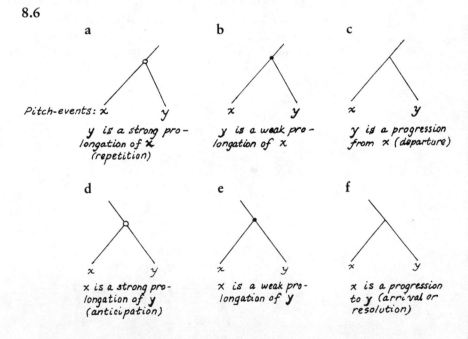

In left branching the pattern is reversed, because left branching signifies a movement toward relaxation. The least relaxing connection is an anticipation of the same event (8.6d), since no change in pitch structure takes place. Somewhat relaxing is the restatement of an event in a more consonant form (8.6e). The most relaxing kind of left branching is a progression to a completely different and more consonant event (8.6f).

It would be possible to devise still other kinds of right and left branchings than those just described, corresponding to the many gradations in tension and relaxation between events. Such a notational enrichment, however, would come at the cost of analytic inclusiveness. For example, one would like to be able to treat the configurations in 8.7, despite surface differences, as functioning similarly in terms of tension and relaxation.

8.7

Under the scheme just outlined, they are all left-branching progressions (as in 8.6f); greater specificity in branching connections would obscure what they have in common. We believe that the three kinds of connection introduced here, together with their right and left branchings, strike the right balance between diversity and generality. As will be seen shortly, the concatenation of these simple relationships will lead to more than enough complexity.

8.2 Preliminaries to Prolongational Trees

The prolongational connections just discussed have been considered only for two isolated events. The Reduction Hypothesis demands that such connections be drawn for all the events in a piece. To do this we must have a conception of the successive stages, or domains, of analysis, in which events become available for connection. In time-span reduction this task was relatively straightforward, since the stages were defined by the time-span segmentation. In prolongational reduction, by contrast, the domains of analysis are less predetermined, and consequently are rather difficult to explain; moreover, they cannot be explained prior to the actual building of trees. It is therefore convenient to circumvent this problem for the moment and to turn to tree building as if the problem were already solved.

Before we can proceed we must satisfy a further demand of the Strong Reduction Hypothesis, namely that events be analyzed in a strict hierarchy. In terms of the tree notation this means that all branchings must be either right or left; there can be no event that is either equivalent to another event or an insertion between two superordinate events. This requirement was not a problem for time-span reduction, where the time-span segmentation always forced a decision one way or the other. The fluidity of analytic domains in prolongational reduction makes it an issue here.

Consider equivalence first. In Schenkerian analysis one might wish to say that two identical events forming a prolongation are somehow the same event at a more background level of analysis. In the tree notation the two events would connect as a strong prolongation, but neither event would dominate the other by right or left branching.[3] Thus there would be no progression toward tension or relaxation, but stasis. The intuitive justification for such a construction might be that at a certain level of abstraction one hears a hierarchy not of discrete events but of harmonic areas.

However, this approach is inadequate. It goes against the grain of the theory as a whole, in which each event is taken in principle as "real" at all relevant levels of analysis. One may hear harmonic areas (these are in any case enclosed within a prolongation), but one also hears all the distinctions among individual events, even those that are strongly prolonged. It is impossible to hear absolute stasis, if only because events take place in time and hence form rhythmic relationships that produce tensing or relaxing effects.

Let us be more specific. At local levels, one has elementary intuitions about "prolongational anticipation" and "prolongational repetition." For example, in 8.8a the first I chord is heard as an anticipation of the second I; but in 8.8b the second I is heard as a repetition of the first. In terms of tension and relaxation, the anticipation (8.8a) relaxes into the following downbeat, whereas the repetition (8.8b) tenses in response to its surrounding stronger beats. Therefore, as the trees in 8.8 indicate, prolongational anticipation receives a left branch, prolongational repetition a right branch.

8.8

a   **b**

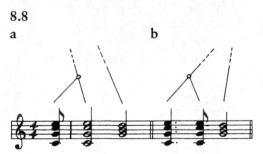

At global levels, on the other hand, the concept of prolongational anticipation makes no sense. For example, the opening tonic in a sonata-form movement is never heard as an anticipation of its restatement at the beginning of the recapitulation; rather, the beginning of the recapitulation is heard as a prolongational repetition of the opening. The beginning of the recapitulation is heard in the context of the opening, and hence must be subordinate to it. Thus all large-scale strong prolongations are right branches.

Next consider the insertion of an event between two superordinate events. To take the general case, let y be an elaboration within the context $x...z$ (8.9).

8.9

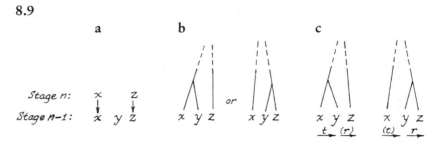

Schenkerian analysis does not necessarily specify y as an elaboration of either x or z; often it suffices that y is inserted between x and z at a subsequent level (8.9a). We, on the other hand, must specify either right or left subordination for all cases (8.9b). If we can intuitively justify this added formal requirement, prolongational reduction will have gained another dimension of structural meaning.

To begin with, it should be understood that y is necessarily less consonant (in the broadest sense of this term) than x or z; if it were not, x or z would be subordinate to it and hence could not already be attached in the tree at more global levels. Therefore, whether y becomes a right branch to x or a left branch to z, the pattern of tension and relaxation is that of a tensing from x to y and a relaxing from y to z (8.9c). This fact suggests the following question: Does one experience y more as a tensing away from x, or more as a relaxing toward z? Alternatively: Is y more closely related to x or to z? These are at bottom the same question; it is a matter of perceptual relatedness, of closeness of connection. If in a given case we can distinguish the relative closeness of y to x and z, then we know which branching to assign.

Let us consider some concrete examples. In monophony, intervallic distance is a significant factor in determining the branching of an intermediate subordinate event. In 8.10a the D connects more closely to (or tenses more in relation to) the previous C, and thus connects as a right branch; in 8.10b the F connects more closely (or relaxes more in relation to) the following E, and thus connects as a left branch. Once harmony is introduced, however, closeness is primarily a function of fundamental bass analysis and distance in terms of the circle of fifths. Therefore the intermediate event in 8.10c is a right branch and the intermediate event in 8.10d is a left branch. Finally, even though the branching decisions in 8.10a–8.10d are already fairly clear, intuition becomes still more definite when chromatic inflections are introduced, as in 8.10e; here the intermediate event belongs to the adjacent event that shares its diatonic collection.

8.10

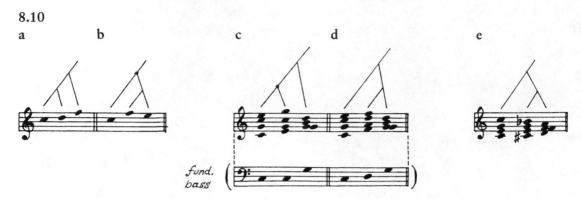

The decision for right or left branching is more problematic for *passing motions* within weak prolongations (that is, within arpeggiations), where the surrounding events are melodically and harmonically equidistant from the passing event. Yet there is a sense in which the passing event tenses or relaxes (as the case may be) primarily in relation to the dominating event in the weak prolongation. For example, the V$_3^4$ in 8.11a and 8.11b is heard primarily in relation to the I, not the I⁶, resulting in a right branch in 8.11a and a left branch in 8.11b. In the quasi-*Ursatz* in 8.11c, the tensing from $\overset{3}{\text{I}}$ to $\overset{2}{\text{V}}$ is less salient than the relaxing from $\overset{2}{\text{V}}$ to $\overset{1}{\text{I}}$, so the V connects to the $\overset{1}{\text{I}}$ as a left branch.

8.11

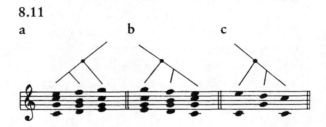

Intuition is weakest for *neighboring motions* within strong prolongations, since the surrounding events are by definition identical in pitch structure. However, as argued above, right or left branching for strong prolongation can be decided from rhythmic factors. As a result, the reasoning about passing motion applies in a weaker form to neighboring motion: the neighboring event tenses or relaxes more in relation to the dominating event in its environment. Now, because strong prolongation is almost always a right-branching structure, it follows that neighboring motion is typically a right branch. This holds true whether the neighboring motion is a locally dissonant note (as in 8.12a), a neighboring chord (8.12b), or, say, a large-scale neighboring motion extending over the B section of an ABA form (8.12c). At these global levels right-branching neighboring motion is particularly obvious: one hears the contrasting section in relation to what has happened, not to what is yet to come. On the other hand, when elaborating a local prolongational anticipation, the result may be left-branching neighboring motion, as in 8.12d.

8.12

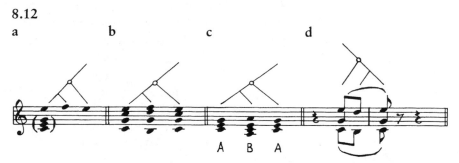

The factors determining right or left branching may, of course, conflict with one another—as, for instance, when melodic and harmonic influences are in opposition. And more factors enter into right and left branching than we have so far discussed. What this account has established is that in all cases there are intuitions concerning right versus left branching, and consequently that mere "in-between-ness" is not a sufficient analytic concept.

We must cover one other issue before building trees. What in general makes one event prolongationally more important than another? For example, how did it come about in 8.9 that y was lower in the tree than x or z? Observe that this is in principle a different question than what we have just been addressing. Up to this point we have been concerned with the mode of connection among events already available for analysis. Now we ask why it is these events that are available in the first place.

One might suppose that absolute criteria of pitch stability provide a hierarchical scale by which prolongational importance can be gauged. But, as we saw in section 5.4, this scale is a necessary but not sufficient condition for prolongational analysis. Rhythmic factors also play a vital role in the perception of prolongational relationships. Specifically, rhythmically unimportant events are heard as prolongationally relatively unimportant, and structural accents are heard as prolongationally relatively important, regardless of absolute criteria of pitch stability. These perceptions can be reflected in the prolongational tree if the prolongational reduction derives not from the musical surface but from its associated time-span reduction, since, in addition to reflecting factors of pitch stability, the latter contains the requisite rhythmic information. The time-span importance of an event thus becomes a governing factor in determining its prolongational importance. From this it follows that, unlike the other components, the prolongational tree must be constructed starting from its largest, most important levels. If it were the other way around, the time-span importance of an event could not be evaluated at any particular stage of analysis.

We do not argue that prolongational importance necessarily corresponds in a one-to-one relationship with time-span importance. Nor does time-span importance dictate the actual prolongational connections. Rather, time-span importance acts as the general regulator of events available for successive levels of prolongational analysis. From this input the optimal prolongational connections can be established.

The close dependence of prolongational reduction on time-span reduction constitutes a major claim of our theory. It asserts that the perceived patterns of tension and relaxation in pitch structure depend crucially on the hierarchy of structurally important events within time-spans as defined by meter and grouping. In other words, the listener's understanding of pitch connections in a piece is a function of how he segments its surface. This claim entails the unification of pitch and rhythm within one overarching theory.

A detailed explanation of prolongational importance and its relation to time-span importance presupposes an understanding of prolongational domains, a full discussion of which is postponed until section 9.3. We have outlined this relationship here only in order to convey a framework within which prolongational trees can be understood intuitively.

8.3 Prolongational Trees

Our course in this section will be initially to consider the most global level of a piece, since prolongational reduction proceeds from global to local levels. From this immediately emerges the conception of the prolongational *basic form* (corresponding to the Schenkerian *Ursatz*), which we then utilize to develop a prolongational structure for antecedent-consequent periods. Narrowing our focus further, we next investigate cadential preparations and some characteristic patterns within the single phrase. Then we show how the tree for a phrase can change, depending on whether the phrase is analyzed in isolation or as part of a larger context. Finally, we draw an important generalization about prolongational trees.

The Basic Form and the Antecedent-Consequent Period

The most global levels of time-span reduction typically yield the structure shown in 8.13a. These events are the first to become available for prolongational analysis. As the prolongational tree in 8.13b shows, the opening I attaches as a weak prolongation to the final I, after which the structural dominant attaches as a resolving left branch to the final I. This V must be a left branch because it is part of the cadence and because the final I is the dominating event in its environment at this stage of analysis.

8.13

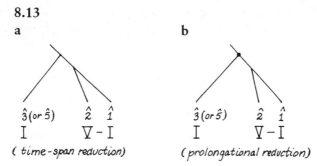

a   b

$\hat{3}$ (or $\hat{5}$) $\hat{2}$ $\hat{1}$ $\hat{3}$ (or $\hat{5}$) $\hat{2}$ $\hat{1}$

I   V – I   I   V – I

(time-span reduction)   (prolongational reduction)

Although the trees in 8.13 look similar, they have contrasting interpretations: 8.13a expresses the arc of tonal motion from the piece's structural beginning to its cadence; 8.13b says first that the piece forms a relaxing prolongation of the tonic and second that the opening I tenses into the V, which in turn relaxes—more strongly than the previous tensing—into the final I.

Tree 8.13b represents the prolongational *basic form* for a typical tonal piece. It is grammatically complete in the sense that it expresses both tonic prolongation and cadential resolution. This form appears not only for whole pieces but—when considered in isolation—also for subordinate grouping levels such as theme groups, periods, and phrases. Much of the unity of tonal music depends on this fact.

Consequently, we can also consider 8.13b to represent the skeleton for a typical antecedent-consequent period in "interruption form." If the time-span analysis for the period yields the structure shown in 8.14a, then 8.14b is the prolongational basic form corresponding to levels *a* and *b* of 8.14a. The next events available for prolongational analysis are the half-cadential V and the opening I of the consequent (level *c* in 8.14a). Although the sheer geometry of the tree permits these two events to connect in a large number of ways, we will consider only a few representative alternatives.

8.14

a   b

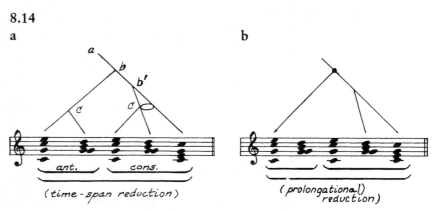

(time-span reduction)   (prolongational) reduction)

First consider some left-branching possibilities. In 8.15a the half-cadential V attaches to the final V, producing a prolongational anticipation. However, as argued above, this makes no sense over such an interval of time: How could the first V relax rhythmically into the second? More plausible would be to make the half-cadential V the most important V in the passage, with the final V as a prolongational repetition (8.15b). But this alternative is dubious because the final V no longer cadences the entire passage (recall the discussion in section 6.5 about the location of the structural dominant).

8.15

a   b

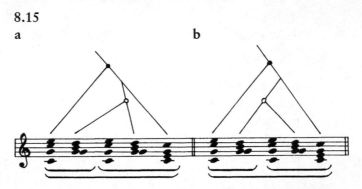

Perhaps most significantly, 8.15a and 8.15b both fail on the grounds that the opening I of the consequent cannot then connect as a right branch with the initial I, because that would result in crossing branches with the half-cadential V. The attachment of the two Is beginning the two phrases seems particularly essential when, as is usually the case, thematic parallelism reinforces the harmonic return of the I; one hears the second I as a repetition—a starting over—of the first I. In prolongational branching this relationship is expressed by a strong prolongational repetition, in which case the half-cadential V must itself be enclosed within a tonic prolongation as in 8.16.

8.16

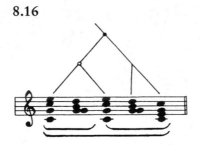

This leaves two possibilities for attachment of the half-cadential V: as a left-branching progression to the opening I of the consequent (8.17a) or as a right-branching departure from the initial tonic (8.17b).

8.17

a   b

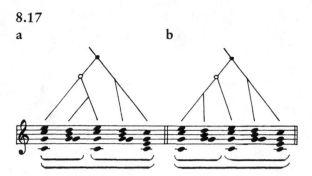

Though 8.17a is plausible when the V leads texturally into the I, much more common is the sense of a syntactic break between the half-cadential V and the opening I of the consequent. As a result, the V is felt primarily as a departure from the initial I. Thus the usual prolongational translation of the time-span tree in 8.14a is the tree in 8.17b. This tree says that, within the basic form as described above, the initial I prolongs into its repetition at the opening of the consequent; and, within this prolongation, the half-cadential V primarily tenses in relation to the initial I.

Cadential Preparation

Now we will consider the single complete phrase as our analytic world. First we will discuss the events leading up to the cadence ("cadential preparation"), and then we will turn to the events in the phrase between the opening tonic and the cadential preparation.

Before directly addressing cadential preparations, we need to interpolate a few remarks about circle-of-fifths progressions. Generally, one wants to say that V is to I as ii is to V and vi is to ii, and so on; each event in the sequence relates similarly to its adjacent events. Because V is less consonant than I (and ii less consonant than V, and so on), a I–V progression receives a right branch and a V–I progression a left branch. Since these relationships apply sequentially, an ascending circle of fifths tends to result in a successively embedded right-branching structure (8.18a) and a descending circle of fifths in a successively embedded left-branching structure (8.18b).

8.18

a   b

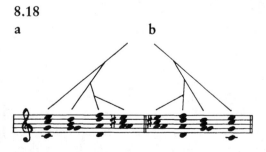

A cadential preparation and a cadence together often produce a descending circle-of-fifths progression in terms of fundamental bass motion. Think of the typical ii⁶–V–I cadential formula; this naturally receives an embedded left-branching structure (as in 8.18b). But not all cadential preparations relate to the V by fifth motion—for example, the IV in the equally typical IV–V–I progression. Yet the ii⁶ and the IV function similarly in these progressions; the difference between the two lies in details of melodic voice leading, not in the harmony, where the essential fact in both is the bass motion from the fourth to the fifth scale degree.

Clearly a generalization about cadential preparations is needed that includes both of these possibilities for cadential preparation and others as well. Traditional harmonic theory is relevant here, with its generalized conception of "subdominant function," some realizations of which are listed in figure 8.19. In all these cases, the chief sense of the "sub-dominant"-to-dominant progression is one of the "subdominant" leading and relaxing into the dominant. Therefore any "subdominant" must attach as a left branch to the following cadential dominant. And because the cadential V–I is also a left branch, the overall progression of "sub-dominant" to dominant to tonic must always take the form of a doubly embedded left-branching progression (8.19). This conclusion seems only proper, since a doubly embedded left-branching progression signifies the maximal decrease in tension among three adjacent events—just as one would expect at the end of a phrase.

8.19

subdominant function (ii⁶, ii⁶₅, IV, vi, aug6, vii⁷/V, etc.)   dominant (V or V⁷)   tonic (I)

Variants on the configuration in 8.19 can weaken or strengthen the cadence. For example, cadences without cadential preparation are comparatively weak (8.20a); cadences with triply embedded left branching tend to be very strong (8.20b,c). The cadential ⁶₄ increases the sense of resolution by adding, at a lower level (since it is a locally dissonant elaboration), a second left branch to the dominant (8.20d). Sometimes, as compensation, a suspension functionally replaces an absent sub-dominant preparation (8.20e) (see the cadential patterns in the Bach chorale "O Haupt" in section 6.6).

8.20

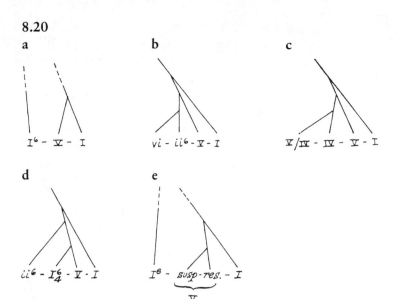

The Complete Phrase

Combining the remarks on cadential preparation with the basic form, we arrive at the structure in 8.21a: a structural beginning plus a nucleus of left branchings at the cadence.

8.21

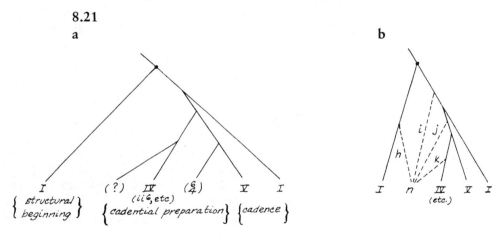

Now suppose that event *n* is the most important event in the phrase between the opening tonic and the "cadential nucleus." There are four geometrically possible ways to connect *n*, labeled *h*, *i*, *j*, and *k* in 8.21b. If branching *k* is chosen, *n* becomes an extended part of the "cadential nucleus" and thus does not carry the phrase functionally beyond 8.21a. If branching *j* is selected, *n* connects to the cadential V without being part of the ongoing, step-by-step process involved in cadencing. Though conceivable, this possibility is difficult to imagine in practice. Branching *i* is unacceptable because it violates the supremacy of the cadence as the goal of the phrase. That leaves branching *b* as the obvious choice. A moment's reflection reveals that this is only logical, since all the branchings in 8.21a are left branches, signifying relaxations at various levels. Clearly there must first be tension if relaxation is to follow; therefore there must be at least one right branch off the opening I, indicating a departure, before the left-branching cadential nucleus.

There are, of course, numerous right-branching possibilities—for instance the ascending circle of fifths in 8.22.

8.22

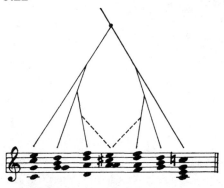

This example in effect combines 8.18a and 8.18b into one. In such a symmetrical case there occurs a point of reversal where the branching could conceivably go either way (hence the dashed branches in 8.22); in practice, the issue can usually be decided on rhythmic grounds or on the basis of structural parallelism.[4]

Far more common than ascending-descending sequential patterns is the right (strong or weak) prolongation of the opening tonic, within which further elaborations proliferate; the tonic prolongation (*n* in 8.21b) is then followed by the cadential nucleus, as shown in 8.23a. Thus the phrase divides prolongationally into more or less unequal halves. Examples 8.23b–8.23e provide four elaborated illustrations of 8.23a, each freely based on a model from the classical literature (8.23b from Schubert's song "Morgengruss," 8.23c from "O Haupt," 8.23d from the K. 331 theme, and 8.23e from the opening of Beethoven's Sonata op. 109).

Some comments on 8.23c–8.23e are in order. According to the branching criteria sketched above, the second event in 8.23c (the IV) should attach not to the ensuing I⁶ but to the preceding I. We have attached it to the I⁶ because of mutually supporting linear criteria in the bass and the soprano. This is a good example of how vertical and horizontal factors can conflict. In 8.23d the point of interest lies in the double neighboring motion of the V⁶ to the I and the "vi⁷" to the V⁶. The neighboring motion is represented in the tree by a right-branching progression enclosed within a right-branching strong prolongation; this

8.23

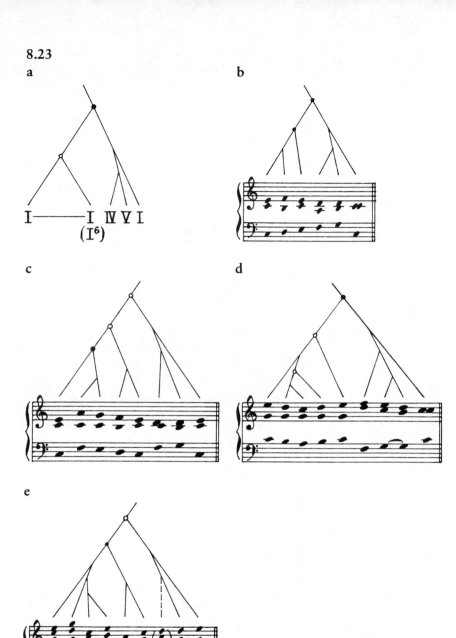

Prolongational Reduction

complex then repeats itself. In 8.23e the ii⁶₅ is in parentheses because it
does not appear in Op. 109. This weakens the sense of closure. It also
creates a balance among pairs of events: as the partial branchings in 8.24
show, the first two pairs of events form right branchings, the second two
pairs left branchings. This symmetry cuts across the larger-level asymmetry of tonic prolongation (six events) plus cadence (two events).

8.24

Local versus Global Hearing

A significant aspect of prolongational branching emerges if one of these
phrasal analyses is considered within a more global context. To illustrate,
let us suppose that 8.23b is the consequent phrase of an interrupted and
completed antecedent-consequent period (8.25).

8.25
a
                              b   c

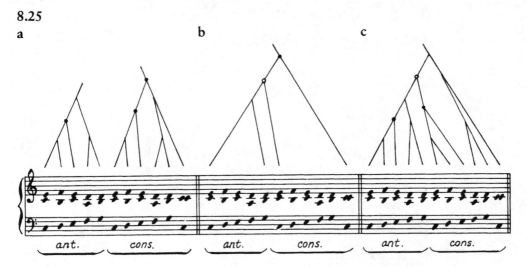

If the two phrases are analyzed separately (8.25a), the antecedent shows
an overall tensing to the half-cadential V and the consequent repeats the
self-contained structure of 8.23b. In the context of the entire period,
however, the consequent must be analyzed differently: the opening I of
the consequent is heard as a prolongational repetition of the initial I of
the antecedent, and the cadence of the consequent is heard as resolving
the period as a whole (8.25b). When the intervening events in the consequent are assigned branches, as in 8.25c, their subordination remains the

same as before, since their function is local. The result is that the branchings of the I, the vii^7, and the I^6 in the consequent diverge from the closing ii^6–V–I of that phrase, and connect instead across the phrase boundary, creating a huge jump in the tree between the I^6 and the ii^6.

Such jumps in prolongational trees have a special meaning: they point to moments in the musical flow where the "structural action" begins to take place (in this case, with the preparation for the final cadence). More generally, a right-branching pattern followed by a left-branching pattern will always create a jump. Such jumps represent major reversals in tension and relaxation, from ongoing progression toward closure.

These features could never appear within a phrase in time-span reduction, bound as it is to the time-span segmentation. Indeed, the tree for the consequent in 8.25c is highly noncongruent, since the time-span tree for this phrase would make its structural beginning subordinate to the final cadence, not to the initial I of the antecedent. Together the two kinds of reduction illuminate the double function of the beginning of any reprise: on one hand, such a moment begins a coherent musical unit (as conveyed by time-span reduction); on the other, it repeats and prolongs an earlier moment (as conveyed by prolongational reduction).

It may be objected nonetheless that the patterns of tension and relaxation for the consequent phrase in 8.25 are most easily revealed by a local analysis, and that therefore 8.25a is preferable to 8.25c. We respond that both analyses are correct, depending on the perspective. A fundamental feature of musical understanding is that it functions simultaneously in varying degrees of fragmentation and integration. One can easily imagine an undeveloped or inattentive listener who hears only partial prolongational hierarchies, either unconnected or insufficiently integrated with each other. The experienced listener, on the other hand, follows the Reduction Hypothesis and integrates all the parts into a whole, while at the same time hearing the aspect of wholeness within each part. This truly complex state of affairs could be represented in our theory by providing multiple preferred analyses signifying different degrees of integration (for example, both 8.25a and 8.25c). Our more modest goal here, however, will be to continue to adhere to the simplifying idealizations set forth in section 1.1, and to develop analyses of only the most global hearings.

Normative Prolongational Structure
Implicit in the discussion so far is that certain tree patterns recur constantly, whereas others virtually never happen. For example, it is most unlikely that a phrase or piece begins in utmost tension and proceeds more or less uniformly toward relaxation (8.26a), or that it begins in relaxation and proceeds toward a conclusion of utmost tension (8.26b), or that it begins and ends in tension with a relaxed midpoint (8.26c). These are suggestive possibilities uncharacteristic of Western tonality.

Rather, a tonal phrase or piece almost always begins in relative repose, builds toward tension, and relaxes into a resolving cadence (8.26d). This is the most essential way in which the idiom achieves the aesthetic effects of balance and closure (8.26a–8.26c would all give an "open-ended" effect).

8.26

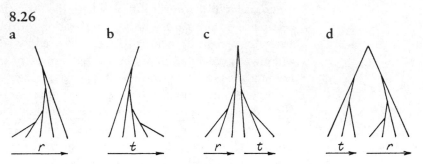

We would like now to make explicit the minimal branching condition, which we will call *normative prolongational structure,* for this tensing-relaxing pattern in tonal music.

First, it should be clear from the "global" treatment of the consequent phrase in 8.25c that the branches of the prolongationally most important events in a phrase or section need not necessarily attach directly. Whether or not they connect depends on their function in the overall context. Therefore, as suggested by 8.27a, such attachment is not a requirement for normative prolongational structure.

8.27

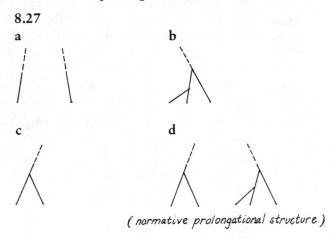

(normative prolongational structure)

Second, it was demonstrated above that a "subdominant" cadential preparation plus a full cadence produces a double left-branching progression. Since this is the norm for closure in tonal music, let us provisionally stipulate that the relaxing part of normative structure demands the structure in 8.27b. Finally, at least one significant right-branching progression is needed to provide sufficient tension to balance the relaxing pattern in

8.27b; this is shown in 8.27c. The resultant minimal branching for normative prolongational structure appears in 8.27d. Any phrase or section that meets this condition possesses a degree of completeness; any that does not sounds unbalanced or unfulfilled in terms of tension and relaxation.

If, in addition, the prolongationally most important events in a given region attach directly as a strong or weak prolongation, the resultant tree combines normative structure with the basic form (8.28a). In other words, this tree shows the basic form elaborated so as to fulfill normative structure. Such a configuration feels more complete than either the basic form or normative structure alone, and typically appears at various levels of tonal structure from the phrase up to the entire piece.

8.28

a   b

(basic form + normative structure)   (basic form/normative structure
                                                     with reprise)

A prevalent formal feature of the high Classical period (as opposed, say, to the Baroque binary form) is the reprise of opening material in the tonic. This causes an extra normative branch to be added to 8.28a, a prolongational repetition that connects to the opening above the departure from the opening (8.28b). In the antecedent-consequent period, this extra branch stands for the beginning of the consequent; in ABA' ternary form, for the beginning of A'; in rounded binary form, for the beginning of the reprise; in sonata form, for the beginning of the recapitulation. (Note, incidentally, the similarity of 8.28b to the characteristic intraphrasal branchings in 8.23, in which the tonic is in one way or another prolonged up to the cadential nucleus. This correspondence illuminates the frequently heard remark that the high Classical forms were based on the nature of the phrase.)

A partial prolongational analysis of the beginning of "La ci darem la mano" from Mozart's *Don Giovanni* will illustrate these various structures. The tree for the antecedent phrase alone is given in 8.29. Note that the branchings separate according to diatonic collection: the ii^6 tenses off the I, and the V^6/V – V and then the V/V all lead as a tonicizing motion to the cadential V. This tree thus displays a tensing-relaxing pattern, but falls just short of normative structure because the uppermost left branch attaches as a weak prolongation, not a progression; the cadence lacks a subdominant preparation. Since the phrase moves from I to V, there is no basic form.

8.29

a

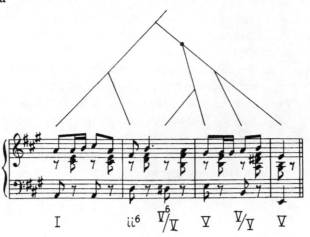

I   ii⁶   V⁶/V   V   V/V   V

b

I   ii⁶   V   I

c

By contrast, the consequent phrase, analyzed in isolation in 8.29b, produces a basic form but lacks the right branch necessary for normative structure. (If, by parallelism with the antecedent, the ii⁶ were analyzed as a right-branching departure, the phrase would lack a subdominant cadential preparation.) This absence of any significant tensing motion makes the consequent in itself sound perhaps less complete than the antecedent. Together, however, the two phrases produce a normative structure, a basic form, and a prolongational repetition indicating the reprise (8.29c). Each half needs the other for completion.

We have found that normative structure in particular constitutes more than a descriptive generalization about prolongational trees. It is also an active force in shaping prolongational relationships. Listeners intuitively seek out this tensing-relaxing pattern even where contrasting hearings might otherwise seem more viable. (Why this is so would make interesting speculation; is it a Western cultural convention, or does it originate in biological factors?) Therefore this principle must become part of the formal grammar; we will return to it in section 9.6.

8.4 A Secondary Notation

The prolongational trees are by now sufficiently complicated that it will help to relate them to a secondary notation developed from ordinary musical notation. For this purpose we will adapt two Schenkerian symbols, the stemless note head and the solid or dashed slur. The stemless note head is useful because it represents pitch-events but is durationally and hierarchically neutral. The slurs reflect the connections and hierarchical distinctions conveyed by the tree.

Only the slurs require explanation. Suppose there are two "adjacent" events x and y; for the moment it does not matter which is prolongationally more important. If they connect as a strong prolongation, a dashed slur is drawn between them in the secondary notation (8.30a). If they connect as a weak prolongation or as a progression, a solid slur is drawn between them (8.30b, 8.30c). If their branches do not directly join in the tree, no slur can be drawn between them (8.30d). Thus, given the three events in 8.30e, slurs are drawn between x and z and between y and z, but not between x and y; and similarly in 8.30f, where no slur is drawn between x and z.

8.30

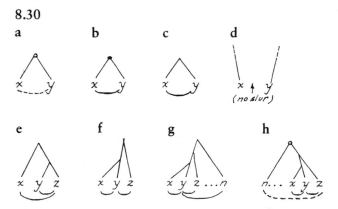

Hierarchical relations among these connected or unconnected events are conveyed much the same as in grouping analysis: slurs "contain" other slurs. For instance, in 8.30e the slur connecting y to z is contained by the slur connection x to z. Even if (as in 8.30f) there is no containing slur, there is bound to be a larger level of analysis that clarifies the situation. Thus in 8.30g y connects to n, turning the connection between y and z into a contained slur and the connection between x and y into an "appended" slur. In 8.30h the strong prolongation contains the connections between x and y and between y and z, and it is deducible that the connection between y and z dominates that between x and y because z is also part of the larger slur. In doubtful cases, one can always refer to the tree.

Because the drawing of slurs among all the voices in a passage would be visually confusing, we will usually include only the bass and soprano lines in the secondary notation. It is also convenient to omit inconsequential (small-level) details. As a clarification, large-level events such as structural beginnings and cadences can be indicated by "white" note heads. Finally, the prolongational tree itself can apply to abstractions like those in 8.30, to the secondary notation, or, where practicable, to the actual notated music. In the last case the secondary notation is placed beneath the actual music. All of these provisions are variously illustrated in 8.31a, the prolongational reduction of the first phrase of "O Haupt," and in 8.31b, a repeat of the antecedent-consequent period in 8.25c repeated in the secondary notation.

8.31

a

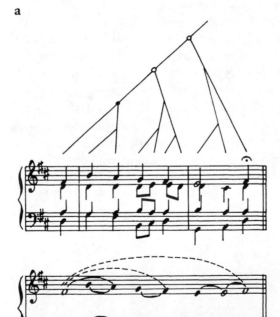

b

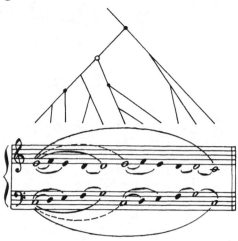

The secondary notation visually conveys the linear dimension of prolongational reduction better than does the tree (a matter of appearance, not substance), and it easily conveys the "prolongational groupings" inherent in prolongational reduction. On the other hand, it does not distinguish between weak prolongation and progression. More important, it is less clear than the tree concerning domination and subordination, and it says nothing about tension and relaxation.

In closing the description of prolongational notation, we observe that there is no labeling of levels in either the prolongational tree or its secondary notation. As discussed in section 6.2, such labeling is meaningful in time-span reduction only because time-spans tend to be fairly regular in duration. No such situation obtains in prolongational reduction. What counts here is the patterns of connection and subordination; these relationships produce the patterns of tension and relaxation. The relative significance of an event is a function of its degree of embedding in the overall structure. For example, in 8.31b the vii^6 in both phrases is deeply embedded, while the final ii^6–V progression is directly subordinate to the most important event in the passage, the final I. The geometric height of a branch is immaterial.

**8.5
A Complete
Prolongational
Reduction**

This section will present the prolongational reduction of a more extended excerpt, the *Chorale St. Antoni* (formerly attributed to Haydn) as arranged by Brahms in his *Haydn Variations,* op. 56b (example 8.32). To put the analysis in context, we begin with the grouping, metrical, and time-span analyses of the theme (8.33). For convenience, the music in 8.33 simplifies the registers from 8.32, and already represents the quarter-note level of time-span reduction plus only those events at the eighth-note level that form separate harmonies. In addition, the grouping

8.33

Prolongational Reduction

overlap and associated metrical deletion at measure 23 are given in their underlying forms so as to facilitate the drawing of the tree.

A few analytic remarks are needed for the grouping and metrical analyses in 8.33. An attractive feature of the theme is its characteristic 5-bar (3+2) phrasing, created by the motivic extension of measure 2 into measure 3 (and similarly for measures 7–8 and 20–21). The most plausible metrical analysis is one that is in phase with this 3+2 grouping analysis, resulting in an irregular second row of dots for the first section (measures 1–10) and, by parallelism, for the reprise (measures 19–23). At measure 23 this interpretation requires the metrical deletion mentioned above. Equally plausible for the reprise, however, is the metrical interpretation placed in curly brackets; this more regular analysis follows "conservatively" from the 4+4 contrasting section (measures 11–18), and leads without complication into the codetta (measures 23–29). The choice is between parallelism and simplicity. In the "conservative" reading, the cadential arrival at measure 23 is rhythmically especially satisfying because it permits the 5-bar phrase finally to be heard in a metrically periodic fashion.

Turn now to the tree in 8.33. Because the time-spans in the piece are irregular and are more deeply embedded in its second half, the specific designations for levels d and e are somewhat arbitrary. We have not bothered to include branchings for events at levels smaller than level g. The rest should be self-explanatory. On the whole, this is one of those pieces where the time-span reduction is less valuable in itself than for its role as an input to the prolongational reduction.

We will develop the prolongational reduction in stages from the time-span reduction. Levels a and b in 8.33 yield the prolongational basic form in 8.34a. At the next stage, level c in 8.33 offers one event for prolongational analysis, the V in measure 11. However, the I in measure 19 appears at level d, only one level smaller than the V in measure 11; and this I, the beginning of the reprise, makes the closest possible connection with the opening I. Therefore, as shown in 8.34b, the I in measure 19 must be selected as a prolongational repetition of the opening I, to which the V in measure 11 then attaches as a departure. Though the tree in 8.34b represents a longer passage of music, the prolongational situation is analogous to the standard antecedent-consequent structure shown in 8.17b. If we then add the essential remaining element of the cadential nucleus for the final cadence, the "subdominant" ii^6 in measure 22, the resultant tree in 8.34c satisfies normative structure as well (compare 8.28b).

The next available events appear at level e in 8.33. First, the full cadence in measures 9–10 prolongs the opening tonic (8.35a). (We have indicated a weak prolongation here because the $\overset{1}{I}$ in measure 10 is heard within the context of a prolonged $\overset{3}{I}$.) Second, the V in measure 18 weakly

a   **b**   **c**

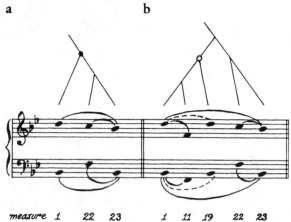

measure 1   22   23   1   11   19   22   23   m. 2   11   19   22   23

prolongs the V in measure 11. Third, the codetta is represented by the tonic prolongational repetition from measure 23 to measure 29. Beneath the secondary notation in 8.35a is shown the (rounded binary) A+B+A′+codetta form of the piece; note how noncongruent it is with the prolongational groupings. From level *f* in 8.33, 8.35b adds the remaining structural accents, the V in measure 5 and the I in measure 6. Also included are the cadential preparations in measures 4 and 9, corresponding to the ii⁶ in measure 22.

The portion of the tree within the dashed area *a*, signifying the antecedent-consequent period of measures 1–10, repeats the global tree in 8.34c; this is a good example of self-embedding. Areas *b* and *c* draw attention to the fact that the I prolongation in measures 23–29 balances the V prolongation in measures 11–18. The coherence of the piece hangs in part on these prolongational relationships.

As all the phrases are now framed by their most important events, we can turn next to their internal structures one by one.

The major point of prolongational interest in the antecedent phrase in measures 1–5 concerns the pivotal role of the vi chord in measure 3. Should it be a right or a left branch? Rhythmic and motivic considerations direct it as a tensing motion off the previous V in measure 3, but harmonically it is already part of the cadential nucleus. The analysis in 8.36c suggests both possibilities with dashed branches. Also worth pointing out in 8.36c is the slight tensing-relaxing motion at the cadence, enclosed within the larger relaxation of the ii⁶–V progression. Finally, observe that the neighboring IV chord in measure 2 attaches as a right, not a left, branch; this is due to the influence of the time-span segmentation, a prolongational principle to be discussed in section 9.4. The consequent phrase in measures 6–10 requires no additional comment.

8.35

a

m. 1   9 10   11   18   19 22   23   29
       A   B   A'   C

b

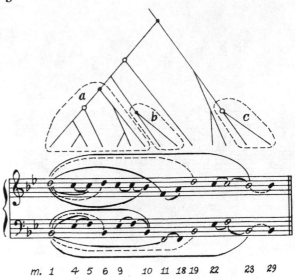

m. 1   4 5 6 9   10 11 18 19 22   23   29

8.36

a

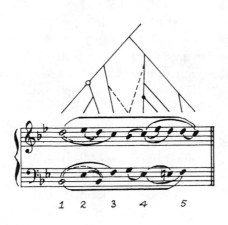

1   2   3   4   5

b

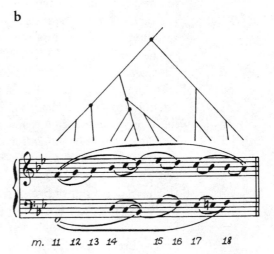

m. 11 12 13 14   15 16 17   18

c

m. 15 16 17   18

d

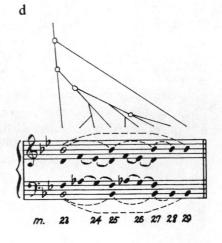

m. 23   24 25   26 27 28 29

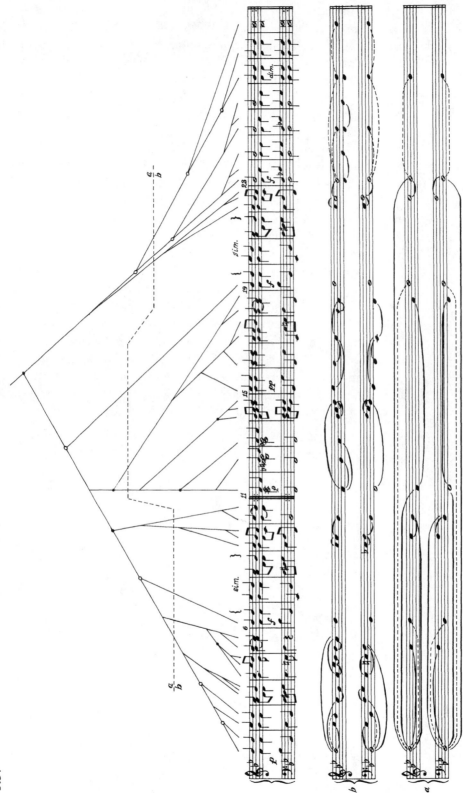

8.37

The branching for measures 11–14, the first half of the contrasting section, proceeds without complication (8.36b). Note that since the entire passage is under a V prolongation, the I in measure 14 must be subordinate to the V in measure 11. The "answer" in measures 15–18, on the other hand, is difficult to analyze, because melodic and harmonic factors conflict and because of the ambiguous function of the I$^6_4$ chord in measure 16. The analysis in 8.36b emphasizes melodic factors; it says that the E♭ in measure 15 is heard as a neighbor note under the prolongation of D from measure 14 to measure 16. Emphasis on harmonic factors leads to the branching in 8.36c, in which the subdominant motion toward the cadential V in measure 18 begins already at measure 15.

The reprise in measure 19–23 needs no comment. The codetta in measures 23–29 produces two sequences of left-branching resolutions—echoes, as it were, of the real resolution at measure 23—within a number of prolongational repetitions (8.36d).

The overall prolongational reduction of the *Chorale St. Antoni* appears in 8.37. As a visual aid, we have divided the secondary notation into two levels, marked *a* and *b*. The dashed line slicing across the tree reflects this division in that all the branching connections made above the line belong to level *a* and all those below the line belong to level *b* (the events in level *a* correspond to 8.35b). It should be apparent from our presentation of the branchings for each phrase that competing "preferred" analyses for local levels are possible, and that our discussion of various prolongational details has not been exhaustive.[5]

9
Formalization of Prolongational Reduction

**9.1
Fundamental
Hypotheses**

In the discussion in chapter 8 of the essential intuitions behind prolongational reduction, we assumed that the Strong Reduction Hypothesis applies to this domain of musical analysis, that is, that it makes sense to describe these intuitions in the form of a unified tree structure. Now we state this assumption overtly:

Prolongational Hypothesis 1 Intuitions about pitch-derived tension and relaxation in a piece can be expressed in terms of a strictly hierarchical segmentation of the piece into *prolongational regions,* such that
a. each region represents an overall tensing or relaxing in the progression from its beginning to its end, and
b. tensings and relaxings internal to each region represent subordinate and nonoverlapping stages in the overall progression.

In our initial discussion of tension and relaxation in section 8.1 we implicitly assumed Prolongational Hypothesis 1, in that we drew diagrams like 9.1a and 9.1b (copies of 8.3a and 8.3b) but none that were like 9.1c and 9.1d.

All of the examples in 9.1 satisfy condition a of Prolongational Hypothesis 1, since each arrow represents an overall tensing or relaxing from its beginning to its end. In 9.1a and 9.1b the regions form a hierarchical structure of the usual sort, whereas 9.1c and 9.1d violate condition b in that they contain overlapping of the sort we have disallowed in other components of musical structure. Prolongational Hypothesis 1 claims that such situations do not occur in musical intuition. Where they seem to occur, it is as a result of structural ambiguity in a piece—two independently viable structures in competition—not as part of a single unified structure. It is this property that permits prolongational reductions to be represented as tree structures.

Chapter 9

9.1

Prolongational Hypothesis 1 raises a crucial question: how are the hierarchical regions in a piece defined? For example, how does one arrive at the difference in the regions appropriate to the hearing of 9.1a and 9.1b? In effect, this was the question asked in section 5.4, where we demonstrated the impossibility of reducing a piece on the basis of the surface sequence of pitch-events alone. As suggested in section 8.2, the answer we propose can be stated as the following hypothesis:

Prolongational Hypothesis 2 The choice of events that define prolongational regions is strongly influenced by the relative importance of events in the time-span reduction.

Prolongational Hypothesis 1 claims that it is possible to build a tree structure; it thus enters into the formulation of the prolongational reduction well-formedness rules, to be stated in the next section. Prolongational Hypothesis 2, on the other hand, deals with the question of which of the many possible tree structures assigned to a piece by the well-formedness rules represents one's actual hearing. It claims that the major axes of tension and relaxation tend to be those events that are most important in articulating grouping structure. This hypothesis, with a number of refinements, will be incorporated into the prolongational reduction preference rules, to be developed in section 9.4.

9.2 Prolongational Reduction Well-Formedness Rules

To define prolongational tree structures over pieces, we need four rules. First, the tree must contain a single most important event, the head. Second, there must be specified ways for events to elaborate other events. As discussed in section 8.1, these are strong prolongation, weak prolongation, and progression. Third, every event in the piece must be attached to the tree. Fourth, branches must not cross. It is the latter two conditions that embody Prolongational Hypothesis 1, guaranteeing the hierarchical embedding of prolongational regions.

For precision, we must state over what string of pitch-events the prolongational reduction is defined. If it is defined over the musical surface, we will be unable to supply two separate functions to those events contained in a grouping overlap. This suggests that the prolongational reduction, like the time-span reduction, should be defined over underlying grouping structure. A further refinement would take account of the extra events present in the time-span reduction that are created by fusion and transformation, since they too have functions in the prolongational reduction. However, we leave their incorporation into this component for future research and assume for the moment that the underlying grouping structure provides the correct string of events from which to construct the prolongational reduction.

To facilitate formal treatment of the prolongational tree, we introduce the following definitions:

An event e_i is a *direct elaboration* of another event e_j if e_i's branch terminates on e_j's branch.

An event e_i is a *recursive elaboration* of another event e_j if it is a direct elaboration of e_j or if its branch leads upward through a sequence of direct elaborations to e_j's branch.

Figure 9.2 illustrates these terms with an abstract tree structure whose branches are numbered.

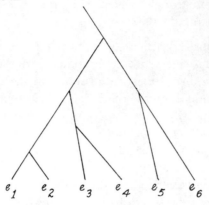

In 9.2, e_2 and e_3 are direct elaborations of e_1, which is in turn a direct elaboration of e_6. Hence e_2 and e_3 are recursive elaborations of both e_1 and e_6. And e_4, which is a direct elaboration of e_3, is therefore a recursive elaboration of e_3, e_1, and e_6. On the other hand, e_5 is not a recursive elaboration of e_1: it branches from e_6, which does not branch from e_1. Similarly, e_2 is not a recursive elaboration of e_3.

With these definitions, we can state the prolongational reduction well-formedness rules.

PRWFR 1 There is a single event in the underlying grouping structure of every piece that functions as prolongational head.

PRWFR 2 An event e_i can be a direct elaboration of another event e_j in any of the following ways:

a. e_i is a *strong prolongation* of e_j if the roots, bass notes, and melodic notes of the two events are identical.

b. e_i is a *weak prolongation* of e_j if the roots of the two events are identical but the bass and/or melodic notes differ.

c. e_i is a *progression to or from* e_j if the harmonic roots of the two events are different.

PRWFR 3 Every event in the underlying grouping structure is either the prolongational head or a recursive elaboration of the prolongational head.

PRWFR 4 (No Crossing Branches) If an event e_i is a direct elaboration of an event e_j, every event between e_i and e_j must be a direct elaboration of either e_i, e_j, or some event between them.

All four rules should be at this point self-explanatory, with the possible exception of PRWFR 4. It says that if e_i and e_j form a closed part of the tree, by virtue of one branching directly off the other, then no event between them may be a branch of an event outside the region. The abstract tree in 9.3 illustrates this.

9.3

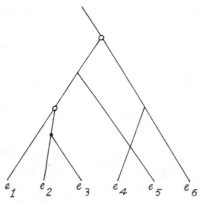

In this tree e_5 is a direct elaboration of e_1, so PRWFR 4 says that all events between them must be direct elaborations of either them or events between them. Since e_2 is a direct elaboration of e_1, and e_3 is a direct elaboration of e_2, these two events satisfy the condition. However, e_4 is a direct elaboration of e_6, which is not between e_1 and e_5. Hence PRWFR 4 is violated and the tree is not well formed.

It may be worth mentioning that these well-formedness rules can easily be modified for a purely melodic idiom such as Gregorian chant. In such a case, the definitions of prolongation would be stated in melodic rather than primarily harmonic terms. In the simplest situation, two events of the same pitch would count as a prolongation and two of different pitches would count as a progression. Intermediate relations, such as that between "primary" and "secondary" tones, might in addition be defined as weak prolongations. Other than these changes, the theory of prolongational trees could be carried over intact.

As in the other components of the musical grammar, the well-formedness rules underdetermine the choice of a most stable analysis for a piece—they simply state the general properties of all possible analyses. We now develop the preference rules by which the most stable tree for a piece is constructed.

Formalization of Prolongational Reduction

General Considerations

As in the case of the time-span reduction, the procedure for determining the most stable prolongational reduction involves constructing the tree piecemeal and finding the most important event in each of the many hierarchically related regions of the piece. The regions of application for time-span reduction were the time-spans, independently determined on the basis of the grouping and metrical structure. However, this is not the case for prolongational reduction; as was pointed out in sections 5.4 and 8.3, it is characteristic of prolongational reduction that its regions cut across group boundaries. This means that the regions for rule application cannot be fixed in terms of information available from other components.

Prolongational Hypothesis 1 suggests the overall principle by which regions of rule application are determined for the prolongational reduction. This hypothesis implies that the function of an event in building or releasing tension depends on its relationship to surrounding events that are prolongationally more important: its role consists of a step in progressing from one of these surrounding events to the other.

This conclusion in turn leads to a radical difference between the construction of the prolongational tree and the other three components of the analysis. Whereas the grouping, metrical, and time-span structures were built from the smallest units up, culminating with the largest elements of the structure, the prolongational structure must be constructed from the top down, starting with the head of the piece and dividing the piece into progressively smaller regions until all events are included. This method is necessary because the prolongational context in which an event e is heard depends on the position and relationships of events that are prolongationally more important than e.

The Prolongational Head

In order to construct the tree from the top down, we must start by finding the prolongational head of the piece. Prolongational Hypothesis 2 says that prolongational importance is in large part tied to time-span importance. This suggests that we begin by identifying the prolongational head with the time-span head of the piece. In other words, the point of maximal prolongational stability—the point of greatest relaxation—is that point in the piece that most strongly articulates the end of the largest group. (In the next section this claim will be incorporated into a preference rule, but for the moment let us just take it for granted.)

The prolongational head is not necessarily the absolute end of the piece, since in some cases a coda may be subordinate in the time-span reduction to the full cadence that precedes it. This occurred in the *Chorale St. Antoni*, discussed in section 8.5. In such cases the end of the coda usually forms a strong prolongation with the prolongational head, so that the very end of the piece is equally a point of maximal relaxation.

But there are cases where even this is not so—for example, the slow movement of Bach's Fourth Brandenburg Concerto or Schumann's song "Im wunderschönen Monat Mai" from *Dichterliebe*—where the piece ends on a nontonic chord that leads into the next movement or song. In these exceptional cases, the point of maximal relaxation occurs before the end, and the very end is a departure from the head.

Having chosen a prolongational head, we have created one or possibly two regions in which a maximally important event must be determined: from the beginning to the head, and (if the head is not at the very end) from the head to the end. In continuing the construction of the tree, we must solve three problems: defining regions of rule application in the general case, finding the prolongationally most important event in a region of rule application, and deciding whether this event is to be attached as a right branch to a preceding event or as a left branch to a following event. All of these problems were treated informally in chapter 8; we take them up in more detail in the next subsection and the following two sections.

Defining Regions of Rule Application

To find the regions in terms of which prolongational stability is determined, let us examine the abstract trees in 9.4. In these examples, e_1, e_2, and so on stand for events in underlying grouping structure. They are numbered to reflect order of elaboration rather than temporal sequence. The symbol # stands for the boundary of the piece; for notational convenience we think of each piece as preceded and followed by the abstract symbol #. Also, for the moment, the manner of attachment (strong or weak prolongation or progression) can be disregarded. Finally, in the following discussion we use the notation (e_i-e_j) to stand for the string of events between, but not including, e_i and e_j.

Suppose that e_1 in 9.4a is the prolongational head, and that e_2 has been chosen, by whatever means, as the most important event in the region $(\#-e_1)$. Because there is no other place to attach it, e_2 must be a direct elaboration of e_1. The piece is now divided into three regions in which prolongational importance must be determined: $(\#-e_2)$, (e_2-e_1), and $(e_1-\#)$, as indicated by the curly brackets beneath 9.4a.

Next, suppose that, by whatever means, a prolongationally most important event e_3 is chosen in the region $(\#-e_2)$. As shown by the dotted lines in 9.4b, the geometry of the tree permits e_3 to be attached either to e_2 or to e_1. However, what happens if e_3 is attached to e_1? Since branches may not cross, e_3 must be attached higher than e_2, which indicates that it is prolongationally more important. But this contradicts the assumption that e_2 was originally chosen as the most important event in $(\#-e_1)$. Thus e_3 can only be attached to e_2; the other attachment violates the musical meaning of the tree structure.

9.4

a

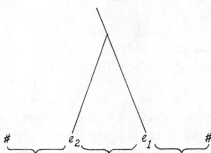

b

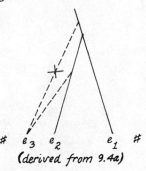

(derived from 9.4a)

c

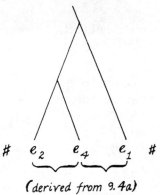

(derived from 9.4a)

d

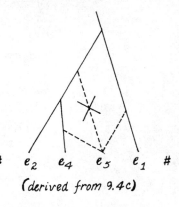

(derived from 9.4c)

e

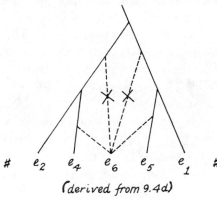

(derived from 9.4d)

For a more complex but similar case consider 9.4c, in which e_4 has been chosen as the most important event between e_2 and e_1; assume that e_4 has turned out to be a direct elaboration of e_2. Then the passage from e_2 to e_1 is divided up into two regions: (e_2-e_4) and (e_4-e_1). Let us focus on the geometry of the latter of these regions.

Suppose that the prolongationally most important event in (e_4-e_1) turns out to be e_5. As shown in 9.4d, e_5 could conceivably be attached in any of three ways: to e_4, to e_2, or to e_1. However, if it is attached to e_2, the prohibition against crossing branches means that it must be attached higher than e_4, and hence that it is prolongationally more important than e_4. But this violates the assumption that e_4 was the most important event in (e_4-e_1). Therefore, e_5 may be attached only to e_4 or e_1 if the musical meaning of the tree is to be preserved.

For the most complex case, suppose that e_5 in 9.4d turns out to be attached to e_1, as in 9.4e. Then, in the region (e_4-e_5), the prolongationally most important event e_6 can geometrically be attached in four different places: to e_4, e_2, e_1, and e_5. But attachment to e_2 would require e_6 to be more important than e_4, violating assumptions; and attachment to e_1 would require e_6 to be more important than e_5, again violating assumptions. Hence only attachment to e_4 or e_5 is possible.

This exercise has established the general procedure for constructing a prolongational tree. The prolongational head e_1 establishes two initial regions, $(\#-e_1)$ and $(e_1-\#)$, of which the second is empty if e_1 is at the very end. We find the prolongationally most important events in each of these regions and attach them to e_1, dividing the piece into at most four regions. In each of these regions, we find the prolongationally most important event and attach it to one of the events that bound the region from which it has been chosen. These then divide the regions in which they were chosen into further regions, and so forth. In general, an event chosen as the most important event in a region (e_i-e_j) must be a direct elaboration of either e_i or e_j; it cannot be a direct elaboration of something e_i or e_j is attached to. If one endpoint of a region is $\#$, the most important event in the region must be a direct elaboration of its other endpoint.

Having worked out this procedure, we can now define a prolongational region in a simple and general fashion:

A *prolongational region* is a sequence of events (e_i-e_j), $(\#-e_j)$, or $(e_i-\#)$ such that all events within the sequence are recursive elaborations of either e_i or e_j.

The reader can easily verify that this definition is valid for all the prolongational regions illustrated in 9.4. In particular, in the most complex case (9.4e), e_6 must be a direct elaboration of either e_4 or e_5; and events chosen subsequently between e_4 and e_5 must in turn be elaborations of e_4, e_5, or e_6 (that is, recursive elaborations of either e_4 or e_5).

Notice that the endpoints of a prolongational region need not attach directly to one another. Again this is illustrated by the region (e_4-e_5).

Given this definition of a prolongational region, we turn to the question of how the prolongationally most important event in a region is chosen. (Henceforth, for convenience, when we refer to an arbitrary prolongational region (e_i-e_j) we will understand this to include the cases where e_i or e_j is replaced by #.)

9.4
Prolongational
Reduction
Preference Rules

In the above discussion of prolongational regions, we took for granted the operation of two separate processes: choosing the prolongationally most important event in a region (e_i-e_j), and determining whether that event is an elaboration of e_i or of e_j. These two problems are addressed by the prolongational reduction preference rules. As will be seen, some of the rules deal with only one problem or the other, and some deal with both.

Influence of Time-Span Reduction
We begin with two preference rules that establish the relation between prolongational reduction and time-span reduction. The first is an explicit statement of Prolongational Hypothesis 2, now localized to the choice of the most important event of a prolongational region:

PRPR 1 (Time-Span Importance) In choosing the prolongationally most important event e_k of a prolongational region (e_i-e_j), strongly prefer a choice in which e_k is relatively time-span-important.

Since PRPR 1 interacts with preferences concerning pitch stability in ways not to be described until the next subsection, we illustrate it here with examples in which pitch stability does not play a role.

An obvious application of PRPR 1 is in choosing the prolongational head of a piece. If we regard the entire piece as a prolongational region (#–#), PRPR 1 says to prefer a prolongational head that is relatively time-span-important—that is, the time-span head.

Next, recall the impossibility of constructing a reduction of the first phrase of the Mozart A Major Sonata solely on the basis of pitch criteria (see example 5.10). There are four root-position tonic chords with C♯ on top, any of which, on pitch criteria alone, might be prolongationally most important. However, PRPR 1 says that the time-span importance of the first chord in the piece establishes its prolongational importance; the relative time-span unimportance of the other three disqualifies them.

A third illustration of PRPR 1 appears in 9.5 (a repetition of 8.8). In each case, the rule selects the I chord that is in a metrically stronger position, hence more important in time-span reduction (by TSRPR 1).

9.5

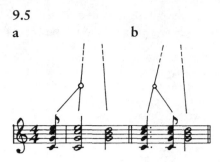

PRPR 1 addresses only the question of which event in a region is most important, not that of which endpoint of the region that event is attached to. Another preference rule deals with this second question in terms of congruence with time-span segmentation: other things being equal, direct prolongational elaborations should not cross time-span boundaries.

PRPR 2 (Time-Span Segmentation) Let e_k be the prolongationally most important event in a prolongational region $(e_i - e_j)$. If there is a time-span that contains e_i and e_k but not e_j, prefer a prolongational reduction in which e_k is an elaboration of e_i; similarly with the roles of e_i and e_j reversed.

One prominent situation in which PRPR 2 applies is illustrated in 9.6.

9.6

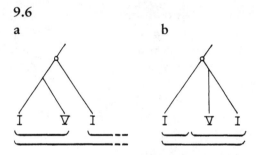

In both 9.6a and 9.6b, assume that e_i and e_j are I chords and e_k is a V adjacent to the second I in the musical surface. However, as the groupings shown in the examples indicate, the V in 9.6a is a half cadence preceding a new phrase beginning on I; by contrast, the V in 9.6b is the dominant of a full cadence resolving on the final I. We argued in section 8.3 that the half cadence is heard as a departure from the initial I, whereas the dominant of a full cadence is a left branch to its resolution. PRPR 2 accounts for this difference in terms of the grouping difference between 9.6a and 9.6b.

PRPR 2 is stated in terms of time-span segmentation rather than time-span reduction branching, in order to accommodate instances in which the branching cannot possibly be congruent yet time-span considerations still affect prolongational branching. Example 9.7 presents a typical case;

Formalization of Prolongational Reduction

the V–vi forms a deceptive cadence at the end of a phrase, and the following progression is a phrase extension that forms a group of its own.

9.7

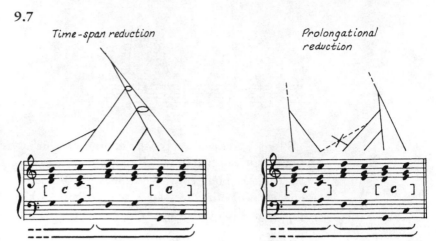

In time-span reduction the vi is more important than the preceding V, since it forms the rhythmic completion of the group. However, in prolongational reduction the V will normally be more important, for reasons of harmonic stability. The problem PRPR 2 addresses is how to attach the vi chord.

At the point in the derivation where the attachment of the vi is being considered, its context is the V on the left and the ii^6 on the right. A harmonic connection in either direction is possible: the vi can in principle be construed either as a departure from the preceding V or as part of the cadential preparation for the final V. PRPR 2, taking note that the first V and the vi are contained in a group that does not contain the ii^6, tips the balance in favor of the right-branching interpretation (departure). In the resulting tree the branching is not congruent with the time-span branching, but it does respect grouping boundaries. PRPR 2 is stated in terms of segmentation rather than branching, then, in order to address just this sort of case.

PRPR 2 is by no means as strong a rule as PRPR 1, since prolongational reductions commonly are noncongruent with time-span segmentation. Its influence appears to be strongest at relatively local levels of segmentation and to fade considerably from the phrase level up. The local strength of PRPR 2 seems to be related to the "locality" condition on fusion in time-span reduction (mentioned in section 7.2), in ways that we cannot at present specify.

If unchecked by other considerations, PRPR 2 would build prolongational trees that expressed tension and relaxation only in terms of each individual phrase, connecting the phrases up in whatever manner the time-span segmentation dictated. Thus PRPR 2 creates pressure toward relatively local, phrase-by-phrase prolongational reductions of the sort discussed in section 8.3. As pointed out there, one of the characteristics of the more sophisticated listener is his ability to overcome this pressure for a "bottom-up" analysis and to hear larger-scale patterns of tension and relaxation that cut across phrase boundaries. We now turn to the evidence such a listener uses for these patterns: the harmonic and melodic connections among events.

Stability of Prolongational Connection

We can state the preference rule for stability of connection in preliminary form as follows:

PRPR 3 (Stability of Connection, preliminary form) Let e_k be the prolongationally most important event in a prolongational region $(e_i - e_j)$. Prefer a prolongational reduction in which e_k is an elaboration of that endpoint with which it forms the more stable prolongational connection.

PRPR 3 conflicts with PRPR 2 if e_i and e_k fall in a group together but e_k and e_j form a more stable connection across a group boundary. Before exploring such conflicts we must refine this preliminary rule in two ways. First, the notion of stable prolongational connection must be clarified (we return to this in a moment). Second, the rule as stated addresses only the case in which the most important event e_k in a region has already been chosen; but numerous cases arise in which e_k cannot be chosen on grounds of time-span importance alone (by PRPR 1). Consider 9.8, a typical antecedent-consequent pattern.

9.8

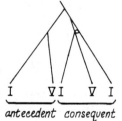

Time-span reduction

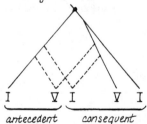

Prolongational reduction

The prolongational tree for the beginning and the final cadence is the "basic form" discussed in section 8.3. The next most time-span important events are the end of the antecedent and the beginning of the consequent. Because these two events are of equal time-span importance, PRPR 1 cannot choose which of them is e_k for the region from the I to the V of the full cadence. Hence PRPR 3 as stated above cannot apply to establish any attachment.

The solution to this difficulty is to restate PRPR 3 so it can affect the choice of e_k as well as its attachment:

PRPR 3 (Prolongational Connection) In choosing the prolongationally most important event e_k in a prolongational region $(e_i - e_j)$, prefer an e_k that attaches so as to form a maximally stable prolongational connection with one of the endpoints of the region.

In applying this form of PRPR 3 to 9.8 we find that the most stable connection is of the intermediate I to the initial I, since this forms a right prolongation; 9.9a is the resulting tree. In turn, the V is now between two Is, so that PRPR 3 is indeterminate. Because of the grouping, however, PRPR 2 applies to attach the V to the initial I, as in 9.9b. The preference rules have thus carried out the derivation discussed in detail in chapter 8 (examples 8.14–8.17).

9.9

a

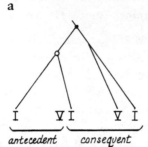

b

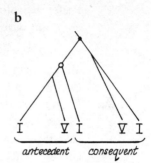

Notice that the attachment of the intermediate I in 9.9a overrides PRPR 2, which would prefer attachment to the following V.

Now we turn to refining the concept of stable prolongational connection. Most of the relevant factors were mentioned in sections 8.1 and 8.2; we will enumerate them here as a set of conditions to which PRPR 3 refers.

Stability Conditions for Prolongational Connection
1. (Branching condition)
   a. Right strong prolongations are more stable than right weak prolongations, which in turn are more stable than right progressions.
   b. Left progressions are more stable than left weak prolongations, which in turn are more stable than left strong prolongations.
2. (Pitch-collection condition)
   A connection between two events is more stable if they involve or imply a common diatonic collection.
3. (Melodic condition)
   a. (Distance) A connection between two events is melodically more stable if the interval between them is smaller (with the exception of the octave, which is relatively stable).
   b. (Direction) An ascending melodic progression is most stable as a right-branching structure; a descending one is most stable as a left-branching structure.

4. (Harmonic condition)

   a. (Distance) A connection between two events is harmonically more stable if their roots are closer on the circle of fifths.

   b. (Direction) A progression that ascends along the circle of fifths is most stable as a right-branching structure; one that descends along the circle of fifths or produces a subdominant-to-dominant relationship is most stable as a left-branching structure.

Condition 1 was discussed in connection with examples 8.5 and 8.6 and requires no further exposition here. Condition 2 was illustrated by a secondary dominant relationship in 8.10e. More broadly, this condition applies not just to local borrowing from other diatonic collections but also to tonicizations at various larger levels of structure. For example, this condition creates pressure to unify the branchings in the dominant region of a sonata movement.

Condition 3a was illustrated in examples 8.10a and 8.10b and needs no more comment. Condition 3b expresses the commonplace intuition that a singer or a trumpeter, for example, must make a greater effort to reach higher pitches; hence ascent and descent correspond to tension and relaxation respectively. The Schenkerian *Urlinie,* a descending stepwise melodic progression, reflects both conditions 3a and 3b.

Parallel to the distance and direction aspects of melodic connection, there are corresponding distance and direction aspects of harmonic connection. Condition 4a was illustrated in examples 8.10c and 8.10d; condition 4b in 8.18 and 8.19.

Condition 4a does not mention relative and parallel major-minor relationships, because they arise from the interaction of condition 4a with condition 2. The relative major-minor relationship is fairly distant on the circle of fifths but close in diatonic collection; conversely, the parallel major-minor relationship is identical on the circle of fifths but dissimilar in diatonic connection. Thus major-minor relationships are more equivocal than tonic-dominant relationships, where conditions 2 and 4a are in mutual agreement.

The ways in which conditions 3 and 4 reinforce or conflict are an enriching factor in the tonal idiom. For example, the harmonic implications of even an unaccompanied melody often override purely melodic factors in determining prolongational connection. Conversely, a harmonic progression as such also produces melodic implications, especially through the motion of the bass. Typically, melodic influences are more marked at smaller levels of reduction, and at larger levels play a relatively insignificant role in comparison with harmonic connection.

The interaction of conditions 1–4 and their refinement could be pursued further, but we will not do so here. In the present context these conditions act as sub-preference rules within the application of PRPR 3, much like the subcases of the local-detail rules in grouping (GPRs 2 and 3) and the length rule in meter (MPR 5). Their behavior will be made clearer in the course of the derivations in this chapter and chapter 10.

In addition to PRPR 3, there is a second principle that relates prolongational attachment to prolongational connections. Section 8.2 motivated this principle in connection with passing and neighboring motions (examples 8.11 and 8.12).

PRPR 4 (Prolongational Importance) Let e_k be the prolongationally most important event in a region $(e_i - e_j)$. Prefer a prolongational reduction in which e_k is an elaboration of the prolongationally more important of the endpoints.

This rule, like PRPR 2, affects only the attachment of e_k, not the choice of e_k, and like PRPR 2 it is a relatively weak principle in comparison to PRPRs 1 and 3 (the major factors in determining the details of prolongational reduction).

Example 8.12d, reproduced here as 9.10, is a case where PRPR 2 conflicts with PRPR 4.

9.10

The initial event and the neighboring motion are contained in a time-span that does not contain the downbeat, so PRPR 2 favors a right-branching construction. Insofar as our judgment of the structure of 9.10 is correct, PRPR 4 has overridden PRPR 2 here. The delicacy of the judgment may reflect a balance between the two rules.

Parallelism

As in the other components of the musical grammar, there is a preference rule for parallelism in prolongational reduction. Imagine an example in which the stability conditions are in conflict, creating an ambiguity between right and left branching for a particular event. The parallelism rule says that no matter how the ambiguity is resolved, parallel passages must resolve it in the same way. Other things being equal, a motive should not have a different prolongational structure when it reappears.

PRPR 5 (Parallelism) Prefer a prolongational reduction in which parallel passages receive parallel analyses.

So far we have presented only one example in which PRPR 3 contributes to the choice of e_k: the antecedent-consequent pattern in 9.8 and 9.9. In this example, PRPR 1 does not provide any preference between the intermediate V and I, so PRPR 3 alone decides between them. However, this example was chosen specifically to isolate the effects of PRPR 3. When we turn to more complex cases, the two rules interact profusely. Their interaction is central to our theory of prolongational reduction.

The Mozart K. 331 theme provides an especially good illustration of the interaction of PRPRs 1 and 3. Example 9.11 presents the time-span reduction for a harmonic sketch of the first four measures; for simplicity, let us assume that level e is the musical surface.

9.11

In forming the prolongational reduction, let us assume that we have already attached the initial I and the cadential V to form a prolongational region, as in 9.12. This is the antecedent portion of the tree derived in 9.9b.

Formalization of Prolongational Reduction

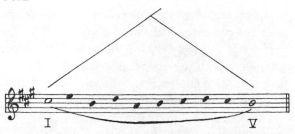

This region contains eight events, from which we must choose an e_k and attach it. PRPR 1 favors the most time-span-important events—the first V^6 and the "vi^7." PRPR 3, on the other hand, favors the I chord, since it forms a strong right-branching prolongation with the initial I. Thus the two rules are in conflict.

In analyzing numerous examples of this sort of conflict, we have found that the following principle accounts for the vast majority of cases:

Interaction Principle In order to make a sufficiently stable prolongational connection, e_k must be chosen from the events in the two most important levels of time-span reduction represented in (e_i-e_j).

The Interaction Principle restricts the conditions under which PRPR 3 can override PRPR 1: no matter what stable prolongational connection can be made to the endpoints of a region, only those events in the highest two levels of time-span reduction represented in the region can be considered for e_k. Thus the Interaction Principle is a more explicit version of Prolongational Hypothesis 2, which states the dependence of prolongational reduction on time-span reduction, and, through time-span reduction, on grouping and metrical structure.

The Interaction Principle allows two levels of time-span reduction to be available for e_k, rather than only one level, because a degree of flexibility must be allowed between time-span importance and prolongational importance. On the other hand, the use of two levels rather than three or more appears empirically to yield just the correct degree of looseness between the two reductions; it prevents unimportant detail from playing too great a role at any particular stage of prolongational analysis.[1]

We return now to the conflict in 9.12. According to the Interaction Principle, the I chord may be chosen as e_k, because it is only one time-span level less important than the V^6 or the "vi^7." (On the other hand, in the original K. 331 passage, the I chord on the third beat of measure 1 is two levels less important than the V^6, and so cannot be considered a candidate for e_k.) The tree resulting from the choice of the I is shown in 9.13.

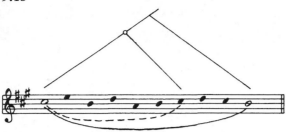

There are now two regions to consider: between the two Is and from the second I to the final V. Let us deal with the latter first. The ii⁶ and the I⁶₄ are equal in time-span importance, so PRPR 1 does not apply. Of the four possible connections between these two chords and the endpoints, the most stable is the left-branching descending fifth progression from the ii⁶ to the V, so the ii⁶ is chosen as e_k. Then the I⁶₄ must attach to either the ii⁶ or the V. Because of the arrival in the bass, it attaches to the V, as in 9.14.

9.14

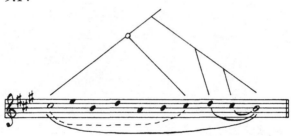

The part of the tree just developed is one of the cadential formulas presented in section 8.3. The ii⁶, despite its relative unimportance in the time-span reduction, has emerged as relatively important in the prolongational reduction: it is the most important left branch of the cadential V.

Next we turn to the region between the two Is in 9.14. The V⁶ and the "vi⁷" are again most time-span-important, but the most stable harmonic connection is from the initial I to the I⁶. The Interaction Principle as applied so far selects the I⁶ as most important; however, intuition favors the V⁶. There are two local influences supporting this intuition. First, the V⁶ is melodically closer to the I than the I⁶ is, and the events involved are at a local enough level here that melodic connection, in both the soprano and the bass, plays a decisive role. Thus PRPR 3 is itself conflicted between harmonic and melodic closeness, so that the I⁶ is not clearly a more stable connection than the V⁶. PRPR 1 therefore prevails, choosing the V⁶ for its time-span importance. The second factor in the choice of the V⁶ involves motivic structure, and will be discussed below.

After the V^6 attaches, the I^6 attaches as a weak prolongation to the initial I. The tree now looks as in 9.15.

9.15

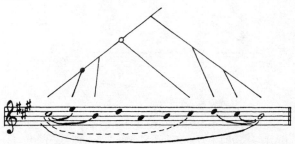

Between the V^6 and the second I, the most time-span-important event is the "vi^7." But the second V^6 forms more stable prolongational connections, either as a strong prolongation of the first V^6 or as a progression into the second I by descending circle of fifths. In either case, the Interaction Principle allows us to choose the V^6, despite its lesser time-span importance; this yields 9.16.

9.16

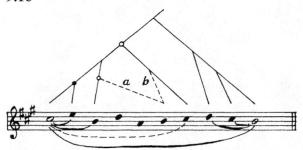

The dashed lines in 9.16 indicate the alternative attachments of the second V^6. We believe the choice is a genuine ambiguity in the piece: Is this event heard as a repetition of the first V^6 (branching a), or as leading into the I (branching b)? Note, however, that PRPRs 2 and 4 both favor branching b, because the I and the second V^6 but not the first V^6 are in the second two-measure group and because the I is more important than the V^6. For this reason, there may be some preference for this attachment.

Between the two V^6s, the most time-span-important event is still the "vi^7," while the strongest harmonic connection is to the V^4_3. As in 9.15, however, linear and harmonic connections conflict, leaving PRPR 1 free to choose the "vi^7" as e_k. If branching a in 9.16 is preferred, there is pressure for the "vi^7" to attach to the previous V^6 because of PRPR 4. If branching b is selected, the "vi^7" attaches unequivocally to the following

V⁶ through the influence of PRPR 2. In either case, by parallelism with measure 1 (PRPR 5), the V_3^4 finally attaches as a right branch to the preceding V⁶. Example 9.17 gives the complete tree for both possibilities, with 9.17a deriving from branching *a* in 9.16 and 9.17b deriving from branching *b*.

Both trees in 9.17 are musically meaningful. That in 9.17a captures the double neighboring motion in the voice leading of the phrase—the V⁶ within a prolonged I and the "vi⁷" within a prolonged V⁶. On the other hand, that in 9.17b better represents the pattern of tension and relaxation in the phrase, with the "vi⁷" and the second V⁶ relaxing into the following I.

9.17

a   **b**

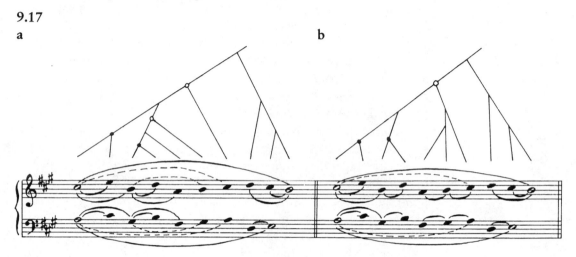

Now let us turn to our promised comment on motivic structure. Although the rule of parallelism (PRPR 5) creates parallel *internal* structure for parallel motives, it does not necessarily prevent a situation like 9.18a.

9.18

　　　　　　　　　　　　a　　　　　　　　　　　　　　**b**

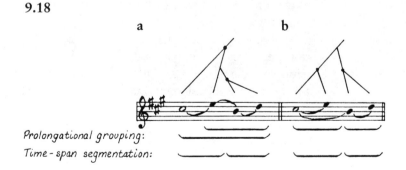

Prolongational grouping:

Time-span segmentation:

In this tree the two occurrences of the motive are internally parallel (in that the second half of each is subordinate to the first half), but the second occurrence is prolongationally an elaboration of an internal part of the other. This is the structure that would have resulted if the I^6 had been chosen ahead of the V^6 in 9.14. Instead we chose 9.18b—at the time, on linear grounds.

But there is another reason not to prefer 9.18a: it implies that the second occurrence of the motive is part of the first, rather than a self-contained entity. PRPR 2 (congruence to time-span segmentation), which is especially effective at these small levels, addresses this difficulty, since 9.18b is congruent to the time-span segmentation and 9.18a is not. This can be seen more clearly in these examples by comparing the time-span segmentation with the "prolongational grouping" (the domains defined by the extent of prolongational elaborations). Thus PRPR 2 has an important effect on the delineation of motivic structure in prolongational reduction: it keeps motives prolongationally intact.

This derivation has illustrated the typical way in which the PRPRs interact. The primary influences on prolongational structure are PRPRs 1 and 3, with PRPRs 2, 4, and 5 helping to decide otherwise indeterminate cases. What makes K. 331 unusual is the number of times the Interaction Principle has to be invoked, resulting in repeated prolongational subordination of the time-span-important "vi^7." Most pieces do not display such a disparity between time-span and prolongational importance, but to the extent that they do, it is as a result of the Interaction Principle, as in this example.

An additional case where the Interaction Principle plays a role is in deriving the prolongational structure of deceptive cadences, illustrated in 9.7. In a deceptive cadence, it is typically the case that the V forms a more stable prolongational connection with its surroundings than does the vi. Because the V is immediately subordinate to the vi in the time-span reduction, the Interaction Principle says that it should be chosen as e_k in the relevant region, with the vi subordinate, as shown in 9.7. Hence deceptive cadences, unlike full cadences, display a reversal of prolongational importance, with the dominant more important than the resolution.

To sum up: the Interaction Principle states how the time-span reduction regulates prolongational importance. In constructing a prolongational reduction, we can, for each prolongational region, simply search for the strongest prolongational connection possible among the events in the two largest levels of time-span reduction represented in the region. Events of less time-span importance need not be considered. In terms of musical cognition, this means that patterns of tension and relaxation are strongly organized by rhythmic articulation—an intuition that seems obvious, but to our knowledge has not previously been formulated explicitly in the theoretical literature. The power of the Interaction Principle in constraining possible prolongational reductions makes it a central part of our theory.

Section 8.3 presented the notion of a normative (or preferred) overall prolongational structure for phrases and larger levels of grouping. The principle was stated as a preference for phrases that contain at least one significant right-branching progression (a departure, increasing tension) and a doubly embedded left-branching progression (a prepared cadence, relaxing the tension). The general structure is shown in 9.19.

9.19

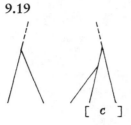

This section will state the principle more precisely and show how it affects the choice of prolongational structure in a number of cases.

Statement of the Rule

To arrive at a better understanding of this principle, we begin by asking two questions: To what groups does the preference for normative structure apply? How is the normative configuration associated with the selected groups?

To answer the first question we note that intuitions about "normal" tension and relaxation are not applicable to small groups such as the first measure of K. 331. Rather they apply to those groups that we designated in section 7.4 as *cadenced groups:* groups that at some level of time-span reduction are represented as a single event (the structural beginning) followed by a cadence (the structural ending). Recall that the smaller levels of cadenced groups correspond to the intuitive notion of phrase, the larger levels to sections, and the largest level to the entire piece. The rule of normative structure should apply to all these cadenced groups.

Consider now the second and more difficult question. The intuition we are trying to express is that from the beginning to the end of a cadenced group there should be a tensing followed by a relaxation. Of course, by "beginning" we cannot mean the *surface* beginning, since, for example, events on upbeats usually do not feel like the point from which the tension starts. In fact, in large-scale cadenced groups, such as the exposition of Beethoven's "Tempest" Sonata (see section 10.2), there may be a rather lengthy structural anacrusis before the point at which the normative structure begins. Similarly, by "ending" we cannot mean surface ending, since, as we saw in the *Chorale St. Antoni* (section 8.5), the prolongational tension is defused seven measures before the end. Hence the rule describing normative structure must refer to some more abstract notion of beginning and ending events than that given by the musical surface.

Formalization of Prolongational Reduction

The appropriate events can be identified as the endpoints of the largest prolongational region entirely contained within a cadenced group. Let us call these events the *prolongational beginning* and *prolongational ending* of the group. They will usually, but not always, coincide with the structural beginning and ending defined by the time-span reduction.

It remains to specify the nature of normative structure. Observe that the double left branching in 9.19 is due to the fact that full cadences already have two events in them, one connected as a left branch to the other. Instead of literally specifying double left embedding, it is advantageous to require simply a cadential preparation, that is, one significant left branch attached to the designated cadence. This formulation generalizes to half cadences, where the normative prolongational ending is a V chord prepared by one previous significant event as its highest elaboration. This was the structure at the half cadence in measure 4 in K. 331 in the previous section, for instance. Such a description of normative form also generalizes to phrases with deceptive cadences, in which the prolongational ending is the V rather than the vi. Here again, one significant left branch is the norm. In nearly all cases, the desired left branch is "subdominant" in function.

Section 8.3 pointed out that for music of the Classical period, but not the Baroque, normative structure also includes a prolongation of the prolongational beginning, standing often for the beginning of a consequent or a reprise. In stating the rule for normative structure, we include this variant in parentheses. We now have the elements necessary for a statement of the rule.

PRPR 6 (Normative Prolongational Structure) A cadenced group preferably contains four (five) elements in its prolongational structure:
a. a prolongational beginning,
b. a prolongational ending consisting of one element of the cadence,
(c. a right-branching prolongation as the most important direct elaboration of the prolongational beginning,)
d. a right-branching progression as the (next) most important direct elaboration of the prolongational beginning,
e. a left-branching "subdominant" progression as the most important elaboration of the first element of the cadence.

PRPR 6 is involved in the derivation of the "basic form" described in section 8.3. Consider a piece whose largest levels of time-span reduction are as in 9.20.

9.20

The prolongational head is naturally the final I. Next, the Interaction Principle allows either the initial I or the cadential V as the prolongationally next most important event. Of these, the V forms a better prolongational connection, since a left-branching progression is more stable than a left-branching weak prolongation. But the resulting tree, 9.21a, does not conform to the normative structure. Moreover, the left-branching I–V progression is highly unstable, since it is an *ascending* circle-of-fifths progression. The alternative, the "basic form" in 9.21b, allows the normative structure to be satisfied.

9.21

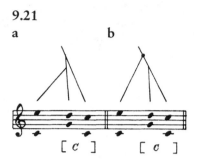

Thus PRPR 6, acting in concert with PRPR 1, overrides the preference of PRPR 3 for a stronger prolongational connection at the highest level of branching.

A second application of the normative structure rule is in establishing the prolongational ending of pieces such as the *Chorale St. Antoni* (discussed in section 8.5). Following the full cadence ending in measure 23, this piece has seven measures of coda over a tonic pedal. PRPR 6 says that the final I of the coda cannot be the prolongational ending for the piece since it does not end a prepared cadence. As a result, the prolongational ending is pushed forward to the last full prepared cadence, and the coda material extends as a right prolongation from the tonic in measure 23. In turn, because of the strong preference for the prolongational head of the piece to be the time-span head as well (PRPR 1), there is pressure on the time-span reduction, through TSRPR 6 ("Prefer a time-span reduction that results in a stable prolongational reduction"), to choose measure 23 as the time-span head also, overriding the usual time-span preference for placing structural endings at the very end. This is an important case of interaction between components.

More generally, PRPR 6 favors a tree like 9.22 for a cadenced group that ends with a prepared cadence plus a number of V–I repetitions (for example, the exposition of the first movement of Beethoven's Fifth Symphony). This accords with the intuition that the first I defuses the major tension of the piece and the additional cadences are simply repetitions. (The repetitions may be further differentiated in prolongational importance, but that does not affect the present point.)

Formalization of Prolongational Reduction

9.22

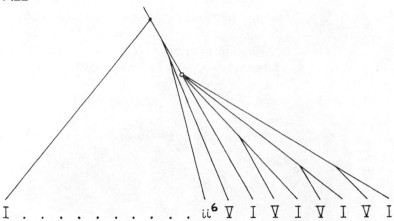

$$\text{I} \quad . \quad . \quad . \quad . \quad . \quad . \quad . \quad . \quad \text{ii}^6 \ \text{V} \quad \text{I} \quad \text{V} \quad \text{I} \quad \text{V} \quad \text{I} \quad \text{V} \quad \text{I}$$

It is important that PRPR 6 does not specify the harmonic function of the prolongational beginning and ending of a cadenced group. In particular, they need not form any sort of prolongation. The prolongational beginning may be a right branch off some earlier event to which the prolongational ending does not connect directly. Such a situation is found in a number of examples already discussed (for instance the consequent of the antecedent-consequent pattern in 9.9b). Moreover, a phrase that modulates may satisfy normative structure. All that is necessary is that the requisite right- and left-branching progressions be present. Example 9.23 illustrates the normative structure in the modulating third phrase of "O Haupt."

9.23

Normative Structure and the *Ursatz*

In appearance, the prolongational basic form approximates the *Ursatz* of Schenkerian theory. In function, however, the concept of normative structure may play a role more comparable to the *Ursatz,* in that normative structure specifies an obligatory pattern that must be fulfilled for a passage to be musically complete. But the statement of the rule in terms of branchings rather than specific progressions allows it to apply to a wider range of situations than the *Ursatz*. The modulating phrase just cited is a simple example. A more complex example appears in 9.24, a harmonic sketch of the Chopin A Major Prelude, part of whose time-span reduction was presented in 7.23 and 7.24. This is an entire piece that satisfies normative structure but is an instance of neither the basic form nor the *Ursatz*.

9.24

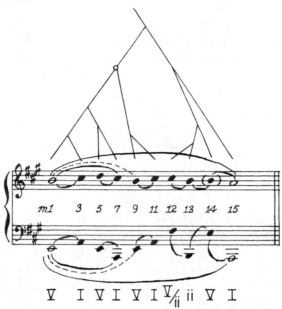

We will first derive the prolongational tree in 9.24, then discuss the musical consequences of the analysis. We assume the time-span reduction given in example 7.24, in which the initial V is the structural beginning of the piece. (As mentioned there, another interpretation is possible in which the first I chord is the structural beginning.)

Since the initial V forms a stable progression to the prolongational head, the final I, it is selected as the highest branch off the head. The next most time-span-important event is the V of the final cadence. In terms of prolongational connection alone, this could attach either as a prolongation of the initial V or as a progression to the final I. But time-span congruence (PRPR 2), prolongational importance of the endpoints (PRPR 4), and above all the cadential structure stipulated by PRPR 6 favor the latter attachment. This yields a structure with the geometry of the basic form but not its specific harmonic content: it is V–V–I rather than I–V–I.

The next attachment is the V in measures 9–10, which becomes a prolongation of the initial V. Within the region from this V to the end (the second phrase), the V/ii and the ii in measures 12–13 form a descending circle-of-fifths progression to the cadential V (PRPR 3) and so attach as left branches. The I in measure 11 is closer in diatonic collection to the preceding V than to the following V/ii, so it becomes a right branch (by stability condition 2 on PRPR 3). As a result, the second phrase in itself constitutes a normative structure.

In the first phrase, the Interaction Principle suggests that the V in measure 5 should attach next, as a prolongation of the initial V. However, a closer approximation to normative structure within this phrase is obtained by attaching the I in measure 7 first, with the V as its left branch. By parallelism (PRPR 5), the I in measure 3 behaves like the I in measure 11, attaching as a right branch to the initial V.

The nonparallelism in branching between the first two V–I progressions reflects the fact that the second is a cadence and the first is not, according to the criteria discussed in section 7.4. Alternatively, parallelism (PRPR 5) might dictate that the importance of the second V–I be reversed. These conflicting applications of PRPR 5 at different levels of structure contribute to the ambiguity of the piece.

The result is a balanced normative structure, altogether similar to the structure of a classical antecedent-consequent phrase like the K. 331 theme with one exception: the roles of I and V are exactly reversed on the largest left branch of the structure and all its elaborations. Thus the whole piece consists not of a I prolongation, as in the basic form, but of a V prolongation leading to a final cadence. The maximal point of tension in the piece, the transition from measure 11 to measure 12, emerges clearly in the tree as a transition from right to left branching.

An oddity of 9.24 is that the Is in measures 3, 7, and 11 are right branches of preceding Vs, a situation we have not previously encountered. This happens because, according to this interpretation, these Is are heard in the context of a V prolongation.

An alternative interpretation, in which the first I is the structural beginning, results in the prolongational reduction in 9.25, which we will not derive.

Although 9.25 satisfies the basic form, it suffers from at least two shortcomings. First, in 9.24 the most important V in the piece is the one in measure 1, which therefore functions both as structural beginning and as structural dominant. In 9.25, by contrast, the initial V is only a local elaboration; the structural beginning is the I in measure 3, and the structural dominant is the V in measure 14. But the weak register of the bass in measure 14 makes it an unconvincing structural dominant in comparison with the Vs in measures 1 and 9. Second, one's sense of parallelism between the two phrases depends more on the identity of the Vs in measures 1 and 9 than on the Is in measures 3 and 11, since the I in measure 11 does not complete its group but progresses on to the V/ii. Example 9.24 brings out the importance of the Vs to the parallelism, whereas 9.25 relies more heavily on the Is. In addition to these problems

with 9.25, it claims that the two major phrases of the piece do not exhibit normative structure. Thus there is some reason to prefer analysis 9.24 over 9.25, despite its nonconformance to the basic form. However, as in the time-span reduction, the piece probably should be ultimately treated as ambiguous between the two readings, with some additional options in the treatment of details.

An interesting feature of the Chopin A Major Prelude is that the melody could have been harmonized throughout with V–I progressions. However, this possibility would have been unacceptable in the tonal idiom, because, under either interpretation, 9.24 or 9.25, there would be no final prepared cadence, and hence no full normative structure. The way that Chopin toys with this possibility and then deviates from it contributes to the charm of the piece.

An even more decisive example of normative structure without basic form is the Brahms Intermezzo op. 76, no. 4. This piece begins on V and contains no occurrences of I at all until the arrival before the coda (measure 45). Thus the prolongational beginning cannot possibly be I. Moreover, there is no authentic cadence at the end; rather the bass descends chromatically to the prolongational ending, which is in turn prolonged by plagal cadences. Thus the piece is a major deviation from the *Ursatz* and the basic form. Nonetheless, it does display the geometry of normative prolongational structure, as shown in the harmonic sketch (9.26). It is this structure that permits the piece to be heard as a coherent (though unusual) example of a standard form, not so different in fact from the *Chorale St. Antoni*. In particular, the "cadential" function of the final $\flat\text{II}^{+6}$–I progression is inferred from its position in the normative structure.

Formalization of Prolongational Reduction

9.26

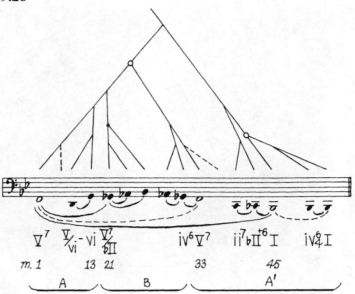

Normative Structure and Musical Complexity

Why should musical grammar include such a rule as PRPR 6? To convey the effect of the rule in a more general context, we observe that all the previous rules of time-span and prolongational reduction consider as maximally stable those structures in which virtually nothing happens. If a piece were to consist entirely of tonic chords and full cadences, these other rules for pitch organization would be blissfully happy, since there would be little if any conflict in pitch stability. Obviously, from the point of view of musical interest, such a piece would be unsatisfactory; *something* must happen. Consider, for example, what the Chopin A Major Prelude would sound like with V–I progressions throughout.

But simply to say that music must deviate somehow from total regularity would leave the shape of pieces virtually unconstrained. PRPR 6 addresses this problem. It requires that a piece have prolongational variety, so that a passage of total stasis (except to confirm a phrase ending) is heard as unusual. But the rule further says that not just any variety is desirable; the variety must be manifested as structured patterns of tension and relaxation. Since the constraint is stated in terms of types of connections among events, and since it is to an extent independent of surface rhythmic considerations, it leaves the composer free to satisfy it in innumerable interesting ways. And insofar as the rule applies to cadenced groups hierarchically from the phrase level up to the entire piece, its multilayered effects create pressure toward a musical surface of considerable complexity—and toward a complexity that increases with the size of the piece.

On the other hand, the complexity the rule engenders is not just gratu-itous complication. Rather, because it is patterned in terms of levels of structure, it produces a higher degree of coherence. Each event has a specific and unique function in the whole, in a way that would not be true of either a uniform string of events such as V–I–V–I–... or a random sequence. It may be inferred from other areas of cognition, such as vision and language (see Koffka 1935; Neisser 1967; Fodor, Bever, and Garrett 1974), that this strong structuring of the parts into the whole enhances comprehension and memory.

9.7
Binary Form and Sonata Form

As additional illustrations of prolongational derivations, this section de-velops trees for the major structural points in binary-form and sonata-form movements.

Figure 9.27 is a harmonic sketch of the larger levels of time-span reduction for a typical binary baroque dance form, Menuetto I of the Bach G Major Cello Suite.

9.27

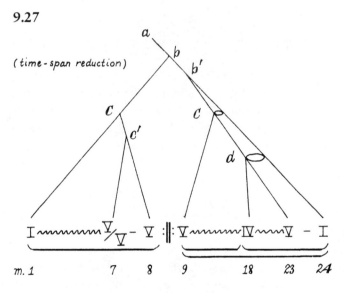

In such a piece, there is no important recurrence of I between the very beginning and the final cadence; thus there can be no large tonic prolon-gation inside of the basic form. The most time-span-important events within the basic form are the dominants in measures 8–9. How should these be attached? Superficially, one might think that they form a domi-nant prolongation to the final cadence, as in 9.28a. But such a structure would claim, counterintuitively, that the tension of the piece begins to defuse by the double bar (the midpoint of the piece). Moreover, in similar pieces in the minor mode, such as the sarabande of the C Minor Cello Suite, the point corresponding to measure 8 has the relative major instead

Formalization of Prolongational Reduction

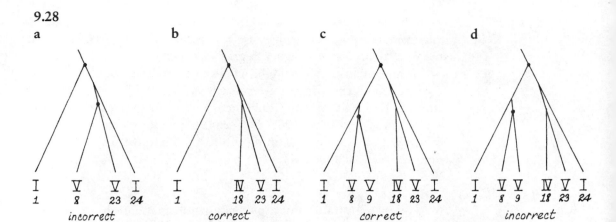

a b c d

I V V I
1 8 23 24
incorrect

I IV V I
1 18 23 24
correct

I V V IV V I
1 8 9 18 23 24
correct

I V V IV V I
1 8 9 18 23 24
incorrect

of the dominant. Here a prolongation to the dominant of the final cadence would be impossible; the relative major is heard as a departure from the initial tonic. One does not hear any great structural difference between the two alternatives, and in fact in the cello suites in minor keys Bach sometimes chooses the dominant minor and sometimes the relative major. Thus, for generality, 9.28a cannot be the correct structure for this piece.

The PRPRs create a different tree. Within the basic form, derived from level *b* of the time-span reduction, the most stable prolongational connection possible in the next two time-span levels is that between the IV chord in level *d* and the V of the final cadence; a weak left prolongation to the V in measure 8 or 9 would be considerably weaker. The Interaction Principle thus selects the IV as the next event added to the basic form, as shown in 9.28b.

Between the initial I and the IV, the dominants surrounding the double bar are most time-span-important. They do not form a strong prolongational connection to the following IV, but can be attached as a departure from the initial I. What is the correct way to do this? Two possibilities appear in 9.28c,d: in 9.28c the end of the first section is superordinate and the beginning of the second section is its elaboration; in 9.28d the reverse is the case.

Intuitively, 9.28c appears to be the correct choice. The end of the first section is a definite point of harmonic arrival, more important to the piece's progress than the beginning of the second section. This is clearer if we compare with structurally parallel pieces such as the sarabande of the C Minor Cello Suite. Here the first section ends on III, and the second section begins immediately with III^{b7}, already a departure from the point of stability. Again under the assumption that at large levels of structure many examples of this genre are structurally parallel, this comparison leads us to conclude that 9.28c is the correct structure for 9.27.

The preference rules favor this result. If the V in measure 9 is chosen first, as in 9.28d, the V in measure 8 must be attached as a relatively unstable left-branching weak prolongation. On the other hand, if the V in measure 8 is chosen first, measure 9 is attached as a right-branching prolongation, a more stable result overall. In other words, the relative weighting of prolongational connections favors making measure 8 a point of arrival for the first section, of which measure 9 is a continuation, rather than treating measure 8 as an anticipation of the second section.

Though it would be interesting to pursue this example further, we are concerned for the moment only with the larger aspects of the form. However, it is worth noting that, when the additional branches are filled in, the tree will satisfy the normative form (with the parenthesized Classical options in PRPR 6 omitted). Note that each section individually as well as the whole piece satisfies the structure, that neither section is a tonic prolongation, and that the prolongational beginning of the second section (the V in measure 9) is not directly connected to the prolongational ending. These three considerations further illustrate the flexibility of normative structure.

The antecedent-consequent and binary forms contain most of the elements necessary for constructing a prolongational skeleton for a movement in sonata-allegro form. Figure 9.29 presents a harmonic sketch for a typical example, with its grouping and time-span reduction. The double bar between the exposition and development is notated for convenience.[2]

9.29

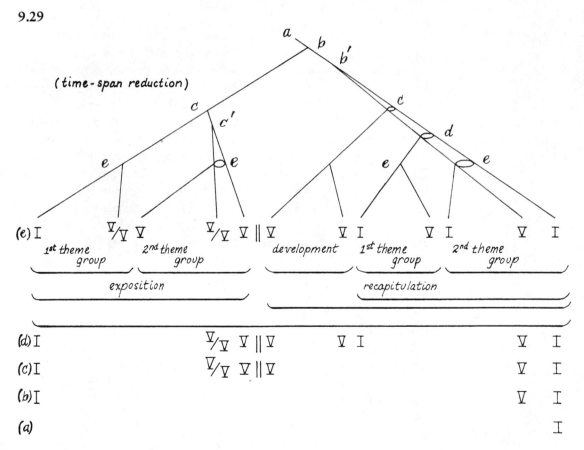

Formalization of Prolongational Reduction

Within the basic form, the most stable prolongational connection is the strong prolongation from the beginning to the start of the recapitulation; the Interaction Principle permits this to be chosen as the most important event in the region, as shown in 9.30. Thus the presence of the recapitulation results in a major difference in prolongational structure from the binary form; the central dominant is no longer the most important event in the interior of the piece, but is displaced by the tonic prolongation.

9.30

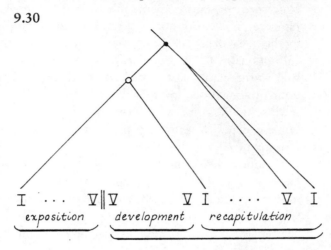

The prolongation in 9.30 breaks the piece into two prolongational regions: the exposition and development together, and the recapitulation. In the region consisting of the exposition and development, we have a situation not unlike the binary form: the highest two levels of time-span reduction contain only Vs and V/Vs, so there is no prominent tonic prolongation. The most time-span-important events are the Vs surrounding the double bar. How should they be attached? For the same intuitive and formal reasons as in the case of the central dominants in binary form, the beginning of the development should be a right branch off the end of the exposition. This leaves the two possibilities shown in 9.31. These are equally consistent with stable prolongational connection as stated so far (PRPR 3), but 9.31a is favored by time-span segmentation (PRPR 2) and the prolongational importance of the initial I (PRPR 4).

In addition, the choice of 9.31a is reinforced by appeal to a distinction among the structural functions of the dominant, not previously incorporated in the theory. As in the binary form, the Vs surrounding the double bar are tonicized Vs; other key areas (most notably III in movements in minor) can be substituted without changing the overall sense of the piece. By contrast, the V at the end of the development is a half-cadential V; the main substitution for it would be a full cadence whose resolution overlapped with the recapitulation.

9.31

a

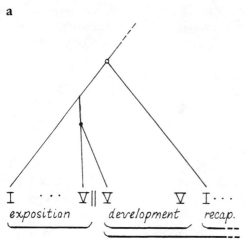

b

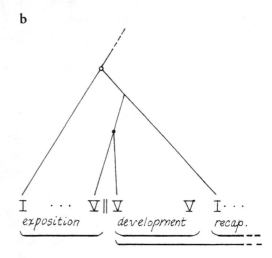

There appears to be a difference in the prolongational behavior of these two V functions. As seen in previous examples, the cadential V can function as either a departure from or a progression to a I, depending on circumstances. But a tonicized V, like other alternative key areas, is heard more naturally as a departure from a preceding I than as a step in relaxing to a following I. This distinction might be incorporated as a refinement in the stability conditions for prolongational connection in order to reinforce the choice of 9.31a over 9.31b. (It would be invoked in binary form as well, reinforcing the structure in 9.28c over other alternatives.)

With the division of the piece by the central dominants, there are now three regions to consider. We deal with the development first. The end of the development attaches either as a prolongation of the beginning of the development or as a progression to the recapitulation. The two possibilities are shown with dashed lines in 9.32.

9.32

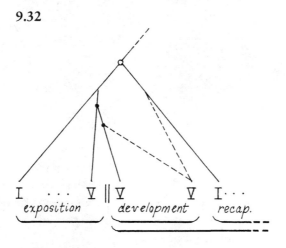

Formalization of Prolongational Reduction

Here movements may differ or be ambiguous. Time-span segmentation (PRPR 2) favors the right-branching reading; prolongational importance (PRPR 4) favors left branching. However, a further consideration often resolves the ambiguity. The half-cadential V at the end of the development is usually heard within the diatonic pitch collection of the following tonic, whereas the V at the beginning of the development is heard within the diatonic collection of the dominant key area. Hence, the half-cadential V forms a stronger prolongational connection with the following I, and attaches as a left branch.

Either of two common variants in sonata movements also favors the left-branching reading. If the development ends with a full cadence that overlaps with the recapitulation, the resolution of the full cadence is very close in time-span segmentation to its V, overriding the connection to the beginning of the development. Likewise, if the development begins (or the exposition ends) in an area other than V, the connection from there to the cadential dominant is less stable, so the left-branching progression to I is again favored. Still, the structures of some developments favor a right-branching ending, as shown by the dashed branch in 9.32.

Next we attach the structural boundaries of the exposition. The problem here is where the beginning of the second theme-group should attach—as a progression away from the initial tonic (9.33a) or as an anticipation of the end of the exposition (9.33b).

9.33

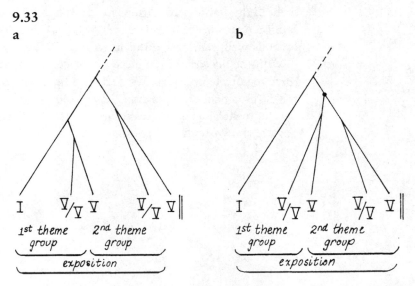

Intuition favors 9.33b, so that the second theme-group in itself exhibits the basic form. For the rules to achieve this result, the conditions for prolongational stability must favor connection through common diatonic collection—even in the relatively unstable left-branching prolongation—over departure to a new key.

This refinement of the stability conditions is useful for other purposes as well, so it is not an arbitrary decision restricted to this case alone. For example, in a minuet whose trio is in a contrasting key, the trio intuitively forms its own independent patterns of tension and relaxation, being heard as a unified insertion between the minuet and the da capo. If we weight stability of prolongational connection strongly in favor of maintaining diatonic collection, the desired result is obtained, as in 9.34.

9.34

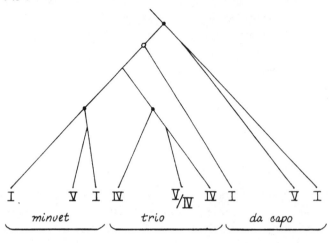

9.35

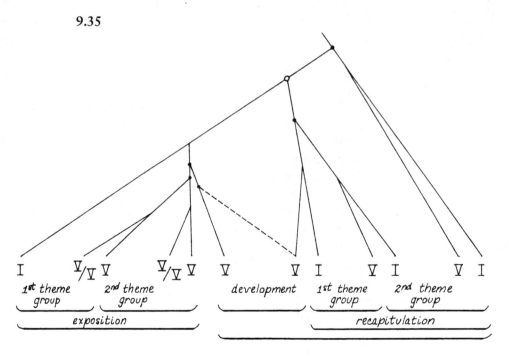

Formalization of Prolongational Reduction

Returning to 9.33, we see that the V/V at the end of the first theme-group forms the most stable prolongational connection as a left branch, as shown in 9.33b. This completes the exposition.

In the recapitulation, the beginning of the second theme-group forms a different connection than in the exposition. Because it is a I rather than a V, its most stable attachment is as a prolongation of the beginning of the recapitulation. In turn, the end of the first theme-group, a V, is now between two Is. It may attach to the earlier I because of congruence with time-span segmentation (PRPR 2). However, it is more usual to hear this event as leading into the second theme-group, by parallelism (PRPR 5) with the exposition.

Putting together all these fragments, 9.30–9.33, we arrive at 9.35 as the tree for the entire movement. This diagram expresses the structural counterpoint between the major grouping divisions of the piece and the major patterns of tension and relaxation.

9.8 Reflections on Musical Cognition and Music as an Art

PRPR 6 (normative structure) is the last of the rules of musical grammar to be developed in this study. As this rule is the first to embody the overarching influence of large-scale prolongational structure on the details of musical form, we regret having to break off our discussion of musical grammar here. Still, there is something important to be learned from our having taken so long to reach this point: how abstract musical intuition is. If our theory of normative structure of musical phrases is correct, the structure is specified in terms of relationships of prolongational connection among structurally significant events, not in terms of any specified sequence of events. Moreover, the structurally significant events are chosen in large part because of their importance in time-span reduction, not just for their superficial melodic and harmonic content. But time-span reduction itself represents a considerable degree of abstraction from the musical surface, since it crucially involves the grouping and metrical structures, which in turn represent properties of the music not directly presented in the surface sequence of pitch-events. We believe that the great complexity of this mapping from the musical surface to prolongational structure, and the comparative lack of prescriptive constraints within that mapping, are among the deeper reasons why tonal music is such a rich art.

Some readers may feel uneasy with the complexity of the apparatus we have introduced to describe musical intuition, particularly that used to derive prolongational structure. Beyond the sheer empirical power of the theory to describe the characteristics of specific pieces and of tonal music in general, we offer three arguments that support this complexity.

First, we have been careful to relate every step in our development of musical grammar to musical intuition. The four components of musical structure each express a different aspect of musical intuition, and almost all of the preference rules have been justified on the basis of readily audible characteristics of straightforward examples. The complexity of tonal music arises from the interaction of these individually fairly simple principles; in particular, many of the possibilities for musical interest arise from conflicts among competing principles. Thus we have tried to show as completely as possible that each part of this complex whole is grounded in what the listener hears.

Second, anyone who has thought about musical structure in any depth ought to expect it to be this complex. One constantly reads statements such as ". . . the interpretation of music—and this is what analysis should be—is an art requiring experience, understanding, and sensitivity" (Cooper and Meyer 1960, p. 9). One is inclined to call an artifact or activity *art* when one cannot consciously decompose or reproduce one's intuitions about it, and when one at the same time senses that these intuitions are complex and subtle. If the principles underlying musical intuition were simple and easily discovered, the sense of music as an art would hardly be so strong. Indeed, the complexity of the grammar presented here is still only part of the story. We have explicitly left open some important aspects of musical structure, and have not even begun to approach the problem of musical affect, so crucial to artistic concerns.

A third justification for the complexity of the grammar is its status as a theory of musical cognition—what the experienced listener knows that enables him to comprehend music (and, for that matter, what an experienced performer knows that enables him to make music comprehensible). Many people find it hard to believe that mental operations could be so elaborate, especially since the structures they manipulate are so far removed from the musical surface. However, we find no difficulty in accepting a grammar of this complexity as a model of human knowledge. In the only other areas of human cognitive function where we are aware of theories whose scope is comparable to the present theory of music, namely visual perception and language, the principles governing mental function have been shown to be of commensurate complexity. In both of these areas one is, if anything, even less consciously aware of the complexity of one's intuitions than in music. Unconscious processes of amazing complexity and subtlety are by no means incompatible with a conscious impression of great ease and fluidity, and with the sense that one learns these cognitive tasks by "just picking them up" from experience with sufficient environmental stimulation. Our theory of music is no different from these other areas in this respect. We would have been surprised if it had proved fundamentally simpler.

10
Some Analyses

In this chapter we present a variety of suggestive analyses generated by the theory. For reasons of space we will not attempt to derive these analyses in any detail, but will confine our remarks to points of special interest. It will be understood that, within a limited range, alternate "preferred" analyses might also be predicted by the rules.

10.1
A Complex Rhythmic Example

Usually the periodicity of metrical structure—whether it is in or out of phase with grouping structure—proceeds in a regular correspondence with grouping structure, so that parallel passages receive parallel metrical analyses (metrical preference rule 1). When groups become irregular in length, either a large-scale metrical adjustment of some kind occurs or large-scale metrical levels simply fail to apply. But Schubert, in the A Major Waltz from his *Valses Sentimentales,* op. 50 (example 10.1), accomplishes the feat of maintaining hypermetrical beats four bars apart throughout, within the irregular grouping context of an AA′BA″ form composed of 10+8+10+10 bars; this is illustrated schematically in 10.2.

In the grouping analysis shown in 10.1 and 10.2, the A and A′ sections are straightforward: the theme twice forms symmetrical units of 2+2+2+2 bars, at the next level 4+4 bars, then 8 bars. However, the two introductory bars of tonic harmony turn the A section finally into a 10-bar group; the A′ section works as an 8-bar group because the equivalent tonic harmony has already been supplied by the final chord of the A section. In the B section, one at first tends—out of a "conservative" hearing of group structure—to hear the grouping as 2+2=4 bars, and so on, parallel to the patterns previously established (the dashed grouping slur in 10.1). But measures 21–24 are repeated exactly in measures 25—28, forming parallel groups (grouping preference rule 6); consequently, a "radical" hearing attaches the crucial 2-bar group in measures

10.1

10.2

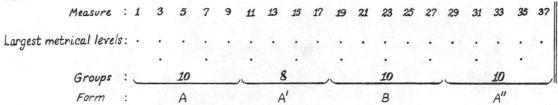

21–22 to the ensuing two bars instead of the previous two bars. The grouping structure of the B section thereby becomes identical to that of the A section $(2+2+2+2+2=2+4+4=2+8=10)$, and likewise (GPR 6) for the reprise. In this light, the right hand in measures 29–30 fills in the space, so to speak, that was left vacant in measures 1–2.

In the metrical analysis in 10.1 and 10.2 we note some conflict concerning the placement of the largest level of beats: Should they occur on the downbeats of measures 1,5,9,... or on the downbeats of measures 3,7,11,... ? Following Schachter 1980, we have chosen the second alternative, even though it results in a cadential $^6_4$ in a relatively weak metrical position (measure 5, etc.); mitigating factors are the more in-phase pattern (MPR 2) and the continuance of regularity (MPR 10) into the B section, where the strongest beats obviously take place on the downbeats of measures 19, 23, and 27. This regularity then persists—though again ambiguously—to the end of the piece.

Under this interpretation, then, the metrical periodicity proceeds uniformly throughout, despite irregularities in grouping structure. A subtle consequence of this analysis is that the motive rising to measure 17 receives a different metrical interpretation in measure 23. More broadly, the large-scale metrical structure of the B section reverses that of the A section: the strongest beat is on the downbeat of its first bar instead of its third, and so on. (The A′ section, because it lacks the two introductory bars and hence begins next to a strong beat, prepares the way for this change.) Finally, because the B section is 10 bars long, the grouping-meter relationship in the A″ section automatically reverts to what it was at the beginning. Thus the larger grouping-meter parallelism is satisfied in the end, despite intervening divergences.

It might be argued that in certain tonal pieces grouping and meter can become completely independent of one another, each going its own way, forming its own articulative structure, and occasionally converging with the other at a structural downbeat.[1] Although such structures are expressible within our analytic system, we have found no example more complex in this regard than this Schubert waltz. In a sense, it can happen here because the piece is a dance—there are enough conventional regularities to permit the perception of significant divergences in patterning between grouping and meter. In other words, it takes a great deal to override MPR 1.

10.2 Motivic Structure and Time-Span Reduction

In this section we illustrate some ways in which time-span reduction can be useful in illuminating motivic relationships.

First consider the rondo theme from Beethoven's *Pathétique* Sonata, op. 13. As indicated by the dashed circles in 10.3, the phrase begins and ends with almost identical motivic material at the musical surface. Yet this obvious relationship is partially obscured because the main notes of the motive assume, respectively, virtually opposite reductional functions: the E♭ on the downbeat of measure 1 is the structural beginning of the phrase, whereas the corresponding E♭ in measure 7 is only part of an embellishing cadential ⁶₄; the D in measure 1 is a passing tone, whereas the corresponding D in measure 7 is part of the cadence for the entire phrase; the C on the downbeat of measure 3 is only part of an unfolding of the opening tonic chord, whereas the corresponding C in measure 8 resolves the whole passage. In the tree of 10.3, parallel treatment of parallel passages (time-span reduction preference rule 4) must give way to the more global factors of the structural beginning and cadence (TSRPRs 7 and 8). This conflict between surface similitude and underlying function gives the theme much of its particular character.

10.3

The opposite case—where reductionally parallel relationships reveal underlying motivic connections not readily apparent at the musical surface—is much more common in music of the Classical period (though not in that of the late nineteenth century). By way of illustration, consider the opening of the minuet of Beethoven's Sonata, op. 22 (example 10.4).

It is evident that the motivic structure of measures 5–8 neatly mirrors that of measures 1–4 (example 10.5); this would emerge explicitly at the eighth-note level of time-span reduction. The phrases of the contrasting section (measures 9–16) expand the phrase-opening motive and retain the cadential formula (other surface connections exist, but we will ignore them here).

10.5

To see in a deeper way what is going on, we must consult relevant portions of the time-span tree and their relations to the grouping and metrical analyses. In the first group at the smallest grouping level, an anacrusis simply moves to a more stable event on the downbeat (tree fragment *a* in 10.6).

10.6

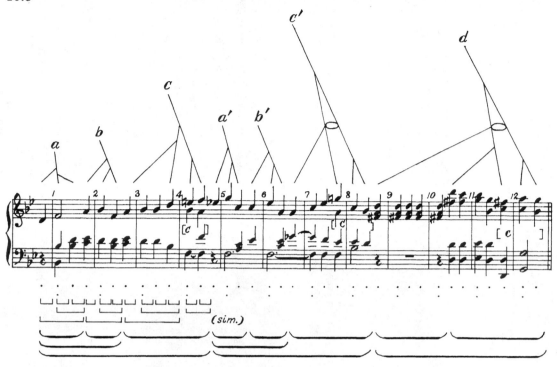

In the second group, however, the event on the downbeat "resolves" to a more stable event on the second beat (TSRPR 2), producing a second left branch at the immediately smaller reductional level (tree fragment *b*). This pattern then continues in the third group, in which the motive is extended to produce a 2-bar group; the anacrusis to measure 3 itself becomes a left branch to the anacrusis to measure 4 (tree fragment *c*). (Note, incidentally, how inappropriate the cadence in measure 4 would be if there were no appoggiatura; this is because it must "rhyme" in the time-span reduction with measure 2.) Similar patterns persist throughout the second phrase (tree fragments *a'*, *b'*, and *c'*). In the third phrase, the pattern is expanded still further to encompass a 4-bar group (tree fragment *d*). In all these cases (except for tree fragment *a*), the underlying "gesture" is one of anacrusis to appoggiatura to resolution, with the anacrusis elaborated in a progressive fashion. In a sense, this abstract tree structure, together with its associated grouping and metrical structures, is the real "motive"—a rhythmic motive—beneath the surface variety of the music.

Now we turn to the beginning of Beethoven's "Tempest" Sonata, op. 31, no. 2 (example 10.7), in which the same "linear motive" emerges

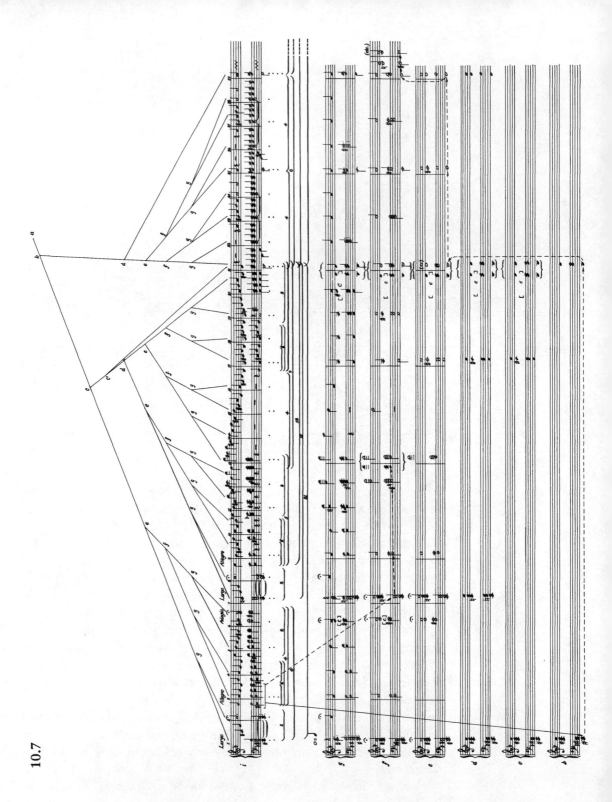

at widely different reductional levels.[2] In measures 2–3 the line C♯–D–E–F appears in the bass (bracketed in 10.7.) The C♯ of this line stems from the registrally isolated low C♯ in measure 1. Only in retrospect does one become aware that this low C♯ itself initiates a large-scale unfolding of the identical motive, so that its quick statement in measures 2–3 seems like a surface foreshadowing. This larger statement is indicated by the dashed arrows in the secondary notation in 10.7. At level *b*, the low C♯ is finally answered in its own register by the D in measure 21, with the large-scale arrival of the tonic. At this point the pace of the motive quickens, the D proceeding to E and F at level *e* (measures 21 and following). Surface motivic associations (the rising arpeggio in measures 1–2, 21–22, and so on) reinforce these connections.

Meanwhile, a version of the motive involving an augmented second has appeared at level *f* (E–F–G♯–A in measures 7–13). This fragment is then picked up, again at level *f*, in the lower register in the sequential passage following measure 21. Finally, the combined pattern extends, beyond the music shown in 10.7, by transposition (D–E–F–G♯–A to A–B–C–D♯–E) to the E pedal beginning in measure 41. The different rates at which this linear motive unfolds provide an important means for unifying the disparate tempi of this movement.

The passage in 10.7 is instructive for another purpose as well: it is a good example of a structural anacrusis (measures 1–20) resolving on a structural downbeat (measure 21), as discussed in section 2.4. Note how the downbeat of measure 21 represents the convergence of three separate parameters: meter (a large-level beat), grouping (large-scale grouping boundaries, in this case strengthened by an overlap), and time-span reduction (a large-scale harmonic arrival). Only where all three conditions are met simultaneously do we speak of a structural downbeat. Note also how the duration of the structural anacrusis, from measure 1 to the downbeat of measure 21, is indicated by the grouping analysis and level *b* of the reduction.

One feature of the reduction itself deserves special comment: the choice of the opening V⁶ as the head of the entire passage. One might instead select the tonic chord in measure 3, on grounds of pitch stability (TSRPR 2). This tonic, however, is heard within the context of a dominant prolongation (see measures 1–6 at level *f*); in other words, TSRPR 6 overrrides TSRPR 2 here. Further supporting the V⁶ are its low bass register (TSRPR 3) and its position in the larger grouping structure as a structural beginning (TSRPR 8). This latter factor also supports the choice of the opening V⁶ over the tonic arrival in measure 21; but the really decisive factor in this case is parallelism (TSRPR 4), since any equivalent to measure 21 is omitted in the recapitulation (in large part because its motivic material is exhausted in the development section). (In order to optimally fulfill normative structure (PRPR 6), the prolongational reduction would reverse the relative prominence of the V⁶ in measure 1 and the i in measure 21.)

Each of the following prolongational reductions will be preceded by the time-span reduction (along with the associated grouping and metrical analyses) from which it is derived. We begin with the opening portion of Mozart's G Minor Symphony, as a reductional addendum to the detailed rhythmic analyses in chapters 2–4. Then we analyze Bach's C Major Prelude from volume I of *The Well-Tempered Clavier* and Schubert's "Morgengruss" from the song cycle *Die Schöne Müllerin;* in both of these cases, issues of general interest arise. Finally, we consider a complex development section, from Mozart's D Major Quintet K. 593.[3]

In example 10.8 (a simplified version of the first 22 bars of the G Minor Symphony), the metrical analysis duplicates that of "hypothesis A" discussed in section 2.2. The grouping analysis is complicated and depends in part on reductional considerations (GPR 7); for example, it would seem reductionally inappropriate to connect the introductory bar (measure 1) at a larger grouping level than that in 10.8. The most difficult grouping decision concerns measures 14–16: should the subsidiary woodwind line receive a separate group, or should we maintain the principle of nonpolyphonic grouping analyses? We have chosen the latter course, with the result that measures 12–16 are analyzed simply as an extended answer (GPR 6) to measures 10–11. Here, and also in measure 1, subgroup bracketing fills the time-span breach where the grouping analysis fails to segment the musical surface beyond a certain level of detail.

In cases where the grouping analysis is so irregular, the assignment of levels in the time-span reduction becomes somewhat arbitrary. We have therefore taken the added step in 10.8 of labeling the groups according to their corresponding reductional levels; in-between grouping levels are given primed letters. (The subgroup bracketings in measures 1 and 16 receive the label *e* because they would have extended through that time-span—the 2-bar level—if they had not been "cut off" by grouping boundaries.)

The secondary notation in 10.8 also requires an adjustment. Normally we notate events over the duration of their relevant group. But this becomes cumbersome when grouping and meter are as out of phase as they are here. Hence we have opted to notate the durations not according to grouping structure but according to metrical periodicity; the secondary notation thereby becomes easier to read and hear. The tree is not affected by this change. At the same time, however, it becomes more difficult to correlate the tree with the secondary notation; so we have added grouping markings within the secondary notation itself to show which events are available for analysis at any given stage. For example, the groups marked *e* beneath level *f* in the secondary notation indicate the selectional possibilities for level *e*.

The prolongational reduction shown in 10.9 follows without complication from 10.8—that is, the prolongational reduction preference rules

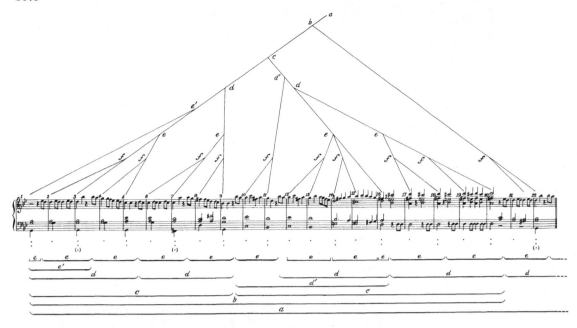

are mutually reinforcing. (Obviously, the prolongational tree could be carried out in more detail.)

10.9

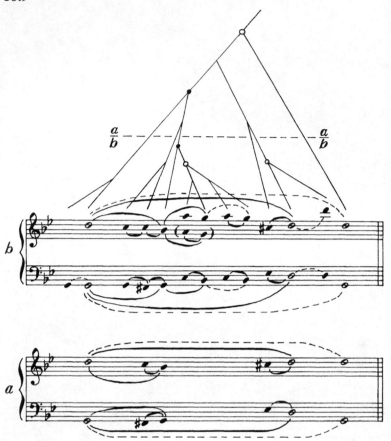

Turning now to the Bach C Major Prelude, represented at the measure level in 10.10, we find that the uniform surface of the music yields an unusual paucity of evidence for the grouping and metrical analyses—and hence for time-span segmentation. But this does not mean that grouping and metrical issues of interest do not arise. Consider first the hypermetrical structure. The piece seems to begin in a hypermetrical 4/4, and clearly proceeds from measure 24 (the dominant arrival) to the end in the same fashion. Thus there must be either a "missing" measure or a hypermetrical adjustment between the beginning and measure 24. In the nineteenth century an added measure was widely accepted between measures 22 and 23 (a i$^6_4$), presumably to rectify the irregularity in metrical periodicity (as well as to eliminate the diminished third in the bass line). Alternatively, one might hear hypermetrical 4/4 bars until measure 21, then a hypermetrical 3/4 until measure 24. At the opposite extreme, Schenker 1932 readjusts the hypermetrical 4/4 already at measure 4, because of the formulaic extension of the tonic in measures 1–4 (measures 1 and 4 are in a sense equal). This, however, produces an idiosyncratically out-of-phase pattern with the grouping structure, which is clearly four bars long at the beginning; MPR 1 militates against this solution. We prefer to locate the change at measure 8, in conjunction with a combined grouping overlap and metrical deletion. Measures 5–6 and 7–8 form parallel groups, as do measures 8–11 and 16–19; thus, by GPR 6, measure 8 functions in both directions. Also, since there is no essential harmonic motion from measure 8 to measure 9, it is plausible to think of measure 8 as an unequivocal suspension, hence in a strong metrical position (MPR 8). The result is shown in 10.10.

The larger grouping levels are difficult to determine. For example, should measures 5–11 belong to measures 1–4, or to measures 12–19, within the larger group of measures 1–19? Should measures 20–23 belong to measures 1–19 or to measures 20–35? In both cases, the issue has been decided by the resultant time-span and prolongational reductions (GPR 7). This is a good illustration of how interactive the individual components are—in short, how holistic musical perception is, hence how difficult it is to develop an algorithm for the derivation of structural descriptions.

A few remarks are needed about the time-span reduction in 10.10. First, the arpeggiations have already been fused (time-span reduction well-formedness rule 3b) at the measure level. Second, we have interpolated a missing chord function (a ii^6_5) (TSRWFR 3c) between measures 21 and 22, since the suspended E in measure 21 does not resolve to a D until measure 23, by which time the chord has changed. In our analysis, this underlying ii^6_5 stands behind the entire subdominant passage (measures 20–23). Third, we have taken the liberty in level *b* of the secondary notation of raising the structural V (measure 24) an octave, to bring it into the "obligatory register" of the piece as a whole. This operation would not be meaningful at smaller levels because of the descent to the lower octave in measures 6–19; the events at the lower octave must be eliminated first. Strictly, this operation is not part of the grammar. We have included it here, however, to show how octave transfers might eventually be incorporated into the theory not just in a general way but at specific reductional levels.

The locus of analytic interest in the Bach C Major Prelude lies in its prolongational reduction (10.11). Beneath its multifarious branchings (which derive by a straightforward application of PRPRs 1 and 3), there is an underlying regularity: doubly or triply embedded left-branching progressions contained within a (strong or weak) prolongation. As the brackets below the music in 10.11 show, every event except the opening tonic is implicated in or subsumed under such a structure. The beautiful coherence of the piece resides to a great extent in this abstract prolongational feature.

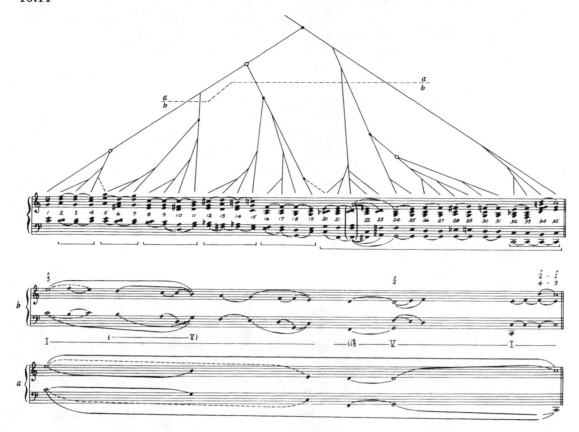

Let us see what this feature means in terms of tension and relaxation. In the first half of the piece, each motion toward tension takes place at a relatively large level (the prolongations of I in measures 4 and 19, the tonicizing movement to V in measure 11). Each of these global tensings subsumes strong local patterns of relaxing; twice these relationships are further elaborated through anticipatory left weak prolongations (measures 5–7 to 8–11, measures 12–15 to 16–19). The very ending (measures 32–35) echoes these local patterns, specifically mirroring the opening (measures 1–4).

The largest levels of the prelude exhibit the same pattern—only here, after the tensing to measure 19, the relaxing pattern also occurs over long spans of time. The music begins its final relaxation already at measure 20. As the tree shows, this enormous expansion of the final cadence is accomplished by successive elaborations of the subdominant (measures 20–23), the dominant (measures 24–31), and the tonic (measures 32–35). But such an expansion of the final relaxation could not be maintained if local levels simultaneously relaxed; so here, especially in the elaboration of the dominant (measures 24–31), the prevailing local pattern is broken by a series of tensing right branches. Thus the uncommon circumstance arises that the moment of greatest tension (that is, the most deeply embedded right branch, measure 29), takes place within the elaboration of the final cadence.

A few words about the secondary notation in 10.11: At level *b* we have slightly transformed the outer voice-leading to show the underlying pattern of descending 10ths in measures 4–19. In measures 24–35 we have added some inner voicing, together with the numbering of scale degrees, to demonstrate how the melodic line resolves simultaneously on the tonic in the upper register and on the third in the middle register. (This analysis corresponds closely to that of Schenker 1932.) Level *a* shows the overall basic form and normative structure (with added right prolongation) (compare 8.28b). It is unusual for these events to spread out so evenly across an entire piece. This, plus the unarticulated musical surface, gives the piece the character of a single overarching phrase.

Before turning to the next example, we must interpolate a remark about harmonic rhythm. As normally conceived, harmonic rhythm is the pattern of durations produced by changes in harmony at the musical surface. This conception can easily be deepened by considering it also to be the pattern of durations created by any given level of prolongational reduction. For example, the harmonic rhythm of the C Major Prelude is not just one harmony per bar, but—among other levels—19 bars of I (measures 1–19), 3 bars of ii$^6_5$ (measures 21–23, with measure 20 as transitional), 8 bars of V^7 (measures 24–31), and 4 bars of I (measures 32–35) (level *a* in the secondary notation in 10.11).

Schubert's song "Morgengruss" also begins its final cadence unusually early, but in this case the harmonic rhythm of its global normative structure is so bizarre that one suspects the actual music to be a deviation from a more prototypical pattern. Before this point can be addressed, however, we must look at its grouping, metrical, and time-span reductional analyses (10.12). (In the example, the introduction and strophic repetitions have been omitted. The music is already reduced to the quarter-note level. The voice and piano have been compressed into one; the parentheses in measures 6–7 and 17–19 indicate the timbrally subordinate repetitions for piano alone.)

To abbreviate this discussion, let us assume as given the metrical and time-span reductional analyses. The grouping, however, deserves special comment. In 10.12 the solid slurs denote the selected groupings, the dashed slurs alternate possibilities. The first ambiguity concerns the status of the piano repetitions in measures 6–7 and 17–19. Are they extensions of two parallel 6-bar phrases (measures 1–6 and 12–17) (GPR 6), or are they echoes of immediately preceding material (measures 5–6 and 15–17) (also GPR 6)? Both are true; we have chosen the latter parallelism because the former would excessively elevate the piano repetitions in the time-span reduction (GPR 7).

The second ambiguity in the grouping has to do with how a 3-part form (ABA') groups at the next larger level. There are three possibilities: ABA'=AB+A'=the piece, ABA'=A+BA'=the piece, or ABA'=the piece (no two-part division). The last possibility is the least interesting because it gives the least structure, so we will disregard it. That leaves AB+A' or A+BA'. The problem again concerns which segments are to be construed as parallel. In 10.12, are measure 1 and measure 12 parallel beginnings (in which case the form is AB+A'), or are measures 6–7 and measures 16–19 parallel endings (in which case the form is A+BA')? (As discussed in note 2 to chapter 9, the same issue arises with sonata form, historically as well as analytically.) Here we have chosen AB+A', largely because the B section (measures 8–11) strongly prolongs the V in measures 5–7 (GPR 7). But the real point is the ambiguity itself. The rhyme scheme (aab/ccb) and the rhythmic patterns in the voice support the parallelism between measures 6–7 and 16–19 (A+BA'), whereas the narrative structure of the first verse[4]—the forthright action of the first poetic line, three anxious questions in the second to fifth lines, followed by the apparent resolution of the sixth line—favors the grouping together of measures 5–11 and the parallelism of measure 1 and measure 12 (AB+A'). Schubert has it both ways.[5]

A consequence of the AB+A' grouping is that the final cadence (measures 11–12) does not function in the time-span reduction (10.12) at any grouping level smaller than the piece itself. This seems intuitively correct, since when the I arrives in measure 12 it seems like the beginning of the reprise (A'), not the structural ending. This peculiar musical situation originates in the dramatic situation, which is best discussed after an examination of the prolongational reduction.

Included with the prolongational tree in 10.13 are the hypermetrical structure and the AB+A' grouping levels. Bar lines are added at measure 5 and measure 12 to emphasize that these are the points of structural arrival (V and I, respectively); motivic detail (as well as the rhyme scheme) supports the association of these two moments. The tree brings out these connections by describing measures 5–11 as a V prolongation and measures 12–19 as a corresponding I prolongation. Thus, from the vantage of prolongational analysis, the final cadence actually begins at measure 5. For this assignment to be made, closeness of pitch connection (PRPR 3) (the strong right prolongation of the V in measures 5–11) must override time-span importance (PRPR 1), since the V in measure 11 is one level more important than the V in measure 6 in the time-span reduction.

The difficulty with this analysis is that the V in measures 5–6 feels like a half cadence, not part of the final cadence. For the rules to predict this intuition, the alternative grouping A+BA' must be adopted to create a time-span reduction in which the Vs in measures 6 and 11 separate at the next smaller level. Then, with added support from PRPR 2 (congruence), PRPR 1 can override PRPR 3. The result appears in 10.14 (sketched at a

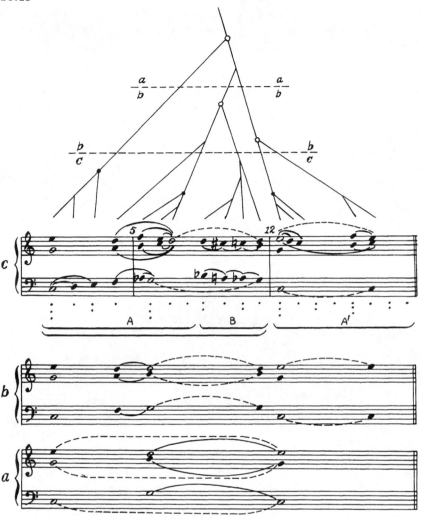

degree of detail comparable to level *b* in 10.13). Here the V at the end of the A section is a right-branching departure, and the V of the B section resolves—preceded by the embedded subdominant progressions in measures 8–10—in a full cadence to measure 12.

10.14

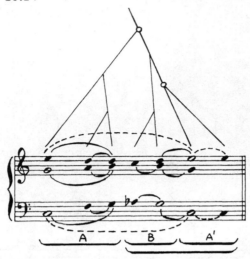

On balance we feel that the strength of the V prolongation in measures 5–11 favors 10.13 over 10.14. Moreover, the dramatic situation supports this preference (this consideration is beyond the predictions of the rules). The hero greets the miller maid; she withdraws, and he fearfully mulls over the reasons for this action over a V prolongation, replete with ominous chromatic upper neighbors in the bass (measure 5, measures 8–10); then he resolves to make a new beginning (A′), but fatally fails to leave, in the form of a harmonically static tonic pedal (measures 12–19). Thus his first crisis of expectation (measures 4–6) is indeed the beginning of the end.

This brings us finally to the odd harmonic rhythm of the global normative structure in 10.13. Usually, as in the piano introduction to "Morgengruss," the initial tonic prolongation covers a relatively long span compared with the left-branching relaxations at the final cadence. But in the song proper, the opposite holds: three bars of I, one bar of ii⁶; but then seven bars of V, followed by eight bars of a I that only begins as if going somewhere. The absence in the A′ section of any subdominant function and of any bass-supported dominant (except in the piano echo) causes the tensing-relaxing branching conditions for normative structure to be found back near the beginning, in measures 2–6. Presumably the hero started with other intentions—either with a quick, resolving I–ii⁶–V–I, as "rehearsed" in the introduction, or with an antecedent-consequent period (measures 1–6 answered by a resolving parallel phrase).

The actual prolongational structure of the song embodies an unexpected deviation from his hopes.

It is an open question how well a formal music theory can incorporate partially extramusical areas such as "dramatic" expectations, fulfillments, and disappointments. Although our theory does not directly address these concerns, we hope that it can be useful as a tool for discussing them precisely.

To conclude this section, we will attempt a prolongational reduction of the development of the first movement of Mozart's D Major Quintet, K. 593. First consider the prolongational reduction of the phrase that both opens and closes the allegro (10.15). The dashed lines at the top of the tree indicate the prolongational alternatives for the head of the phrase, depending on its position in the time-span reduction (PRPR 1), which in turn follows from the grouping. The chief reason this phrase can end as well as begin the allegro is that it amply fulfills the tensing-relaxing pattern of normative structure; it provides the prolongational criterion for closure. As will be seen, the development section functions as an enlargement of this phrase.

Figure 10.16 repeats the schematic prolongational tree for sonata form developed in section 9.7. We are concerned here with the prolongational region bracketed (x) — from the tonicized V at the end of the exposition to the I at the beginning of the recapitulation. As discussed in section 9.7, the V at the end of the development might attach either as a prolongation of the V at the end of the exposition or as a progression to the I beginning the recapitulation (see the dashed branch attaching at either a or b in 10.16).

Now turn to 10.17, an already highly reduced version of the development section of K. 593. The circled Roman numerals at the far left and right signify the opening tonic and the final cadence, respectively; the dashed line slicing across the upper region of the tree isolates the global normative structure of the entire movement. The region bracketed (x) beneath the music and the branching attachments marked a and b correspond to the identical labelings in 10.16. As the tree in 10.17 indicates, we have selected attachment a for the structural V at the end of the development (measure 138), because it is locally tonicized and hence forms a strong prolongation (PRPR 3) with the structural V at the end of the exposition (measure 89). (However, this local tonicization is undermined by the previous descending-fifths sequence having progressed all the way to the subdominant (measure 133); so attachment b is also plausible.)

Thus both the opening phrase (10.15) and the development (10.17) are contained within prolongations. But the analogy goes much farther than this. In motivic and grouping structure, the development forms two parts (measures 106–122 and 123–144) corresponding exactly to the two parts of the opening phrase (measures 1–4 and 5–8 in 10.15). (Measures

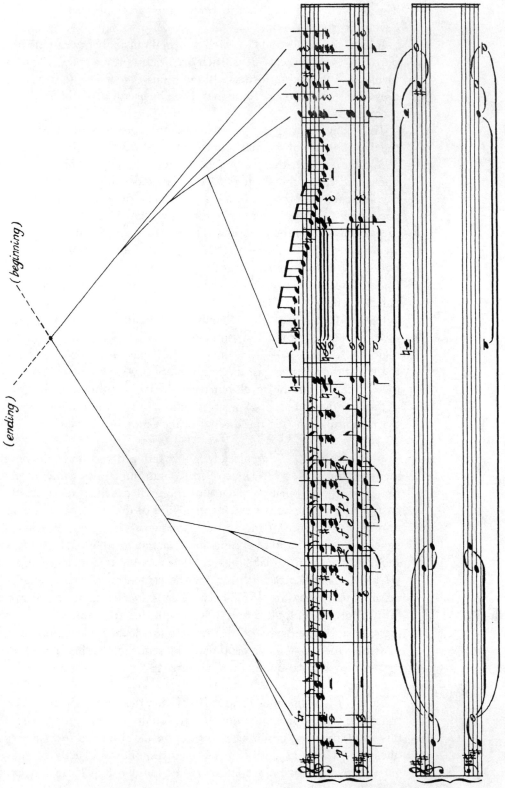

(beginning)

(ending)

10.15

10.16

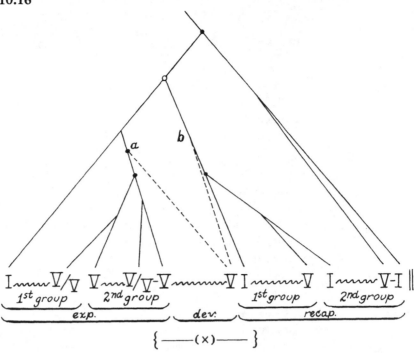

10.17

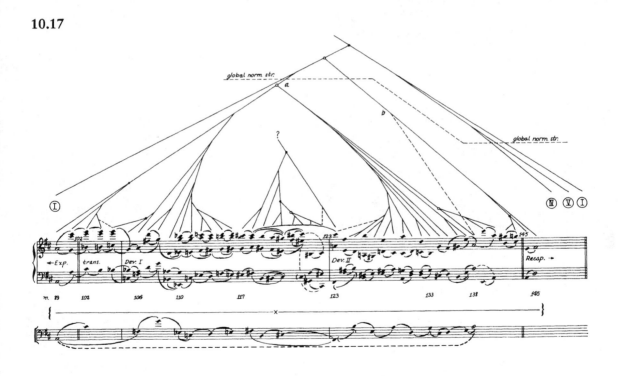

102–104 are transitional.) Moreover, the F major chord in measure 106 and the motivic extensions off it (measures 106–116) form successively embedded right branches (destabilizing departures) corresponding to measures 1–4 of 10.15. This is balanced by the successively embedded left branches (stabilizing progressions; the descending circle of fifths) of the second part of the development, which correspond to measures 5–8 of 10.15. In sum, the development section, beneath its chromatic complexities, is not only a motivic expansion of the opening phrase but also an elaboration of its prolongational tree.

The analogy falters with respect to the central F♯ minor section of the development (measures 117–124). As the sketch in 10.18 of the time-span reduction of the development shows, the half cadence in measure 119 and the F♯ minor arrival in measure 123 are time-span globally important events. (The cadence in measure 119 dominates the cadence in measure 121 because the latter is a prolongational extension of the former (TSRPR 6).) As a consequence of the grouping structure, the cadence (measure 119) is a right branch in the time-span reduction and the F♯ minor arrival is a left branch. Because of their structural importance, these two events must also be prolongationally important (PRPR 1). So far the analogy succeeds. But in the prolongational reduction these events cannot connect as right and left branches, respectively, because they and the other events in measures 117–124 form among themselves a powerful prolongational region (PRPR 3) (10.17). Hence this region is prolongationally isolated from the embedded right and left branching patterns described above.

10.18

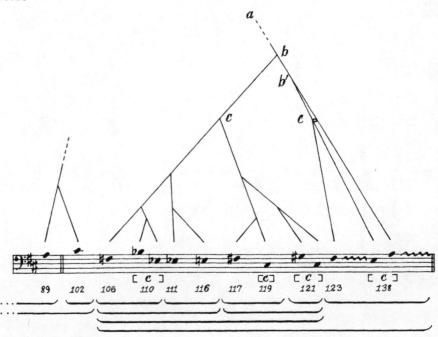

Furthermore, where is the prolongational head of this region, the F♯ minor arrival in measure 123, to attach? Of the possibilities available from 10.18, it seems nonsensical to connect it as a departure from the F major chord (measure 106) or as a direct progression to the V at the end of the development (measure 138). Somewhat more plausible would be to attach it as a direct departure from the V ending the exposition (measure 89). Most plausible, by parallelism with the ensuing descending circle of fifths (measures 123–133), would be to attach it to the B minor chord in measure 125 (the dashed branch in 10.17); but this event is too local in the time-span reduction to be available for prolongational connection (PRPR 1).

Thus the rules in their present state do not predict an intuitively adequate connection for this F♯ minor complex. In a way this nonsolution seems fitting, since as a tonal region it is both near to and remote from the V prolongation within which it is embedded. It is near because it is the relative minor within the prolongation; it is remote because of the way it is approached. This ambiguity is reflected in the application of the rules.

10.4 Possible Refinements in Prolongational Reduction

We discern two general ways in which the prolongational component might be further enhanced.

First, it should be possible to incorporate underlying voice-leading features in a more satisfactory way. For example, in 10.15 the voice leading of the melody would seem to be an unstable version of a more stable structure. Specifically, the high C and B in measures 5 and 7 are registral displacements, and the melody as a whole is composed of two independent lines. If we fuse the F♯ and the A in measure 1 (TSRWFR 3b), understand the B on the fourth beat of measure 2 to carry over into the following downbeat (TSRWFR 3c), lower the C and the B in measures 5 and 7 an octave (by an as yet unstated transformational rule), and invoke criteria about primary, subsidiary, and "contrapuntal" lines (single lines that form two or more linear structures), 10.15 converts into the coherent voice leading of the prolongational reduction in 10.19.

At level b it is apparent that the C in measure 5 is an upper neighbor to surrounding bs in measures 3 and 7. At level a the upper line emerges as a linear ascent from $\hat{5}$ to $\hat{8}$, over the more basic $\hat{3}-\hat{2}-\hat{1}$ descent (the whole notes) in the middle voice.

There are three reasons why we have not yet developed this aspect of pitch structure. First, we believe that principles of "coherent" voice leading depend to a great extent on the rhythmic and reductional factors already explicated in this book. To be sure, Schenker develops such principles in a (for the most part) intuitively satisfying way; but to give a rule-based account one must incorporate these other factors. We have only now reached the point where this is possible. Second, to make

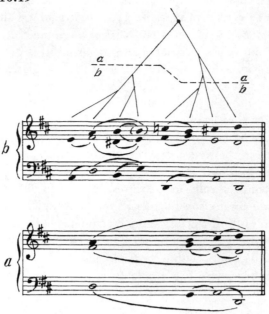

changes in the music such as converting 10.15 into 10.19 would involve an extensive use of transformational rules (TSRWFRs 3b and 3c are in effect transformational rules). This is a direction we have so far avoided because of the difficulty in constraining the application of such rules. Moreover, it is dangerous in a theory of musical intuition to alter the musical surface too much in the pursuit of a coherent underlying model; one can lose touch with the actual music. We have found it method-ologically prudent to err in the direction of adhering to musical surfaces as the basis for assigning hierarchical descriptions. Third, it is hard to arrive at general principles for the determination of primary, subsidiary, and "contrapuntal" lines. This is obviously a significant area of musical intuition, and it plays a crucial role in the perception of underlying voice leading. We have not explored this area in any detail.

Assuming that these problems can be overcome, we surmise that the assignment of "coherent" voice-leading structures will take place not as a last step in prolongational derivation, but at various stages of time-span and prolongational derivation. These transformational operations, of course, will apply only where cognitively meaningful. To the degree that such operations will be needed for a given musical passage, the listener's task of comprehending the musical signal will naturally be seen to be much more complicated.

The second enhancement of the prolongational component concerns a partial separation of melodic from harmonic reductional function. As stated in section 5.3, a purely hierarchical approach to pitch structure demands that a piece be viewed as a sequence of discrete events. Each "event," in both its harmonic and melodic aspects, assumes a unique position in the overall hierarchy. In our theory harmonic criteria have generally (though not always) overridden melodic criteria when the two have been in conflict, because melodic features are for the most part heard within a harmonic context. But even if this approach succeeds in a wide variety of cases, it is a simplification of musical reality.

Consider, for example, the progression shown in 10.20.

10.20

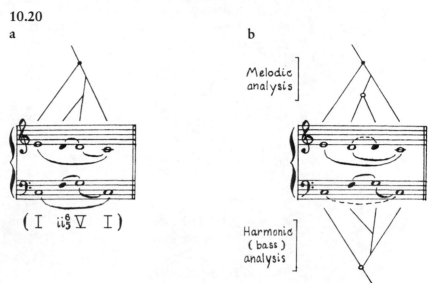

Obviously the melody depends on the harmonic context: the sequence E–D–C is heard in C major (rather than, say, E minor or F major, in which it would receive differing reductional functions); the D is heard as passing between (and hence subordinate to) notes of the tonic triad. Our standard prolongational analysis appears in 10.20a. But the melody and the harmony are also heard somewhat differently. As illustrated in 10.20b, the melodic D in the V chord is a prolongational repetition of the D in the ii$_5^6$, and the final I is a prolongational repetition of the initial I. (Here the reader must get accustomed to reading trees upside-down.) Thus, if separate but related trees are assigned to the melody and the harmony, each tree in 10.20b differs from the tree in 10.20a.

Especially significant in 10.20b are the implications of the largest levels of branching. Most tonal pieces progress from the tonic to a more stable tonic; this is represented in 10.20a and in the melodic analysis in 10.20b. But in another sense most pieces are prolongational extensions of the initial tonic; this is represented in the harmonic analysis in 10.20b.

Consider also a typical deceptive cadence, $\overset{\hat{2}}{V}$–$\overset{\hat{1}}{vi}$ or $\overset{\hat{7}}{V}$–$\overset{\hat{8}}{vi}$. Here the melody resolves to the tonic while the harmony tenses away from the tonic. In such cases, our single tree analysis has emphasized the motion toward harmonic instability. A double tree analysis would in addition show the melodic resolution, thus giving a fuller characterization of the deceptive cadence.

Before we draw any theoretical conclusions from these examples, let us examine another familiar passage. Suppose one "prefers" Schenker's reduction of the first phrase of K. 331 (Schenker 1925, 1935) to the ones offered in section 9.5 (see also the remarks in section 7.3 concerning the melodic primacy of C♯ or E in measure 1). Schenker's is certainly a plausible reading; in our secondary notation it looks like 10.21.[6]

10.21

How could our theory generate 10.21? One might grant the prominence of the E due to its relative height (TSRPR 3), or, alternatively, fuse measure 1 (and measure 2) (TSRWFR 3b). But there are more serious difficulties: the bass (that is, the harmony) and the melody must receive contrasting structural descriptions. In measures 1–2, in the bass the first events dominate the second (A over C♯, G♯ over B), but in the melody the second events dominate the first (E over C♯, D over B). In measure 4 two events in the melody (C♯ and B) over the V must be structurally important, but the C♯ is not harmonically well supported (a cadential $^6_4$). (This particular situation is common in Schenkerian reduction, and has caused dissent; in its defense, it is not the melodic note in these cases that forms the dissonant fourth with the bass.) In short, to arrive at Schenker's analysis, one must assign related but different trees to the melodic and harmonic structures, as in 10.22.

Preliminary investigation has indicated that in some passages the discrepancy between harmonic and melodic trees can be much greater than in 10.20b and 10.22. On the other hand, we feel that Schenker sometimes ascribes too great an independence to the outer voices (for example, in the first phrase of the Bach chorale "Ich bin's, ich sollte büssen" in Schenker 1932). The problem is to find the right balance—to let the bass, which governs the harmony, control the connective possibilities in the melodic tree, yet allow a certain leeway for melodic notes to form their own connections. At this point we are unclear whether such double analyses should derive as a second stage of prolongational reduction from the single prolongational trees so far developed in the theory, or

whether they should derive directly from time-span reduction (which, in any case, will remain with a single-tree analysis, by virtue of the time-span segmentation). It would certainly make for a simpler theory if the latter possibility obtained.

At issue, ultimately, is the perceptual status, in terms of tension and relaxation, of music viewed as a sequence of discrete events. Insofar as music is indeed heard this way, the prolongational component as developed in chapters 8 and 9 would seem to stand up fairly well. Yet a special aspect of tonal music is that the principles of harmonic (bass) motion and of melodic motion, though interactive, are distinct. A single-tree analysis must compromise these distinctions. The notion of a double-tree analysis offers the possibility for expressing in a rule-governed way both the interactive and the distinctive aspects of melodic and harmonic prolongational relationships.

11
Musical Universals and Related Issues

This chapter presents a retrospective overview of the theory developed in chapters 2–9, focusing on the issue of musical universals and their implications for musical cognition.

11.1
What is a Musical Universal?

To forestall misunderstanding, we should make clear at the outset what we mean by the term "musical universal." A musical universal need not be readily apparent in all musical idioms. We are concerned here rather with universals of musical *grammars*—the principles available to all experienced listeners for organizing the musical surfaces they hear, no matter what idiom they are experienced in. The relation between a musical universal in this sense and the nature of particular musical idioms is somewhat subtle and bears explanation.

Each rule of musical grammar is sensitive to certain features of the musical surface (such as presence of attack points or relatively consonant pitch events) or to certain aspects of musical structure (for example, symmetry, parallelism, and stability of other components of the analysis). If the relevant feature is present, the rule applies to mark a certain structure as well formed or preferred (depending whether the rule is a well-formedness or a preference rule). Essentially, we can claim a rule to be universal if it applies in the same way in every idiom that employs the distinctions to which the rule is sensitive. For example, we feel fairly confident that metrical preference rule 4, the stress rule, is universal; we suspect that there is no idiom that uses local stresses in which these stresses do not tend to be heard as strong beats, other things being equal. In particular, there is no idiom in which stresses are marks of weak beats.

There are two kinds of apparent counterexamples to this claim, both of which are taken into account in our definition. First, an idiom in which stresses do not occur (for example, some varieties of Renaissance music) does not argue against the universality of the rule. The stylistic norms of the idiom simply do not give the rule opportunities to apply. An analogous situation can be found in the visual arts: one would not claim, because a particular artistic idiom made use only of black and white, that the intended viewers could not make use of principles of color perception.

A second kind of apparent counterexample might involve an idiom like jazz in which cross-accents and syncopation are a prominent characteristic. One might be tempted to claim that in such an idiom an accent or a stress is indeed a mark of a weak beat, violating the putative universal. However, closer examination suggests that such a solution would be incorrect. The stylistic norm is not simply stresses on weak beats; it consists rather of a number of strategies aimed at increasing local metrical tension. The normal preference rules do not fail to apply; in fact they are exploited as a means of creating the desired metrical tension, which results from a conflict among rules. In short, the mere fact that a particular idiom makes particular stylistic choices cannot itself contradict a claim of universality for a rule; these choices may simply reflect the way the idiom uses the interaction of universal rules to create interesting musical structures.

A case can be made for genuine idiom-specificity of rules, however, if there are two idioms for which similar aspects of the musical surface give rise to distinct kinds of musical structure. Two obvious examples are the rules for pitch stability and the metrical well-formedness rules. In the former case there is no question that particular pitch configurations are treated as consonant by one idiom and dissonant by another (see section 11.5). In the latter case an idiom that permits metrical regularities, say, at a distance of seven beats (such as much Balkan folk music) will analyze as metrically stable a passage that in classical Western tonal music would be complex and irregular. Thus it is not hard to make a case for some aspects of musical grammar being idiom-specific.

However, the idiom-specific features of the grammar we have developed seem to be considerably fewer than one might at first surmise.[1] Though this may in part be a function of our own ignorance of other idioms, we have shown why a superficial examination of another idiom will not necessarily disprove our conjectures. To invalidate our claims, it is necessary to demonstrate that our principles of grammar cannot be applied to the idiom to yield analyses that correspond to the intuitions of experienced listeners. This is a task of no less complexity in other idioms than in classical Western tonal music. In short, a genuine test of our claims of universality would appear to require serious historical and ethnomusicological research.

Investigation of other idioms may be expected to yield a further benefit. We have just noted that not all idioms make use of accentual distinctions to which the metrical preference rules are sensitive. Similarly, many idioms do not make use of pitch simultaneities (harmony), so that they do not engage those parts of the time-span and prolongational reduction rules that are sensitive to harmonic stability. One might wonder if there are universals of musical grammar that are similarly not exploited by classical Western tonal music and whose presence we have therefore not suspected here. A study of other idioms would help to reveal the existence of such principles.

Beyond the specific claims about universality of particular rules discussed in preceding chapters, we present here some overall hypotheses about universals that emerge from the theory—general features that remain intact beneath any modifications of the rules themselves.

1. Musical intuitions are organized along the four hierarchical dimensions treated here: grouping, metrical structure, time-span reduction, and prolongational reduction. Each of these (with specified exceptions such as overlaps) is a strictly hierarchical structure that includes every pitch-event in a piece.
2. The structure of a piece in each component is determined by the interaction of well-formedness rules, preference rules, and transformational rules, applying in essentially the way we have illustrated in previous chapters.
3. The four components interrelate basically in the ways developed here:
    a. Grouping and meter are independent (though different idioms constrain their interaction in varying degrees).
    b. Time-span segmentation depends on meter at small levels, grouping at large levels, and the combination of the two at intermediate levels.
    c. Time-span reduction depends on a combination of pitch stability and time-span segmentation.
    d. Prolongational regions and prolongational importance are determined largely in terms of time-span importance and stability of pitch connection.
    As a consequence of b–d, the listener's understanding of global pitch structure is strongly influenced by his local segmentation of the musical surface.
4. In order for hierarchical decisions to be made within the two reductional components, there must be criteria for the relative stability of pitch-events. This means that a given idiom must supply both a tonal center for a piece (not necessarily a tonic as defined in classical Western tonality, but a center of pitch gravity) and a scale of distance of other pitch-events from the tonal center.
5. Structural beginnings and endings of groups form significant articulation of a piece's structure; structural endings are marked by conventional formulas (cadences of some kind).

Each of these points is embodied in the form or content of our grammar for classical Western tonal music. The first two specify the overall form of the grammar; 3a is represented by the absence of well-formedness rules linking grouping and meter; 3b is a generalized statement of the time-span segmentation rules; 3c concerns certain aspects of time-span reduction preference rules; 3d concerns aspects of the prolongational reduction preference rules; 4 states a presupposition of the preference rules for both reductions; 5 is represented rather directly by TSRPRs 7 and 8 and indirectly by PRPR 6 (normative structure).

One might wonder why we are so concerned with universals of musical grammar, particularly in the sense of "universal" defined at the beginning of this section. The reason is that universals of this sort are crucial to the question of the innateness of musical cognitive capacity, a topic to which we now turn.

11.2 Musical Innateness

In outlining our goals for music theory in chapter 1, we distinguished two sorts of inquiry. The first was to describe the experienced listener's knowledge of a musical idiom by means of a musical grammar for the idiom; the second was to explicate the source of this knowledge. We argued there that, to the degree that the listener's knowledge is complex and abstract with respect to the musical surface, it becomes more difficult to explain his acquisition of this knowledge on the basis of simple generalization over presented musical surfaces (the "stimulus generalization" of empiricist psychology).

Having developed a grammar of tonal music in considerable detail, we are now in a position to make the argument more pointed. If the rules we have proposed correspond at all closely to principles unconsciously known and used by the experienced listener, one must ask how the listener manages to learn them. And of all the possible organizations one could attribute to tonal music (including all the incorrect ones posited by us music theorists), why does the listener infer the ones he does? The only answer that we find defensible is that one does not have to learn the entire grammar from scratch. Rather, one has no choice about much of it; many aspects of the grammar are simply the only (or easiest) ways that one's mental abilities make available for organizing a musical signal.[2] In other words, much of the complexity of musical intuition is not learned, but is given by the inherent organization of the mind, itself determined by the human genetic inheritance.

In trying to separate those aspects of musical intuition that are innately given from those that are learned, we have two independent sources of evidence. First, as just argued, it would appear implausible that someone could construct the entire grammar solely on the basis of presented musical surfaces. In particular, those parts of the grammar that are especially remote from the surface evidence are strong candidates for innateness. It is unlikely, for instance, that one could infer from a number of unanalyzed musical surfaces even the existence of a prolongational component; thus on grounds of learnability we would argue that the presence of such a component in musical grammar represents a contribution of innate musical capacity, even if some of its particular rules must be learned.

A second kind of evidence for innateness appeals to the existence of universals of musical grammar, in the sense defined in the preceding section. Though it is possible to attribute grammatical universals to cultural diffusion or to mere historical accident, another explanation is that they reflect cognitive similarities among all human beings—innate aspects of mind that transcend particular cultures or historical periods. Thus universals of musical grammar, especially those of the abstract sort presented here, can be taken to represent innate aspects of musical cognition, and the differences among grammars can be taken to represent learned aspects of musical idioms. (As suggested in the preceding section, claims of universality are empirical, and are subject to verification or falsification by historical and ethnomusicological research.)

The range of variation among rules in different idioms also constitutes grounds for hypotheses about innateness. For example (to consider an extreme case), though idioms differ in metrical and intervallic possibilities, we feel safe in conjecturing that there is no idiom that makes use of metrical regularities 31 beats apart, or for which the most stable melodic interval is the thirteenth. Rather, given the number of conceivable options, the differences among idioms fall into a relatively constrained set. These constraints on variation give an indication of the limitations of human musical cognition—the possibilities for structuring the musical surface available to someone learning an idiom.

As many readers will no doubt be skeptical of our claim that a great deal of musical grammar is innately specified, let us see what it would take to falsify the claim. Beside providing evidence from other idioms for the nonuniversality of particular rules of musical grammar, one might take issue with the argument in three other ways.

First, someone who grants the existence of a musical grammar in the mind of the experienced listener might still deny that it is in part innate. But it is not enough to deny innateness on the basis of methodological preference; it is incumbent on such a critic to explain how all the complexities of musical grammar might otherwise be learned.

Alternatively, one could simply deny the existence of as rich a musical grammar as we have claimed, proposing instead a theory of musical intuition with much simpler and hence (perhaps) more learnable principles. Such a criticism, however, calls for an explanation of all the musical intuitions we have discussed in motivating our theory. In short, we believe it would be extremely difficult to overcome the argument for the innateness of a substantial body of musical grammar, even if many of our formulations of the rules should prove incorrect.

A third criticism, and one to which we would be more receptive, might ask why evolution should have provided us with such complex innate machinery, for which there is no evident survival value. A conceivable answer might be that many of the principles of musical grammar are not specific to music; that musical grammar is a confluence of a number of factors independently needed for more essential aspects of cognitive ability. (There might, nevertheless, be a residue of musical cognition that is a product of nonadaptive evolutionary accident.) We have already mentioned a few such possibilities: the principles of grouping (section 3.2), the use of stress (phenomenal accent) and length as indications of accent in both music and language (section 4.2), and the phenomenon of auditory stream segregation and its relation to fusion in time-span reduction (section 7.2). Chapter 12 will explore such correspondences in more detail.

However, such an argument does not make musical grammar any simpler; it just shows that musical grammar, in all its richness, need not be isolated from the rest of cognition. In fact, it should be worthwhile to pursue these connections in the opposite direction, using the complexity of musical grammar as evidence for the complexity of cognition in general.

11.3
Summary of
Rhythmic Features

To buttress our claim for the complexity and hence the possible innateness of much of musical intuition, we summarize in this section the contributions of our theory to an area commonly thought to involve "natural" abilities: musical rhythm. It is also an area where musical properties carry over to other dimensions of human experience. In addition, this overview provides the opportunity from a purely musical standpoint for gathering together ideas, scattered throughout the book, on a topic of great importance.

At the beginning of chapter 2 we implied that many writers have treated the subject of rhythm inadequately because they have tried to reduce its many aspects to a few simple notions. We have proposed instead that rhythm is multidimensional and interactive. Below are the aspects of rhythm that our theory addresses. Some of these aspects emerge directly as part of the structural description assigned to a piece by the formal grammar, others indirectly as interpretations based on the structural description.

1. The *grouping component* assigns the segmentation into musical units inferred by the listener from the musical surface. The local hierarchical distortions of *overlap* and *elision* are given special treatment within the grouping component by means of transformational rules.
2. The *metrical component* assigns the pattern of strong and weak beats heard by the listener. Metrical accents are distinguished from *phenomenal accents,* which are an input to metrical structure, and *structural accents,* which are represented in time-span reduction. *Syncopation* arises when phenomenal accents conflict with the inferred metrical

periodicity. A special metrical level is designated as the *tactus*. This level is the perceptually most salient metrical level; it is regular, and is usually at a moderate tempo. At comparatively small and large levels, metrical irregularities of a limited kind can take place. One kind of irregularity, *metrical deletion,* occurs in connection with grouping overlap, and is treated by a corresponding transformational rule. The perception of meter fades at global levels.

3. A group at a small or intermediate grouping level can have a strongest beat, around which other beats within the group "cluster" (this phenomenon is central to Cooper and Meyer 1960). Whether a weak beat within the group is heard as an *upbeat* or as an *afterbeat* is a function of its position in the grouping structure. The time-span from an upbeat to its associated downbeat is an *anacrusis.* More generally, the listener hears as perceptually significant the interaction of grouping structure with the time-spans from beat to beat at each metrical level. When these two kinds of temporal articulation coincide, grouping and meter are *in phase;* when they do not, grouping and meter are *out of phase.* Out-of-phase patterns can be slight or acute.

4. The listener hears pitch-events in the context of rhythmic units composed of a combination of metrical and grouping time-spans. The *segmentation rules* develop these rhythmic units in terms of metrical time-spans at small musical levels, of a combination of metrical and grouping time-spans at intermediate levels, and of grouping time-spans at large levels.

5. In a broad sense, the function of *time-span reduction* is to relate rhythmic structure and pitch structure to each other. It does this by assigning a hierarchy of structural importance to pitch-events within rhythmic units as defined by the segmentation rules. At small time-span reductional levels, right and left branchings convey the relation of structurally important events to *metrical* structure. The four pitch-meter paradigmatic situations of section 6.2 exhaust the relational possibilities of a head and its direct elaboration(s) to strong and weak beats. At large levels (from the phrase up), right and left branchings signify the dominance and subordination of structural beginnings and structural endings (cadences) as they function within *grouping* structure. Structural beginnings and cadences relate cyclically across groups at successive levels of global segmentation. These "arcs of tonal motion" normally begin and end at or near the endpoints of the groups for which they function, and hence stand in accentual opposition to the periodicity of metrical structure. Such *structural accents* can occur at metrically strong or weak points.

6. A *structural downbeat* represents the instantaneous confluence of a grouping boundary (often in conjunction with an overlap), a hypermetrical strong beat, and a structurally important event in time-span reduction. A *structural anacrusis* covers the span from the previous

event at the appropriate time-span reductional level to the event at the structural downbeat.

7. *Prolongational reduction* expresses one of the most basic rhythmic intuitions: the breathing in and out, the tensing and relaxing, inherent in the motion of pitch-events. This component places pitches in a dynamic relationship. The different kinds of branching signify relative degrees of tensing and relaxing. *Normative structure* supplies the minimal branching structure for the tensing-to-relaxing motion fundamental to all tonal pieces.

8. The events contained under a prolongational branching complex can be thought of as a *prolongational grouping*. *Harmonic rhythm* as traditionally conceived is a special, surface instance of the interaction of prolongational grouping with metrical structure. In this theory harmonic rhythm is the durational pattern of all levels of prolongational grouping.

9. Time-span reduction and prolongational reduction can be in a *congruent* or *noncongruent* relation to one another. Because time-span trees correlate with grouping structure (via the segmentation rules), congruence is best understood as the relationship between events heard within grouping structure and events heard within prolongational groupings. The latter can cut across subphrase groupings, across phrases, and across global segmentations, producing varying degrees of noncongruence. Noncongruent relationships promote continuity over division.

All of these features can, in a general sense, be termed "rhythmic." Nor is the list complete. First, it has not included the nuances of individual preference rules and the ways they interact in a conflicting or reinforcing fashion. Second, it has not included the rhythmic patterns at the musical surface: its patterns of attack points, durations, and rests; its patterns of pitch-rhythmic repetitions and parallelisms. These features are an input to the theory, not part of it. Yet these surface patterns themselves form rich rhythmic relationships with all the inferred aspects of rhythmic structure enumerated above, complicating the rhythmic picture still further. Third, the rhythmic effect of *contour* patterns has not been discussed. Fourth, we have neglected the impact of timbral factors on rhythmic perception. No doubt there are other rhythmic features that we have not thought to mention here.[3]

It must be emphasized that none of the rhythmic features discussed here is reducible to any other. One's intuitive understanding of, say, a particular musical "gesture" is a product of the minute interaction of these multifarious dimensions—their presence or absence, their conflicting or reinforcing structures. As Seymour Shifrin once remarked, "Cross-accentuation is the life-blood of rhythm."

11.4
Motivic "Trans-
formations," ·
"Deep Structures,"
and Musical
"Archetypes"

Though we have made heavy use of motivic relationships in motivating and stating the preference rules of the theory, we have not addressed the important issue of how to formalize these relationships. Indeed, it may seem odd, given our linguistically oriented methodology, that we have not proposed a component of thematic and motivic "transformations"— after all, transformations are so central to linguistic theory (though see note 10 to chapter 1).

To explain why we have avoided this approach, we must first point out that the word *transformation* does not normally mean the same thing in music as it does in linguistics. Its linguistic usage is adapted from mathematics and denotes the conversion of one syntactic construction into another, semantically related construction. Our usage has been similar, in that a transformational rule in our theory converts one musical structure into another structure that retains the "sense" of the former. In both cases, the number of transformations is finite. In musical parlance, however, *transformation* is used in a more general sense: it signifies any thematic, motivic, or other change in musical material such that the result of the transformation is recognized as a modification of the previous state of the material.

This more generalized usage poses difficulties if it is to be treated in a systematic fashion. Let us put the problem in the following way: Given any two sets of pitches and durations, it is possible logically to "transform" one into the other, and to do so in any number of ways. Every musician has been confronted with analyses that relate musical materials indiscriminately. As recognized by Meyer (1973), the problem is to constrain the admissible relations, to limit the permissible transformations. Presumably a theory that purports to describe the musical intuitions of the experienced listener should be able to treat this matter. It may in fact be possible to construct a system in which only certain musical ideas can be related only if certain transformations (in the general sense) take place; such a system would establish the relative proximity or distance of musical ideas. There are two reasons why we have skirted this area in favor of the four domains of analysis developed here, both alluded to in section 1.4.

First, themes, motives, and other musical ideas (in the limited sense in which they are usually meant) are relatively local patterns that are subsumed under more generalized perceptions of rhythmic structure and pitch elaboration; that is, they are heard within the context of a metrical organization, a set of grouping boundaries, and the two hierarchies of pitch importance. If these ideas were developed compositionally without respect to context, the result would be largely chaotic; in the work of sophisticated composers, they often seem inextricably bound up with context. It would be pointless to discuss them without a theory of the structures in which they are embedded.[4]

Second, we have restricted ourselves in this study to a formalization of the hierarchical aspects of musical structure. For the most part, the development of musical surface material is not a hierarchical phenomenon. For example, that motive A has been transformed into A', and A' into A'', does not mean that any of them has hierarchical priority over the others. Rather, they are a sequence of musical units that are perceived simply as being related to one another in certain ways. Insofar as there is a sense in which a hierarchical relation might exist among these motivic forms—if, for example, A' is heard for contextual reasons as more "basic" or "characteristic" than A—the resulting hierarchical description would not be of the kind that has been under consideration here, namely an exhaustive partitioning into hierarchical, nonoverlapping segments or elements.

The discussion in section 3.3 suggests an alternative attack on the problem of motivic "transformation": motivic relatedness counts as an instance of *parallelism*. There we advocated seeking a set of preference rules to pick out parallelisms. Such rules would take into account not only the obvious factors of surface pitch contour and rhythmic configuration, but also more contextual or global considerations, such as position of the motive in grouping structure, its metrical pattern, and its reductional structure. Intuitions about motivic relatedness display all the characteristics we have come to associate with phenomena governed by preference rules, in particular the gradations in judgment due to the interaction of diverse factors. Thus our theory provides a formal possibility for expressing motivic relatedness through preference rules, which circumvents the difficulties engendered by a more traditional "transformational" approach.

Another question that may arise in connection with our methodology concerns "deep structure"—a technical term that has been widely misunderstood. It should first be pointed out that the largest levels of our reductions are in no sense analogous to deep structures in linguistics. Rather, they are analogous to stages of phrase-structure analysis as represented in linguistic trees. Thus the highest level in one of our reductions (always the tonic chord) roughly corresponds to "Sentence," our second largest level (the "basic form" in prolongational reduction) roughly corresponds to "Noun Phrase + Verb Phrase," and so forth. However, as pointed out in section 5.3, musical trees represent elaborations rather than *is-a* relations among grammatical categories, so even this analogy should not be pushed too far. (A more apt linguistic analogy to reductional trees is discussed in section 12.3.)

In a transformational generative grammar, "deep structure" refers to underlying phrase structures that have not been subjected to transformations (in the technical sense). "Surface structure" refers to the constituent structure of actual linguistic expressions. Transformations convert deep structures into surface structures. In our music theory the well-formedness rules describe hierarchical organizations that correspond roughly to linguistic phrase structure, and, as mentioned earlier in this section, the musical transformational rules are analogous to linguistic transformations (though, as mentioned in section 3.4, the operations they perform more closely resemble phonological than syntactic transformations). Therefore, to the limited extent that musical transformational rules are necessary—such as for grouping overlaps and elisions, metrical deletions, and missing harmonic functions—our theory does embody a notion of "deep structure"; the transformations convert underlying disentangled overlaps and the like into the musical surface.

For some, there might be an intuitive sense in which "deep structure" implies a representation of simple, normative, archetypal forms. While rejecting the applicability of the term in this sense, we agree that the study of archetypal patterns is a matter of serious interest. All experienced listeners intuitively apprehend a phrase, for example, as relatively normal or unusual.

It might be supposed that an archetypal pattern is best systematized in terms of a deep structure (in the technical sense), which would then be converted by means of transformational rules into the musical surface. For example, a five-measure phrase might be seen as derived from a deep-structural four-measure phrase, a noncongruent phrase such as the opening of Mozart K. 331 might be seen as derived from a congruent phrase, and so forth. One can see versions of such derivations, in varying degrees of formality, in Schenker 1935, Komar 1971, Snell 1979, Keiler 1978a, and Schachter 1980. Although such an approach seems initially plausible, we have found it impracticable both musically and formally. Musically, it is easy to conceive of rather simple irregularities such as five-measure phrases and harmonic substitutions as distortions from an archetypal form; but in dealing with a passage of any complexity or length it is hard to specify what archetype the music is a transformation of. This musical difficulty is reflected in a formal difficulty similar to the one concerning thematic transformations: in order to derive various surface structures from a deep structure, it would be necessary to admit an almost unconstrained class of permissible transformational derivations. Furthermore, there are the problems of positing a universe of archetypal forms, choosing the correct deep structure for any complex piece, and systematically specifying the derivation from archetype to musical surface for any given passage. None of the approaches cited above makes a serious attempt to solve this collection of formal difficulties.

Rather than develop an archetypal deep structure, with its attendant problems, we propose (as hinted in section 3.6) that archetypal patterns emerge as a consequence of the preference rules for the four components of the musical grammar. A passage in which the preference rules maximally reinforce each other, within each component and across components, will be heard as "archetypal." As more conflict appears among preference rules, the passage deviates more from archetypal form and is heard as musically more complex.

Let us provisionally suggest some features of the archetypal phrase in terms of the components of our theory:

1. Each larger-level group is divided into two groups of equal length.
2. The larger levels of metrical structure are uniformly duple.
3. The grouping and metrical structures are maximally in phase, in the sense described in section 2.3. This not only excludes all but the lowest-level upbeats, but also guarantees that the measure lengths of groups are in powers of 2.
4. In the time-span reduction, the structural beginning of a phrase is its first event and is a tonic chord in root position; the cadence of the phrase is its last two events and is a tonic perfect cadence.
5. The prolongational reduction yields a normative structure, in the sense described in sections 8.3 and 9.6.
6. The time-span and prolongational reductions are congruent, in the sense described in section 5.4.

These six properties of archetypal phrases maximally satisfy those preference rules that address the abstract structure of the phrase: grouping symmetry (GPR 5), binary metrical regularity (MPR 10), correlation of grouping and meter (MPR 2), choice of cadences and structural beginnings (TSRPRs 7 and 8), prolongational normative structure (PRPR 6), and correlation of the two reductions (PRPRs 1 and 2). This list is not exhaustive; moreover, one could find "archetypal" patterns emerging from mutually reinforcing preference rules at levels both smaller and larger than the phrase. In short, archetypal patterns are not represented directly in the grammar, but emerge as ideally stable structural descriptions produced by the grammar.

A further advantage of our approach to the issue of archetypes is that it relates at every point to more general musical and psychological issues, such as the relation of tonal music to other idioms, the distinction between learned and innate aspects of musical idioms, and the relation of musical cognitive capacity to other cognitive capacities. A "deep structural" approach to archetypes could in principle address these issues, but they are not a concern in the approaches we have seen; nor is it at all obvious to us how they could naturally be integrated into the formal mechanisms these approaches imply. By contrast, the preference-rule formalism was motivated from the start (section 3.2) on psychological grounds.

In the chapters on reductions we have simply assumed the conventional notions of harmony and counterpoint for classical Western tonal music, without attempting to provide the principled basis for these notions that a complete theory of musical cognition would require. This section sketches some essential features of a foundation for the system of pitch relationships in tonal music and tonal idioms in general.

Historically, the most prevalent approach to explaining the basis of tonality has been an appeal to the natural overtone series. The argument goes back at least to Rameau; two recent advocates have been Hindemith (1952) and Bernstein (1976). Although we agree that tonality reflects an innate organization of the pitch structure of music, we will review why the overtone series has only a limited influence on this ability.

One part of the argument involves simultaneously sounded tones. We observe that, next to singing in unison with each other, people find it easiest to sing in octaves, often doing so without conscious effort. People sometimes even sing in fifths, thinking that they are singing in unison, but this phenomenon is less prevalent than that at the octave. These results are not confined to humans: apparently, if dogs are trained to respond to a particular pitch, and their responses are then tested on different pitches, a pitch an octave away from the original elicits much greater response than surrounding tones.

To account for these results, it has been observed that the octave and the fifth are intervals formed by the first two overtones of the natural harmonic series, as shown in figure 11.1.

11.1

fundamental   1st   2nd   3rd   4th   5th   6th   7th   8th   9th   10th
overtone   overtone

The theory is that we can consider two pitches similar, or that we find their combination less dissonant, more pleasing, or easier to sing, if one of them forms a unison with an overtone of the other or if they are overtones of a common fundamental. Thus, goes the argument, the intervallic inventory of music has grown gradually more complex or sophisticated as people have come to make use of more overtones.[5]

This hypothesis appears to account for certain developments in the history of Western music, since the next harmonic interval to appear after the fifth, during the Middle Ages, was the fourth—the interval between the second and third overtones. After that, the major third began to appear—the interval between the third and fourth overtones. By sounding simultaneously the overtones up through the fourth, we arrive at the major triad, the fundamental building block of Western tonal music. By building a major triad on the second overtone as well as on the fundamental, we get the opposition of dominant to tonic that is indispensable to classical harmony. Then we can add to the vocabulary the dominant of the dominant, the subdominant (whose second overtone is the original fundamental), and so on. Eventually we have the complete system of Western tonality, all allegedly arising from consonances generated by the overtone series. So goes the argument of Bernstein (1976, pp. 35–37); Helmholtz (1885) follows similar lines, with great care.

Closer examination reveals difficulties. There was indeed an early period in the history of Western music in which the fourth was consonant and the third dissonant. But not long after the introduction of the major third as a consonance, a fourth between the bass and another part came to be treated as dissonant, requiring resolution. This was its status in the classical period. Furthermore, there is no way to derive the minor triad from the overtone series. It is true that the minor triad can be thought of as somewhat less stable than the major; historically, it was not until the eighteenth century that pieces ended with any frequency on the minor triad. But in the Classical period it was treated as a consonance. Since the fourth (generated by the overtone series) is dissonant and the minor triad (not generated by the overtone series) is consonant, derivation from the overtone series is neither a sufficient nor a necessary condition for consonance, even in the musical idiom most familiar to us.

Another argument of Bernstein (1976, pp. 27–29) concerns the simplest version of the pentatonic scale (11.2), widespread throughout the world.

11.2

This pitch collection is quite close to that provided by the first eight overtones (ignoring octave transpositions); hence the overtone series may be thought to predict this scale directly. The one minor discrepancy is the last note, A, which is to correspond to the sixth overtone of C, a flattened B♭. What is not explained is why, in so many cultures, the A is not the pure overtone but is much closer to the A of the diatonic scale, a fifth above D. To argue that this is because the sixth overtone is "in the cracks" of the natural scale and the ear has difficulty hearing it is in effect to abandon the hypothesis of the primacy of the overtone series, replacing with some other principle (probably the circle of fifths).

A further consequence follows from this hypothesis about the pentatonic scale: if an idiom has a smaller inventory of pitches, they should be selected from those below the eighth overtone. Thus the most highly favored system with only three distinct pitches should be the one in 11.3.

Musical Universals and Related Issues

11.3

This prediction is not correct. Except in the idiom of bugle calls, something like 11.4 is more likely, according to the survey of folk-music idioms by Nettl (1973); this is also the pitch collection of the widespread children's "teasing chant."

11.4

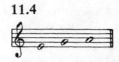

Example 11.4 might be described as the fifth, sixth, and seventh partials of the hypothetical fundamental C. But such an explanation weakens the principle upon which the pentatonic scale is supposedly based, namely using the lowest overtones first. Thus the hypothesis of the primacy of the overtone series is not only somewhat incorrect in its prediction about the simplest pentatonic scale, but also seriously questionable with respect to tritonic scales.

Moreover, the overtone series provides no direct account of versions of the pentatonic scale containing minor seconds, such as these two cited by Bernstein:

11.5

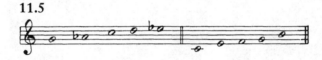

Because the minor second appears in the overtone series only as the interval between the fourteenth and fifteenth overtones, one well might ask what happened to all the intervening intervals that are supposedly easier to hear.

To make things still worse, there are musical idioms in which the overtone series seems to play no significant role at all. Rouget and Schwarz 1970 describes a Sudanese idiom whose scale divides the octave into seven equal intervals, each slightly smaller than a whole step; thus no intervals other than the unison and the octave are present from the overtone series. The two-part music of the island of Krk in Yugoslavia[6] includes, besides the unison and the octave, only multiples of some interval smaller than the half-step, intervals completely foreign to Western ears. Yet both of these idioms unmistakably have a tonal center.

Thus, beyond the octave, the fifth, and perhaps the major third, it is difficult to make any useful connection between the overtone series and the universality of tonality. In a sense, this result is more significant than if the overtone hypothesis were correct, for it shows that tonality is not simply man's response to physical facts about sound. Rather, like language, tonality in music provides evidence for a cognitive organization with a logic all its own. The mind is not simply following the physical path of least resistance, as the overtone hypothesis would have it, but is creating its own way of organizing pitch combinations into coherent patterns.[7]

It is interesting that Helmholtz (1885), after studying the acoustics of tonality and the overtone series in great detail, arrives at a rather similar conclusion (pp. 364–365):

... the principle of tonal relationship [through the overtone series] did not at all times exclusively determine the construction of the scale, and does not even yet determine it exclusively among all nations. This principle must, therefore, be regarded to some extent as a *freely selected principle of style* [Helmholtz's italics]. ... the construction of scales and of harmonic tissue is a product of artistic invention, and by no means furnished by the natural formation or natural function of our ear, as it has been hitherto most generally asserted.

In seeking an alternative account of tonality, one can imagine any number of possible sets of first principles from which to build the pitch system of classical Western tonal music. The question arises as to which of the possible methods of deriving the system accurately reflects the experienced listener's unconscious knowledge of the tonal pitch system. One kind of evidence that bears on this question comes from an examination of the pitch structures of other tonal idioms of the world (possibly excluding consciously "invented" systems). If one finds a set of first principles that can be elaborated equally into any of these various systems, this is more likely to be a description of psychological interest, for it represents all tonal systems as different realizations of the same cognitive capacity.

The above statements should be explained in more detail. We claim that listeners use their musical cognitive capacity to organize music they hear, and further that musical idioms will tend to develop along lines that enable listeners to make use of their abilities to organize musical signals. Therefore, if there is some kind of organization that is especially "natural" (that is, favored by musical cognitive capacity), we should expect this sort of organization to be widespread among musical idioms. (On the other hand, we do not expect all idioms to exploit all aspects of musical cognition equally. For example, the Macedonian folk idiom mentioned in section 4.4 makes heavier use of certain metrical possibilities than classical Western tonal music, which in turn uses more possibilities of pitch organization than many other idioms.)

Thus we believe that a basis for classical Western tonality should be developed in part by searching for the underlying features it shares with other tonal systems. (Section 4.4 suggested similar investigation with respect to metrical structure.) We have made no extensive survey of other tonal idioms, but a preliminary examination suggests three elements that enter into the definition of a tonal system: a pitch collection or scale, a member of the pitch collection designated as tonic, and a measure of relative stability among members of the pitch collection (particularly with respect to the tonic). Let us consider these in turn.

Pitch Collection

In certain simple tonal systems the pitch collection consists simply of a given number of distinct pitches, related only by relative height, without fixed intervals between them. Some varieties of gamelan music described in Becker and Becker 1979 have such an organization (though this music is very complex in other respects). Assuming differentiation among drum sounds, it is possible to think of drum music in these terms as well.

The next refinement is to specify the intervallic relationships among the available pitches, as in any number of familiar tonal systems. If the pitch collection in such an idiom spans more than an octave, two possibilities appear. First, the upper octave may contain different intervals (or pitch classes) than the lower; Nettl 1960 (p. 10) cites Cheremis music as an example of such a system. Alternatively, as in classical Western tonal music, a principle of octave equivalence may be invoked, so that the pitch collection extends indefinitely upward and downward by successive octave transpositions.

Among the options in the definition of pitch collection is the possibility of contextual variation, such as different pitches in ascending and descending contexts. This is familiar in classical Western tonal music from the inflection of the sixth and seventh degrees in the minor scale, but it occurs as well in other idioms, for instance in certain Indian ragas (Cooper 1977).

The specification of pitch collections for classical Western tonal music might begin with the major and minor diatonic scales, together with their possible chromatic inflections (in contrast to starting with the chromatic scale, which does not provide enough internal structure). In addition, a recursive principle based on the circle of fifths relates the scales by transposition. A very different and more complex system appears in raga, where traditional Indian theory describes the several hundred distinct thātas, or pitch collections, in terms of relationships to "parent scales." Cooper 1977 shows that it is of theoretical interest to treat these relationships as generative principles of some subtlety (see also Powers 1977). To do so is to claim that the choice of pitch collections is not arbitrary, but follows from the interaction of simple principles.

Of course, there are many idioms that employ far simpler pitch collections than the two just mentioned. One would eventually hope to characterize in a constrained way the range of possibilities across "natural" tonal idioms.

Tonic

The second element of a system of tonality is the designation of a particular member of the pitch collection as the major point of stability, or *tonic*. (Some authors have used the term "basis tone" to avoid any implications of classical Western tonality.) All other pitches are heard in terms of their relation to this pitch, and it is normally the pitch on which a piece must end. In addition, there may be another designated pitch that serves as a secondary point of stability, which, following Nettl 1973, we will call the "dominant." In classical Western tonal music it is a fifth above the tonic, but in other traditions other intervals appear. For example, in different Indian ragas the "dominant" (samvādī) is often a fourth or a fifth above the tonic (vādi); in Torah chant, the "dominant," where "half cadences" end, is a second above the tonic.

Different scales may result from choosing different members of the pitch collection as tonic. For example, the range of medieval modes results in large part from designating different members of the same pitch collection as tonic. The same principle applies in deriving various Indian ragas (scales) from a single thāta (pitch collection).

The claim that all pitches of a piece are heard in relation to the tonic can be concretely demonstrated in the many musical traditions where the melodic line is accompanied by a drone, which is invariably pitched on the tonic and/or "dominant." But even where the tonic is not blatantly present in this fashion, its identity is usually clear from such factors as the nature of cadential structure and the overall shape of melodic lines. Furthermore, if the reduction hypothesis of chapter 5 is correct, the most background level of reduction for every piece is a statement of the tonic; hence the tonic is in some sense implicit in every moment of the piece.

Measure of Relative Stability

The third element of a system of tonality is a measure of relative stability (or, broadly speaking, of relative consonance and dissonance) for various pitch configurations. We have already discussed above the limited extent to which the overtone series influences criteria of intervallic stability. Thus many aspects of a measure of stability will be a matter of convention.

The simplest imaginable measure of stability would include only one distinction: that between the tonic and any other pitch. The tonic would be stable, and all other pitches equally unstable. In such an idiom, the tonal system as such would place no constraints on the choice of pitches within a piece, except for the last note, which, presuming a piece must end stably, would have to be the tonic. Van der Werf 1972 argues that the chansons of the thirteenth-century *trouvères* are a case of this kind of tonal organization.

In classical Western tonal music, the principles of relative stability are highly elaborated. There are three distinct sorts of principles involved, each addressing a different way of combining pitches. First, principles of *melodic* stability define the relative stability of intervals in the horizontal motion of a single voice. Second, principles of *harmonic* stability define the relative stability among possible vertical combinations of pitches. These two differ in various respects—most markedly in their treatment of the interval of the second, which is the most stable melodic motion but highly dissonant harmonically. Third, the horizontal and vertical dimensions combine in principles of *harmonic progression* (such as relatedness by the circle of fifths). Traditional theory has employed all three of these kinds of principles, usually without clearly distinguishing them. We too have made use of these principles in stating the preference rules for the two reductional components, without feeling obliged to spell them out in detail since they are so well known. Obviously a complete theory of the idiom would be as explicit in this area as we have been in others.

Though open to wide variation, these three general characteristics are essential to any notion of tonality, no matter how broadly conceived. Their pervasiveness suggests that they form an important part of the cognitive organization with which listeners structure musical experience. However, the differences among tonal systems represent aspects of musical structure that a listener must learn (for the most part unconsciously) in order to become "experienced." At the same time, the fact that certain trends appear among simpler tonal systems (for example, the frequent use of small-ratio intervals as points of harmonic stability, and the prevalence of some kinds of pentatonic scales over others) suggests the possibility of an innate system of preferences among tonal systems analogous to the principles of markedness in phonological systems of language proposed in Trubetzkoy 1939 and Jakobson 1941. These would not dictate the specifics of tonal systems, but would aid the learner in the selection of hypotheses about the tonal system he is trying to learn. In other words, one could regard the "inexperienced listener" as seeking a grammar to organize some corpus of musical surfaces that he hears; the markedness principles would guide him toward certain possibilities and away from others. We leave a more thorough investigation of this topic for future research.

11.6 Remarks on Contemporary Music

A limited amount of the world's music, particularly a great deal of twentieth-century art music, would appear to be an exception to the musical universals proposed in this chapter. Even where there is a tonal center, much contemporary music does not offer a coherent measure of relative pitch stability; much of it denies a tonal center altogether. Moreover, a regular metrical hierarchy is often not conveyed, even if the music is notated in traditional terms. Through extreme motivic "transformations" or even the avoidance of motivic content, much of this music withholds evidence for structural parallelism that would lead to any rich hierarchy of grouping structure. At bottom, all of these trends are manifestations of a tendency to avoid repetition.

We do not wish to address the cultural or aesthetic reasons for this tendency, nor do we want to make value judgments. But it is in the spirit of our inquiry to ask what the cognitive consequences of these kinds of organization are for the listener, assuming he is using the principles of musical cognition we have proposed.'

As pointed out in section 11.1, the absence of some kind of organization in the musical signal eliminates the influence of the relevant preference rules. Consider first the absence of a tonal center. In this case, none of the preference rules that refer to pitch stability will be applicable to the musical surface. As a result, the choice of important events in the time-span reduction will be constructed almost exclusively on rhythmic grounds. Pitch enters only through consideration of linear connections (TSRPR 6) and registral extremes (TSRPR 3). The absence of cadential formulas of some kind removes an important indicator of larger-scale time-span reductional structure.

In the prolongational reduction, linear relationships are greatly weakened, with the partial exception of melodic or harmonic identities (strong prolongations). Thus the connection with time-span reduction (PRPRs 1 and 2), itself determined mostly on rhythmic grounds, remains as the chief determinant of prolongational structure. In other words, the theory predicts that intuitions of tension and relaxation, which the prolongational reduction is designed to express, are based less on pitch factors than on rhythmic, dynamic, and timbral considerations, and that large-scale pitch connections do not play a great role in the listener's comprehension of the music.

Suppose in addition that, as often happens, there is little evidence for a regular metrical structure. Then, as discussed in section 4.4, the metrical well-formedness rules fail to impose any extrinsic organization on the pattern of phenomenal accents in the musical surface. The resulting metrical structure follows the irregularities of local detail and hence cannot be extended to any depth. (Recall from chapter 4 how the presumption of regularity was fundamental to the construction of a metrical hierarchy, especially for the larger levels of complicated examples.) An immediate consequence is that metrical tensions such as syncopation become hard to project. Furthermore, the mutual interaction of meter and time-span reduction is weakened: not only are there fewer metrical distinctions available to affect choice of time-span heads (through TSRPR 1), but, because of the absence of pitch stability, there are fewer time-span distinctions available to affect metrical choices (through MPR 9). Insofar as the time-span reduction is weakened by metrical irregularity, the prolongational reduction is weakened too.

All these factors contribute to the weakening of grouping organization. Since the music in question usually avoids symmetry and overt repetition, and since more abstract forms of parallelism intimately involve reductional and metrical considerations, the evidence on which to base grouping judgments is predominantly that of local detail (GPRs 1–3). As a consequence, little multileveled global grouping can be constructed beyond the most obvious textural divisions. And if local detail results in irregular group lengths, metrical structure is further weakened through the influence of grouping parallelism on meter (MPR 1). Some varieties of contemporary music even cloud evidence for local grouping judgments.

In sum, to the degree that the applicability of these various aspects of musical grammar is attenuated, the listener will infer less hierarchical structure from the musical surface. As a result, nonhierarchical aspects of musical perception (such as timbre and dynamics) tend to play a greater, compensatory role in musical organization. But this is not compensation in kind; the relative absence of hierarchical dimensions tends to result in a kind of music perceived very locally, often as a sequence of gestures and associations. Its complexity often resides in the extreme refinement of individual nuances. Alternatively, many composers take recourse in constructing very complicated musical surfaces in terms of the sheer number and variety of events per unit of time. This too is by way of compensation for the lack of sufficient hierarchical organization, but is not a replacement for it.

All of this discussion presupposes that the listener uses the principles of musical cognition set forth in our theory for structuring his perception of such music. One might alternatively suppose that he is using different principles. What might these principles be? One possibility is that he is somehow capable of inferring the organization that the composer, through his compositional method, has consciously built into the piece. For example, a composer might use statistical principles of molecular motion to determine compositional choices. We find it unlikely that the listener can hear according to such radically different principles.[8]

A more plausible case might be made for serialism in pitch organization as a possible principle of musical cognition. Let us see what this would entail. First of all, serialism is a permutational system, in which the function of each pitch is determined by its position within the complete set (usually a twelve-tone row). This means that local elaboration of a particular pitch is not an available option within the compositional technique in any direct way. Such ornamentation could be devised by adding further principles to the system, but they would not be intrinsic to serialism as such.

To be sure, serialism does provide means for elaborating structure, in the form of basic operations on the set such as transposition, inversion, and retrograde. These are global operations on the set as a whole, and as such are transformational (in the technical sense) rather than phrase-structure-like, as our trees are. Hence these operations provide only a set of relationships among different occurrences of the set or portions of it;

they do not, in any direct sense, create a large-scale hierarchy of importance among these occurrences. In other words, these operations play a role more like motivic "transformations" than like reductions in organizing a piece. Thus our hypothetical listener who uses serial principles to organize his hearing has little counterpart to the elaborational structures of tonal music, either at local or at global levels.

Granted that serialism is a vastly different kind of organization for music, as observed in Babbitt 1960, one could ask whether a human being could ever become the hypothetical listener we have posited. Could a listener, through experience, acquire serial principles in such a way as to be able to comprehend the serial structure of novel pieces in the idiom? We find little reason to believe this possible, inasmuch as no serial composer has this ability beyond a very limited extent. Most serial composers, in fact, readily acknowledge the discrepancy between compositional and perceptual organization; that is, they do not defend the necessity for our hypothetical serial listener. Ultimately this is not a matter of opinion or even a purely theoretical question; it is an empirical question, to be decided on psychological grounds. (See Meyer 1967, Ruwet 1972, and Dowling 1972 for a preliminary critique of the cognitive relevance of serial principles.)

But if principles of serialism are not claimed to be cognitively relevant, this leaves open the question of what principles the listener actually uses when he hears serial music. We believe that among the most important principles he falls back on are the musical universals we have proposed; he fits the musical surface of a serial piece to structures described by these principles as best he can.

In addition, it is possible that some of the concepts of recent atonal theory could be developed into a richer theory of how experienced listeners perceive atonal music. Writers such as Forte (1973) and Rahn (1980) have laid a systematic groundwork for atonal music (including serial music) roughly comparable to a formal description of the diatonic system for tonal music. A fundamental concept of such analysis is that of a *set*, a collection of pitches analyzed as (or perceived as) belonging together. Sets, like the groups of the present theory, include collections of contiguous events, but they differ in that individual pitches rather than pitch simultaneities are taken as the smallest units. Thus, as an extreme case, a set may consist of two pitches chosen from one pitch-event plus three from the next pitch-event, while the other pitches in these pitch-events belong to different sets altogether.

These approaches to atonal theory do not specify criteria for what constitutes a set in a given instance, that is, how an experienced listener segments a musical surface into its constituent sets. In order to flesh out a theory of atonal musical cognition, one would first have to develop well-formedness rules for possible segmentations. As suggested above, pitches could belong together if in some sense they were contiguous.

Overlapping as well as vertical, horizontal, and diagonal configurations would have to be allowed. Then, out of these possible segmentations, preference rules would select sets actually heard by the experienced listener. Here parallels to the grouping principles of proximity (GPR 2), similarity (GPR 3), and parallelism (GPR 6) would be relevant. Sets selected at the smallest level would then be related to one another, or combined into larger sets, according to principles of relatedness already partly developed in the atonal theoretical literature. There would undoubtedly be interaction between choice of larger-scale sets and grouping structure as developed here.

A further step might involve partial pitch hierarchies. By implication, current atonal set theory regards all pitches contained within a set as somehow equal. To the ear, however, this is not so. Even without a general scale of pitch stability, structural importance tends to be attributed to events perceived as salient at the musical surface (for example, events that are loud in their contexts, or notes at registral extremes). In other words, structural importance in atonal music may be induced in large part from phenomenal accent. The most salient event in a set could thus be analyzed as its head. In turn, the heads of contiguous sets might go on to form sets at the next level. Unlike the events at the smallest level, these events would not have to be contiguous at the musical surface. Thus we would arrive at a kind of reduction of the piece, stated over set structure instead of time-span segmentation. But it is doubtful that such reductions could be carried very far.

To pursue these ideas further would take us beyond the scope of this book. We have tried only to show how our approach might bear on atonal theory. Most theory about contemporary music has been occupied either with the description of compositional systems or with the systematization of analytic procedures not directly related to the listener's understanding. Our approach emphasizes that there is a crucial distinction between the principles by which a piece is composed and the principles by which it is heard (that is, those that permit the listener to construct a mental representation of the piece). As theorists, we are concerned only with the latter.

The relevance of this distinction to the description of atonal and serial music pertains with equal or greater force to probabilistic methods of composition, to aleatoric methods, to serialism extended to the rhythmic dimension, or to any other procedures that do not directly engage the listener's ability to organize a musical surface. In each of these cases, the gulf between compositional and perceptual principles is wide and deep: insofar as the listener's abilities are not engaged, he cannot infer a rich organization no matter how a piece has been composed or how densely packed its musical surface is. It is in this sense that an apparently simple Mozart sonata is more complex than many twentieth-century pieces that at first seem highly intricate.

Suppose someone were to deny this distinction and to claim that any arbitrary method of composition can create organizations that may become cognitively salient to a listener with sufficient exposure. To be sure, one's ability to structure input improves with exposure; this is implicit in our idealization to the experienced listener. But the assertion that exposure alone suffices for learning is tantamount to blind faith in the most radical form of behaviorism: it attributes to the learner little if any innate organization (disposition to learn certain types of organization rather than others) beyond the ability to respond to reinforcement. There is an overwhelming amount of evidence throughout all areas of psychology that human ability to structure the environment is genetically highly predetermined. We see no reason why musical capacity should be any exception.

It is important not to misunderstand the relevance of this discussion to aesthetic issues. Some critics of serialism, such as Hindemith (1952) and Bernstein (1976), have seized on its perceptually more dubious aspects as arguments against its validity as a compositional method. One could make analogous objections to aleatoric and probabilistic techniques. But such arguments miss the point. No one has offered a concrete theory of how cognitive capacity bears on issues of aesthetic value. All that the argument above implies is that listeners will find it difficult to assign any rich structure to music composed by these techniques. This conclusion is plausible, and it may account in part for the relative inaccessibility of this music. But accessibility per se is not a measure of value. Some of the world's greatest art is highly inaccessible; most of the most ephemeral art is readily accessible. Both tonality and contemporary techniques have produced acknowledged masterpieces; both have produced trash.

In short, our theory says nothing about the relative value of compositional techniques. Nor do we advocate our theory as a novel compositional method. In any case, it could not be applied directly as a generator of pieces, because of the presence of preference rules. Obviously, whatever helps a composer compose his music is of value to him. We believe, nonetheless, that our theory is relevant to compositional problems, in that it focuses detailed attention on the facts of hearing. To the extent that a composer cares about his listeners, this is a vital issue.

12
Psychological and Linguistic Connections

In chapter 1 we said that one of the criteria for adequacy of our theory of music is its ability to shed light on more general psychological issues. In this chapter we present some ways in which the formal theory developed in chapters 3, 4, 7, and 9 reveals clear connections with existing theories in psychology and linguistics, and we reflect on the possible consequences of these connections.

Neisser 1967 (pp. 245–248) points out an important similarity in spirit between generative linguistics and the Gestalt psychology of the 1920s to the 1940s. As we said in chapter 1, our theory is conceived with the same general goals as generative linguistics: to give an account of one aspect of (largely unconscious) human knowledge, explicating the character of a certain class of intuitions, and to divide this knowledge into innate and learned parts. Thus our theory of music is another instance of the sort of cognitive theory discussed by Neisser. One burden of this chapter will be to use the theory of music to forge a more than merely spiritual connection between generative linguistics and Gestalt psychology. Section 12.1 reviews the similarities presented in chapter 3 between the rules of musical grouping and the processes involved in visual form perception. This leads to some discussion of how some of the defects of Gestalt theory can be overcome in the light of contemporary linguistics and the present music theory. Finally, we survey recent work in vision whose general form resembles our music theory.

One of the striking differences between music theory and linguistic theory, mentioned in chapter 1, is the presence in music theory of preference rules, a rule type foreign to generative-transformational grammar. Section 12.2 suggests some cases of current issues in linguistic theory where the preference-rule formalism appears to provide insightful solutions, suggesting that linguistics and music theory are not as different in this respect as might otherwise have been supposed.

Section 12.3 describes a strong parallel between certain aspects of musical and linguistic structure. Recent work in phonology has proposed an analysis of the sound structure of language in terms of hierarchical structures that resemble time-span reductions. We will show how closely these phonological structures are formally related to time-span reductions, then show that they are the result of largely analogous rule systems, even though the entities the rules manipulate are quite different.

12.1
Gestalt Theory and Visual Form Perception

Recall the parallels between visual and auditory grouping pointed out in section 3.2 and 3.4. That such parallels exist was observed by Wertheimer (1923); Köhler (1929) conjectured that they are a result of similar physiological organization in the two domains. Lashley (1951) also argued that essentially similar mental representations serve for both spatially and temporally sequenced memory. However, none of these psychologists had much systematic to say about the structure of temporal organization per se, beyond the enumeration of a certain amount of highly suggestive evidence. Having developed a formal theory for one type of temporal organization, we are in a position to examine the parallelism more closely.

Wertheimer 1923 presents examples almost exactly analogous to our illustrations of visual and musical grouping in section 3.2 (examples 3.6–3.13), and suggests that three general characteristics are involved in these judgments: greater proximity and greater similarity enhance grouping judgments, judgments are less certain when the principles come into conflict, and under certain conditions one principle can override the other. These are exactly the characteristics we have used to motivate the preference rule formalism. Similar observations with a considerable number of other principles occur throughout Koffka's (1935) discussion of shapes, the figure-ground opposition, and three-dimensionality. Wertheimer and Koffka demonstrate the influence of such factors as symmetry, the continuation of lines along regular curves, the ability of a pattern to enclose space, and even the viewer's intention. In general, they state their principles with the same degree of informality that we adopted in section 3.2; more formal rules like those of section 3.3 do not appear.

The work of Wertheimer and Koffka demonstrates the fundamental claim of Gestalt psychology: that perception, like other mental activity, is a dynamic process of organization, in which all elements of the perceptual field may be implicated in the organization of any particular part. They are at pains to point out and prove two crucial aspects of this claim. First, perception is not simply a product of what is in the environment: the viewer plays an active, though normally unconscious, part in determining what he perceives. Second, the totality of the field as perceived cannot be built up piecemeal as a mere accumulation of the perception of its parts each taken in isolation.

The general underlying principle that forms the basis of the Gestalt account of perception was formulated by Wertheimer as the Law of *Prägnanz*. In Koffka 1935 (p. 110) it is stated briefly:

Psychological organization will always be as "good" as the prevailing conditions allow. In this definition the term "good" is undefined. It embraces such properties as regularity, symmetry, [and] simplicity.

In other words, the various principles of visual perception that Koffka demonstrates are explications of the notion of "good" organization.

The preference rule component of the generative theory of musical grouping resembles Wertheimer's and Koffka's account of vision in more than the way individual rules apply and interact with each other. It also has overall properties that make it a Gestalt theory in the sense just described. First, it is mentalistic: it claims that perceived grouping is not present in any direct way in the musical surface. In fact, the events of grouping structure are not even in one-to-one correspondence with the musical surface, since in grouping overlap one surface event appears twice in underlying grouping structure, and in grouping elision an event appears in grouping structure that is absent from the musical surface. These noncorrespondences are made possible by claiming that grouping structure is a mental construct, associated with the musical surface by unconscious rules.

But the theory of grouping is not just mentalistic. It is specifically Gestalt, in that it claims that grouping structures cannot be built up strictly from their parts. Three of the preference rules are indeed concerned with local details, and the information they provide is of undeniable importance. But the rule of intensification (grouping preference rule 4) involves comparison of scattered potential group boundaries, the rule of symmetry (GPR 5) involves the total internal structure of groups, and the rule of parallelism (GPR 6) can invoke the mutual influence of regions spaced arbitrarily far apart. Furthermore, there are cases—such as the opening theme of Mozart's G Minor Symphony, at transition 8–9 (example 3.19)—in which the interpretation of a low-level local detail is overridden by considerations of parallelism.

Other components of the musical grammar show even more clearly that global considerations are essential for musical perception. For example, in syncopation, preference rules for local metrical detail are overridden by global requirements on metrical well-formedness. A choice of head for a time-span is often influenced by a cadential function at some larger level. Global considerations pervade prolongational reduction as a result of its "top-down" construction.

The overall function of the preference rules is to select a structure that is maximally stable; that is, they define what assignments of structure to a musical surface are perceptually "good." Thus the preference rules in effect constitute an explicit statement of the Law of *Prägnanz* as it applies to musical perception.

Having shown that the theory of musical grouping is an instance of Gestalt theory, what are we to make of this relationship? This question must be approached with a certain amount of care, in view of the present status of the Gestalt tradition: though its importance is widely acknowledged, it has hardly been prominent in the literature of the past quarter century. If we are to attach any significance to the similarity of musical grammar and the Gestalt theory of vision, it seems wise, if only for self-protection, to ask why Gestalt psychology has lost influence.

The sociological (irrational) difficulties have already been largely overcome. One gets the impression that Gestalt theory could not withstand the powerful antimentalistic bias prevalent in American psychology during the 1940s and 1950s, and it seems to have been written out of existence by the more "scientific" behaviorist school. Similarly, in the psychology of music, Seashore's (1938) behaviorism was far more prestigious than Mursell's (1937) Gestalt-influenced work. Now the shoe is on the other foot. The success of generative linguistics has played a large role in rekindling interest in mentalistic theories, while behaviorist psychology has been to a great extent discredited by arguments rather similar to those advanced 40–60 years ago by the Gestaltists. (Chomsky 1959 seems to have been a significant turning point.) Thus the atmosphere is now more conducive to a sympathetic reading of Gestalt work than it has been in the past.

More substantive difficulties with the Gestalt tradition arose from the problem of how to couch a mentalistic theory in a rigorous and explanatory fashion. First, it was felt (perhaps partly in response to behavioristic arguments) that no mentalistic theory could be worthwhile without an account of its mechanism, and in this respect Gestalt theory, like all psychological theories past and present, was unquestionably deficient. Koffka compares the Law of *Prägnanz* to physical principles that minimize energy at boundaries between substances. Köhler 1940 tries to make this sort of analogy into a theory by claiming a direct correspondence between the stabilization of perceptual fields and the stabilization of electrical fields in the brain. But, as has been widely recognized, this physiological reduction is far too crude for the finely tuned observations it is meant to explain.

Generative linguistics has again prepared the way for a resolution of the problem, by demonstrating the virtues of dividing a psychological theory into description of knowledge (competence model), description of mechanism (performance model), and physiological reduction. It has come to be widely accepted that a theory may address only competence (as much linguistic theory does) or only competence and performance (as many theories in psycholinguistics and artificial intelligence do), and still be of great explanatory value. Thus Gestalt theory may now be regarded as a theory of knowledge or of processing, which frees it of the stigma of its weak attempts at physiological explanation.[1]

The other stumbling block to Gestalt theory was a lack of formalism. Generative formalisms modeling mental representation had not yet been developed, so a physically based treatment was probably the only way available for going beyond the informality of most Gestalt theorizing. Needless to say, this too no longer presents a problem. Although the formalisms of transformational grammar do not lend themselves to the purposes of visual theory, certain recent work in psychology can be viewed as steps toward a generative theory of vision.

Suppose we think of a theory of vision as a description of the viewer's ability to comprehend the presented visual field. Among the components of such a theory will be a theory of visual structure, an abstract organization that, like musical structure, is mentally generated but attributed to or projected onto the presented field. This structure is the visual world as perceived, that is, the terms in which visual experience presents itself to consciousness. The possibilities for visual structure will be described by principles analogous to musical well-formedness rules.

In addition, the theory will need to describe the mapping between the presented visual field and visual structure. In general, the presented evidence will underdetermine the choice of visual structure; that is, the visual field will in general be highly ambiguous. Therefore the mapping function will have to include a system of preferences that choose the most highly favored analysis or analyses for a presented visual field. The Gestalt laws of organization can be construed as informal statements of various aspects of this system of preferences.

More recent work illustrates parts of such a theory. The detailed topological constraints of Shiman (1975, 1978) are involved in the definition of a well-formed visual structure; they essentially guarantee the orderly decomposition of a field into regions by placing global conditions on the network of boundaries that establish the decomposition. By working through the mathematical consequences of the visual intuition that a boundary is "oriented" (that it belongs specifically to only one of the regions that it adjoins), Shiman derives, among other things, the possibility of certain classical visual figure-ground ambiguities and the impossibility of a three-dimensional interpretation for certain well-known "impossible figures."

The research cited in Shepard 1980 and the theory presented there are very close in spirit to the sketch of visual theory given above. Shepard states clearly the need for a theory of internal mental representation of the visual field upon which computations such as "mental rotations" can be performed. He further shows the necessity for a system of preferences because of the underdetermination of representation by the visual field. Shepard's approach is to derive preferred structures in terms of a metric over a topological manifold whose dimensions correspond, in our framework, to the domains of preference rules. He also alludes to musical problems, describing a topological manifold in which geometrical distance corresponds roughly to relative stability of prolongational connection (that is, of harmonic and melodic relationship).

The most highly detailed work on visual theory in this vein is that reported in Marr 1982. Marr divides the mapping from the presented visual field to visual structure into a number of steps, each of which is a mapping between two discrete levels of structure. Each of the levels of structure he posits is defined explicitly, and the mappings between them are equally explicit, to the point where a meaningful computer simulation is possible. Although Marr's model does not extend all the way to the level of object recognition, those steps he has described are successful in accounting for many important properties of visual perception. Elements of this theory have been incorporated into subsequent work such as Ullmann 1979 and Kosslyn 1980.

In its overall form, Marr's theory is similar to our theory of music. Each level of visual structure is characterized by a set of principles analogous to well-formedness rules. Moreover, the mappings between levels of visual structure rely on principles that operate exactly like our preference rules. Principles may reinforce each other or conflict; when there is conflict, the outcome may be ambiguous or one principle may override the other, depending on their relative strengths of application.

Thus, within modern theories of human visual information processing, many features of Gestalt theory have survived and many analogs to our music theory have emerged. Moreover, the mentalist and innatist position of Gestalt theory is quite in tune with contemporary work. For example, Shepard 1980 contains repeated references to our ability to perceive the world as we do in terms of the outcome of evolution shaping the innate nature of the visual system.

What has not survived from Gestalt psychology is its attempt at physiological reduction. But when viewed as computational principles, the Gestalt laws of organization seem inevitably to play a role. Thus our appeal to principles of Gestalt psychology is not anachronistic. We have used them in a fashion compatible with modern work in visual theory. We have found it useful to refer to the earlier work, despite its lack of explicitness, because of its directness and clarity in addressing some of the more fundamental issues of psychological inquiry that are simply assumed by more recent work.

12.2 Preference Rules in Linguistic Theory

As promised in chapter 1, the generative music theory developed here does not look much like generative linguistics. This section will point out certain formal relationships that are not immediately obvious.

The difference in methodology between the two theories, mentioned in section 1.2, is symptomatic: whereas linguistic theory is highly concerned with grammaticality, music theory is much more concerned with preference among a considerable number of competing well-formed (grammatical) structures. The closest analog to linguistic grammaticality in music theory is adherence to well-formedness rules. These rules resemble linguistic rules in that they either establish a branching or hierarchical structure (like phrase-structure rules in syntax) or characterize permissible distortions of the branching structure (like transformations). This suggests that the bulk of a linguistic grammar consists of well-formedness rules—from phonology through syntax to semantics. Even the lexicon can be considered a part of the well-formedness rule component, in that it establishes well-formed matchings between phonological, syntactic, and semantic form at the terminal nodes of branching structures. The well-formedness rules for music, even considering all four components of the musical grammar, hardly approach the linguistic well-formedness rules in complexity. This reflects the much greater role of grammaticality in language than in music.

The question thus arises as to whether linguistic theory contains any rule systems comparable to preference rules in music. It turns out that a number of phenomena discussed in the linguistic literature have properties appropriate to such rules. We present three of these briefly.

Relative Scope of Quantifiers

Within the rules relating syntactic form to semantic representation, there is a subsystem that deals with establishing the correspondence between the syntactic position of quantifier words such as *every, all, some,* and *many* and their scope in logical form. The effect of scope difference is illustrated in the following pair of sentences, discussed in many places in the linguistic literature. (Emphasizing *two languages* in example 12.1b aids interpretation.)

12.1
a. Every person in this room knows at least two languages.
b. At least two languages are known by every person in this room.

In 12.1a each person may know a different two languages, but in 12.1b two particular languages are known to everyone in the room. The difference is notated formally in terms of relative embedding of quantifiers; the "logical forms" of 12.1a and 12.1b are (informally) 12.2a and 12.2b, respectively.

12.2
a. Every person x in this room is such that [there are two languages y and z such that [x knows at least y and z]].
b. There are two languages y and z such that [every person x in this room is such that [x knows at least y and z]].

The rules relating syntactic quantifier position and relative embedding of quantifiers in logical form have been discussed at great length in both the philosophical and linguistic literature. But among the difficulties in most accounts (including Jackendoff 1972) has been the assumption that these rules are well-formedness rules—that is, that there are principles of the usual grammatical sort that clearly determine the relationship. Ioup 1975 shows that this assumption is false, and that the relationship is in part mediated by what in the present context appear to be preference rules.

Ioup takes seriously the observation, made occasionally in the literature, that ambiguous sentences containing two quantifiers often have a preferred reading.[2] Her preference rules can be stated as follows:

Preference Rule 1 Given two quantifiers in the same surface clause, preferably assign larger scope to the quantifier that is higher on the following scale, or hierarchy: *each>every>all>most>many>several>some> a few*.

Preference Rule 2 Given two quantifiers in the same surface clause, preferably assign larger scope to the one in more salient surface position, defined as the hierarchy topic>deep and surface subject>deep or surface subject but not both>indirect object>preposition object>direct object.

Ioup shows these preferences to hold over a wide range of languages (where the hierarchy in rule 1 is defined over the closest translations of the quantifiers), and claims that they are universal. Furthermore, the hierarchy of syntactic positions is almost the same as one independently motivated for other purposes, so it is not totally *ad hoc* in this rule. Though Ioup does not work out very fully the interaction of the two rules, the overall pattern looks very much like what we expect from preference rules: variable strength application, which yields strongly preferred interpretations when rule applications reinforce, ambiguity when rule applications of commensurate strength conflict, and exceptions to a rule when its weak application is overridden by strong application of another rule.

The preference rules for quantifier scope are a relatively small subsystem embedded in a large system of well-formedness rules. The next examples are more extensive, though they have the disadvantage of not having been given as satisfactory a formal treatment.

Pragmatics

Under normal circumstances we use sentences to mean what they mean literally. But a substantial body of literature under the rubric "pragmatics" has discussed utterances in which the speaker does not literally mean what he says. Among the best-known examples are the uses of the sentences in 12.3, which are literally requests for an answer of *yes* or *no*, as requests for the salt.

12.3
Can you pass the salt?
May I ask you to pass the salt?
Would you mind passing the salt?

Many principles of pragmatics appear to have the nature of preference rules. Grice 1975 presents a particularly clear case in which a number of "maxims" for conversation are stated as preferences on utterances of sentences; for example, "Make your contribution as informative as required," "Do not say what you believe to be false," "Avoid ambiguity," and "Be relevant." Although these are stated as maxims for the speaker, they apply equally to the process of interpretation by the hearer, where they appear as preferences on how to construe the speaker's intended meaning. In this form, the four maxims just quoted can be stated as in 12.4.

12.4
a. Prefer to assume that the speaker is telling you all he knows.
b. Prefer to assume that the speaker believes what he intends to convey.
c. Prefer to assume that the speaker has only one meaning in mind.
d. Prefer to assume that the speaker is conveying something relevant.

To these must be added the rule whose violation motivates the entire system:

12.5
Prefer to assume that what the speaker says is what he intends to convey.

The inclusion of "prefer to assume" in all these principles is what makes them not necessary and sufficient conditions but preferences on interpretation.

Grice works through a number of cases where the speaker violates maxims for special effects of various sorts (just as the composer brings about conflicts among preference rules to avoid clichés in music). The problem for the hearer is to decide what it is that the speaker intends, given the context. Just in case the overall demands of the situation call for rule 12.5 to be overridden, the hearer must construct a plausible intended message that is in some way related to what is said. Grice calls this construction a *conversational implicature.*

Here are a few simple examples: An utterance of an ambiguous sentence presents the hearer with an apparent violation of rule 12.4c. The rule of relevance 12.4d suggests the proper choice of reading in most cases, and choosing only one reading (in partial violation of rule 12.5) permits rule 12.4c to be satisfied. On the other hand, in the case of a pun *both* readings are relevant, and 12.4c is abandoned in favor of complete satisfaction of 12.5, with humorous effect.

Grice presents the case where the speaker says "X is a fine friend," where the hearer knows, and the speaker knows that the hearer knows, that the speaker dislikes X. Here, if rule 12.5 is obeyed, rule 12.4b is violated. This interpretation—that the speaker is lying—might be appropriate if there were a third party in the conversation who was a friend of X and did not know the speaker's relation to X and whom the speaker did not wish to offend. Alternatively, the interpretation in which 12.4b is obeyed and 12.5 is violated is ironic: the speaker is saying just the opposite of what he means.

The rules presented in 12.4 and 12.5 do not deal with utterances that are questions, such as 12.3. A rule must be introduced that addresses the speaker's sincerity in requests, parallel to 12.4b for declaratives. A reasonable first approximation is 12.6.

12.6
Prefer to assume the speaker needs what he requests.

In 12.3, if the question is taken literally, in accordance with rule 12.5, the utterance is a request for information that the hearer can be fairly sure the speaker does not need, in violation of 12.6. The interpretation that does least violence to the literal reading of 12.3 but satisfies 12.6 is to read it as a request for the salt.

The interaction of these rules is analogous to the interaction of musical preference rules. A major difference in Grice's theory, though, is that it lacks a formal characterization of the set of structures out of which possible intended meanings are chosen; such a characterization would correspond to the well-formedness rules of music theory. In particular, when literal interpretation is abandoned, a new interpretation is chosen that is close to the literal one according to a highly complex but unspecified metric of closeness. Nonetheless, the similarity of Grice's pragmatic rules to preference rules for music points to a qualitative difference between pragmatics and the bulk of semantics, syntax, and phonology. The example of musical grammar provides a precedent from another cognitive domain for maintaining the distinction between pragmatic rules and other rule types in linguistic theory. Bach and Harnish (1979, chapter 8) develop a treatment of Gricean principles not unlike what we have proposed here.

Word Meanings
One of the fundamental problems for a theory of word meaning is to explicate the intuitions behind a judgment that a given individual (thing or person) or a given category (class of things or persons) is or is not an instance of the category named by a given word. Where the category is named by a noun, these judgments take the form of assessing the truth of sentences of the forms given in 12.7.

12.7
a. That [*pointing*] is a y.
b. X is a y. [where X is a proper name or definite description]
c. An x is a y. [where x is a common noun]

Example 12.7a asserts category membership of an individual designated nonverbally; 12.7b asserts the category membership of an individual designated verbally; 12.7c asserts the inclusion of one category in another. Judgments of type 12.7b and 12.7c are basic to most theories of entailment, analyticity, and so forth. Jackendoff (forthcoming) gives evidence that all three sentence types present essentially the same problems to a theory of word meaning.

Most theories of word meaning treat categorization as an open-and-shut case. But this is an oversimplification. Many judgments are uncertain—for example, those in 12.8a–12.8c, which correspond to sentence types 12.7a–12.7c, respectively. Connoisseurs of linguistic semantics will notice that appealing to insufficient scientific knowledge, fuzzy logic (see Lakoff 1972), or division of linguistic labor (Putnam 1975) will not help account for the uncertainty in these examples.

12.8

a. That [*pointing*] is $\begin{cases} \text{a lake (not just a pond).} \\ \text{a boulder (not just a stone).} \end{cases}$

b. George Bush is a fool.

   The signs Washoe (the chimpanzee) makes are a language.

c. An australopithecus is a human.

   A piano is a percussion instrument.

An adequate theory of word meaning must allow for such uncertain judgments.

A related problem is pointed out in Wittgenstein 1953. In his well-known discussion of the word *game,* Wittgenstein shows that there cannot be necessary and sufficient conditions for something to be a game, since there are no properties shared by all games that are not also shared by other activities that are not games. Similar arguments can be applied to most words in the language: for almost any condition one can place on the members of a category, there are individuals that are exceptions to the condition but are still intuitively judged to be members of the category. Thus necessary and sufficient conditions are generally too strong a requirement on a theory of word meaning. Wittgenstein argues that word meanings should be characterized in terms of a system of overlapping "family resemblances"—characteristics that members of a category may, but need not, share. This suggestion has been investigated experimentally in the work of Eleanor Rosch (see particularly Rosch and Mervis 1975). These results suport the family-resemblance hypothesis, showing in addition that the members of categories that are considered most prototypical of that category are those with the most attributes in common with other members of the category and the fewest attributes in common with members of other categories.

These arguments suggest that the proper formalization of word meanings is as a combination of well-formedness rules and preference rules, much as in the theory of musical structure. For example, there are no necessary and sufficient conditions for a portion of the musical surface to be judged a group. The grouping well-formedness conditions are necessary conditions on groups, but not sufficient. Each preference rule is an attribute that creates family resemblances among grouping structures, but since every preference rule can be overridden by the proper confluence of circumstances, it is a sufficient condition only in the absence of conflicting evidence. Where preference rules come into conflict, dubious judgments of grouping result; where a great number of preference rules reinforce each other, a stereotypical grouping structure results. Thus the theory of preference rules accounts for the productivity of the system, the existence of family resemblances, the existence of dubious judgments, and the existence of stereotypical examples.

To see how directly this result bears on a theory of word meanings, observe that the grammar of musical grouping presented in chapter 3 can be taken as a theory of the meaning of the term *(musical) group*. One would expect meanings of other words to be commensurately complex. In particular, it is plausible that the well-formedness conditions would at least fix the semantic field of a word. The preference rules would, among other things, carry out discriminations along dimensions of continuous variation. For example, color terms would presumably have well-formedness conditions identifying them as denoting colors; the exact discrimination among colors would be carried out by preference rules. On the other hand, some classes of terms might lack any interesting preference rules. Kinship terms, for instance (including terms of non-kinship like *bachelor*), seem to be such that well-formedness conditions on configurations of primitives such as *male, female, descendant of,* and *spouse of* largely suffice. Thus we would expect the balance between well-formedness and preference rules to differ from word to word, with well-formedness rules never entirely absent.[3]

Other Phenomena

We mention briefly three other areas in which the characteristics of preference rules have been observed. One of these is *phonetic perception.* Liberman and Studdert-Kennedy (1977) speak of a "trading relation" among the acoustic cues that distinguish such phrases as *gray ship, gray chip, great ship,* and *great chip.* In particular, the duration of the silence after the vowel of the first word (between 0 and 100 milliseconds) and the duration of the fricative "sh" noise (between 60 and 180 milliseconds) must be evaluated in relation to each other in order to predict which phrase is heard. This behavior closely resembles the assignment of metrical weight in music, for example, where stress and length interact in similar fashion.

Another area of grammar for which the notion of preference rules seems especially apposite is the statement of *markedness conventions:*

conditions that establish preferred forms for rules of grammar but may be violated by particular grammars. Principles of markedness have been appealed to especially in phonology (see, for example, Trubetzkoy 1939; Chomsky and Halle 1968), but syntactic theory has also often made use of the characteristic marked-unmarked distinction. A more general form of markedness conventions is the *evaluation metric* for grammars, proposed by Chomsky (1965). The evaluation metric embodies a set of preferences that enable the child to choose a grammar from among numerous possibilities, where the choice is underdetermined by the linguistic evidence available to the child. It is a fundamental component of contemporary theories of generative grammar.

Finally, the theory of *parsing strategies*—part of the study of linguistic performance—has frequently made use of heuristic strategies that make a "best guess" about the structure of a sentence being processed (see Kimball 1973; Wanner and Maratsos 1978; J. D. Fodor 1978). Again, preference-rule-like behavior is clearly observable, in the way that syntactic and semantic evidence interact to determine which of many potential structures is to be selected.

Thus, although the general notion of preference rules and the characteristics of preference-rule systems have not been recognized as such within linguistic theory, a number of linguistic phenomena do display the requisite properties. In general, generative linguistics, perhaps because of its historical roots in the theory of computability, has stressed only the contribution of well-formedness rules. By contrast, much research on vision has concentrated on the equivalent of preference rules. The theory of musical cognition developed here highlights the necessity for both types of rules, not only for music, but for language and vision as well.

**12.3
A Deep Parallel
Between Music
and Language**

This section will show that the formalism developed in chapters 5–7 to express time-span reduction is a notational variant of a formalism in linguistics called *prosodic structure*. After demonstrating the relationship we will ask whether the relationship is an accident or whether it rests on a principled basis. In an effort to answer this question we will compare the theory of prosodic structure with the theory of time-span reduction. Our conclusion will be that these theories are closely related in form, though not in substance. The implications of this parallel for more general issues of cognition are discussed in the last part of this section.

Prosodic Structure

The theory of phonology has traditionally assumed that the sound pattern of language is determined simply in terms of the linear string of phonological segments (or phonemes). However, under this assumption (developed in greatest detail in Chomsky and Halle 1968) many phenomena of stress placement, stress subordination, vowel harmony (in languages such as Turkish), and syllable structure proved resistant to perspicuous treatment. A recent line of research in phonology, first proposed by Liberman (1975) and Liberman and Prince (1977), has developed a theory of *prosodic tree structures* (sometimes also called *metrical structures*) that overcomes these difficulties. This theory has stimulated a great deal of work developing and refining the initial formulation.[4] Although there are several variants of the theory already in the literature, enough basic agreement exists that we can present a composite version that does justice to the literature and brings out those characteristics most like time-span reduction.

It is well known that there are two simultaneous and independent kinds of organization in the phonetic string—morphological and syllabic—and that these two do not divide up the phonetic string in the same way. For example, the word *originality* divides up morphologically as *origin+al+ity,* but syllabically as *o+ri+gi+na+li+ty.* Notice that the syllables *na* and *li* cut across morpheme boundaries. Kahn (1976) was the first to give a satisfactory theory of syllable structure in generative phonology; Chomsky and Halle (1968) had tried rather successfully to do without the notion of syllable in their theory.

The rules determining position of word stress in various languages often make use of distinctions among syllable types. This suggests that stress rules should apply not to the simple phonological string, nor to the morphological structure (as in Chomsky and Halle 1968), but to the syllabic structure. Moreover, the existence of numerous languages that place stress on every second (or third) syllable of a word suggests that in these languages syllables are themselves organized into larger units, which have been termed *feet.* The complete prosodic organization of the word results from aggregating the feet together.

A tree notation developed in Liberman and Prince 1977 expresses the aggregation of syllables into feet and of feet into words. In their notation, each node of the tree dominates either a surface syllable or two other branches, one strong (*s*) and one weak (*w*). For example, 12.9 illustrates their tree structures for the English words *reconciliation* and *contractual.*

12.9

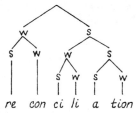 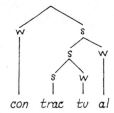

The purpose of the *s* and *w* markings is to express relative degrees of stress. In Chomsky and Halle 1968, as in previous traditions, stress was marked numerically on vowels: [1 stress] was greater than [2 stress],

Psychological and Linguistic Connections

which in turn was greater than [3 stress], and so forth. In addition, all numbered degrees were treated as greater in stress than [unstressed]. To employ this formalism in rules, elaborate conventions had to be developed that had little to do with the linguistic insight they were intended to express. In the tree notation, by contrast, main stress falls on the syllable dominated only by *ss* in the tree (the *designated terminal element*), subsidiary stresses fall on syllables immediately dominated by *s*, and unstressed syllables are all immediately dominated by *w*. In *reconciliation*, for instance, the main stress falls on the penultimate syllable, subsidiary stresses fall on *re-* and *-cil-*, and the remaining syllables are unstressed; in *contractual*, only the single syllable *-trac-* is stressed. Thus the tree notation represents relative stress as explicitly relational; that is, in terms of hierarchical oppositions of *ss* and *w*s. For many reasons this is clearly superior to the theory that assigns stress in terms of numerical values; and for once a major change in linguistic theory has not met with vociferous opposition.

We can now make an initial comparison of time-span reduction and prosodic structure. Abstracting away from the musical and linguistic material at the bottoms of the trees, let us examine the trees themselves. In both sorts of trees, each branch divides into branches that are classified according to a binary opposition. In the time-span-reduction tree, the opposition is head versus elaboration; in the prosodic tree, the opposition is strong versus weak.[5] This similarity leads to the observation that the two tree notations are essentially notational variants. Taking the time-span reduction notion of *head* as parallel to the prosodic notion of *strong*, we can establish the equivalence of structures shown in 12.10.

12.10

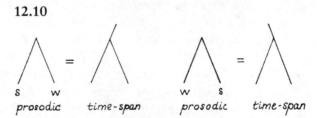

With this equivalence, we can convert a prosodic tree into time-span reduction notation by systematically substituting time-span configurations for the corresponding prosodic ones at each node in the tree; that is, a right branching for an *s-w* configuration and a left branching for a *w-s*. Alternatively, we can convert time-span reductions into prosodic notation by reversing the process. Figure 12.11 is the time-span notation corresponding to the analyses of *reconciliation* and *contractual* given in 12.9. It can readily be seen that Liberman and Prince's notion of designated terminal element (that unit dominated only by *ss* in a tree) translates into time-span notation as the head (that unit from which all others branch). Hence the primary stress in 12.11 is indicated by the longest branch in the tree.

12.11

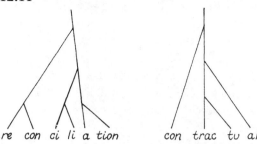

It is at least an interesting coincidence that two theories, developed independently to deal with totally dissimilar phenomena, should have arrived at equivalent notations to express their analyses. To establish a preliminary sense of the strength of the equivalence, it is useful to compare time-span and prosodic trees with syntactic trees. Both the time-span and prosodic trees represent a hierarchy of binary oppositions: head versus elaboration and strong versus weak. By contrast, syntactic trees represent a hierarchy of abstract syntactic categories, such as sentence, noun phrase, and verb phrase. Thus the form of time-span and prosodic trees is not an inevitable consequence of strict hierarchical structure alone, since there are other imaginable hierarchical organizations that lead to different types of tree structures.

Does the equivalence of the two notations mean that there is a similarity between the intuitions the two theories address? As a step toward answering this question, we will compare the rule systems that determine time-span reductions and prosodic trees, and show that they share important formal properties and even some substantive properties. By demonstrating this more extensive parallelism, we will have shown that the equivalence of notations is more than a coincidence.

Prosodic Segmentation Rules

We begin by summarizing the grammar of time-span reduction developed in chapters 6 and 7. There are three subcomponents. First, the segmentation rules (section 7.1) produce an exhaustive hierarchical segmentation of the musical surface into time-spans. The time-spans form what might be called a layered hierarchy. At the most local levels are the time-spans we have called *subgroups,* those determined by metrical structure alone and by metrical structure interacting with grouping. Next, there are one or more levels of *uncadenced groups;* and at the largest levels the time-spans are all *cadenced groups.* These layers are fixed in order from smallest level to largest and cannot mix; for example, there cannot be a level of subgroups intervening between two levels of groups. This layering, though not stressed as such in chapters 6 and 7, is important for the comparison with prosodic structure.

The well-formedness rules (section 7.2) make up the second subcomponent of the grammar of time-span reduction. They determine a set of possible time-span reduction trees, such that every time-span has a head selected out of the heads of the time-spans it immediately contains. Third, the choice of head for each time-span is determined by the preference rules (sections 7.3 and 7.4), which are sensitive to metrical, harmonic, voice-leading, and cadential properties of the events in the time-span.

The version of hierarchical phonology most similar to the grammar of time-span reduction is that developed by Selkirk (1978, 1980). More than other approaches, Selkirk's makes clear the distinction between rules of segmentation, rules that build tree structures on the basis of the segmentation, and rules that determine relative prominence of sister branches in the trees (though these distinctions are implicit in all the other approaches). To bring out the parallelism with music, we will present a version of Selkirk's theory, slightly modified from her presentation but preserving its essential insights.

Although the pioneering study by Liberman and Prince (1977) makes use of the notions of syllable and foot, their formal role in the theory is left somewhat unclear. Selkirk, however, argues that syllables and feet must be explicitly marked as *prosodic categories,* and that these categories play a role in the formal statement of various phonological processes. In addition, Selkirk argues for the existence of other, larger, prosodic categories of *word, phonological phrase, intonational phrase,* and *utterance.* The result is a segmentation of the phonological string into a complex hierarchy that corresponds only in part to syntactic structure. For example, 12.12 is the segmentation of the sentence *In Pakistan, Tuesday is a holiday.* The levels to the left identify the prosodic categories.

12.12

	In Pa ki stan Tues day is a ho li day
syllable level	
foot level	
word level	
phon. phr. level	
int. phr. level	
utterance level	

An important way in which this structure is unlike syntactic structure and like time-span segmentation is that, whereas in syntactic structure a category may recur inside one of its constituents (for instance, NP inside PP inside NP), this is impossible in the phonological segmentation.

Words, for example, may contain feet but may not be contained in them. Thus phonological segmentation is a hierarchy that is "layered" in the same sense as time-span segmentation.

As in the case of the time-span categories *subgroup* and *group,* each of the phonological categories has a different principle of segmentation. The principle for segmentation into syllables is approximately as follows: Each language has a characteristic class of syllable onsets. For example, in English, syllables (hence words) can begin either with no consonant, with any single consonant, or with a variety of clusters such as *st, tr, spl,* etc. but not including *zd, pk,* etc. The basic principle in forming the syllabic segmentation is to set syllable boundaries so as to maximize the length of syllable onsets, in conformance with the principles of basic syllable composition of the language. So, for example, in *Pakistan,* a syllable boundary is placed before *st,* since it is an allowable syllable onset. However, in *Tuesday,* the medial cluster *sd* (phonetically *zd*) is not a possible syllable onset of English, so the boundary is set between the two consonants.[6] Syllable boundaries are of course set between words as well.

The principles for segmentation into feet vary among languages. Selkirk argues that French essentially has primarily monosyllabic feet. Vergnaud and Halle (1979), examining the literature on a wide variety of languages, find three other sorts of foot-formation rules: those establishing bisyllabic feet, those establishing trisyllabic feet, and those establishing feet of unlimited length (bounded by word boundaries or syllables of a specified type). English appears to have monosyllabic, bisyllabic, and trisyllabic feet, depending on the content of the syllables gathered up into a foot. The relevant factors are the tenseness of the syllable's vowel and the nature of the consonants, if any, at the end of the syllable. So far as is known, syllable types are not distinguished for prosodic purposes in any language by the nature of their initial consonant(s).

Some examples are given in 12.13. Example 12.13a is a monosyllabic foot; 12.13b is a bisyllabic foot; 12.13c is a trisyllabic foot, which, like all trisyllabic feet in English, begins with a bisyllabic foot; 12.13d, by contrast with 12.13b, is a bisyllabic word consisting of two monosyllabic feet—the difference between this and 12.13b accounts for the fact that its second syllable bears secondary stress and that of 12.13b does not.

12.13

	a *flounce*	**b** *modest*	**c** *Pamela*	**d** *gymnast*
syllable level	⌞____⌟	⌞__⌟⌞__⌟	⌞_⌟⌞_⌟⌞_⌟	⌞__⌟⌞__⌟
foot level	⌞____⌟	⌞_____⌟	⌞____⌟	⌞__⌟⌞__⌟
word level	⌞____⌟	⌞_____⌟	⌞_____⌟	⌞_____⌟

For our present comparison, an interesting aspect of English foot formation is the behavior of unstressed syllables at the beginning of a word. In one proposed treatment of them, the structure of words like *attire, vanilla,* and *America* is as in 12.14 (though the mechanism for deriving this structure has been open to dispute—see Selkirk 1980).

12.14

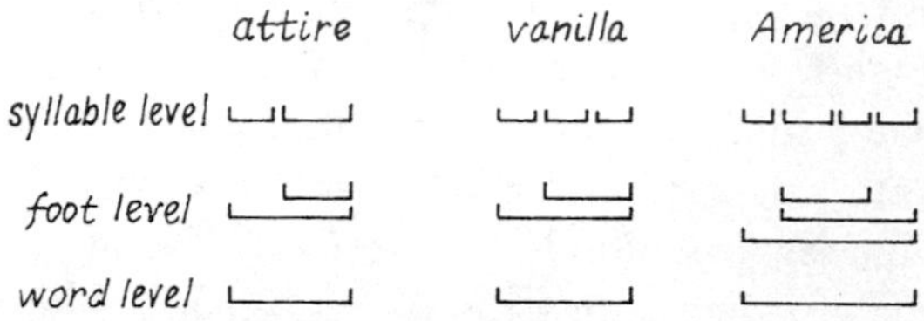

In 12.14 we find an unstressed initial syllable preceding a monosyllabic, a bisyllabic, and a trisyllabic foot. The initial syllable is not simply an odd syllable added at the beginning of the word, but is adjoined to the rest as the beginning of an extra foot level. For us this solution is particularly significant because of its parallel with the treatment of upbeats in time-span segmentation (see examples 6.4 and 6.5 and section 7.1). In each case a weak segment separated by a major boundary (a group boundary in music, a word boundary in language) from the preceding strong segment is instead adjoined to the following segment. Hence, beyond the formal parallel of a layered hierarchy in both grammars, the segmentation rules display an interesting substantive parallel.[7]

At the next layer of the hierarchy the segmentation into words is obvious. We only have to note that compounds such as *blackboard* and *labor union* have two word levels, as shown in 12.15.

12.15

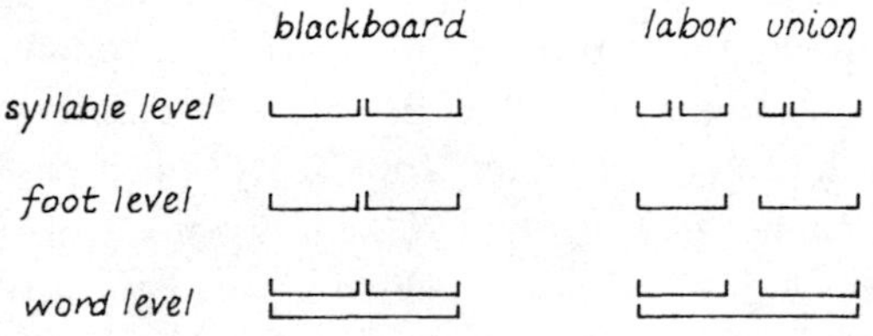

However, it remains to be shown how the feet of a multifoot word are structured. Selkirk, following Liberman and Prince, gathers the two rightmost feet into a segment, then gathers that with the next to the left, and so on until the left-hand boundary of the word is reached. For example, *reconciliation,* with three feet, receives the structure shown in 12.16. (Selkirk's notation does not accord the segment *-ciliation* the label "foot," but there appears to be no harm in it.)

12.16

reconciliation

syllable level ⌷_⌷__⌷_⌷⌷⌷_⌷

foot level ⌷____⌷_⌷__⌷_⌷

word level ⌷_____⌷

Looking at a large variety of languages, Vergnaud and Halle (1979) conclude that the rule for structuring the feet of an English word is typical. The only major difference that appears is that in some languages the gathering of feet begins at the left and works rightward, in the mirror image of the English rule.[8] Morris Halle has suggested (personal communication) that one should expect similar mirror-image phenomena in time-span segmentation in music. Recall that the normal gathering of subgroups into larger subgroups places the strong beat on the left. However, as mentioned at the end of section 7.1, there is a musical idiom in which the strong beat appears to be on the *right* end of subgroups: the gamelan music described by Becker and Becker (1979). Hence the cross-linguistic possibilities for foot formation parallel the cross-idiom possibilities for subgroup formation.

The larger levels of the prosodic structure—phonological phrase, intonational phrase, and utterance—have been less extensively studied than syllables, feet, and words. Selkirk's preliminary work indicates that the rules determining segmentation at these levels are not terribly different from the rules discussed so far, except that they make use of syntactic as well as phonological properties to establish boundaries.

To sum up: We find that prosodic structure, like time-span reduction, is based on a segmentation of the surface string into a layered hierarchy. Each layer (subgroups, uncadenced groups, and cadenced groups in music; syllables, feet, words, and the like in language) in itself exhaustively analyzes the string, and of course there may be more than one such level.

We next turn to the principles that define the possible trees associated with a phonological segmentation.

Prosodic Well-Formedness Rules

The principles of segmentation apply in such a way that each segment at each level immediately contains either one or two segments of the next smaller level (this should be evident from examination of the structures in 12.12–12.16). Thus it is simple to construct a tree that reflects the segmentation. Each of the smallest segments (syllables in the version of the theory presented here) is attached to the bottom of a branch. If a segment *x* is the only segment immediately contained in the segment of the next larger level, nothing happens in the tree. If segments *x* and *y* are both

Psychological and Linguistic Connections

immediately contained in the same segment z of the next larger level, the branches corresponding to x and y are joined into a branch corresponding to z; one of the two constituent branches is labeled s (strong) or w (weak). If this process is carried out recursively, all the way to the largest levels of segmentation, the result is a well-formed tree of the sort illustrated in 12.9 above, expressing the relative prominence of all the segments of the phonological string.[9] This process parallels exactly the construction of a time-span tree.

It is worth noting that the binary relationships the two trees express are not strictly parallel. The relationship *head* versus *elaboration* in time-span reduction trees is a relationship between events in the musical surface; a branch in a tree represents a single event. For example, the uppermost branching in the tree for a piece stands for a relation between the piece's structural beginning and structural ending, not between its first and second halves. By contrast, the relationship *strong* versus *weak* in prosodic trees is a relationship between segments of the phonological segmentation; each branch in the tree represents a syllable, foot, or word. For example, the uppermost opposition of w and s in *reconciliation* (12.9) is a relationship between *recon-* and *-ciliation*. We will discuss below whether this disparity between the two theories is genuine, or whether a more complete parallelism can be obtained.

So far we have simply constructed a set of possible prosodic trees corresponding to a particular segmentation. What is needed in addition is a set of rules of prominence to ascertain, for each branching in the tree, which branch is s and which w.

Prosodic Rules of Prominence
Each of the layers in the prosodic hierarchy has a characteristic rule or set of rules for determining relations of prominence. Starting from the innermost layer, the aggregation of syllables into feet, the rule for English is as follows (in present terms[10]):

Prominence Rule 1
a. In a foot that immediately contains two syllables, the first syllable is strong.
b. In a foot that immediately contains a foot and a syllable, the foot is strong.

This rule results in the trees shown in 12.17 for *flounce, modest, Pamela, attire, vanilla,* and *America* (the segmentation is from 12.13 and 12.14). Recall that main stress goes on the syllable dominated only by ss.

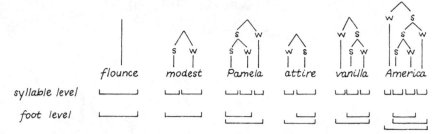

Vergnaud and Halle (1979) show that there are languages in which the counterpart of rule 1a has the reverse effect, marking the second syllable strong. Rule 1b could conceivably have a mirror-image counterpart, making the foot weak; however, the empirical need for such a rule is as yet unclear.

The next layer in the hierarchy is the aggregation of feet into words. Liberman and Prince (1977) give the following rule for English:

Prominence Rule 2 (Lexical Category Prominence) In a segment immediately containing two feet, the second is strong if and only if it branches.[11]

This rule results in the trees in 12.18 for *gymnast, reconciliation, anecdote,* and *anecdotal*. Notice in particular the contrast between the last two of these, where the extra syllable *-al* causes the second foot of *anecdotal* to branch, in turn altering the tree and shifting stress to *-do-*.

12.18

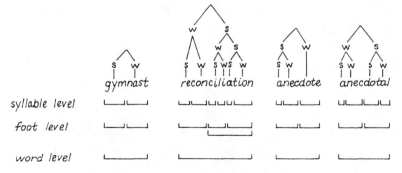

A similar rule governs the aggregation of words into larger words:

Prominence Rule 3 (Compound Stress) In a word immediately containing two words, the second is strong if and only if it branches into two words.

This rule accounts for the contrast between main stress on *Rorschach* in *Rorschach blot* and on *ink* in *Rorschach ink-blot*. In the latter only, the second word on the next-to-largest level of segmentation branches into

Psychological and Linguistic Connections

two words. (Segmentation and tree structure are shown only from the word level up in 12.19.)

12.19

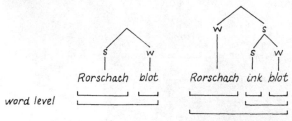

Notice that the rule specifies branching into two *words,* rather than just branching as in the previous rule. The reason for this is that the rule is not sensitive to the number of syllables or feet in the constituent words. For example, in both *labor day* and *labor union,* main stress falls on *labor,* even though in the latter case *union* branches into two syllables. (Nonetheless, one can imagine generalizing prominence rules 2 and 3 into a single rule if proper attention is paid to stating limitations on the ability of rules to cross layers in the hierarchy.)

Finally, the aggregation of words into phonological phrases is governed by this rule from Liberman and Prince 1977:[12]

Prominence Rule 4 (Nuclear Stress) In a phonological phrase that immediately contains two phonological phrases or words, the second is strong.

This rule accounts for the stress patterns of phrases like *three red hats* and *John ate Bill's peach* (represented only from word level up in 12.20).

12.20

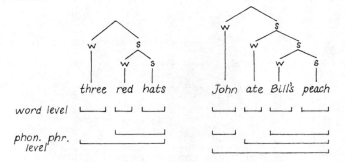

At the level of phonological phrase there is also a prominence rule that bears a more patent resemblance to rules of musical structure than the four preceding rules. This is Liberman and Prince's rule of Iambic Reversal, also commonly called the Rhythm Rule. Its effect is to shift stress leftward in certain situations. For example, the words *thirteen* and *Tennessee* have strongest stress on the last syllable when spoken in isolation;

but in the phrases *thirteen men* and *Tennessee air* their strongest stresses are on the initial syllable. Liberman and Prince explicate the rule in terms of a metrical structure not unlike the musical metrical structure described in chapters 2 and 4.

The general idea behind the Rhythm Rule is that the stresses of a linguistic phrase form a hierarchical metrical pattern, with relatively heavy stresses corresponding to relatively strong beats and relatively weak stresses corresponding to relatively weak beats. The ideal metrical structure is one in which relatively strong and relatively weak beats alternate; in particular, two relatively strong beats are preferably not adjacent to one another. Just such a situation arises in the juxtaposition of *thirteen* with *men* and *Tennessee* with *air:* the strongest stress is on the second word, and the next strongest is on the final syllable of the first word. The Rhythm Rule alters this undesirable situation by reversing the largest *w* and *s* of the first word, thereby separating the second-strongest stress from the strongest by a relatively weak stress. Thus, instead of 12.21a and 12.21b (the tree structures one would expect given the stress patterns of the individual words), the Rhythm Rule yields the structures in 12.21c and 12.21d. Beneath the segmentation is the metrical structure (in our notation) assigned to the tree; the number of dots below a syllable is proportional to its relative prominence in the tree.

12.21

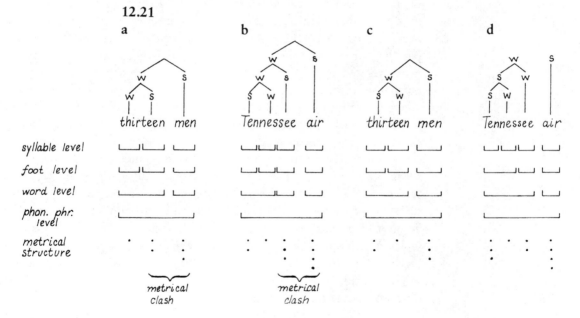

The Rhythm Rule can therefore be thought of as a rule that makes prosodic structure conform more closely to an ideal metrical pattern. Despite the differences in formulation, there is a clear kinship between this rule and the rules relating metrical structure to time-span reduction (MPR 9, TSRPR 1, and especially TSRPR 5). The major difference between music and language in this respect is that musical events are organized around a fixed and regular metrical structure that must be maintained throughout. In language, by contrast, the rhythm is flexible and is not required to conform to any particular pattern.

Either of these practices may be altered. In recitative, fixed meter is abandoned by dropping MWFR 3 (the spacing of strong beats two or three beats apart) and MWFR 4 (the equal spacing of beats), and more flexible, speechlike rhythms appear. In poetry, a fixed metrical pattern is imposed to which the linguistic stresses correspond; in effect, a counterpart of MWFRs 3 and 4 is adopted (see Halle and Keyser 1971 and Kiparsky 1977 for discussion).

Thus we can conclude that the relation of relative prominence to metrical structure is substantially the same in music and language. The difference between the relevant musical preference rules and the prosodic Rhythm Rule is a function largely of the different metrical practices of the two media.

Some Discrepancies

The last three subsections have shown that time-span reduction and prosodic structure are not just represented by equivalent tree notation; they are the products of grammars that carry out formally parallel operations on musical and phonological strings. In each case, the string is segmented into a layered hierarchy, in which each layer provides an exhaustive segmentation. A set of possible tree structures is defined in precisely parallel fashion over the segmentations, and preference rules or prominence rules determine which of the possible trees is the correct one. Furthermore, two substantive parallels have appeared: the treatment of augmented time-spans and augmented feet, with group boundaries and word boundaries playing equivalent roles; and the relationship of metrical structure to choices made by the prominence rules.

Of course, the nature of the strings being segmented and most of the substance of the rules in the two theories are quite different. This only serves to make the formal parallels still more striking, particularly since the two theories were developed independently and were designed to account for radically different sorts of intuitions (though there has been interfertilization of the two theories with respect to the treatment of metrical structure). Before drawing further conclusions, however, we should consider some formal respects in which the two theories differ and discuss how the differences might be resolved.

First, although the parallelism was first motivated by the equivalence of the tree notations, the two notations actually differ somewhat in expressive power. Our discussion has shown the equivalence of prosodic trees to the plainest form of time-span trees, where only *ordinary reduction* has taken place. But in section 7.2 we showed that there are three other relationships that can obtain between the head of a time-span and

the events within it: *fusion,* in which the head represents the simultaneous sounding of two or more events from the time-span; *transformation,*
in which the head is a composite of the events in the time-span; and
cadential retention, in which two successive events forming a cadence are
both retained. Prosodic theory has no equivalent for these three additional relationships. Thus, if it were desirable to adopt a uniform notation for the two theories, time-span notation would be more appropriate;
phonological theory would merely adopt the restrictive form with only
ordinary branching. On the other hand, Morris Halle has informed us
(personal communication) that recent developments suggest the possibility of other relationships in phonology not shared by music. In other
words, phonology and music might share a common core of hierarchical
structure but diverge in various specifics.

A second formal difference between the two theories concerns the
plurality of branching. In time-span theory, most of the branching we
have discussed has been binary; each time-span above the smallest level
contains two time-spans of the next smaller level. However, in a triple
meter (such as the 6/8 of Mozart K. 331), ternary branching appears at a
certain subgroup level. It is also not inconceivable for a group to contain
three or more smaller groups: for example, in strophic songs and variation forms, the largest segmentation of the piece is often into as many
groups as there are verses or variations.

On the other hand, prosodic theory has been formulated in terms of
strictly binary branching. Where a foot, for example, contains more than
two syllables, the segmentation and the resulting tree are constructed
using recursive binary branching, as in 12.22a, rather than multiple
branching, as in 12.22b. Is this a real difference between language and
music, or is it just a consequence of the way the two theories happen to be
stated?

12.22

a   b

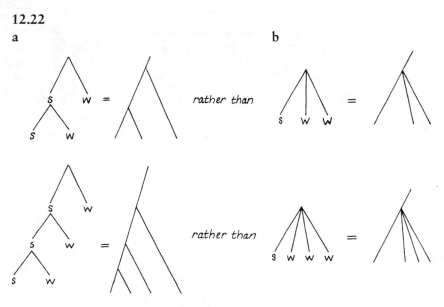

Psychological and Linguistic Connections

Here it is not clear to us which theory should give way, or even if either should. On one hand there seems to be only one use in prosodic theory for recursive binary-branching trees that cannot be equally coded into multiply branching trees: the assignment of relative degree of subsidiary stress (Liberman and Prince 1977, p. 259), which is certainly an important function. But in sections 3.4 and 3.5 of the paper Liberman and Prince suggest that subsidiary stresses are assigned by reference to the metrical structure instead (or in addition). Thus the restriction of prosodic segmentation and trees to strictly binary branching does not have as much explanatory value as might be expected.

On the other hand, there is some potential justification for strict binary branching in time-span trees. At subgroup levels, where ternary branching occurs in connection with ternary meter, there is often motivation for an additional segmentation into 2 + 1 (♩ ♪) or 1 + 2 (♪♩) (the typical "oom-pah-pah" accompaniment can be thought of as a special case of the latter). Although this subgrouping would not be adhered to consistently throughout a piece, as the meter is, it could be supplied in each ternary subgroup by appropriately stated preference rules for time-span segmentation, a rule type we have so far managed to avoid.

At larger levels, intuition seems to support the grouping of multiply branching forms such as variations by twos, in the absence of evidence to the contrary. An odd variation at the end would be adjoined to the group consisting of the previous two variations—parallel to the segmentation of trisyllabic feet in English. Thus there might be some advantage to imposing strict binary branching on time-span reductions.[13] Whatever the outcome, the discrepancy between prosodic and time-span theory does not seem irreconcilable, or even particularly serious.

A much more important difference is in the interpretation of time-span and prosodic trees. As observed above, a branch at any level of a time-span tree stands for a single pitch-event, which is elaborated by all the events whose branches are subsidiary to it. In a prosodic tree, however, a branch is taken to stand for an entire prosodic constituent containing strong and weak parts. If the trees are interpreted so differently, can the theories really be parallel?

The contrast between the two interpretations is not unlike that between two interpretations of metrical accent in music itself. One view, that of Cooper and Meyer 1960, is that metrical weight is (in our terms) a property of time-spans—that metrical weight has duration. In section 2.3 we argued against such a view and for one in which metrical weight is a property of beats (points in time) rather than time-spans. We said there, essentially, that subsidiary elements of "strong" time-spans (time-spans beginning on a relatively strong beat) are in fact no stronger than subsidiary weak elements of "weak" time-spans. For example, in a 4/4 measure, the second beat does not receive more weight than the fourth by virtue of being in the "strong" time-span 1–2 as opposed to the "weak" time-span 3–4. The same argument applies to time-span reduction: low-level elaborations of relatively important events are themselves no more important than equally low-level elaborations of less important events. In other words, strength relative to other time-spans inheres only in the head and not in the time-span as a whole. Thus it would be incorrect to change the interpretation of time-span trees to conform to phonological theory.

On the other hand, it does make some sense to reinterpret prosodic structure in time-span reductional terms. When main stress is applied to a phrase on the basis of a prosodic tree, it is not spread over an entire strong constituent but is applied to the designated terminal element (the head) alone. Unstressed syllables are of equivalent strength whether they are in a relatively strong or a relatively weak constituent. Hence aspects of our argument against Cooper and Meyer's interpretation of metrical weight in music are germane here, which suggests that the musical interpretation of the hierarchical structures common to time-span and prosodic theory is the correct one.

At first glance the notion that a phonological string has a reduction like a musical string may seem rather odd. For example, the tree for *reconciliation* (12.11) indicates a level of reduction of the form *re—ci—a,* one of the form *re—a,* and finally one consisting of the main stressed syllable *a* alone. This is hardly comprehensible in morphological, syntactic, or semantic terms. However, at the phonological level of linguistic representation, we are dealing not only with linguistic information but also with its perceptual and motor organization. It is not at all impossible to think of a prosodic reduction as determining the way a phonological string is perceived, say by identifying relatively strong syllables first. It could also affect the way a string is produced, say by treating the stronger syllables as the axes around which other speech movements are marshaled. If this is a plausible view, the parallelism between music and language is still deeper.

General Implications
No matter how the discrepancies just discussed are eventually resolved, the similarity between the theory of time-span reduction and the theory of prosodic structure seems to us to be a much more significant parallelism between music and language than has ever, to our knowledge, been pointed out. Its persuasiveness arises from the point-by-point correspondence of abstract aspects of the proposed grammars, rather than from superficial analogies between the two media. To see the force of the argument, notice, by contrast, that similarities between syntactic and musical structure—for example, those proposed by Bernstein (1976)—have not proved to be fruitful avenues of investigation. The differences be-

tween syntactic and musical trees, discussed in section 5.3, are too great for such a grammatical comparison to be meaningful.

Why should there be such a parallelism? Given that both theories are attempts to account for human cognitive abilities, the existence of parallelism between them implies a claim that these areas are a respect in which human musical and linguistic capacities overlap. In other words, both capacities make use of some of the same organizing principles to impose structure on their respective inputs, no matter how disparate these inputs are in other respects.

However, if this claim is true, it would be surprising if music and language were the only human abilities so structured. Rather, we should be led to look for something closely analogous to time-span structure in many human abilities under the rubric of "temporal patterning," from event perception to motor control to the planning of extended strategies of behavior. In particular, we should expect a hierarchically articulated notion of *head/elaboration* to figure prominently in psychological theories of temporal organization.

One bit of suggestive evidence for this hypothesis is Lasher's (1978) finding that sequences of ballet steps are invariably interpreted as a sequence of major movements, each preceded by preparatory movements. Such a description is easily seen to be a variant of time-span reduction principles, with the major movements serving as heads of larger segments and the preparatory movements as their elaborations. Notice how this description is more highly structured than one articulated only in terms of "chunking," since it accords one element of each "chunk" the privileged status of head.

Whether or not other kinds of organization eventually prove amenable to more rigorous treatment along these lines, our main point should be clear: The similarity between prosodic and musical structure can be used as a point of triangulation for approaching an account of other temporally structured cognitive capacities.[14]

12.4
A Remark on
Brain Localization

Some readers may ask how the parallel between music and phonology comports with evidence of brain localization. It is well known that the left hemisphere of the brain (in right-handed people) subserves specialized linguistic functions, and that the right hemisphere is implicated in musical perception. Bever and Chiarello (1974) report that in musically naive listeners the right hemisphere seems to be dominant for certain tasks of melodic perception, whereas in musically experienced listeners the left hemisphere is dominant. They argue therefore that "being musically sophisticated has real neurological concomitants, permitting the utilization of a different strategy of musical apprehension that calls on left hemisphere function," namely a more analytic and less holistic or Gestalt form of processing.

Given this evidence, one might conclude that the parallel of time-span reduction and phonology should be explained as follows: Time-span reduction is an analytic function in musical perception; it is therefore confined to musically sophisticated listeners; and it is localized in the left hemisphere, perhaps even in the same place as phonological functions. We would consider such a conclusion hasty, for at least two reasons.

First, we must take issue with the commonly made dichotomy between "analytic" and "holistic" processing. It should be obvious from the present study that every aspect of musical cognition involves an intricate interweaving of local and global evidence. Perception of "Gestalt" properties requires a great deal of "analytic" processing, and vice versa. Hence the musical evidence suggests that it is more difficult to make a sharp division between the functions of the hemispheres along these lines than has often been thought. One would not expect physiological functions to be any more localized than the corresponding psychological ones.

Second, we have repeatedly emphasized that the analytic structures we postulate are not confined to experienced listeners. Even the most naive listeners undoubtedly hear music as grouped; and they know where to tap their feet in time to the music, so they have assigned metrical structure. Moreover, our impression of children's errors in singing songs and of regional variants of folk songs is that they reveal intuitions of reductional structure. Typically it seems to be reductionally unimportant pitches that are omitted or changed, while the structural skeleton remains intact. We believe, therefore, that differences among listeners concern how complex and conflicted the structures are that they can handle. This accords with Bever's (1980, p. 206) assessment that musical sophistication is actually associated with an advantage in *both* hemispheres.

Thus we are reluctant to draw any immediate connections between studies of hemispheric localization and the reduction-phonology parallel. However, given our conjecture in the preceding subsection that some form of reductional structure is a more general element in temporal patterning, we can envisage two distinct hypotheses about brain localization. First, it is possible that all functions involving reductional structure are localized in the same place. In computational terms, this would amount to a claim that reduction is a "parameterized subroutine" to which various processes refer. Alternatively, the parallel could be due to a conservatism in developing new functions; that is, reductionlike structures could appear as parts of numerous different capacities and be differently localized. Computationally, this would be like saying that many copies of essentially the same routine are present, each serving different functions. We are in no position to assess these alternatives. We do think, however, that the parallelism between the grammars of time-span reduction and prosodic structure presents an interesting challenge to any general theory of mental and neurological processing.

Recently a composite discipline called "cognitive science" has been emerging out of parts of psychology, linguistics, neurophysiology, philosophy, and computer science. As its name implies, this discipline is concerned with characterizing the cognitive capacities of humans and other organisms. Perhaps its most important goal is to understand the nature of mental representation. Insofar as the goals we have set for the present study are consistent with such a program of research, we have in effect claimed for music theory a place among the branches of cognitive science.

Our approach to music theory has not been concerned with questions of memory capacity, real-time processing, brain localization, and the like. We have restricted ourselves to a formal characterization of the listener's intuitions about musical structure (that is, of his mental representation of music). Although the theory is far from complete, it is detailed enough and explicit enough to account for a rich range of musical intuitions, from very elementary ones about grouping and meter to very sophisticated ones involving prolongational structure. That alone would suffice to justify music theory as a cognitive science.

Though it could have been the case that musical cognitive capacity had nothing in common with other aspects of human behavior about which anything is known, this chapter has shown that music theory begins to bridge the gap between two other capacities that have been studied much more extensively: visual perception and language. Moreover, the strong parallel between time-span reduction and prosodic structure appears to provide the starting point for a more general theory of temporal patterning. That our study has managed to touch base with visual and linguistic theory in such a striking fashion is in itself a vindication of the idealizations implicit in our approach.

Thus music theory is by no means a curious side branch of cognitive science. We believe we have shown that it can provide central evidence toward a more organic theory of mind.

Notes

Chapter 1

1. This consideration militates against Goodman's (1968) characterization of a piece as the set of performances in conformance with its score.

2. We concur with Arnheim's view (1974, p. 5) that "Far from being a mechanical recording of sensory elements, vision [and other sorts of perception] proved to be a truly creative apprehension of reality—imaginative, inventive, shrewd, and beautiful. . . . the qualities that dignify the thinker and artist distinguish all performances of the mind."

3. The distinction underlying this idealization corresponds to one sense of Chomsky's (1965) distinction between competence and performance. However, since these terms have been used in many senses and have been subject to fruitless polemics, we prefer to avoid this terminology, and wish our idealization to be understood strictly in the terms outlined here.

4. One means of testing beyond the kinds presented in this study is by laboratory experiment, as in the research reported by Dowling (1972, 1978), Deutsch (1977), Bamberger (1980), and Bever (1980). On the nature of scientific standards for a theory of mental structures such as ours, see Chomsky 1980.

5. Among music theorists, Narmour (1977) has been a vocal critic of the methodology of generative linguistics in music theory. However, Narmour's extensive criticism of transformational linguistics does not seem to be based on any great acquaintance with the field, as the only primary source he cites in his bibliography is Chomsky 1957; furthermore, his discussion contains many elementary errors. One reason for this might be that Narmour's main source seems to have been Robinson 1975, accurately assessed in Green 1977.

6. In particular, we will not be concerned whether or not our theory can readily be converted into a computer program—one of the more fashionable criteria of formalization. Though we are not opposed in principle to computational embodiments of formal theories, we will argue that various aspects of the theory cannot be so formalized on the basis of present understanding of the issues (see section 3.3).

7. Sundberg and Lindblom 1976, Kassler 1963, and Smoliar 1974 are examples of this approach. Babbitt 1972 makes similar assumptions in his discussions of music theory based on generative linguistics. Winograd 1968 is an interesting

exception; although musically limited, his "analytic" approach to musical grammar is in some ways more like ours than the "synthetic" grammars cited above.

8. An intrinsic advantage of our "analytic" approach to generative music theory over the "synthetic" approaches listed in note 7 is that we can deal from the start with a far wider range of literature than the musically extremely limited sample each of them generates.

9. This is a point often missed by musical laymen. For example, Hofstadter 1979 speaks of music as expressing the "structure of emotions," but the only musical structures actually discussed are the canonic and fugal structures of such works as Bach's *Musical Offering*. Although we do not deny the interest of these structures, they are superficial to an understanding of Bach's or any other composer's art. Their significance lies, rather, in how they mesh with the more fundamental, and very different, kinds of musical structure discussed here. The affective content of music, we believe, lies in its exploitation of the resources of the tonal system to build dramatic structure. For an influential discussion of musical affect in terms of structural "expectations," see Meyer 1956.

10. Recent developments in generative linguistics (for example, Jackendoff 1972; Bresnan 1978) have considerably weakened the role of transformations in favor of enriched phrase-structure grammar, lexicon, and semantic interpretation. In this respect our music theory more closely resembles current linguistic theory than that of Chomsky 1957, in that it accounts for structure in terms of the interaction of several components which individually are relatively restricted. For another possible notion of musical transformational rule, which we reject, see section 11.4.

Chapter 2

1. Andrew Imbrie (personal communication) has suggested possible examples of overlaps like *j*. We are inclined to regard them as structural ambiguities, that is, passages where two competing plausible groupings can be assigned. Though section 3.4 treats only overlaps like *i*, the theory could easily be expanded to accommodate case *j* should this prove necessary.

2. Sessions (1951, pp. 82–92) makes essentially the same distinctions; his "accent of weight" corresponds to structural accent, and, in a more restricted sense, his "expressive accent" corresponds to phenomenal accent. Cooper and Meyer (1960, pp. 6–8) distinguish between "stress" (phenomenal accent) and "accent," but do not adequately define the latter term; they appear to intend it to mean metrical accent combined with aspects of grouping structure and of structural accent.

3. Imbrie (1973, p. 53) and, in effect, Komar (1971, p. 52) precede us in observing that beats are durationless points in time. The spatial analogy comes from Imbrie. Komar (p. 36) also uses the term *time-span* in the sense we intend.

4. Yeston 1976 (p. 67) also points this out.

5. Because Komar (1971), by analogy with Schenker's pitch theory, attempts to develop a metrical theory derived from "background" metrical levels, let us enumerate a few more general reservations we have about this approach. First, it is an unacceptable simplification to argue, as Komar must, that harmonic arrival (structural accent) and large-scale metrical accent must coincide. This requirement becomes especially problematic when one must choose between structural beginnings and cadences, which together form spans that are anything but equidistant. (We treat this matter in section 2.4.) Second, with pieces having any sectional irregularity at all (that is, with most pieces), how an analysis gets from

hypothetical large-scale equal divisions to the local sense of metrical regularity is bound to be conceptually difficult and arbitrary. (See the discussion of "archetypes" in section 11.4.) Third, there is no *a priori* reason why metrical structure should behave like pitch structure with regard to "background" structures. It is topsy-turvy to develop an entire metrical theory from an assumption—global "metrical" divisions—so remote from the listener's actual experience of a piece of music. A metrical theory should first of all be based on the immediate sensation of strong and weak beats.

6. For example, Bruno Walter's performance (Columbia MS 6494) gives interpretation *A;* Leonard Bernstein's (Columbia MS 7029) gives interpretation *B*. Epstein (1978, pp. 68–70) develops a similar analysis of this passage in somewhat different terms.

7. Bernstein (1976) attempts such a model for this passage (with unconvincing results, as he notes).

8. Contemporary theories of versification no longer rely on the crude categories of traditional prosody; see Halle and Keyser 1971 and Kiparsky 1977. We have criticized Cooper and Meyer only in order to clarify theoretical issues. Their work on rhythm is seminal.

9. There has been a tendency in some recent writing on rhythm (for example, Komar 1971; Westergaard 1975) to downplay grouping in favor of meter, by concentrating on the hierarchy of time-spans between beats and ignoring the hierarchy of time-spans produced by grouping structure. It should therefore be noted that the elementary distinction just made between upbeat and afterbeat would be theoretically inexpressible without the interaction of grouping and meter.

10. A great deal has been written about this issue. For instance, Riemann (1903) construes all groupings as end-accented; that is, as leading from an upbeat to a downbeat (as in hypothesis B). Cooper and Meyer's assertion of discontinuity between hierarchical levels is an improvement: whereas local groupings may be either beginning-accented (trochaic, etc.) or end-accented (iambic, etc.), phrases must be end-accented, because the cadence is the goal of the phrase. Thus they end up with a version of hypothesis B (Cooper and Meyer 1960, p. 61). On the other hand, writers as different as Tovey (1935) and Schenker (1935), by extension from the hierarchy of beats within a measure, have inclined in most cases toward analyses of phrases as beginning-accented (hypothesis A). Cone 1968 (pp. 26–31) is the most persuasive proponent of hypothesis C—though he goes on to accept the essentials of Cooper and Meyer's methodology, with all its attendant problems. Westergaard 1975 (pp. 309 ff.), despite an improved notation and a different terminology (his "first primary downbeat" corresponds to Cone's "initial downbeat," his "second primary downbeat" to Cone's "cadential downbeat"), also proposes a version of hypothesis C. Komar is caught between a commitment to the identification of structural accent with metrical accent (hypothesis C) and a contrary commitment to equal metrical division, with a leaning toward hypothesis B over hypothesis A. Because his system of metrical generation does not otherwise allow for initial upbeats (needed for hypothesis B), he is forced, implausibly, to postulate a nonexistent metrically strong measure, which then is erased by a subsequent operation (Komar 1971, p. 155). Morgan 1978 provides a cogent critique of some previous approaches, but ends up ignoring metrical accent and talking only about structural accent. The most sensible discussion on this and related issues that we have seen in print is Schachter 1976.

11. Schenker's brief remarks about pitch-metrical relations (1935, especially paragraph 288) are consonant with the views set forth here. Also see his rhythmic analysis of the first movement of Beethoven's Fifth Symphony (1921, pp. 27–37). On the other hand, no clear distinction is made between grouping and meter.

Chapter 3

1. In this and succeeding examples, we include the rest between groups as part of the earlier group. This is not just a convention, but corresponds to the intuition that a group normally begins with its first note. To make the intuition clearer, consider a case like measures 124–127 of the *Eroica* Symphony, where one clearly has the opposite sense: the rests on the downbeats of these measures are heard as part of a group that includes the two *following* beats. Such a striking exception makes the intuition in the normal case more evident by contrast. Apparently, then, the assignment of rests to groups is rule-governed. However, we will not pursue the details of this phenomenon here.

2. The term *preference rule* should not mislead the reader into thinking that preference rules model *conscious* preferences. Much of musical understanding is unconscious and hence seems automatic. A "preferred" analysis represents how a musical passage is coherent to a listener.

Proximity and similarity are of course only two of many principles involved in visual and auditory perception. Another well-known principle is *good continuation,* one musical analog of which is the rule of prolongational connection (PRPR 3) in prolongational reduction. This rule picks out as structurally important those events that form the best connection with (are the best continuation of) surrounding structurally important events.

3. Tenney and Polansky (1980) develop a theory of "temporal gestalt-units" that corresponds in some respects to our theory of grouping preference rules. Their system includes an equivalent of GPR 1, though they make the rule a prohibition of single-element groups rather than an avoidance. They have a rule of proximity that is in essential respects identical to our attack-point rule (GPR 2b), and a rule of similarity that is close to our register and dynamics rules (GPRs 3a and 3b). Furthermore, they make clear that grouping perception relies on the interaction of the various principles. Their treatment attempts more than ours in one respect: they quantify strengths of rule application, so that grouping judgments can be simulated by a computer program. The reasons we have not taken this step are explained later in this section.

Chapter 4

1. See Cone's (1968) remarks on differences in importance of hypermeasure levels through the history of classical Western tonal music.

2. Metrical preference rule 2, the "downbeat early" rule, predicts in addition that structure *i,* with the strong beat on the first note of each group, should be slightly more natural than structure *ii.* This seems to conform to intuition. However, if the second eighth note and the rest are replaced by a quarter note, structure *ii* is considerably more natural than *i.* We take up this effect in the next subsection. A similar situation occurs in 4.17a below.

3. Because of their similarity, it would be possible to generalize MPRs 3 and 4 into a single rule. We keep them separate only for convenience.

4. Though the use of the time-span reduction in 4.32 is clear, we have not gathered definitive evidence for what in general constitutes a "relevant" level of time-span reduction for the length rule. We believe that the rule may use any time-span level that is smaller than the metrical level currently being derived.

5. The applications of MPR 5e at beats 2, 6, and 10 seem to have something to do with the rhythmic restlessness of the theme at a very local level. Notice that the second half of the quoted passage, where the pitch repetitions reinforce rather than contradict other metrical preference rules, seems rhythmically more stable.

6. The pervasiveness of certain standard accompanimental patterns can in part be explained as a reinforcement of MPR 6: the "oom-pah-pah" pattern (i) naturally expresses 3/4, and the Alberti bass (ii) not only places the lowest note on the first 16th but places the second-lowest note on the third 16th, that is, on the metrically intermediate beat within the pattern.

7. The distinction between this rule and the parts of MPR 5 (length) that make use of time-span reduction needs some clarification. In the length rule, levels of time-span reduction smaller than the metrical level currently being derived help define what counts as a repeated pitch or prolonged harmony. In MPR 9, by contrast, hypotheses about metrical structure are tested for their consequences for levels of time-span reduction equivalent to and larger than the metrical level currently being derived; a more stable time-span outcome affects metrical choice.

8. The question arises as to why the harmonic changes could not be assigned to the eighth notes immediately preceding the chords on the eighth-note metrical level. To answer this objection, we would argue that harmonic progression is not heard as significant at metrical levels smaller than the tactus, which at the speed this passage is performed (♪ = at least 240) turns out to be the quarter-note level. Thus MPR 5f (harmonic rhythm) is properly restricted in application to harmonic changes in the time-span reduction at the tactus level and higher, eliminating the potentially offending applications at beats 5, 11, 17, and 23. (This restriction eliminates the applications of MPR 5f below the half-note level in the derivation of the Mozart G Minor Symphony above. Because of the other metrical evidence, this does not change the derivation.)

9. In Lerdahl and Jackendoff 1977 we spoke of metrical overlaps rather than metrical deletions. As Andrew Imbrie has pointed out (personal communication), beats are points in time and hence cannot overlap—as opposed to groups, which have duration. Hence the terminology is changed.

10. This analysis follows the metrical interpretation given in Lerdahl and Jackendoff 1977. In another interpretation, where the downbeats of odd-numbered bars are stronger than those of even-numbered bars, this metrical irregularity does not occur.

Chapter 5

1. See for example the brief remarks by Babbitt (1965, 1972) on these parallels. Briefly: If one downplays the Hegelian and Romantic sides of Schenker's thought and emphasizes its more systematic aspects, Schenker can be construed (especially in *Der freie Satz*) as having developed a proto-generative theory of tonal music—that is, as having postulated a limited set of principles capable of recursively generating a potentially infinite set of tonal pieces. But, remarkable and precursory though his achievement was, he did not develop a formal grammar in the sense one would expect nowadays of a generative theory. Moreover, his

orientation was not psychological (as that of generative linguistics is), but artistic; the chief purpose of his theory was to illuminate structure in musical masterpieces. Though our proposed theory also aspires to such illumination, its focus is on musical cognition. Despite these differences, we are profoundly indebted to Schenker's work—as, indeed, anybody in the field must be. Readers unfamiliar with Schenker's work can find a good introduction in Forte 1959 or Jonas 1954.

2. See Kassler 1963, 1976 and Sundberg and Lindblom 1976 for studies along these lines.

3. Smoliar 1980 and Snell 1979 are examples of such an approach.

4. Keiler (1975, 1978a), whose broad theoretical perspective seems to resemble our own, makes this kind of transference of linguistic trees, replete with grammatical categories such as "tonic prolongation," "tonic completion," and "dominant prolongation." From our viewpoint, the resultant musical trees suffer from the sort of superficial analogy between music and language for which he rightly criticizes Bernstein (1976). One also wonders how in principle Keiler's proposed theory will be able to generalize beyond classical tonal music. A musical grammar must be conceived on a more abstract basis if it is to be relevant to the fundamental issue of musical cognition.

Even in the restricted context of classical tonal music, there are severe shortcomings in the descriptive adequacy of Keiler's proposed trees (see for example Keiler 1978a, pp. 212–221). We give three examples: (1) Keiler's trees cannot assign structure to nonharmonic tones, thus missing obvious generalizations such as the similar function of a passing chord and a passing tone. (2) Keiler's trees cannot assign structure to such prevalent forms as an antecedent phrase or an antecedent-consequent period, because his formalism requires every "tonic prolongation" to have a "tonic completion." But it is precisely a characteristic of "interruption" forms that at a certain point the tonic is *not* completed. (3) Keiler's trees cannot assign structure to such common progressions as I–vi–I and IV–V–I, because the only categories available are "tonic" and "dominant." Plainly a "subdominant" category is needed. (The subdominant category would also apply to the ii^6 in a ii^6–V progression, dubiously analyzed by Keiler as "dominant" to "tonic" under a "dominant prolongation.")

Finally, we must distance ourselves from Keiler's generative approach in one absolutely essential respect: Keiler does not develop, nor does he propose to develop, a system of rules that pairs musical surfaces with heard musical structures. He has only developed an analytic notation. Thus, despite the linguistic ambience of his work and the "syntactic" nature of his trees, he is not engaged in constructing a generative grammar in any sense normally intended by the term. (See Jackendoff and Lerdahl 1980 for further discussion.)

5. However, such an assignment does occur in the musical surface in conjunction with grouping overlap, where event x in 5.7c is represented twice in underlying structure. The underlying tree has one branch to each occurrence of x and is therefore well formed; hence x is assigned two distinct functions. See section 7.1.

6. The angles made by these branchings convey no information; they are simply a fortuitous result of where an event is on the page in relation to the geometry of the tree.

7. We discuss this already overdiscussed passage because, beneath its brevity and apparent simplicity, it is unusually useful in presenting issues of general significance. Reductions of a wide variety of pieces will be presented in the following chapters.

8. Schenker's (1925, 1935) more complex solution for the first "event" is discussed briefly in section 7.3 and more extensively in section 10.4. Such refinements may be disregarded at this stage of our presentation.

9. The conception of time-span reduction is not new with us, though a number of refinements are totally our own. To our knowledge, the time-span approach to reduction has been developed, in various ways and to varying degrees, by Barnett (1972), Komar (1971), Lewin (1974), Schachter (1980), Westergaard (1975), and Yeston (1976). Our particular inspiration, for which we are most grateful, was Lewin's unpublished essay on Schubert's song "Morgengruss."

10. Schachter 1976 (pp. 330–334) also draws attention to this characteristic conflict in "groupings."

Chapter 6

1. Lewin 1974, Komar 1971, and Schachter 1980 are examples of a metrical approach to time-span reduction. Schachter restricts his version of time-span reduction (called "durational reduction") to relatively short and regular examples in order to avoid hypothetical constructions. None of these works addresses the question of out-of-phase passages.

2. Schenker himself wavers on this issue. In *Der freie Satz* (figure 21; paragraph 90) he advocates the interrupted V, but many of his graphs (such as the one of Bach's chorale "Ich bin's . . ." in Schenker 1932) prescribe the final V. Komar (1971), in keeping with his "background" metrical theory, appears to favor any salient V that approximately bifurcates the passage in question (see the analysis in the appendix of Komar 1971 of the slow movement of Beethoven's *Pathétique* Sonata). Schachter (1976, pp. 290–298) argues eloquently against the necessary association of structurally important events with roughly equal time-spans; yet he concedes (1980, pp. 211–214) that when a centrally located V is sufficiently prolonged near the musical surface, it might serve as the structural dominant. We think this concession confuses surface salience with reductional function.

Chapter 7

1. Even in recitative and similar metrically unstructured music, the sequence of attack points produces a minimal, possibly irregular, metrical level in terms of which time-spans can be defined. However, such music often has a less highly articulated hierarchy of time-spans than metrically more structured music.

2. Example 7.8 contains several examples of a notational abbreviation we have adopted. Where a particular beat determines both a regular and an augmented time-span, only the reduction of the latter is given in the secondary notation. On the other hand, the tree indicates the complete reduction. For example, the reduction of the first three sixteenths takes place in two steps: the A and the B are reduced to B alone in the regular time-span marked w; then the G and the B are reduced to G alone in the augmented time-span marked x. The branching in the tree reflects these two steps, but the musical notation shows only the outcome of the second step.

3. In the case of a melody accompanied by an Alberti bass, the bass undergoes fusion while the melody undergoes ordinary reduction. Although the intuitions are clear, we have not attempted to incorporate such situations into our theory, for the same reasons we avoided contrapuntal grouping structures: a formalism to represent independent structures for separate voices becomes much too cumbersome to work with.

4. Some additional examples of transformation appear in the analysis of the Schumann song "Wehmut" in Lerdahl and Jackendoff 1977.

5. One might wonder whether optional chords of dominant preparation might be retained in a time-span reduction along with the obligatory penult and final of full and deceptive cadences or with the obligatory V of half cadences. We have found that retention of the dominant preparation adds little to a time-span reduction's ability to convey the sense of a phrase. The importance of dominant preparation will be reflected in prolongational reduction. See sections 8.3 and 9.4.

6. This rule differs from TSRPR 1, which considers only the metrical structure within one time-span at a time. This rule considers the overall relation of a reductional level to metrical structure, a more global consideration.

7. On the other hand, occasions arise in which the cadential resolution is not at the very end of a group, but is prolonged to the end of the group. This occurs, for instance, at the end of the *Chorale St. Antoni*, discussed in section 8.5; the functional final cadence occurs in measures 22–23, and the final tonic is prolonged through two V⁷/IV–IV–I sequences to the end in measure 29. A much more extreme situation arises in the finale of Beethoven's Fifth Symphony, where the structural cadence for the entire movement occurs long before the end; the rest is a prolongation of the resolution. These exceptions are due to the influence of prolongational reduction. See section 9.6 for discussion.

Chapter 8

1. The following account of prolongational reduction differs from that in Lerdahl and Jackendoff 1977. We feel that the present version is a major improvement, but even so it remains less finished than the other three components. In section 10.4 we outline two possible future developments in prolongational reduction.

2. Various writers have found patterns of tension and relaxation to be fundamental to the nature of rhythm. For example, Sessions (1951, p. 84): "The principle of tension and relaxation is perhaps the most important single principle of musical rhythm, and its bearing on all questions of musical expression cannot be overestimated." Also see Schachter 1976 (pp. 333–334). For a much different approach to tension and relaxation, see Hindemith's theory of "harmonic fluctuation" (1942, pp. 115–121).

3. We originally adopted this formulation (Lerdahl and Jackendoff 1977, p. 140).

4. Rhythmic factors might instead lead to a different analysis of 8.22, in which the V/ii would be embedded within a weak prolongation of ii.

5. The reduction in 8.39 agrees in essentials with Schenker's analysis of the piece (1935, figures 42,2 and 138,3). Our main disagreements—intuitive as well as technical—concern Schenker's elevation of the V in measure 11 (the bass) to the level of the *Ursatz* and his treatment of the melodic E♭ in measure 15 as superordinate within its local environment (he makes it a neighboring motion at the background). In both cases Schenker radically separates bass and melodic functions; we discuss this matter in section 10.4.

Chapter 9

1. In the course of numerous analyses we have encountered only one or two cases where one might conceivably want to choose an event *two* time-span levels down. Without more serious examination of a number of such cases, it is hard to determine what motivates this extremely rare weakening of the Interaction Principle.

2. We have shown here only one of two possible grouping structures for sonata form. The ambiguity concerns how the three groups consisting of exposition, development, and recapitulation are to be further grouped. The grouping in 9.29 emphasizes the parallelism in endings between exposition and recapitulation, and is similar to the grouping of the binary form out of which sonata form in part grew historically (see Rosen 1980 on the origins of the sonata style). On the other hand, an emphasis on the parallelism between the *beginnings* of the exposition and recapitulation would result in grouping the exposition and development together. Such a grouping seems more typical of late classical sonata forms, in which the development is balanced by a long coda to give four major sections grouped by twos: exposition-development and recapitulation-coda. In such forms the beginning of the recapitulation is usually a more dramatic point than in earlier sonata movements, emphasizing the major grouping boundary; also, the repeat of the exposition is often omitted, deemphasizing the group boundary between it and the development. The interested reader can verify, however, that the first two steps in deriving the prolongational tree neutralize the grouping ambiguity: in either grouping the prolongational structure is the same.

Chapter 10

1. Andrew Imbrie has suggested this possibility (personal communication).

2. In the secondary notation in 10.7 we have quartered the note values beginning at level *g* in order to show hypermetrical relations more clearly. This practice is convenient only where hypermetrical beats are quite regular.

3. Along with these analyses should be mentioned the time-span reduction of Schumann's song "Wehmut" in Lerdahl and Jackendoff 1977, pp. 154–155 (though now we would prefer an out-of-phase analysis with hypermetrical beats on the downbeats of odd, not even, measures). The prolongational reduction (pp. 156–157), on the other hand, represents an earlier and less satisfactory version of that component, and should be disregarded.

4. "Guten Morgen, schöne Müllerin!
   Wo steckst du gleich das Köpfchen hin,
   Als wär' dir was geschehen?
   Verdriesst dich denn mein Gruss so schwer?
   Verstört dich denn mein Blick so sehr?
   So muss ich wieder gehen."

5. Lewin 1974 discusses these musical-poetic relationships at great length and with considerable insight. Aspects of our analysis duplicate Lewin's.

6. Schenker wants to bring out linear-motivic relationships involving third spans: the ascending C♯–E and B–D in measures 1–2 elaborated into A–B–C♯ in measures 3–4, combined with the descending E–D–C♯ in measures 1–4 followed by D–C♯–B in measure 4. Schachter (personal communication) has argued that this in itself is enough to favor Schenker's analysis. Such a proposal might be incorporated into our theory by invoking another preference rule supporting prolongational reductions that emphasize linear-motivic connections of a certain kind. In other words, it is a matter of weighting preference rules, involving once again the problematic issue of parallelism. We, on the other hand, have tried as much as possible to separate reductional and motivic structures; they are interactive, not equivalent, modes of organization.

Chapter 11

1. All the rules developed in chapters 2–9 are listed in the rule index, and the parts of rules that we conjecture to be idiom-specific are indicated by asterisks.

2. This does not, however, exclude the possibility that one can use other, non-musical, auditory principles to organize a musical surface. One is presumably doing this, for instance, when one hears a piece in an unfamiliar idiom as noise rather than music.

3. That our list covers as much ground as it does is due in part to a reading of Schachter 1976. This paper suggested to us that our theory could express more aspects of rhythm than we had realized.

4. The dubious aspects of Reti's (1951) study of thematic transformations are due to his frequent disregard of hierarchical function.

5. Schoenberg (1911) even uses this "evolutionary" argument to support his writing of highly dissonant harmonies.

6. Some of this music is available on Lyrichord LL189.

7. A related and perhaps more satisfactory hypothesis has been suggested by writers as different as Mursell (1937) and Partch (1949). They maintain that the perception of relative intervallic stability is a correlate of frequency ratios: the simpler the ratio, the easier to comprehend, or the more stable, an interval is. (Johnston 1964 extends this approach to durational patterns.) Their appeal is not to a direct physical cause such as the overtone series, but to an arithmetical, mentalistic one. We take no position here on this interesting line of reasoning, except to observe that cultural convention and musical context are also critical factors. To the extent that a musical idiom does not utilize simple ratios, convention and context will play comparably greater roles.

8. Another example: We understand there is now a pocket computer that can store and play back tunes. Since the tunes are stored numerically, one can take the square root of a tune and play that back! We doubt, however, that such "transformations" are musically very useful.

Chapter 12

1. One must still resist the temptation to try to account for Gestalt principles at too shallow a level. Hochberg 1974, an admirable reassessment of the Gestalt tradition, suggests a number of hypotheses, among which are "Organization can be identified with the structure of the programs of the efferent commands that would be needed to perform the oculomotor behaviors that are normally appropriate to a given stimulus pattern" and "Many of the laws of organization may simply be good cues as to which way occlusion or interposition occurs." There is an obvious difficulty in attributing the laws of organization to programs in the visuomotor system: these laws generalize in a quite straightforward manner to the auditory domain, where there is no corresponding motor activity. We are somewhat surprised that these generalizations, cited in the earliest research in Gestalt theory, have been ignored even by specialists. Their existence seems to us to argue that the laws of organization must be formulated at a level of mental organization where spatial and temporal information are represented compatibly—the level that Lashley 1951 posits. We know of no general theory of this level.

2. Katz and Postal (1964) observe that each sentence in 12.1 is ambiguous between the readings in 12.2, but different meanings are highly preferred. By calling this difference a stylistic matter, they claim to escape the consequence that

transformations change meaning. This is, however, an evasion; see Jackendoff 1972, chapter 8.

3. The material in this subsection is treated in greater depth in Jackendoff (forthcoming).

4. See for example Kiparsky 1977, 1979; Selkirk 1978, 1980; Vergnaud and Halle 1979; and the papers in Safir 1979.

5. One difference, however, is that the prosodic trees permit only one weak branch per node, whereas the musical trees sometimes permit more than one elaboration per node. We return to this difference later in this section; it is immaterial to the discussion here.

6. There are numerous exceptions to this principle, as shown by contrasts in English like *or-che-stra* versus *or-ches-tral*. A complete account of rules of syllabification is as yet unavailable.

7. The structures in 12.14 are derived from the structure given in Selkirk's (1980) example 28b. In her alternative structure (28c), which is identical to Liberman and Prince's treatment, the initial syllable is simply adjoined at the word level. Though this choice always makes a difference in segmentation, it will only make a difference in tree structure in the case of multifoot words such as *Monongahela*. In such a case the 28b structure will adjoin the initial syllable to the foot *-nonga-*, whereas the 28c structure will adjoin it to the combination of the two feet *-nonga-* and *-hela*. We know of no empirical arguments for one or the other, beyond the musical parallel. Incidentally, Selkirk 1980 notes that feet augmented by an initial unstressed syllable occur only at the beginning of a word, not word-internally, and argues that this fact should not have to be stipulated by the theory that derives such structures. However, it is exactly parallel to the musical case, where an augmented subgroup may occur only at the beginning of a group. The parallelism suggests that the stipulation against which Selkirk inveighs is not so offensive after all.

8. Selkirk raises the possibility that in fact the directionality of the English rule is only a preference rather than a necessity. This allows for the observed alternate stressing in complex words such as *Ticonderoga,* by means far too complex to describe here.

9. Readers familiar with hierarchical phonology will notice that our tree does not contain category labels such as syllable and foot; these are present only in the segmentation. This separation of functions avoids a notational problem that arises in current conventional practice, where some nodes in the tree have only category labels, some have only *s* or *w,* and some have both.

10. This formulation has been designed to generalize to "upbeat" syllables, which receive separate treatment in Selkirk's exposition. In Liberman and Prince's account, the prominence contour of a foot is determined by the same rule that creates the segmentation; the two functions are not distinguished.

11. Prominence rule 2 is subject to a number of classes of exceptions, discussed at length by Liberman and Prince.

12. We have not discussed the constituency of the phonological phrase. Liberman and Prince, following Chomsky and Halle (1968), take it to be essentially identical to nonlexical syntactic categories (NP, VP, etc.). However, Selkirk 1978 argues that a more complex relationship is involved. For the examples here, the two views are indistinguishable.

13. For what it is worth, Kiparsky 1977 shows that so-called triple meters in poetry (dactylic and anapestic) must be treated as duple meters with a divided weak position. The consequences of this for music are unclear.

14. In this we agree with Liberman (1975, pp. 313–314), who, after demonstrating the importance of metrical structure (in our terms) to language, makes the following observation:

There is some reason (evolutionary parsimony, if nothing else) to suppose that the cases of language, music, and dance demonstrate, in a more intuitively accessible way, a system which in fact is the organizing principle of all temporally ordered behavior. . . . [This supposition] suggests that the source and origin of "rhythm" is quite abstract, especially with respect to the fundamental division between event-structure [our time-span structure] and time-structure [our metrical structure]. . . .

It is worth pointing out that this tremendously advantageous system does seem to impose one requirement—that the behavior in question be abstractly segmented into discrete subunits. An interesting consequence of this is that there could be no music without notes (structured, say, [into continuous contours]), no language without words and phonemes (in which the meaningful units were irretrievably smeared throughout a temporally unsegmented noise), and no dance without "steps."

Rule Index

Note: Rules marked with an asterisk are idiom-specific. We believe the rest are universal.

Grouping Structure

GWFR 1 (p. 37)
Any contiguous sequence of pitch-events, drum beats, or the like can constitute a group, and only contiguous sequences can constitute a group.

GWFR 2 (p. 38)
A piece constitutes a group.

GWFR 3 (p. 38)
A group may contain smaller groups.

GWFR 4 (p. 38)
If a group G_1 contains part of a group G_2, it must contain all of G_2.

GWFR 5 (p. 38)
If a group G_1 contains a smaller group G_2, then G_1 must be exhaustively partitioned into smaller groups.

GPR 1, alternative form (p. 43)
Avoid analyses with very small groups—the smaller, the less preferable.

GPR 2 (Proximity) (p. 45)
Consider a sequence of four notes $n_1 n_2 n_3 n_4$. All else being equal, the transition n_2-n_3 may be heard as a group boundary if
a. (Slur/Rest) the interval of time from the end of n_2 to the beginning of n_3 is greater than that from the end of n_1 to the beginning of n_2 and that from the end of n_3 to the beginning of n_4, or if
b. (Attack-Point) the interval of time between the attack points of n_2 and n_3 is greater than that between the attack points of n_1 and n_2 and that between the attack points of n_3 and n_4.

GPR 3 (Change) (p. 46)

Consider a sequence of four notes $n_1 n_2 n_3 n_4$. All else being equal, the transition $n_2 - n_3$ may be heard as a group boundary if

a. (Register) the transition $n_2 - n_3$ involves a greater intervallic distance than both $n_1 - n_2$ and $n_3 - n_4$, or if

b. (Dynamics) the transition $n_2 - n_3$ involves a change in dynamics and $n_1 - n_2$ and $n_3 - n_4$ do not, or if

c. (Articulation) the transition $n_2 - n_3$ involves a change in articulation and $n_1 - n_2$ and $n_3 - n_4$ do not, or if

d. (Length) n_2 and n_3 are of different lengths and both pairs n_1, n_2 and n_3, n_4 do not differ in length.

GPR 4 (Intensification) (p. 49)

Where the effects picked out by GPRs 2 and 3 are relatively more pronounced, a larger-level group boundary may be placed.

GPR 5 (Symmetry) (p. 49)

Prefer grouping analyses that most closely approach the ideal subdivision of groups into two parts of equal length.

GPR 6 (Parallelism) (p. 51)

Where two or more segments of the music can be construed as parallel, they preferably form parallel parts of groups.

GPR 7 (Time-Span and Prolongational Stability) (p. 52)

Prefer a grouping structure that results in more stable time-span and/or prolongational reductions.

Grouping Overlap (p. 60)

Given a well-formed underlying grouping structure G as described by GWFRs 1–5, containing two adjacent groups g_1 and g_2 such that

g_1 ends with event e_1,

g_2 begins with event e_2, and

$e_1 = e_2$,

a well-formed surface grouping structure G' may be formed that is identical to G except that

it contains one event e' where G had the sequence $e_1 e_2$,

$e' = e_1 = e_2$,

all groups ending with e_1 in G end with e' in G', and

all groups beginning with e_2 in G begin with e' in G'.

Grouping Elision (p. 61)

Given a well-formed underlying grouping structure G as described by GWFRs 1–5, containing two adjacent groups g_1 and g_2 such that

g_1 ends with event e_1,

g_2 begins with event e_2, and

(for left elision) e_1 is harmonically identical to e_2 and less than e_2 in dynamics and pitch range or

(for right elision) e_2 is harmonically identical to e_1 and less than e_1 in dynamics and pitch range,

a well-formed surface grouping structure G' may be formed that is identical to G except that

it contains one event e' where G had the sequence e_1e_2,

(for left elision) $e' = e_2$,

(for right elision) $e' = e_1$,

all groups ending with e_1 in G end with e' in G', and

all groups beginning with e_2 in G begin with e' in G'.

Metrical Structure

MWFR 1 (revised) (p. 72)
Every attack point must be associated with a beat at the smallest metrical level present at that point in the piece.

MWFR 2 (revised) (p. 72)
Every beat at a given level must also be a beat at all smaller levels present at that point in the piece.

MWFR 3* (p. 69)
At each metrical level, strong beats are spaced either two or three beats apart.

MWFR 4 (revised)* (p. 72)
The tactus and immediately larger metrical levels must consist of beats equally spaced throughout the piece. At subtactus metrical levels, weak beats must be equally spaced between the surrounding strong beats.

MPR 1 (Parallelism) (p. 75)
Where two or more groups or parts of groups can be construed as parallel, they preferably receive parallel metrical structure.

MPR 2 (Strong Beat Early) (p. 76)
Weakly prefer a metrical structure in which the strongest beat in a group appears relatively early in the group.

MPR 3 (Event) (p. 76)
Prefer a metrical structure in which beats of level L_i that coincide with the inception of pitch-events are strong beats of L_i.

MPR 4 (Stress) (p. 79)
Prefer a metrical structure in which beats of level L_i that are stressed are strong beats of L_i.

MPR 5 (Length) (p. 84)

Prefer a metrical structure in which a relatively strong beat occurs at the inception of either

a. a relatively long pitch-event,

b. a relatively long duration of a dynamic,

c. a relatively long slur,

d. a relatively long pattern of articulation,

e. a relatively long duration of a pitch in the relevant levels of the time-span reduction, or

f. a relatively long duration of a harmony in the relevant levels of the time-span reduction (harmonic rhythm).

MPR 6 (Bass) (p. 88)

Prefer a metrically stable bass.

MPR 7 (Cadence) (p. 88)

Strongly prefer a metrical structure in which cadences are metrically stable; that is, strongly avoid violations of local preference rules within cadences.

MPR 8 (Suspension)* (p. 89)

Strongly prefer a metrical structure in which a suspension is on a stronger beat than its resolution.

MPR 9 (Time-Span Interaction) (p. 90)

Prefer a metrical analysis that minimizes conflict in the time-span reduction.

MPR 10 (Binary Regularity) (p. 101)

Prefer metrical structures in which at each level every other beat is strong.

Metrical Deletion (p. 104)

Given a well-formed metrical structure M in which

i. B_1, B_2, and B_3 are adjacent beats of M at level L_i, and B_2 is also a beat at level L_{i+1},

ii. T_1 is the time-span from B_1 to B_2 and T_2 is the time-span from B_2 to B_3, and

iii. M is associated with an underlying grouping structure G in such a way that both T_1 and T_2 are related to a surface time-span T' by the grouping transformation performed on G of

    (a) left elision or

    (b) overlap,

then a well-formed metrical structure M' can be formed from M and associated with the surface grouping structure by

(a) deleting B_1 and all beats at all levels between B_1 and B_2 and associating B_2 with the onset of T', or

(b) deleting B_2 and all beats at all levels between B_2 and B_3 and associating B_1 with the onset of T'.

Time-Span Reduction

Segmentation Rule 1 (p. 146)

Every group in a piece is a time-span in the time-span segmentation of the piece.

Segmentation Rule 2 (p. 147)

In underlying grouping structure,

a. each beat B of the smallest metrical level determines a time-span T_B extending from B up to but not including the next beat of the smallest level,

b. each beat B of metrical level L_i determines a *regular* time-span T_B, which is the union (or sum) of the time-spans of all beats of level L_{i-1} (the next smaller level) from B up to but not including

(i) the next beat B' of level L_i* or

(ii) a group boundary,

whichever comes sooner, and

c. if a group boundary G intervenes between B and the preceding beat of the same level, B determines an *augmented time-span* T_B', which is the interval from G to the end of the regular time-span T_B.

TSRWFR 1 (p. 158)

For every time-span T there is an event e (or a sequence of events e_1e_2) that is the *head* of T.

TSRWFR 2 (p. 158)

If T does not contain any other time-span (that is, if T is at the smallest level of time-spans), then e is whatever event occurs in T.

TSRWFR 3 (p. 159)

If T contains other time-spans, let $T_1,...,T_n$ be the (regular or augmented) time-spans immediately contained in T and let $e_1,...,e_n$ be their respective heads. Then:

a. (Ordinary Reduction) The head of T may be one of the events $e_1,...,e_n$.

b. (Fusion) If $e_1,...,e_n$ are not separated by a group boundary ("locality" condition), the head of T may be the superimposition of two or more of $e_1,...,e_n$.

c. (Transformation) If $e_1,...,e_n$ are not separated by a group boundary, the head of T may be some mutually consonant combination of pitches chosen out of $e_1,...,e_n$.*

d. (Cadential Retention) The head of T may be a cadence whose final is e_n (the head of T_n—the last time-span immediately contained in T) and whose penult, if there is one, is the head of a time-span immediately preceding T_n, though not necessarily at the same level.*

TSRWFR 4 (p. 159)

If a two-element cadence is directly subordinate to the head e of a time-span T, the final is directly subordinate to e and the penult is directly subordinate to the final.

TSRPR 1 (Metrical Position) (p. 160)
Of the possible choices for head of a time-span T, prefer a choice that is in a relatively strong metrical position.

TSRPR 2 (Local Harmony) (p. 161)
Of the possible choices for head of a time-span T, prefer a choice that is
a. relatively intrinsically consonant,
b. relatively closely related to the local tonic.

TSRPR 3 (Registral Extremes) (p. 162)
Of the possible choices for head of a time-span T, weakly prefer a choice that has
a. a higher melodic pitch,
b. a lower bass pitch.

TSRPR 4 (Parallelism) (p. 164)
If two or more time-spans can be construed as motivically and/or rhythmically parallel, preferably assign them parallel heads.

TSRPR 5 (Metrical Stability) (p. 165)
In choosing the head of a time-span T, prefer a choice that results in more stable choice of metrical structure.

TSRPR 6 (Prolongational Stability) (p. 167)
In choosing the head of a time-span T, prefer a choice that results in more stable choice of prolongational reduction.

TSRPR 7 (Cadential Retention) (p. 170)
If the following conditions obtain in a time-span T, then label the progression as a cadence and strongly prefer to choose it as head:
  i. There is an event or sequence of two events $(e_1)e_2$ forming the progression for a full, half, or deceptive cadence.*
  ii. The last element of this progression is at the end of T or is prolonged to the end of T.
  iii. There is a larger group G containing T for which the progression can function as a structural ending.

TSRPR 8 (Structural Beginning) (p. 170)
If for a time-span T there is a larger group G containing T for which the head of T can function as the structural beginning, then prefer as head of T an event relatively close to the beginning of T (and hence to the beginning of G as well).

TSRPR 9* (p. 174)
In choosing the head of a piece, prefer the structural ending to the structural beginning.

Prolongational Reduction

PRWFR 1 (p. 214)
There is a single event in the underlying grouping structure of every piece that functions as prolongational head.

PRWFR 2 (p. 214)
An event e_i can be a direct elaboration of another event e_j in any of the following ways:
a. e_i is a *strong prolongation* of e_j if the roots, bass notes, and melodic notes of the two events are identical.*
b. e_i is a *weak prolongation* of e_j if the roots of the two events are identical but the bass and/or melodic notes differ.*
c. e_i is a *progression to or from* e_j if the harmonic roots of the two events are different.*

PRWFR 3 (p. 214)
Every event in the underlying grouping structure is either the prolongational head or a recursive elaboration of the prolongational head.

PRWFR 4 (No Crossing Branches) (p. 215)
If an event e_i is a direct elaboration of an event e_j, every event between e_i and e_j must be a direct elaboration of either e_i, e_j, or some event between them.

PRPR 1 (Time-Span Importance) (p. 220)
In choosing the prolongationally most important event e_k of a prolongational region (e_i-e_j), strongly prefer a choice in which e_k is relatively time-span-important.

PRPR 2 (Time-Span Segmentation) (p. 221)
Let e_k be the prolongationally most important event in a prolongational region (e_i-e_j). If there is a time-span that contains e_i and e_k but not e_j, prefer a prolongational reduction in which e_k is an elaboration of e_i; similarly with the roles of e_i and e_j reversed.

PRPR 3 (Prolongational Connection) (p. 224)
In choosing the prolongationally most important event e_k in a prolongational region (e_i-e_j), prefer an e_k that attaches so as to form a maximally stable prolongational connection with one of the endpoints of the region.

Stability Conditions for Prolongational Connection (p. 224)
1. (Branching condition)
  a. Right strong prolongations are more stable than right weak prolongations, which in turn are more stable than right progressions.
  b. Left progressions are more stable than left weak prolongations, which in turn are more stable than left strong prolongations.

2. (Pitch-collection condition)*
A connection between two events is more stable if they involve or imply a common diatonic collection.

3. (Melodic condition)
  a. (Distance) A connection between two events is melodically more stable if the interval between them is smaller (with the exception of the octave, which is relatively stable).
  b. (Direction) An ascending melodic progression is most stable as a right-branching structure; a descending one is most stable as a left-branching structure.

4. (Harmonic condition)*
  a. (Distance) A connection between two events is harmonically more stable if their roots are closer on the circle of fifths.
  b. (Direction) A progression that ascends along the circle of fifths is most stable as a right-branching structure; one that descends along the circle of fifths or produces a subdominant-to-dominant relationship is most stable as a left-branching structure.

Interaction Principle (p. 228)
In order to make a sufficiently stable prolongational connection, e_k must be chosen from the events in the two most important levels of time-span reduction represented in (e_i-e_j).

PRPR 4 (Prolongational Importance) (p. 226)
Let e_k be the prolongationally most important event in a region (e_i-e_j). Prefer a prolongational reduction in which e_k is an elaboration of the prolongationally more important of the endpoints.

PRPR 5 (Parallelism) (p. 226)
Prefer a prolongational reduction in which parallel passages receive parallel analyses.

PRPR 6 (Normative Prolongational Structure)* (p. 234)
A cadenced group preferably contains four (five) elements in its prolongational structure:
  a. a prolongational beginning,
  b. a prolongational ending consisting of one element of the cadence,
(c. a right-branching prolongation as the most important direct elaboration of the prolongational beginning,)
  d. a right-branching progression as the (next) most important direct elaboration of the prolongational beginning,
  e. a left-branching "subdominant" progression as the most important elaboration of the first element of the cadence.

Bibliography

Arnheim, Rudolf. 1974. *Art and Visual Perception (The New Version)*. Berkeley: University of California Press.

Babbitt, Milton. 1960. Twelve-tone Invariants as Compositional Determinants. In *Problems of Modern Music*, Paul Henry Lang, ed. New York: Norton.

———. 1972. Contemporary Music Composition and Music Theory as Contemporary Intellectual History. In *Perspectives in Musicology*, B. S. Brook et al., eds. New York: Norton.

Bach, Kent, and Robert M. Harnish. 1979. *Linguistic Communication and Speech Acts*. Cambridge, Mass.: MIT Press.

Bamberger, Jeanne. 1980. Cognitive Structuring in the Apprehension and Description of Simple Rhythms. *Archive de Psychologie* 48: 171–199.

Barnett, David. 1972. *The Performance of Music*. New York: Universe.

Becker, Judith, and Alton Becker. 1979. A Grammar of the Musical Genre *Srepegan*. *Journal of Music Theory* 23.1: 1–44.

Bernstein, Leonard. 1976. *The Unanswered Question*. Cambridge, Mass.: Harvard University Press.

Bever, Thomas. 1980. Broca and Lashley Were Right: Cerebral Dominance Is an Accident of Growth. In *Biological Studies of Mental Processes*, D. Caplan, ed. Cambridge, Mass.: MIT Press.

Bever, Thomas, and Robert J. Chiarello. 1974. Cerebral Dominance in Musicians and Nonmusicians. *Science* 185: 537–539.

Bregman, A. A., and J. Campbell. 1971. Primary Auditory Stream Segregation and Perception of Order in Rapid Sequences of Tones. *Journal of Experimental Psychology* 89: 244–249.

Bresnan, Joan. 1978. A Realistic Transformational Grammar. In *Linguistic Theory and Psychological Reality*, M. Halle, J. Bresnan, and G. Miller, eds. Cambridge, Mass.: MIT Press.

Chomsky, Noam. 1957. *Syntactic Structures*. The Hague: Mouton.

———. 1959. Review of Skinner's *Verbal Behavior*. *Language* 35.1: 26–58.

———. 1965. *Aspects of the Theory of Syntax*. Cambridge, Mass.: MIT Press.

————. 1972. *Language and Mind*. New York: Harcourt, Brace & World.

————. 1975. *Reflections on Language*. New York: Pantheon.

————. 1980. *Rules and Representations*. New York: Columbia University Press.

Chomsky, Noam, and Morris Halle. 1968. *The Sound Pattern of English*. New York: Harper & Row.

Chomsky, Noam, and George Miller. 1963. Introduction to the Formal Analysis of Natural Languages. In *Handbook of Mathematical Psychology,* vol. II, R. D. Luce, R. Bush, and E. Galanter, eds. New York: Wiley.

Cone, Edward T. 1968. *Musical Form and Musical Performance*. New York: Norton.

Cooper, Grosvenor, and Leonard B. Meyer. 1960. *The Rhythmic Structure of Music*. University of Chicago Press.

Cooper, Robin. 1977. Abstract Structure and the Indian Rāga System. *Ethnomusicology* 21.1: 1–32.

Deutsch, Diana. 1977. Memory and Attention in Music. In *Music and the Brain,* M. Critchley and R. A. Henson, eds. London: Heinemann.

————. 1980. Music Perception. *Musical Quarterly* 66.2: 165–179.

Dowling, W. J. 1972. Recognition of Melodic Transformations: Inversion, Retrograde, and Retrograde-Inversion. *Perception and Psychophysics* 12: 417–421.

————. 1978. Scale and Contour: Two Components of a Theory of Memory for Melodies. *Psychological Review* 85.4: 341–354.

Epstein, David. 1979. *Beyond Orpheus*. Cambridge, Mass.: MIT Press.

Fodor, Janet D. 1978. Parsing Strategies and Constraints on Transformations. *Linguistic Inquiry* 9.3: 427–474.

Fodor, Jerry A. 1975. *The Language of Thought*. Cambridge, Mass.: Harvard University Press.

Fodor, Jerry A., Thomas Bever, and Merrill Garrett. 1974. *The Psychology of Language*. New York: McGraw-Hill.

Forte, Allen. 1959. Schenker's Conception of Musical Structure. *Journal of Music Theory* 3.1: 1–30.

————. 1973. *The Structure of Atonal Music*. New Haven, Conn.: Yale University Press.

Goodman, Nelson. 1968. *Languages of Art*. New York: Bobbs-Merrill.

Green, Georgia. 1977. Review of Robinson, *The New Grammarians' Funeral*. *Language* 53.4: 406–410.

Grice, Paul. 1975. Logic and Conversation. In *Syntax and Semantics,* vol. 3, P. Cole and J. Morgan, eds. New York: Academic.

Halle, Morris, and Samuel Jay Keyser. 1971. *English Stress*. New York: Harper & Row.

Helmholtz, Hermann. 1885. *On the Sensations of Tone*. New York: Dover, 1954.

Hindemith, Paul. 1942. *Craft of Musical Composition*, vol. 1. Mainz: Schott; Melville, N.Y.: Belwin-Mills.

————. 1952. *A Composer's World*. Garden City, N.Y.: Doubleday.

Hochberg, Julian. 1974. Organization and the Gestalt Tradition. In *Handbook of Perception,* vol. 1, E. C. Carterette and M. P. Friedman, eds. New York: Academic.

Hofstadter, Douglas. 1979. *Gödel, Escher, Bach.* New York: Basic.

Imbrie, Andrew. 1973. "Extra" Measures and Metrical Ambiguity in Beethoven. In *Beethoven Studies,* A. Tyson, ed. New York: Norton.

Ioup, Georgette. 1975. Some Universals for Quantifier Scope. In *Syntax and Semantics,* vol. 4, J. Kimball, ed. New York: Academic.

Jackendoff, Ray. 1972. *Semantic Interpretation in Generative Grammar.* Cambridge, Mass.: MIT Press.

———. 1977. Review of Bernstein, *The Unanswered Question. Language* 53.4: 883–894.

———. (forthcoming). *Semantics and Cognition,* Cambridge, Mass.: MIT Press.

Jackendoff, Ray, and Fred Lerdahl. 1980. Discovery Procedures vs. Rules of Musical Grammar in a Generative Music Theory. *Perspectives of New Music* 18.2: 503–510.

———. 1981. Generative Music Theory and its Relation to Psychology. *Journal of Music Theory* 25.1: 45–90.

Jakobson, Roman. 1941. *Child Language, Aphasia, and Phonological Universals,* tr. A. Keiler. The Hague: Mouton, 1968.

Johnston, Ben. 1964. Scalar Order as a Compositional Resource. *Perspectives of New Music* 2.2: 56–76.

Jonas, Oswald. 1954. Introduction to Schenker's *Harmony.* University of Chicago Press. MIT Press paperback edition, 1973.

Kahn, Daniel. 1976. *Syllable-Based Generalizations in English Phonology.* Ph.D. diss., MIT.

Kassler, Michael. 1963. A Sketch of the Use of Formalized Languages for the Assertion of Music. *Perspectives of New Music* 1.2: 83–94.

———. 1976. The Decidability of Languages that Assert Music. *Perspectives of New Music* 14.2: 249–251.

Katz, Jerrold J. 1972. *Semantic Theory.* New York: Harper & Row.

Katz, Jerrold J., and Paul Postal. 1964. *An Integrated Theory of Linguistic Descriptions.* Cambridge, Mass.: MIT Press.

Keiler, Allan. 1977. The Syntax of Prolongation I. *In Theory Only* 3.5: 3–27.

———. 1978a. Bernstein's *The Unanswered Question* and the Problem of Musical Competence. *Musical Quarterly* 64.2: 195–222.

———. 1978b. The Empiricist Illusion. *Perspectives of New Music* 17.1: 161–195.

Kimball, John. 1973. Seven Principles of Surface Structure Parsing in Natural Language. *Cognition* 2: 15–47.

Kiparsky, Paul. 1977. The Rhythmic Structure of English Verse. *Linguistic Inquiry* 8.2: 189–248.

———. 1979. Metrical Structure Assignment is Cyclic. *Linguistic Inquiry* 10.3: 421–442.

Koffka, Kurt. 1935. *Principles of Gestalt Psychology.* New York: Harcourt, Brace & World.

Köhler, Wolfgang. 1929. *Gestalt Psychology.* New York: Liveright.

———. 1940. *Dynamics in Psychology.* New York: Liveright.

Komar, Arthur J. 1971. *Theory of Suspensions.* Princeton, N.J.: Princeton University Press.

Kosslyn, Stephen M. 1980. *Image and Mind.* Cambridge, Mass.: Harvard University Press.

Lakoff, George. 1972. Hedges: A Study in Meaning Criteria and the Logic of Fuzzy Concepts. In Papers from the Eighth Regional Meeting of the Chicago Linguistics Society, University of Chicago Linguistics Department.

Lasher, Margot. 1978. A Study in the Cognitive Representation of Human Motion. Ph.D. diss., Columbia University.

Lashley, Karl. 1951. The Problem of Serial Order in Behavior. In *Cerebral Mechanisms in Behavior,* L. A. Jeffries, ed. New York: Wiley.

Lees, Robert B. 1960. *The Grammar of English Nominalizations.* The Hague: Mouton.

Lenneberg, Eric. 1967. *Biological Foundations of Language.* New York: Wiley.

Lerdahl, Fred, and Ray Jackendoff. 1977. Toward a Formal Theory of Tonal Music. *Journal of Music Theory* 21.1: 111–171.

———. 1981. On the Theory of Grouping and Meter. *The Musical Quarterly* 67.4: 479–506.

Lewin, David. 1974. Analysis of Schubert's song "Morgengruss." Unpublished manuscript.

Liberman, Alvin, and Michael Studdert-Kennedy. 1977. Phonetic Perception. In *Handbook of Sensory Physiology,* vol. VIII: *Perception,* R. Held, H. Leibowitz, and H.-L. Teuber, eds. Heidelberg: Springer.

Liberman, Mark. 1975. The Intonational System of English. Ph.D. diss., MIT.

Liberman, Mark, and Alan Prince. 1977. On Stress and Linguistic Rhythm. *Linguistic Inquiry* 8.2: 249–336.

Marr, David. 1982. *Vision.* San Francisco: Freeman.

Meyer, Leonard B. 1956. *Emotion and Meaning in Music.* University of Chicago Press.

———. 1967. *Music, the Arts, and Ideas.* University of Chicago Press.

———. 1973. *Explaining Music.* Berkeley: University of California Press.

Morgan, Robert P. 1978. The Theory and Analysis of Tonal Rhythm. *The Musical Quarterly* 64.4: 435–473.

Mursell, James. 1937. *The Psychology of Music.* New York: Norton.

Narmour, Eugene. 1977. *Beyond Schenkerism.* University of Chicago Press.

Nattiez, J. J. 1975. *Fondement d'une sémiologie de la musique.* Paris: Union Générale d'Éditions.

Neisser, Ulric. 1967. *Cognitive Psychology.* Englewood Cliffs, N.J.: Prentice-Hall.

Nettl, Bruno. 1960. *Cheremis Musical Styles*. Bloomington: Indiana University Press.

———. 1973. *Folk and Traditional Music of the Western Continents,* second edition. Englewood Cliffs, N.J.: Prentice-Hall.

Partch, Harry. 1949. *Genesis of a Music*. Madison: University of Wisconsin Press.

Powers, Harold S. 1977. The Structure of Musical Meaning: A View from Benares. *Perspectives of New Music* 14.2/15.1: 308–334.

Putnam, Hilary. 1975. The Meaning of Meaning. In *Language, Mind, and Knowledge* (Minnesota Studies in the Philosophy of Science, vol. 7), K. Gunderson, ed. Minneapolis: University of Minnesota Press.

Rahn, John. 1980. *Basic Atonal Theory*. New York: Longman.

Reti, Rudolph. 1951. *The Thematic Process in Music*. New York: Macmillan.

Riemann, Hugo. 1903. *System der Musikalischen Rhythmik und Metrik*. Leipzig: Breitkopf und Härtel.

Robinson, Ian. 1975. *The New Grammarians' Funeral*. New York: Cambridge University Press.

Rosch, Eleanor, and Carolyn B. Mervis. 1975. Family Resemblances: Studies in the Internal Structure of Categories. *Cognitive Psychology* 7: 573–605.

Rosen, Charles. 1972. *The Classical Style*. New York: Norton.

———. 1980. *Sonata Forms*. New York: Norton.

Rouget, Gilbert, and J. Schwarz. 1970. Transcrire ou décrire? Chant soudanais et chant fuégien. In *Échanges et communications, hommage offert à Claude Levi-Strauss,* vol. 1. Paris: Mouton.

Ruwet, Nicolas, 1972. Contradictions du langage sérial. In Ruwet, *Langage, musique, poésie*. Paris: Seuil.

Sachs, Curt. 1962. *The Wellsprings of Music*. The Hague: Martinus Nijhoff.

Safir, Ken, ed. 1979. MIT Working Papers in Linguistics, vol. 1. MIT Department of Linguistics and Philosophy.

Schachter, Carl. 1976. Rhythm and Linear Analysis: A Preliminary Study. In *The Music Forum,* vol. IV, F. Salzer, ed. New York: Columbia University Press.

———. 1980. Rhythm and Linear Analysis: Durational Reduction. In *The Music Forum,* vol. IV, F. Salzer, ed. New York: Columbia University Press.

Schenker, Heinrich. 1921. *Der Tonwille I*. Vienna: Tonwille-Flugblätter (tr. in *Beethoven: Symphony No. 5 in C minor,* E. Forbes, ed. New York: Norton, 1971).

———. 1925. *Das Meisterwerk in der Musik,* vol. 1. Munich: Drei Masken.

———. 1932. *Fünf Urlinie-Tafeln*. Vienna: Universal Edition; New York: Dover, 1969.

———. 1935. *Der Freie Satz*. Vienna: Universal Edition (tr. Ernst Oster, New York: Longman, 1979).

Schoenberg, Arnold. 1922. *Harmonielehre*. Vienna: Universal Edition (English translation, Berkeley: University of California Press, 1978).

Seashore, C. E. 1938. *Psychology of Music.* New York: McGraw-Hill.

Selkirk, Elisabeth. 1978. On Prosodic Structure and its Relation to Syntactic Structure. Mimeographed. Department of Linguistics, University of Massachusetts, Amherst.

————. 1980. The Role of Prosodic Categories in English Word Stress. *Linguistic Inquiry* 11.3: 563–606.

Sessions, Roger. 1951. *Harmonic Practice.* New York: Harcourt, Brace & World.

Shepard, Roger. 1980. Psychophysical Complementarity. In *Perceptual Organization,* M. Kubovy and J. Pomerantz, eds. Hillsdale, N.J.: Erlbaum.

Shiman, Leon. 1975. Grammar for Vision. Ph.D. diss. (mathematics), MIT.

————. 1978. The Law of Perceptual Stability. *Proceedings of the National Academy of Sciences* 75.4: 2049–2053 and 75.5: 2535–2538.

Singer, Alice. 1974. The Metrical Structure of Macedonian Dance. *Ethnomusicology* 18.3: 379–404.

Smoliar, Stephen. 1974. Process Structuring and Music Theory. *Journal of Music Theory* 18: 308–336.

————. 1980. A Computer Aid for Schenkerian Analysis. *Computer Music Journal* 4.2:41–59.

Snell, James L. 1979. Design for a Formal System for Deriving Tonal Music. Master's thesis, State University of New York at Binghamton.

Sundberg, John, and Bjorn Lindblom. 1976. Generative Theories in Language and Music Description. *Cognition* 4: 99–122.

Tenney, James, with Larry Polansky. 1980. Temporal Gestalt Perception in Music. *Journal of Music Theory* 24.2: 205–241.

Tovey, Donald Francis. 1935. *Essays in Musical Analysis.* London: Oxford University Press.

Trubetzkoy, N. S. 1939. *Principles of Phonology* (tr. C. Baltaxe, Berkeley: University of California Press, 1969).

Ullmann, Shimon. 1979. *The Interpretation of Visual Motion.* Cambridge, Mass.: MIT Press.

Van der Werf, Hendrik. 1972. *The Chansons of the Troubadours and Trouvères.* Utrecht: A. Oosthoek.

Vergnaud, Jean-Roger, and Morris Halle. 1979. Metrical Structures in Phonology—A Fragment of a Draft. Mimeographed. MIT.

Wanner, Eric, and Michael Maratsos. 1978. An ATN Approach to Comprehension. In *Linguistic Theory and Psychological Reality,* M. Halle, J. Bresnan, and G. Miller, eds. Cambridge, Mass.: MIT Press.

Wertheimer, Max. 1923. Laws of Organization in Perceptual Forms. In *A Source Book of Gestalt Psychology,* W. D. Ellis, ed. London: Routledge & Kegan Paul, 1938.

Westergaard, Peter. 1975. *An Introduction to Tonal Theory.* New York: Norton.

Winograd, Terry. 1968. Linguistics and the Computer Analysis of Tonal Harmony. *Journal of Music Theory* 12.1: 2–49.

Winston, Patrick. 1970. Learning Structural Descriptions from Examples. Report, Project MAC, MIT.

Wittgenstein, Ludwig. 1953. *Philosophical Investigations*. Oxford: Blackwell.

Yeston, Maury. 1976. *The Stratification of Musical Rhythm*. New Haven, Conn.: Yale University Press.

Index

Consonance and dissonance, 117, 119, 160–162, 185, 290–292, 295–296. *See also* Pitch stability
Contemporary music, 18, 296–301
Cooper, G., 26–27, 249, 284, 328, 334, 335
Cooper, R., 294

Deceptive cadence, 138, 158, 222, 275–276
Deep structure, 5, 287–288
Deutsch, D., 333
Direct elaboration, 214, 215, 219
Dit le Bourguignon (anonymous), 66–67
Dowling, W. J., 111, 299, 333
Downbeat, 129, 284. *See also* Structural downbeat
Dynamics, 9, 45–46, 63, 80–81, 297–298

Elaboration, 105, 113–114, 116, 287, 298, 322, 330
direct and recursive, 214, 215, 219
Elisions, grouping, 9, 14, 38, 55–62, 99–104, 283, 304
Epstein, D., 7, 335
Evaluation metric, 314
Evolution, 282–283, 307, 344
"Experienced listener," 1, 3, 53, 112, 178, 197, 223, 274, 278, 281, 293, 296, 301, 330–331
Extrametrical events, 72, 74

Final of cadence, 156–159
Fodor, J. A., 241
Fodor, J. D., 314
Forte, A., 299, 337–338
Fusion (TSRWFR 3b), 153–155, 159, 167, 213, 327, 339

Gamelan music, 150, 294, 321
Generative grammar, 5–6, 9, 62, 111–113, 249, 286–289, 302–303, 305, 307–330
Gestalt psychology, 40–43, 111, 302–307, 336, 342
Goodman, N., 333
Green, G., 333
Gregorian chant, 18, 215
Grice, P., 310–311

Grouping Preference Rules, 37, 43–55, 62
GPR 1, 43–44, 46–49, 52, 64–65, 298, 336
GPR 2, (proximity), 40–42, 44–49, 51–52, 54, 63–67, 298, 300, 336
GPR 3 (similarity/change), 41–42, 45–49, 63–67, 298, 300, 336
GPR 4 (intensification), 49–51, 63–67, 304
GPR 5 (symmetry), 49–51, 55, 65–67, 92, 101, 289, 297, 304
GPR 6 (parallelism), 43, 51–55, 62–67, 92, 99, 124, 250, 252, 258, 261, 264, 266, 298, 300, 304
GPR 7 (time-span and prolongational stability), 52, 54, 258, 261, 264, 266
Grouping structure, 8, 12–18, 21, 25–67, 74–76, 92, 99, 119–128, 132–138, 146–151, 154, 168, 203–206, 216, 228, 243, 248, 250–266, 269, 283, 289, 297–298, 304, 313. *See also* Cadenced group; Elision; Overlap
underlying and surface, 60–61, 147, 174, 206, 213
Grouping Well-Formedness Rules, 36–39, 55–62
GWFR 1, 37
GWFR 2, 38
GWFR 3, 38
GWFR 4, 38, 55, 59–61
GWFR 5, 38, 147
Grundgestalt, 7

Halle, M., 85, 314, 315, 319, 321, 323, 326, 327, 335, 343
Harmonic rhythm, 74, 84–85, 87, 95, 121, 130, 164–165, 264, 268, 285
Hauptmann, M., 1
Haydn, Franz Joseph
Quartet, op. 76, no. 6, fourth movement, 90–96
Symphony no. 104, first movement, 58, 101; minuet, 26–28
Trio in G minor, 109
Head. *See also* Prolongational head
of time-span, 120, 124, 152–177, 284, 322
of phrase, 136
of piece, 174, 216, 220

"conservative" and "radical"
  hearings, 22–25, 206, 250–252
in language. *See* Prosodic structure
Metrical Well-Formedness Rules,
  68–74, 90, 96–99, 279
  MWFR 1, 69–73, 86, 97
  MWFR 2, 69–73, 97
  MWFR 3, 69–73, 97–99, 326
  MWFR 4, 69–73, 86, 97–99, 326
Meyer, L., 7, 26–27, 63, 249, 284,
  286, 299, 328, 334, 335
Miller, G., 6
Minuet and trio form, 247
Morgan, R., 335
Motivic structure, 9, 12, 13, 16–17,
  27, 43, 50–51, 62, 65, 92,
  116–117, 125, 231–232, 252–257,
  266, 269, 286–289, 296, 341
Mozart, Wolfgang Amadeus
  "La ci darem la mano" (*Don
  Giovanni*), 199–201
  Quintet in C major, K. 515, first
  movement, 99
  Quintet in D major, K. 593, first
  movement, 269–274
  Sonata, K. 279, first movement, 55,
  62, 103
  Sonata, K. 331, first movement,
  32–33, 63, 70–71, 88, 118–123,
  134–135, 138, 140–141, 156–157,
  162–165, 167–168, 171–174, 194,
  227–232, 276, 338, 339, 341
  Symphony no. 40 in G minor,
  K. 550, first movement, 22–25,
  27–28, 37, 39, 47–52, 74, 85–87,
  89–90, 96, 121, 127, 163,
  258–260, 304, 337
  Symphony no. 41 in C major
  ("Jupiter"), fourth movement,
  73
Mursell, J., 305, 342
Musical intuition, 1–4, 7–8

Narmour, E., 106, 333
Neighboring motions, 186, 194, 226
Neisser, U., 241, 302
Nettl, B., 292, 294, 295
Network notation, 116
Normative prolongational structure,
  197–201, 233–241, 243, 264, 268,
  269, 285, 289

Overlap, grouping, 14, 38, 55–62,
  99–104, 147, 174, 206, 246, 257,
  261, 283, 284, 304, 334, 338
Overtone series, 1, 290–293, 295

Parallelism, 50–53, 75, 163–164,
  226, 287, 296, 341. *See also* GPR
  6; MPR 1; PRPR 5; TSRPR 4
Parsing strategies, 314
Partch, H., 342
Passing motions, 186, 226
Penult of cadence, 156–159
Performance, musical, 7, 25, 63–64,
  70, 84
Phenomenal accent, 17, 21, 78–79,
  96, 283
Phonetic perception, 313
Phonology, 6, 62, 85, 314–330
Phrase, 12, 119, 133–137, 168,
  191–197, 199, 233–241, 289
Pitch collection, 224, 246–247,
  291–292, 294
Pitch stability, 117–118, 160–162,
  224–226, 279, 295–297,
  342
Poetic accents, 19, 26–27, 85, 344
Polyphony (counterpoint), 37, 87–88,
  92, 116, 117, 273–277, 339
Postal, P., 342
Powers, H., 294
Pragmatics, 309–311
Preference rules, 9, 39–43, 287–289,
  296, 302, 304, 306–314, 326, 336.
  See also Grouping Preference
  Rules; Metrical Preference Rules;
  Prolongational Reduction
  Preference Rules; Time-Span
  Reduction Preference Rules
in linguistic theory, 307–314
Prince, A., 315–328, 343
Processing, musical, 3
Progression, 181, 214, 215, 224
Prolongation, strong and weak, 182,
  214, 215, 224
Prolongational beginning and ending,
  234–236, 239
Prolongational groupings, 121, 203,
  207, 231–232, 285
Prolongational head, 214, 216–219,
  220
Prolongational Hypothesis 1,
  211–213

Time-Span Reduction
  Well-Formedness Rules (cont.)
  TSRWFR 4 (cadential retention),
    158–159
Time-span segmentation, 119, 122,
    124–133, 146–151, 221–223, 281,
    284. *See also* Segmentation Rule 1;
    Segmentation Rule 2
Tonality, 117, 139, 290–301
Top-down conditions, 170, 216, 304
Torah chant, 295
Tovey, D., 335
Transformation, musical, 11, 60–62,
    70, 99–104, 273–274, 286–289,
    297–299
  in time-span reduction (TSRWFR
    3c), 142, 155, 159, 167
Transformational grammar. *See*
  Generative grammar
Tree notation, 112–117, 128–138,
    152, 154–155, 181–201, 211, 214,
    274–277, 315–317
Trouvère music, 295
Trubetzkoy, N., 85, 296, 314

Ullmann, S., 307
Universals of music, 4, 18, 36, 64,
    69, 96, 99, 150, 178, 278–301
Upbeat, 28, 126–127, 129, 147–150,
    284, 320, 343
Urlinie, 139, 225
Ursatz, 111, 139–140, 180, 186,
    188, 236–239
Underlying grouping structure,
    60–61, 147, 174, 206, 213

Van der Werf, H., 295
Vergnaud, J.-R., 319, 321, 323, 343
Vision, 13, 36, 39–43, 58–59,
    302–307
Voice-leading, 116–117, 161–162,
    165–167, 224–225, 273–277

Wanner, E., 314
Well-formedness rules, 9, 281, 308,
    312–314. *See also* Grouping
    Well-Formedness Rules; Metrical
    Well-Formedness Rules;
    Prolongational Reduction
    Well-Formedness Rules; Time-Span
    Reduction Well-Formedness Rules
Wertheimer, M., 40–42, 303–304

Westergaard, P., 335, 339
Winograd, T., 333
Winston, P., 54
Wittgenstein, L., 312

Yeston, M., 334, 339

U.C.B.
LIBRARY